THE WRONG DOOR:
THE COMPLETE PLAYS OF NATALIA GINZBURG

Translated by Wendell Ricketts

The Wrong Door is the first English-language translation of the complete plays of Italian writer Natalia Ginzburg (1916–1991). Bringing together the eleven plays Ginzburg wrote between 1965 and the months before her death, this volume underscores Ginzburg's unique talent as a dramatist.

Ginzburg's plays, like her novels and short stories, are incisive, finely tuned studies of family drama, of the breakdown of relations between the sexes, and of the tribulations of Italian domestic life. The plays showcase Ginzburg's fearless social commentary, her stark and darkly comic observations of Italian life, and her prescient analyses of the socioeconomic changes that have transformed modern Italy. Along the way, Ginzburg creates memorable female characters in a series of fascinating roles. In this fluent and faithful translation, Wendell Ricketts highlights Ginzburg's scalpel-sharp dialogue and lays bare the existential absurdities that lie at the heart of her plays.

Including an introduction by the translator and two essays by Ginzburg on her approach to the theatre, *The Wrong Door* adds a new dimension to the literary portrait of one of Italy's most significant modernist writers.

(Toronto Italian Studies)

WENDELL RICKETTS is a writer and translator living in Italy. He holds an MA in English and creative writing from the University of New Mexico.

THE WRONG DOOR

*The Complete Plays of
Natalia Ginzburg*

Translated by
WENDELL RICKETTS

UNIVERSITY OF TORONTO PRESS
Toronto Buffalo London

© University of Toronto Press Incorporated 2008
Toronto Buffalo London
www.utppublishing.com
Printed in Canada

ISBN 978-0-8020-9848-1 (cloth)
ISBN 978-0-8020-9569-5 (paper)

Printed on acid-free paper

Toronto Italian Studies

Library and Archives Canada Cataloguing in Publication

Ginzburg, Natalia
The wrong door : the complete plays of Natalia Ginzburg /
translated by Wendell Ricketts.

(Toronto Italian studies)
ISBN 978-0-8020-9848-1 (bound). ISBN 978-0-8020-9569-5 (pbk.)

1. Ginzburg, Natalia – Translations into English. I. Ricketts, Wendell
II. Title. III. Series.

PQ4817.I5A2 2008   852'.912   C2008-902140-1

Publication of this book is assisted by the Istituto Italiano di Cultura, Toronto.

University of Toronto Press acknowledges the financial assistance to its publishing program of the Canada Council for the Arts and the Ontario Arts Council.

University of Toronto Press acknowledges the financial support for its publishing activities of the Government of Canada through the Book Publishing Industry Development Program (BPIDP).

Contents

The plays by Natalia Ginzburg translated into English in this volume were originally published in Italian as *Ti ho sposato per allegria e altre commedie* (1970), *Teatro* (1990), and *Tutto il teatro* (2005) by Giulio Einaudi Editore, Turin, Italy.

Acknowledgments

The publication of this volume represents ten years' labour, and thus my appreciation is spread widely, though not, for all that, thinly. To begin, Professor Tony Mares's seminar at the University of New Mexico *nel lontano* 1997 was the ideal space in which to experiment with language – and to learn that translation was equal parts art, skill, and discipline. I continue to be grateful to Donold Lourie, John Shepley, William Weaver, and the PEN American Center for granting me the Renato Poggioli Translation Award in 2000 – the first tangible sign that interest in the plays of Ginzburg went beyond my circle of friends. The contagious enthusiasm of Catherine Coray and Elana Greenfield at the hotINK Festival/Tisch School of the Arts (which sponsored staged readings of two of these translations in 2004), together with the generosity, kindness, and insights of director Kent Paul and the fine actors he assembled, allowed me to hear Ginzburg on stage and in English for the very first time, a gift whose value I cannot overestimate. The Italian Cultural Institute of Toronto provided material support for these translations, and I am very grateful. The novelist and translator Lynne Sharon Schwartz was generous with her time and her personal contacts and gave me a sorely needed boost when morale flagged. For curiosities of language, I benefited from the patient assistance of Silvia Poli, Elvira Politano, and Rachele Duke, even as colleagues on the professional translators' list, Biblit, responded promptly to my many queries. Silvia Colombo, at the Piccolo Teatro di Milano, was both extremely helpful and astonishingly fast in providing us with the image of Alessandro Haber and Giulia Lazzarini that graces the cover of this collection. Finally, I owe a debt of thanks to Ron Schoeffel, to the University of Toronto Press, and to the Press's three anonymous reviewers, who found, in a draft of these plays, something of the *allegria* that Ginzburg had hidden there.

'Letter to Visconti from Natalia Ginzburg'

by Peg Boyers

Luchino,

I am nervous about the play.
Forgive me. I am nervous
about your direction of my play.

I worry about your complex
reading of my simple, stupid characters.
I made them dry,

inert sticks adept
at avoiding fires,
for fear they'll ignite.

You will fill them with fluid, with life.
They will sprout
leaves and flowers and god knows what.

I fear you will paint them with decadent colours,
give them conscience and desire.
You will make their teeth rotten, their appetites vast.

In the winter of 1969, the Italian director Luchino Visconti, best known for such films as
The Leopard (1963), directed Ginzburg's second play, *L'Inserzione* (*The Advertisement*), at
the Teatro San Babila in Milan. In this poem from her collection, *Hard Bread* (University
of Chicago Press, 2002), written in the voice of Ginzburg, Boyers imagines Ginzburg's
anxiety. Used by kind permission of the author.

Luchino, you love a motive too much.
My characters act from the sheer emptiness of their souls.
In truth, they have no souls.

In a sense they are pure.
On your stage corruption will explain
reticence. Blemished complexions

will acquire meaning.
On a smooth cheek you'll place a scar.
What smiles they manage you'll twist.

Luchino, accept the transparency of action.
Sometimes a pipe is just a pipe.
Put the festering symbols aside

for once.
My play is a laconic, idle thing,
· its breath the breath of absent purpose.

Choke it with Meaning and it will die.

Ti ho tradotto per allegria:
The *Commedie* of Natalia Ginzburg

To read an author over the course of time – and to go back to her often with respect and appreciation – may be, as one commonly says of a favourite writer, to love her, but to attempt to translate faithfully a large body of her work is closer to entering into a marriage. Natalia Ginzburg would surely have considered such an assertion sentimental. Her own description of translation (she translated Proust and Flaubert, among others) puts the emphasis squarely on its workmanlike qualities: 'What a job of ants and horses translation is,' she said with characteristic phlegm. 'One has to be as exact and industrious as an ant and have the impetus, the strength, of a horse to pull ahead' (Boyers, 153).

Strength and industry are necessary to any translation, but no more so than with Ginzburg. The eminent scholar and translator William Weaver, in an essay-review of *È difficile parlare di sé* (*It's Hard to Talk about Yourself*), a collection of interviews with Ginzburg published after the writer's death, noted that Ginzburg's prose was 'elusive,' 'resist[ing] translation' (144); and Ginzburg herself suggested that her tendency to be 'too bound by subtle details of style or tone' posed a liability for the potential translator (Boyers, 134).

In fact, even those who value Ginzburg's work rarely fail to acknowledge its difficulties. Cesare Pavese, for example, the family friend who published Ginzburg's first and second novels and who evidently held both her and them in high regard, once famously opined that Ginzburg's style amounted to a *lagna* (a whine or complaint); and Clotilde Soave Bowe, noting Ginzburg's habit of blurring 'subject and manner,' argues that Ginzburg's prose derives its unique power precisely from the fact that it 'borrow[s] the ... atmosphere of the effect which it aim[s] to produce':

Ginzburg sets out, like Flaubert in *Madame Bovary*, to reproduce the colour grey and will always run the risk of being accounted a failure because she succeeds in depicting greyness absolutely. (789)

Critics have sometimes responded to Ginzburg's 'greyness' with displeasure, even with what seems like genuine anger. Alan Bullock, in his discussion of the cool reception Ginzburg's first two novels received, cites the damning judgments of a dozen Italian and British reviewers: 'full of understatement and jerkiness,' 'a dryness which often becomes impoverished when applied to dialogue,' 'a deliberate striving for effect … no longer spontaneous but mannered and insincere,' 'skeletal writing,' 'over-simplification' (25–6). In a similar vein, the conclusions of Giorgio Pullini, who reviewed *La porta sbagliata* (*The Wrong Door*) in 1974, are emblematic of the negative reactions of those who found Ginzburg's theatre craft no more appealing than her prose:

As a playwright, Ginzburg remains at a point of stagnation … [She] makes no pretense of developing events, but rather is content to present a limited series of types who, employing a discursive dialogue, comment on themselves, rehearse tics and manias, [and] take pleasure in regarding their reflections in the mirror and parroting themselves … But the stage remains empty, and the poetry of 'emptiness' is insufficiently intense to satisfy dramatic demands (as in Chekhov), nor is the humour sufficiently adroit to create fireworks. (470; my translation)

Ginzburg, I am convinced, would have found no reason to defend herself against such judgments. Indeed, writing in the 1989 'Note' to the Einaudi collection of her later *commedie*, Ginzburg recalls Elsa Morante's violent reaction to a draft of *Ti ho sposato per allegria*, Ginzburg's first and best-known play, noting that

I knew [her] rages would not persuade me to re-envision my play or to rewrite it, but only to thoroughly explore its total demolition. The strange thing is that total demolition can be immensely beneficial to someone who writes, in the same measure that complete approval can be immensely beneficial.

Ginzburg expanded on her relationship to criticism in her essay of the same name:

I don't say critics' views should be taken with total indifference: the writer may find it useful to compare what they think with what he thinks of his own work ... and to try to see how far his own judgment is a result of the way he instinctively forgives his own faults, how far it is a result of clear knowledge, and how far that of pride and excessive enthusiasm ... [But] as far as our work is concerned, we feel we have really heard nothing that we didn't know before. (78–9)

Let us leave it to Ginzburg herself then to give us – albeit unintention-ally – what I consider to be the most accurate description of her own prose style. In a passionate encomium to one of her favourite authors, the English novelist Ivy Compton-Burnett, written on the occasion of the latter's death in 1969, Ginzburg recalled that

[Compton-Burnett] wrote many novels and they are all alike, so that it is hard to isolate them and remember them individually: with their compli-cated, careful plots, they form, together, a huge rambling building ...

Nature and places are invisible in her novels, because she spends not a syllable on descriptions of them ... Occasionally she pauses for a moment to describe her characters' features very briefly. If she does not stop to de-scribe people and places, it is not through haste or impatience but because of a ... fastidious rejection of what is superfluous ...

In [the] inexorable clarity [of the novels], impenetrable beings sat pinned down in their appalling conversations, exchanging words that seemed like snake bites ...

I could never see any poetry in these novels, yet I felt that it must be there ... and then I realised that the presence of poetry was there like the presence of nature ... Poetry was there like the boundless, gloomy sky that opened up behind those evil, lonely actions. ('La grande signorina,' 89–91)

The reader – or the translator – who enters the huge, rambling build-ing of Ginzburg's own oeuvre contends with all of this – the colour grey; the 'invisible' poetry; the obsessive reworking of plot and the-matic elements; dialogue which, reminiscent of Compton-Burnett's snake bites, comes across 'like a whip or a slap' (Ginzburg's descrip-tion of her characters' speech in her first novel, *La strada che va in città*) (Wilde-Menozzi, 128); her lack of interest in physical scene-setting (she didn't 'much like writing descriptions,' Ginzburg told an interviewer in 1987) (Furman, 37); the sustained tone of complaint and discord that defines the atmosphere of her plays perhaps even more markedly than it does the language of her fiction.

In her eleven *commedie*, in fact, we encounter Ginzburg at her most Ginzburghian. That is no accident, because theatre provided Ginzburg with the solution to a problem she had identified in her writing: the need 'to move beyond autobiography' and to escape the first person, which 'threaten[ed] to become obsessive' (as she wrote in her preface to *Ti ho sposato per allegria*). Indeed, chafing against that 'obsessive' I, Ginzburg experimented with the 'me-not-me' voice in her novels as well. Two of the best known, in fact – *Caro Michele* (1973; *No Way*, 1974) and *La città e la casa* (1984; *The City and the House*, 1986) – are epistolary novels in which the '*io*' (the 'I') of a series of letter writers serves to diffuse the narrative's autobiographical impulse. In *La città e la casa*, letters are exchanged among no less than nine characters, some of whom Ginzburg allows to relate a slightly different version of the same event to different correspondents, just as Sofia – to lift but one example from the *commedie* – so memorably does in her long telephone monologues in *The Secretary*.

Nearly a quarter of a century after the preface to *Ti ho sposato per allegria*, Ginzburg continued to reflect on the process that had, by then, resulted in the completion of nine additional plays and on her increasing comfort with the narrative possibilities of writing for the stage. In her 1989 'Note,' she recalled that:

> In plays, I could use the first person in a non-autobiographical way, which gave me a sense of great freedom. It might be a man who said 'I' or a woman completely different from me. Plays had become a means of expression for me.

In the context of Ginzburg's *commedie*, the word 'freedom' may seem deliberately ironic. The worlds Ginzburg creates in her theatre are founded on claustrophobia and catastrophe; on inertia; on bitterness; on the unrevenged slight; on the wrong turn that has ruined everything; on the past that cannot be gotten over; on the compulsive rehearsal of long-ago hurts; on the vestigial life that survives in stifling, shrinking rooms – in short, on anything but freedom. There are deaths in abundance: either those that predate the action of the play (and the number of widows and orphans in Ginzburg's *commedie* is remarkable) or that involve important (but virtually always unseen) characters. There is a murder in *The Advertisement*, a successful suicide in *The*

Secretary (alongside the countless threatened or attempted others that are mentioned throughout the plays), a heart attack in *A Town by the Sea*, and a car accident in *The Interview*, to mention a few. Over and again, Ginzburg introduces us to characters who live in borrowed or requisitioned housing, who do not know where they will go next, who are divorced or separated or frozen in crumbling relationships, who have run out of money, who knock on doors where they are very likely to be unwelcome but who nevertheless insist on going in. ('Families don't exist anymore,' Titina says in *The Secretary*. 'People come, people go, the door is always open to anyone … Strangers show up at your house and start making a nest.')

All of that being the case, it perhaps goes without saying that no one is ever happier at the end of a Ginzburg play than she or he was at the beginning (with the possible exception of *I Married You to Cheer Myself Up*, which is also Ginzburg's only true comedy). And yet her characters cling with remarkable tenacity to their wrecked lives – to the houses where food has run out (the ill-provisioned kitchen, from which even staples like coffee and bread are absent, is a typical Ginzburghian metaphor for psychic chaos), to relationships marked by infidelity, indifference, or fatalistic entrenchment.

No less paradoxical is Ginzburg's paring down of language, a manipulation that exposes her to the charge that her deceptive plainness is merely offhanded. Her characters frequently employ similes and metaphors that seem just a few degrees off the mark (one character moves with the 'simplicity of a goatherd'; another's 'lack of mystery' is to be expected in someone who is 'like a polenta'; others are as 'indecipherable as a lizard' or 'dull as olive oil'); or they return compulsively to a limited stock of words and catch phrases, clinging to them as if to life rafts, such that the translator's initial impulse is to try to leaven the dialogue by varying the language.

To do so, however, would be a fatal betrayal. Such repetitions and linguistic hiccups are what Ginzburg wrote in lieu of stage directions and physical descriptions; they reveal to us the ruts into which her characters' minds have fallen. Her characters repeat their stories, almost verbatim, to anyone who will listen; the skein of their tales of resentment, loss, and failure pays itself out like so much carefully tended fishing line, and any hapless captive is welcome. They can no more speak differently than they can *behave* differently, and that is Ginzburg's point.

On the subject of language, I would like to say a word regarding the kind of English in which I believe an anglophone public deserves to encounter Ginzburg. In the end, of course, translation is as much a matter of personal choice and taste (and here I risk uttering a blasphemy) as it is of anything else. Granted, a *casa* would be a house in almost any setting; a *sigaro* is just a cigar, even in Italian; and if an animal appears and begins to *miagolare*, it is fairly bound to be a cat and not much choice about it. But on a more comprehensive scale – the overall tone or register of a text – there, the translator has enormous powers to accent or to modulate, to transilluminate or to underexpose, to oxygenate or to stifle.

That said, I must admit my feeling that the problem with Ginzburg in English is that her translators have often made choices whose ultimate impact is to recreate a Ginzburghian world that is overly formal, crabbed, dated, and anglicized. As a result, I would go so far as to suggest that a good deal of Ginzburg might well benefit from being retranslated with an ear for what she herself called the 'even, normal, functional, real language we customarily speak' (Scarpa, 411; my translation).[1]

On the topic of Ginzburg's language, one hears the argument that her novels and plays are characterized by a profound linguistic democracy: maids speak no differently from lawyers; wealthy characters are not 'marked' by a more correct or 'class-inflected' Italian; and dialect, which might reveal regional or social distinctions, is effectively absent. All of this may be true as far as it goes, but one might just as easily see in such a deliberate 'levelling' of language a device of characterization and not a political stance. Her characters express themselves identically because they are, fundamentally, identical. Their meanness, ineptness, and narcissism, their lack of tact and their suffering are their shared qualities, and they speak, literally and metaphorically, with one voice.

It is sometimes said, similarly, that another aspect of Ginzburg's 'democracy' of language is that her characters do not make grammatical errors, which is both patently false and illogical on the face of it: the 'real language ... we customarily speak' is full of small mistakes in grammar and syntax, which is part of what makes it 'real.' For an excellent case in point, the reader is invited to study *L'Intervista* in Italian: the characters rather rigorously eschew the use of the subjunctive, a linguistic 'softening' that is virtually impossible to reproduce in English, from which the subjunctive has all but disappeared.

There can be no question: the great challenge of Ginzburg – which expands exponentially in the *commedie* – is precisely her tendency toward claustrophobia and inwardness; her obsessive focus; her deliberate repetition; her non sequiturs and the tangible staccato of her dialogues and monologues (but *staccato* in the literal sense of the Italian: detached, unfastened) – all of which is born, as it must be, in her use of language. But let us attempt to separate the local from the eternal.

As Italian moves toward English in the process of translation, what emerges is what I would be so bold as to call a certain natural tendency: Italian becomes more succinct, it condenses (literally: the English translation of an Italian text is generally some ten per cent shorter than the original), it loses (unless the translator compensates) a certain elasticity. To the Italian reader or listener, English may seem brusque, unrhetorical, unpleasantly unambiguous. Conversely, Italian can strike the anglophone as indirect, turgid, or overly contingent. These specific impressions are, of course, mine alone, but the general point – that what we mean when we talk about a 'foreign' language includes the way that language indigenously shapes discourse and transmits extraverbal content – strikes me as linguistically sound. I am not aware of many attempts to apply Robert Kaplan's theories of contrastive rhetoric in a systematic way to translation (see, however, Granger, passim), but they certainly deserve to be.

Speaking still generally, then, an additional feature of modern written Italian is its tendency to abhor repetition. From grade school to university, Italian students learn that repetition is stylistically flawed, and 'advanced' users of this technique sometimes go to extraordinary lengths to avoid repeating a verb, a noun, a place or proper name, or even the subject of related clauses in proximity to a prior use.

One thus recognizes, well before translation, that Ginzburg's stylistics are *already* marked by an active resistance to 'proper' literary Italian. Her 'dryness,' her 'skeletal' prose, her obsessive repetitions, then, may never strike a native English speaker in quite the same way as they do a native Italian speaker, precisely because contemporary English tends to 'like' (so to speak) directness and concision, tends to consider a certain amount of repetition rhetorically comforting, and tends to 'dislike' excessive semantic ornament. And yet here is another paradox. Because contemporary English tends to be more concise and straightforward, Ginzburg's stripped-down Italian occasionally requires a kind of softening to keep her 'whips and slaps' from becoming truly unbearable. Those are the ants and horses of translating Ginzburg, but they are also its joys and rewards.

And what lies wrapped in these riddles of language is another of the great treasures of Ginzburg's plays: their humour, their immense sense of (if I may say) camp – by which I mean, among other things, that her characters unerringly single out whatever is least important in their lives and focus melodramatic, exaggerated attention on precisely that. Ginzburg's humour – gallows humour, if one likes – is surely accessible to those who experience the plays only through reading them, but to flower fully that humour almost demands that the plays be heard out loud. Ginzburg did, after all, intend her words to be spoken.

I had the opportunity to validate that assertion on two occasions, the first in November 2003, when, in one of those coincidences that sometimes come along in life, I stepped off the airport shuttle at the Milan train station only to come face to face with a wall of posters advertising a production of *Ti ho sposato per allegria* at the elegant Teatro Manzoni, just down from La Scala. Though I had learned portions of the play by heart (as a translator will), the waves of laughter that washed over the audience at all the right moments still took me by surprise, and I experienced something like relief as Giuliana's relentless lunacy and Pietro's studied dispassion were skilfully modulated by the humanity of live actors. I felt Ginzburg patiently reminding me that she had known what she was doing all along.

The second occasion came a few months later, when I attended a staged reading of my translation of *The Wrong Door*, chosen for inclusion in the January 2004 hotINK Festival at New York University's Tisch School of the Arts. Director Kent Paul, as well as the actors themselves, convinced me to reimagine the entire translation with an ear for its sly humour, for – quite literally – the sound of it. I think it is a better effort as a result.

Twenty years ago, Jorge Luis Borges suggested to an Argentine radio interviewer that he almost preferred his work to be read in translated versions:

> I've been translated into many languages, and someone who reads those translations may think, 'Well, this isn't much, but the original might be acceptable.' For that reason it's to my benefit to be read in translation, because people are disposed more kindly toward me then, such that all mistakes are attributed to the translator and all the good to me. (198)

I am delighted if this translation leaves the reader feeling more kindly disposed toward Ginzburg and especially so if it moves her or him to encounter the plays in Ginzburg's original, remarkably accessible Italian. Any errors or failures in this translation are, of course, mine; and whatever is good about the plays belongs to Ginzburg. I wish more than anything that the availability of a complete English version of her works for theatre might lead to more readings and productions. Natalia Ginzburg's *io* is so fully woven into the tapestry of her plays, and she is so fully present, that to speak them out loud is to hear again, as Ginzburg described in her 1989 'Note,' a beloved voice whose sound we thought we had lost.

Wendell Ricketts
Bologna, Italy

Note

1 For those who don't have Italian, Lynne Sharon Schwartz's lovely *A Place to Live and Other Selected Essays of Natalia Ginzburg* is a good place to start.

References

Borges, Jorge Luis. 1986. *Conversazioni con Osvaldo Ferrari*. Edited by Francesco Tentori Montalto. Milan: Bompiani.

Bowe, Clotilde Soave. 1973. 'The Narrative Strategy of Natalia Ginzburg.' *The Modern Language Review* 68: 788–95.

Boyers, Peggy. 1992, Fall. 'An Interview with Natalia Ginzburg.' *Salmagundi*: 130–56.

Bullock, Alan. 1991. *Natalia Ginzburg: Human Relationships in a Changing World*. Oxford: Berg Publishers.

Furman, Laura. 1987, Winter. 'An Interview with Natalia Ginzburg.' *Southwest Review* 72: 34–41.

Ginzburg, Natalia. 1966. 'Prefazione.' In *Ti ho sposato per allegria*. Turin: Giulio Einaudi Editore, 5–8.

– 1973. 'Criticism.' In *Never Must You Ask Me*. Trans. Isabel Quigly. London: Michael Joseph, 77–80. (First published, 1970.)

– 1973. 'La Grande Signorina.' In *Never Must You Ask Me*. Trans. Isabel Quigly. London: Michael Joseph, 88–91. (First published, 1970.)

– 1990. *Teatro*. Turin: Einaudi.

– 2003. *It's Hard to Talk about Yourself*. Trans. Cesare Garboli. University of Chicago Press.

Granger, Sylviane. 2003. 'The Corpus Approach: A Common Way Forward for Contrastive Linguistics and Translation Studies?' In S. Granger, J. Lerot, and S. Petch-Tyson, eds, *Corpus-Based Approaches to Contrastive Linguistics and Translation Studies*. Amsterdam: Rodopi, 17–29.

Pullini, Giorgio. 1974, Winter. 'La stagione teatrale 1973–74 in Italia.' *Italica* 51(4): 465–82.

Scarpa, Domenico. 2005. 'Bibliografie.' In D. Scarpa, ed., *Natalia Ginzburg: Tutto il Teatro*. Turin: Einaudi, 411–27.

Schwartz, Lynne Sharon. 2002. *A Place to Live and Other Selected Essays of Natalia Ginzburg*. New York: Seven Stories Press.

Weaver, William. 2000, July. 'The Return of Natalia Ginzburg.' *The Yale Review* 88(3): 135–47.

Wilde-Menozzi, Wallis. 1994, Winter. 'Anchoring Natalia Ginzburg.' *The Kenyon Review*: 115–30.

Preface: *Ti ho sposato per allegria*

Last summer I wrote this little play. I had never written a play before. I'd begun quite a few of them, but I generally stopped after the second line. Generally, what happened is that, after two lines, the characters in my plays developed an enormous desire to stop talking. You can't make a play with silence. But this time I found that the characters were talking and to me it seemed a miracle. In fact, I realized they were talking too much. I felt in danger of being swept away, overwhelmed by their waves of speech. The ease and the speed with which they were speaking and I was writing made me suspicious. Such ease is born not out of the joy of creation but from the blindness of inexperience.

What's more, every time I had tried to write a play, a sensation of shyness came over me, and I felt myself freeze up, as if all of the bones in my body had been fused by shame and repulsion. This time, too, I felt shame and repulsion after the first lines. I decided to pay no attention to it and I went ahead just the same, but I suddenly understood where the sensation was coming from. It was coming from the fact that, as I wrote, I was thinking about a public, about a theatre. I was thinking, that is, about an audience.

Writing a story or a novel, I didn't think about the audience, or, rather, what I had in front of me – those to whom I entrusted what I wrote – took on the shape of a confused assemblage of disembodied shadows, a dark, vague cloud where friends, loved ones, and strangers all mingled together. I was tied to it by a secret accord; my relationship with that dark, vague cloud was secret, profound, and utterly private. Writing something that wasn't a novel but a play, on the other hand, what I had in front of me were my fellow human beings, not in the shape of a dark cloud but real, flesh-and-blood people, strangers to me and somehow hostile; and my relationship to this group of real people – to the public, I mean – was a relationship neither profound nor secret but transparent, superficial, and mundane. Such a relationship left me uneasy and inspired shyness and loathing. That was how I understood why I had never before written plays.

That sense of uneasiness was absurd and I knew it. In fact, the people to whom I addressed and entrusted my novels so they might be read were really the same people to whom one would entrust a play so that it might be heard. And yet I still felt that uneasiness and it wasn't anybody's fault: neither mine nor anyone else's. I tried to get beyond it, and, little by little as I wrote, I forgot that I wasn't writing a story but a play. Still, I believe that some of the defects in this play derive precisely from that initial sensation of loathing and unease.

In my personal case, my relationship with the theatre can be described as follows:

When I was six years old, I was taken to the theatre for the first time. I saw a play entitled *Peg o' My Heart*, which left me profoundly excited: an excitement in which the dramatic events of the play combined with the grandeur of the theatre – which I believe was the Teatro Carignano in Turin, with its mirrors and red velvet and its gilded ornamental mouldings – leaving behind a singular impression of solemnity and splendour.

I was taken to the theatre on other occasions during my childhood, but I was never particularly excited about it. I slowly forgot what had happened during *Peg o' My Heart*, remembering only that a girl with an enormous straw hat was always on stage.

At the time, still under the spell of *Peg*, I tried writing something that I called 'a dialogue.' My family told me that it wasn't a dialogue but a play, however, because there weren't just two speaking characters but lots of them – to be exact, every single person who lived in my house, all of whom appeared with their real names and said the lines they really used to say. I never managed to finish this 'dialogue' – in part because nothing whatever happened in it. The characters simply entered and exited, saying what they always said in real life, and, once they'd exhausted their little store of lines, they had nothing else to add. That had been, in any event, my most extensive attempt at playwriting, because after that, as I say, I always quit after the first few lines, or else after I had written 'a table, with a door on the left.' At that point I always stopped and asked myself, 'Why on the left? Why not on the right?' It went on like that until last summer.

Whenever I've had the occasion to go to the theatre in my life, I've always thought that I couldn't even dare wish to be able to write some little play. It would have been impossible.

I've never been one who went to the theatre much and, anyway, I have no sort of theatre culture whatever.

Reading and rereading the plays I loved, I read them like short stories and I never had any interest in problems related to how they could be performed.

If I must be honest, in fact, my way of looking at the theatre has always been fundamentally careless and distracted. Now I think a sort of inferiority complex lay hidden beneath that carelessness. Starting from when I saw *Peg*, perhaps, the world of the theatre had seemed regal and solemn, inaccessible and out of bounds to ordinary mortals.

One evening, a few years ago in London, I went to see a play entitled *The Caretaker*. It seemed quite wonderful. Not only that, it struck me as the kind of play that I might have wanted and been able to write. Since I don't understand English all that well, I went back two times, then I went to see other plays by the same author, whose name is Harold Pinter. When I came back to Italy, I was convinced I was the only one who knew who he was, but then I discovered that he was extremely famous.

A few months ago – last June, to be precise – an actress-friend of mine came to see me in Rome and asked me to write a play for her. The actress's name is Adriana Asti.

Not long after my friend came to see me, I went to a debate about writers and the theatre. There was someone there whose argument was this: that writers don't write for the theatre because they're afraid of the public. To me, that seemed true enough, but I also thought it was wrong to consider such a fear ignoble or contemptible. You can't get rid of a fear like that simply by telling yourself to be brave. I thought that writers were afraid not just of the public but of the actors, the directors, the lights, and the noise, of everything that happens to a play when it is put on the stage. And writers, if they are to write, cannot be afraid – in other words, they cannot be troubled and annoyed by outside issues. Furthermore, as far as writers and the theatre are concerned, the question isn't some vulgar fear of failure, but of something else entirely. It's a fear of not being able to substitute, within one's very soul, a private and secret relationship (which is the relationship a writer has with his reader – the one we customarily have with the people for whom we write) for a public relationship, shameless, clamorous, and fully exposed to the light of day.

One might well respond that countless writers have written for the theatre without experiencing uneasiness or loathing. Given the reality we live in today, however, intimacy and the inclination toward a private existence are a precious commodity that we see trampled and crushed continuously. A writer's relationship with his fellow human beings remains one of the few surviving examples of human good and is something we can preserve.

As for the little play I wrote last summer, I'll say only that it is not – and it isn't meant to be – anything more than a story. Nothing happens in it, and there shouldn't be anything wrong with that. But it doesn't mean anything either, and that does seem like something I should apologize for, because the absence of meaning always (and justifiably) generates disappointment. All the same, I enjoyed writing it, and so I hope that someone, hearing it performed, might enjoy himself a little. I enjoyed myself even if, as I've said, at the beginning I was in the grip of shyness and loathing.

What stayed with me, though, was the desire to write a real play – genuine, adult, serious, with all the undertones and meanings that such things deserve to have. I don't know if I'll ever write it. One thing I now know for sure is that writing plays requires one to forget that there will be voices and people and noise. It requires one to seek out that private relationship with his fellow human beings – moving along as it does in darkness and silence – that private relationship which is the only one that makes creation possible.

This play, my first, is dedicated to the actress Adriana Asti. If she hadn't come to see me that day, to ask me to write a play, I'd never have done it and perhaps I'd have stopped, as I always had before, after two lines. She was the one who induced me to conquer shyness and loathing. It was she because, through the image I had of her, which was part of my normal life, I could conceive of the theatre as normal and ordinary. I could conceive of it within a private relationship. For several days I lazed about, my thoughts buzzing with images of my friend – her hair, her eyes, her clothes, the way she moved. In the end, that image took up residence in the story that developed around her.

Of course, that was simply the external event, and, in fact, I was spurred to write a play by a need that is directly related to my writing – that is, to the desire to find a way to move beyond autobiography.

(Lately, in fact, I haven't been able to write other than in an openly auto-biographical form. I've always written in the first person, but lately the first person threatens to become obsessive.) Still, the external event was significant for me and I wanted to call attention to it.

Natalia Ginzburg
1966

Note

by Natalia Ginzburg[1]

Collected in this volume – not chronologically but in random order – are the plays I wrote between 1968 and 1988. The plays written earlier – that is, between 1964 and 1967 – are collected in another volume.

In all I have written, to date, ten plays: The first in July 1964;[2] the last in August 1988. The first for Adriana Asti; the last for Giulia Lazzarini. The others in between for no one.

The first is *I Married You to Cheer Myself Up*. I believe it may be the most light-hearted of my plays. *The Interview* is the last.

I wrote the first soon after I responded to a question that a theatre magazine had posed to writers: Why don't you write plays? I answered that I didn't write them because I couldn't imagine not instantly detesting any play I had written. It was true. Thinking about a play I might write provoked a profound sense of discomfort in me. Other writers responded that plays didn't suit them, citing a variety of reasons. Soon afterward, they set themselves to the task of writing plays. So did I. Quite a few plays were generated by the question in that magazine.[3]

Around that time, when the magazine came out with the various writers' answers, the actress Adriana Asti came to see me. She was someone I knew very well, and she told me to write a play with a part in it for her. I told her I thought it was unlikely. After that, I left for the country. I was alone there and I was bored and I started thinking about what kind of play I could write. I was curious to see whether my discomfort persisted or disappeared.

At the outset, I had in mind the following things: the face of Adriana Asti and her ironic smile; and the Carignano Theatre in Turin, where I had been for the first time when I was eight years old to see a play that had seemed to me magnificent. I don't remember anything about it except the title – *Peg o' My Heart* – and a young, slender girl with a huge straw hat.[4] Perhaps that's why I began a play that opened with a hat. In the first drafts, a hat appeared, but it turned into a man's hat. Little by little as I wrote, the Carignano Theatre disappeared. I felt no discomfort at all. From Adriana Asti I fashioned a young girl, slender and fragile. Adriana Asti was slender and fragile, but I made the girl in my play more slender and more fragile than Adriana Asti ever was. From her, I fashioned a girl who was very small, untidy, and rootless. I watched as a rather cheerful play emerged. How in the world it was cheerful, I don't know. I was not cheerful. But perhaps it came out that way as a result of the huge and delightful sense of astonishment one feels when one does something she has commanded herself never to do. Or perhaps the play came out cheerful because I was writing in haste, either without giving in to gloom or stopping to experience it only for brief moments. I wrote in haste, out of the fear that I wouldn't manage to finish. Hurriedly and out of boredom. Of course I knew that one must never write out of boredom; boredom is almost always infertile. Boredom is not to be obeyed. But little by little as I wrote, my boredom disappeared. I finished the play in a week. At certain times, when one writes, you stand still; at certain times you walk, and at certain times you run. This time I had the sensation not of running but of gliding. I just let things happen, as I did when I was very young, when I wrote blindly and without knowing where in the world I wanted to end up. It seemed to me I had been thrust back into my childhood.

It was a play with interminable monologues. I thought no actress would ever be able to commit them to memory. As plays, they seemed to me completely unusable.

The house where I was staying was new and they hadn't yet put in the telephone. In order to get to a telephone, one had to walk some twenty minutes along dirt paths and through vineyards. The public telephone was in a bar on the street. There was no direct dialling, and in order to call Rome one had to make a telephone appointment and wait a few hours. I called Adriana Asti several times. Once to tell her that I had finished a play but that the monologues were too long and that she wouldn't be able to memorize them. She told me to send it to her and I did. While I was in the bar or else walking through the vineyards as I came and went, I discovered that I was in some way very attached to the play I had written out of boredom and in haste and while gliding along and just letting things happen, and I very much hoped that someone might perform it. Another time I called Adriana Asti and she told me that the play suited her fine and that the long monologues posed no problem at all.

When I returned to Rome, I gave the play to Elsa Morante to read. She didn't like it at all. She invited me and Adriana Asti to supper in a restaurant in order to let us know just how little she had liked the play. She found it fatuous, foolish, saccharine, affected, and false. She began by saying to me, 'I'll tell you the truth.' It was something she used to say, repeating the phrase whenever she reprimanded someone. That evening, her reproaches were particularly harsh and severe, and it was as if I had committed not an ugly play but an ugly deed. She was angry with me, but also with Adriana Asti, who seemed to her somehow complicit in my guilt. But she was angry above all with me. I heard that phrase, 'I'll tell you the truth' – pronounced in her shrill, silvery voice – quite a few times during the course of that supper, at the table in the restaurant, in the open air under a pergola, in the cool, humid, end-of-September air.

My relationship with Elsa was very similar to my relationship with my sister. When Elsa was angry with me and she scolded me, I went mute because anything I might say seemed as useless to me as a pile of rags. The same thing happened with my sister. I loved Elsa, and everything that came to me from her seemed good, even when it was painful. In her rages I always sensed something that was healthy and invigorating. One emerged from those rages of hers dazed and astonished, feeling like a dog who has fallen into an irrigation ditch and comes back to dry land, shaking the water from his fur. One went away dazed, but not injured and not humiliated. That evening, like many others, I thought that, for me, being with Elsa was like being with my sister. My sister's rages, like Elsa's rages, were violent, impetuous, and generous. They left neither injuries nor wounds nor blood. On that occasion, I knew those rages would not persuade me to re-envision my play or to rewrite it, but only to thoroughly explore its total demolition. The strange thing is that total demolition can be immensely beneficial to someone who writes, in the same measure that complete approval can be immensely beneficial. Those who write are both vain and depressed. Demolition and approval keep the writer company and support him, nurturing him, sustaining him while he bounces back and forth between his depressions and his dreams of glory. What really hurts a writer, on the other hand, is a rain of courteous, gloomy, opaque, and soporific indifference. I read my play again through Elsa's eyes and I found it just as she had said. Fatuous, saccharine, affected, and perhaps false. I salvaged a few

short passages from it – sections into which people and events from my
life had insinuated themselves. I thought perhaps these few short passages would escape Elsa's notice. I didn't rip the play up or hide it in a
drawer. I was attached to it. I continued to wish to see it in a theatre. It
was staged in the winter. Adriana Asti performed.

Shortly afterward I wrote a second play. It was called *The Advertisement*. In its structure, it resembled the one that had preceded it, with
interminable monologues, but it was different in its substance and tone,
which was dark. It had its humorous passages but was in no way cheerful. Again, I gave it to Elsa to read and she told me it was a little better
than the other. One felt in it, she told me, 'something of true pain.' But
she told me not to write any more plays because it wasn't my cup of tea.
She didn't say it like that; I don't remember how she said it, but that was
the gist of it. Meanwhile, something was happening to me. I was finding
it difficult at times to write novels and stories. I preferred to try to write
plays. In plays, I could use the first person in a non-autobiographical
way, which gave me a sense of great freedom. It might be a man who
said 'I' or a woman completely different from me. Plays had become a
means of expression for me. So I wrote several plays over the course of
some time. Elsa didn't read them. The years passed, and that evening
on which she'd spoken so harshly to me in the restaurant seemed lovely
and far away. 'I'll tell you the truth.' Those words are preserved in my
memory, though the sound of her voice has been lost.

When we spent evenings having supper in restaurants, Elsa used to
order spinach, and she would say that she wanted it boiling hot. She
repeated 'boiling hot' two or three times in a shrill, imperious voice,
frowning. But then she didn't go out to supper anymore or at least not
with me. She stopped getting angry with the people around her. She
was too sick and too bitter to involve herself passionately and angrily
with the people she knew and with their mistakes. All of it – people and
their mistakes and their foolish ideas and their gossip – all of it must
have appeared distant and useless, like a swarm of gnats. And it was. It
was, in the place where she was then. A long time has passed since I've
heard her shrill, silvery voice at supper in the evening dampness. 'Boiling hot. I want it boiling hot.' 'Now I'll tell you the truth.'

I haven't written many plays. Only ten over the course of many
years.

At times, my plays have been produced. I would sit with the other
members of the audience, and sometimes I loved the words I had written, sometimes I detested them. One play was produced at the Cari-

gnano Theatre in Torino, the theatre of my childhood, the theatre where I had seen *Peg o' My Heart*. I had always remembered the red velvet seats, the balconies, the mirrors, the theatre curtain with its gold borders. But because they were now putting on one of my plays, it seemed to me that the theatre no longer held any of its former grandeur. My play rendered the place inhospitable and familiar at the same time. I could no longer perceive either solemnity or prestige there. Besides, by then I knew everything that lay behind the theatre curtain. The thick, black cords snaking across the floor. The metal stepladders in the corners. The long, narrow hallways. But I was acquainted above all with the fear that playwrights feel in a theatre, the fear that the people who come to see the play will be bored or that something unforeseen may happen. The actors feel that fear, which reigns in the midst of the red velvet seats and extends beyond the curtain. The public ignores it, but those to whom the play belongs, in one way or another, are well acquainted with it. The person who wrote the play watches the faces of the audience like a spy and hears them whispering. Sometimes, the things they whisper are appalling.

I was thinking about plays then the way I thought about novels, about short stories. The point of departure was the same for both. What was different was what came after. You write a novel and when you've finished it you offer it to an editor. If the editor publishes it, everything goes along fairly smoothly. You don't detest anyone. Or it could be that you detest the editor when he puts an ugly cover on your book or prints something stupid on the inside flap, or else when he forgets about your book and immediately stops sending it to bookstores, or else, finally, when he doesn't give you the money you are owed. But even then, you detest just one single person. If a play is produced on the stage, your lot then is to love or to hate quite a few people: the actors, the director, and the various others who live within the orbit of the theatre. You love them or you detest them. If a novel goes badly, on the other hand, the suffering is just for two – the editor and you. If it goes well, the celebration is for two. But if a play goes badly, you feel the rancour and unhappiness of many weighing down on you. If you're lucky, if people clap their hands, if the newspapers speak highly of your play, you can share your joy with lots of others. And you have, directly before your eyes, the audience, a visible, tangible audience about whom you had completely forgotten while writing your play, but which is now seated in the orchestra seats, terrifying you because you might bore them. Books are capable of sneaking off on their own, calmly and quietly.

Plays generate, within whomever has written them, strong ramifica-
tions of love and hate, and they make their way forward in the midst
of noise.

In my first plays, there were women who chattered tirelessly. After
that, I felt the desire to portray silent women. Then the men chattered.
The women spoke very little. It's not easy, in a play, to carry along a
character who speaks very little. But sometimes it's both wonderful and
necessary.

I'm used to imagining women as small, fragile, untidy, and rootless.
But theatre plays nasty tricks on you. Sometimes, there were women
I'd been thinking of as small, but the people who produced the plays
couldn't have cared less that I'd said I imagined small women, and
chose actresses who were tall and rather massive. And at times I'd been
thinking of poor characters, but on the stage would appear people with
beautiful clothing and a privileged air. I would protest, but it wasn't in
me to argue. They would tell you that the theatre has its own laws. At
times, these laws are absurd and inexplicable and carry us some distance from what was born in our imagination.

One day a young man by the name of Luca Coppola came to see
me. He was a small man, with huge tortoise-shell glasses and a lock of
black hair that danced back and forth across his eyes. He wore a blue,
brushed-cotton T-shirt. I had seen him once at Elsa's house. They were
friends, and he was working then as a theatre director. By the time he
came to see me, Elsa had been dead for perhaps a year. He told me he
had read a short play of mine entitled *Dialogue*, had liked it, and wanted
to put it on stage. *Dialogue* had been produced years before, on television and in a theatre. I was very pleased that this young man had liked
it and that he wanted to produce it again. For a moment I thought that
Elsa, through her friend, had absolved me. But it was a stupid thought
and I immediately swept it from my mind. She hadn't absolved me in
the slightest.

Luca Coppola and I became friends. We used to talk not just about
plays but about everything. I felt comfortable with him, and I didn't
realize that I was old and he was young. One evening, he came to visit
me with a friend of his, the actor Giancarlo Prati. We spent many hours
in conversation that evening on the terrace of my home.

He staged *Dialogue* – the play of mine that he had liked – in Cagliari
months later. He was very nervous and very happy.

They were murdered, Luca Coppola and his friend Giancarlo Prati,
last summer in a Sicilian town called Mazara del Vallo. They were
beaten, chased while they tried to escape and then murdered, at night,

on the seashore. The scene, the deception, and the murder resembled the assassination of Pasolini.[5]

Luca Coppola was someone with whom I talked happily and at length. Even today, it occurs to me to ask him questions. *The Interview* is a play I wrote a short time after he died. I dedicate it to him.

I wrote *The Interview* so that Giulia Lazzarini, an actress whom I admire and love, might perform in it. I thought of Giulia Lazzarini as I had thought of Adriana Asti in those years that are, by now, so far in the past. I thought of Giulia Lazzarini, trying to picture her profile, her eyes, her way of making her way through the world. I saw her as small, quiet, delicate, and fragile, and I sought to weave an episode around her fragility. Her, too, I made distracted, innocent, and rootless. Anyway, even when you write novels and short stories, you wind up thinking intensely of a person or of several people who are real. It's no different with plays.

In this play, there are three characters on stage and three who are only spoken of. Both groups are essential.

In all my plays there are, as here, some characters of whom much is said but who never put in an appearance. Being absent, they are silent. So, in the end, there is someone who is silent.

The Interview was produced at the Piccolo Teatro di Milano last May. I attended the performance on two very happy evenings. I was happy and so were the others. The direction was by Carlo Battistoni. The actors were Giulia Lazzarini, Alessandro Haber, Orsetta De Rossi, and Giulia Zanoni.

In all that we have written, whether plays or novels or something else, is hidden and preserved the time we lived through as we were writing. In plays, that time is hidden and preserved more diffusely and more intensely. Plays have a before and an after. A long train of events trails behind them, and a crowd of people and places revolves around them. Perhaps there isn't much about some of the plays that matters to us anymore, but that which is hidden and preserved within them and which revolves around them is forever dear. Houses or rooms we inhabited while writing and thinking about them. Sometimes they are houses or rooms in which we are no longer allowed or that we wish never to enter again. Towns to which we won't return. Theatres. Thick, black cords snaking across the floor. Friends we no longer spend time with. Voices to which we once listened devotedly and whose sound has been lost. Beloved faces. The memory of the dead.

July 1989

Notes

1 Ginzburg's *Nota* appeared in the second volume of her plays, *Teatro*, published by Einaudi in 1990.

2 The date on *Ti ho sposato per allegria*, as published by Einaudi in 1970, is July 1965.

3 In his notes to Einaudi's complete edition of Ginzburg's plays (*Natalia Ginzburg: Tutto il Teatro*, 2005), Domenico Scarpa identifies the article in question: 'Tre domande agli intellettuali. Gli scrittori e il teatro' ('Three Questions to Intellectuals – Writers and the Theatre'), which appeared in *Sipario*, no. 229 (May 1965). Typically, Ginzburg's responses to *Sipario*'s questions pulled no punches: 'There have always been very few plays written in Italy, and those few, it seems to me, are terrible. If we consider approaching the theatre, we are immediately overcome by a rush of unpleasant memories of terrible Italian plays … If … we begin outlining the possibility of a play set in our contemporary Italy, in our reality, what comes to mind is a grey compendium of the greyest, most terrible, most bloodless plays of Italian theatre.' The problem of Italian theatre, Ginzburg asserted, was first and foremost a problem of language: the best-known playwrights wrote in dialect (she cited Goldoni and De Filippo), but dialect was 'unusable' for those who wanted to write in 'Italian prose.' Too, written Italian was so markedly different from spoken Italian that the question became, What language should characters speak in plays? 'First, we had better learn how to create novels that are written in the even, normal, functional, real language we customarily speak. After that maybe we'll even try writing plays.' As for her 'current attitude, as an author, regarding the theatre,' Ginzburg responded that she would very much have liked to write a play, but 'every time I've tried to write, at the top of a page, "Piero: Where's my hat?" I nearly died of shame and I had to stop, overwhelmed by an acute attack of disgust. Because that Piero, that colon, that 'Where's my hat?' reflected all the terrible Italian plays I'd read and seen in my life.' ('Bibliografie,' 411–12; my translation.)

4 A comedy by the British playwright John Hartley Manners, *Peg o' My Heart* played on Broadway between 1912 and 1914 and thereafter enjoyed a long run in London. Manners also adapted the play into a novel (1913) and collaborated on all three film versions: W.C. DeMille's 1919 silent; a 1922 King Vidor remake with Manners's wife Laurette Taylor in the starring role; and a 1933 Robert Z. Leonard vehicle for Marion Davies. The careful reader will observe that, in her 1989 'Note,' Ginzburg writes that she saw the play when she was eight years old and not six, as she says in the 1966 'Preface'

to *Ti ho sposato per allegria*. Behind this discrepancy lies a small but interesting mystery (and here I am indebted to Pietro Crivellaro of the Teatro Stabile di Torino, whose painstaking research provided the information that follows). *Peg o' My Heart* was translated into Italian as *Peg del Mio Cuore* by Silvano D'Arborio and Luigi Motta and first published in 1924 by the Milan-based publisher Sonzogno. In October/November 1922, the Emma Gramatica company performed *Peg* both at the Teatro Manzoni in Milan and for three weeks at the Teatro Carignano in Turin as part of a repertory season that included various other plays; we cannot be sure whether *Peg* actually premiered in Milan or Turin, though a 4 November 1922 review of the Milan production in the *Corriere della Sera* provides a strong argument for that city. In any case, the Milan theatre magazine *L'Arte Drammatica* reported, at the end of 1922, that box-office receipts for *Peg* exceeded those of any other of the season's productions. Judging from Motta's preface to the 1924 edition of the translation of *Peg*, the play was apparently much more successful with the public than with critics, to whom Motta rather heatedly responded. All that said, it seems likely that Ginzburg did, indeed, first see the play when she was six and not eight.

5 In November 1975, Pier Paolo Pasolini, the radical Italian writer and film-maker, was murdered on the seashore in the coastal village of Ostia near Rome. A seventeen-year-old man, Giuseppe Pelosi, was arrested and convicted of the murder. Even at the time, many believed that Pasolini had been lured into a trap by Pelosi but murdered by a number of unknown others. Indeed, in 2005 Pelosi retracted his confession, and an investigation into Pasolini's death was reopened. Before their deaths, Luca Coppola and Giancarlo Prati had collaborated in translations and other projects related to the work of gay Argentine playwright Copi (Raúl Damonte Taborda), who died of AIDS in 1987.

THE WRONG DOOR:
THE COMPLETE PLAYS OF NATALIA GINZBURG

I Married You to Cheer Myself Up[1]

A PLAY IN THREE ACTS

Cast:
Pietro
Giuliana, Pietro's wife
Vittoria, a maid
Pietro's Mother
Ginestra, Pietro's sister

The first production of this play occurred in February 1965 at Santa Vittoria d'Alba, under the direction of Luciano Salce and with the following performers: Adriana Asti, Renzo Montagnani, Itala Marchesini, Gabriella Giorgelli, and Rita Guerrini. The scenery and costumes were by Luca Sabatelli.

ACT ONE

[*A middle-class apartment in Rome, late morning.*][2]

PIETRO: My hat, where's my hat?
GIULIANA: You have a hat?
PIETRO: I used to. Now I can't find it.
GIULIANA: I don't remember any hat.
PIETRO: Maybe you can't remember. I haven't worn it for a while. We've only known each other for a month.
GIULIANA: Don't say it like that – 'We've only known each other for a month' – as if I weren't your wife.
PIETRO: You've been my wife for a week. In that week, and during the

entire month before that, I never wore my hat. I only wear it when it's raining hard or when I go to funerals. Today it's raining and I have to go to a funeral. It's a soft, brown hat. A fine hat.

GIULIANA: Maybe it's at your mother's house.

PIETRO: Maybe. You haven't seen it by chance, mixed in with all my other things?

GIULIANA: No. But I had all your things put in mothballs. Could be your hat was in there, too. You're going to a funeral? Who died?

PIETRO: A guy died. How many days has Vittoria been with us?

GIULIANA: Since Thursday. Three days.

PIETRO: And right away you had her put all our winter things in mothballs?

GIULIANA: Yours. I don't really have any winter things. I have a skirt, a sweater, and a raincoat.

PIETRO: You had all my winter things put in mothballs? Right away?

GIULIANA: Right away.

PIETRO: Very clever. Brilliant. But now let's fish out my hat. I have to go to this funeral. With my mother.

GIULIANA: Tell me who died.

PIETRO: A guy named Lamberto Genova. He was a friend of my family. He died the other day of a coronary thrombosis. Quite suddenly. In the bathroom, while he was shaving.

GIULIANA: Lamberto Genova? I knew him. I knew him very well. He's dead?

PIETRO: Yes.

GIULIANA: In the bathroom! Lamberto Genova! I'm telling you, I knew him. He even lent me some money once.

PIETRO: Impossible. He was a very tight-fisted man.

GIULIANA: But he lent me some money. He was in love with me.

PIETRO: Vittoria! See if you can manage to find a hat, a brown hat, a soft, furry one. The Signora says you may have put it in mothballs.

VITTORIA: (*Entering.*) It must be in the Four Seasons wardrobe.

PIETRO: What's a Four Seasons wardrobe?

GIULIANA: It's the wardrobe in the hallway. It's got four compartments. Vittoria says that's what it's called.

VITTORIA: But we'll need the stepladder. I'll have to go get it from the cellar. The winter clothes are all up on top and I won't be able to get all the way up there with just a chair.

PIETRO: Can it possibly be this difficult to get your own hat back?

Vittoria exits.

GIULIANA: Now that I think of it, I remember very clearly the last time I saw....

PIETRO: But you told me you'd never seen it!

GIULIANA: I wasn't talking about the hat. I was talking about Lamberto Genova. You know when I saw Lamberto Genova for the last time?

PIETRO: When?

GIULIANA: A few days before I met you. It was January. I was taking a walk in the rain and I was feeling this immense desire to die. I was walking on the bridge and I was planning to throw myself in the river, and I was thinking that I'd leave my raincoat on the railing of the bridge, with a letter in the pocket for my friend Elena, so that way they'd give her the raincoat. Really, it's a beautiful raincoat and I didn't like the idea that it might get lost.

VITTORIA: (*Entering*). Here's your hat. (*Exits.*)

PIETRO: Damn, it really stinks of mothballs. (*He puts it on his head.*)

GIULIANA: Then I see him, Lamberto Genova, coming along the bridge, this tiny, tiny man, with fat cheeks, and that smile of his....

PIETRO: No. Your Lamberto Genova wasn't the one I knew.

GIULIANA: Why? The one you knew wasn't a tiny man with big, fat cheeks?

PIETRO: No.

GIULIANA: Mine was. He was a tiny man, his hair completely white, with these two big, fat cheeks. So, you know, as I was saying, I thought to myself the moment I saw him that morning: 'Damn. I owe him some money.' And I thought, 'Let's hope he invites me to lunch.' And then I thought some more, 'For the time being, I won't kill myself.' And in fact he did take me to lunch. You know where?

PIETRO: Where?

GIULIANA: To the Grotte del Piccione. And while I ate I was thinking, 'This guy here is in love with me, and I might even marry him. Then he'll pay all my bills and I can live a peaceful life in a nice, warm house, with this little old man – a good, calm, dignified man. He'll be like a father to me. That's what I was thinking.

PIETRO: My Lamberto Genova had a wife and children.

GIULIANA: Mine had a wife and children, too. But he might have been willing to get a divorce.

PIETRO: There is no divorce in Italy.

GIULIANA: He would have left the country. He was really in love with me. He said he'd never felt such a strong attraction for a woman.

PIETRO: And then?

GIULIANA: Then what?

PIETRO: Then. After the Grotte del Piccione.

GIULIANA: Then nothing. He took me back home in his car. I talked to him about whether he could help me find a job. So he said he would introduce me to a friend of his, a marchesa who ran a big fashion house and might be looking for a *vendeuse*.

PIETRO: My Lamberto Genova was a doctor. He didn't have women friends who ran fashion houses, absolutely not. He was busy and he didn't have time to waste on girlfriends. He was a very serious person, a very highly esteemed professional man. He was a friend of mine, and anyway, he isn't the one you're talking about. Now I need to go because my mother's expecting me. We have to go to this funeral.

GIULIANA: How cheerful, going to a funeral with your mother.

PIETRO: Why do you always use such a bitchy tone when you talk about my mother?

GIULIANA: No, I was just saying how cheerful to go to a funeral in the company of someone who's as much fun as your mother.

PIETRO: Could you leave my mother out of it, please?

GIULIANA: Don't you want to know if I went to see that friend of my Lamberto Genova about a job?

PIETRO: Tell me, but hurry up because I'm late.

GIULIANA: I didn't go because then I met you. But I was ready to marry anyone, you understand, when I met you. Even Lamberto Genova. With his big, fat cheeks and his owl eyes. Anyone. I was ready to do anything.

PIETRO: So you've told me.

GIULIANA: Anything. I wanted to get out of that situation. It was drink or drown.

PIETRO: Understood.

GIULIANA: So I married you. *Also* for the money. You understand?

PIETRO: Yes.

GIULIANA: And you married me *also* because you felt sorry for me. Isn't it true that you married me *also* because you felt sorry for me?

PIETRO: True. (*Exits.*)

GIULIANA: (*Shouting after him.*) So I guess that means our marriage isn't exactly sound!

VITTORIA: (*Entering.*) What shall I make for lunch?

GIULIANA: Eggplant parmesan.

VITTORIA: Again today?

GIULIANA: Yes, again today. Why?

VITTORIA: I've been here three days and we always make eggplant parmesan. Will you be getting up?

GIULIANA: Not right now.

VITTORIA: Will the attorney be home late?

GIULIANA: I don't know. He went to a funeral.

VITTORIA: Someone died?

GIULIANA: This guy named Lamberto Genova died. I knew him too, though it might be that the one I knew wasn't named Lamberto. Maybe he was named Adalberto. I can't remember very well. I don't have a good memory for names. Do you remember names?

VITTORIA: I do. I have an incredible memory. When I was in school, I learned everything really fast – the rivers, the capitals, the wars, everything. The teacher used to say, 'Let's all listen to Vittoria, who knows her capitals so well.' It would have been nice to stay in school. I went up until fourth grade, then I had to go off to work in the country. I had eight brothers and sisters.

GIULIANA: Me, I never liked studying. My mother wanted me to become a teacher, but I wanted to be an actress or a ballerina. So when I was seventeen, I ran away from home.

VITTORIA: You ran away? And you never went back?

GIULIANA: I go back every now and then, but not too often. I don't get along with my mother. As soon as we're together, we start arguing. I disappoint her because I didn't become a teacher, or an actress, or a ballerina.

VITTORIA: But now that you're married, your mother must be very happy.

GIULIANA: I wrote her that I was getting married. She wrote me back to be careful because there was a lot of riff-raff running around. My mother is very pessimistic.

VITTORIA: But haven't you taken the attorney to meet her?

GIULIANA: Not yet. I sent her some money. But you know, I'm afraid my mother won't spend the money I sent her. I'm afraid she's put it all into interest-bearing bonds. For me. For some day when I might need it. She's always been a maniac for putting her money into bonds as soon as she manages to save any.

VITTORIA: There is a lot of riff-raff running around, it's true. Your mother's right. I've been engaged three times and all three times it

turned out bad because they weren't decent people and my mother
wasn't very happy about it. My mother's opinion counts for a lot
with me, you have no idea. I'd walk through fire for my mother.

GIULIANA: Where do you live?

VITTORIA: My family lives in Fara Sabina.[3] I'll take you with me one
of these days. Do you like pork? This year we had such a beautiful
pig that everyone was envious. But now you've got to let me get
back to work. You're keeping me here talking and I'm going to get
behind.

GIULIANA: Can't you stay and chat a little longer? The house is already
so clean. You cleaned it yesterday. You know, I've never had a maid.
You're the first. I find that a maid is a great convenience around the
house.

VITTORIA: You've discovered the wheel!

GIULIANA: Really a huge convenience.

VITTORIA: Didn't you have a maid in your mother's house?

GIULIANA: Not in our wildest dreams.

VITTORIA: Me, I'm good at every kind of work. I don't know how I
manage to do everything so well. In the houses where I've been,
when I left, they always missed me.

GIULIANA: My mother lives in Romagna, in a town called Pieve di
Montesecco. That's where I was born. It was a little house, dark,
damp, and my mother filled it entirely with furniture so you
couldn't move inside. I slept with my mother in an enormous bed,
under a yellow quilt. My mother makes pants.

VITTORIA: She makes pants? Your mother?

GIULIANA: Yes.

VITTORIA: You're almost like me, then. You were born poor, too.

GIULIANA: Only we didn't have a pig. We didn't even have a hen or
a rabbit. We didn't have anything at all. We were really poor, and
every once in a while my mother would go across town to ask my
father for some money, because he had a general store. My father
lived with another woman, and he and the woman had a bunch of
children together. So he didn't have much money either. They used
to fight, him and my mother, in the general store, and my father's
children were there, all frightened, plus the other woman, skinny
as a rake, with this big bun of kinky hair piled up on her head, and
she'd start yelling at my mother and waving these long arms of hers
in the air.... My mother would leave in a rage, a tiny little woman
all bent over, with her umbrella stuck under one arm and her purse

full of coffee and sugar, because my father used to give her pasta
and sugar and coffee, but she wanted some money, too. She came
back home, still furious, red in the face, and she'd start fussing
around the house, this tiny little woman in a Japanese robe that my
father gave her as a gift when they were still together.... She used
to make these soupy mixtures out of bran and milk, because my
father always gave her a lot of bran, and then these concoctions,
sort of compotes, out of prunes and apples, and if she had any
leftovers after she cooked, she'd put them in little saucepans and
cups on the windowsill. She always has a row of saucepans on the
windowsill. And she's crazy for old newspapers besides. She saves
all her newspapers. She has piles of them under the bed, under the
tables, and if she likes certain pages or photographs she tears them
out and pastes them on the wall. Above her bed she has all these
torn-out pages from the newspaper with photos of Pierino Gamba,
that young boy who became a prodigy as an orchestra conductor.
When I was seventeen years old, I ran away. My father gave me the
money.

VITTORIA: So then what?

GIULIANA: So then I ran away and I came here to Rome to stay with
my friend Elena, who was working as a sales clerk in a stationery
store. I ran away because I wanted to become an actress or else a
ballerina. And also because I didn't want to see all those saucepans
and newspapers anymore. And my mother, when she saw that I'd
run away, she raced over to my father's to get him to come after
me. And my father told her he wouldn't even dream of it, and that
maybe I'd get lucky, maybe become a famous actress for real and I'd
support all of them – him, my mother, that other woman of his and
their children. And my mother went back home and must have had
to console herself with thinking that I was going to turn out like
Pierino Gamba or Greta Garbo.

VITTORIA: And you, in the meantime?

GIULIANA: And in the meantime I was here. At first I was happy because I wasn't at Pieve di Montesecco anymore, but in Elena's room
on the Campo dei Fiori instead. I didn't know how to go about
becoming an actress, but I thought it would be enough if I walked
around on the streets because then someone could stop me and say,
'You're exactly what I'm looking for in my film!' So in the beginning
I didn't do anything, I strolled around the streets and waited and
used up all the money that my father had given me. Then I started

working at the stationery store, too. Then one day I spilled a big bottle of ink on a customer's dress. I didn't do it on purpose. It was really heavy and my hand slipped. But the owner of the stationery store was furious and she fired me on the spot.

VITTORIA: I'll bet she did!

GIULIANA: It wasn't my fault. I was standing on a stepladder, the woman was right there down below me, and the cap on the bottle wasn't sealed right and all the ink poured onto the woman's dress. We tried to get the stain out with milk, but it was useless. The woman got so mad and so did everyone else. They fired me. For a little while I was without a job, then I was taken on by a guy who had a record store, a guy named Paoluccio. He was really in love with me.

VITTORIA: You, too?

GIULIANA: Not me. In the record store I happened to meet someone. This guy who always came in to listen to records. He had a black moustache and a pale face with dark eyes that were so, so sad. He never laughed.

VITTORIA: Never?

GIULIANA: Never. He had this black oversized sweater with the edges done in suede, also black. A beautiful sweater. I think I fell in love with that sweater first.

VITTORIA: And then?

GIULIANA: Then I fell in love with him. His name was Manolo. And Elena said, 'No, no, don't fall in love with that one! I don't like him! He's so black, so black he looks like the Black Knight!' And I said: 'And who's the Black Knight?' And she said: 'I don't know.'

VITTORIA: And so?

GIULIANA: So this Manolo was always sitting on an armchair in the record store, listening to music and smoking his pipe, and looking around with these dark eyes that were so sad, so sad. And then once he took me to his house. He had an apartment on Via Giulia. He lived alone there with a cat.

VITTORIA: Black?

GIULIANA: White. A white cat, fat as a sheep, with a tail that went on forever. We didn't really make love that time. He made me tea. And then he just sat there with the cat in his arms, petting it, looking at me with that sad face of his.... And I was sitting on the rug and I loved him, and the sadness was just consuming me. And he told me that he wasn't capable of love anymore. Because he was always

thinking about his wife, who had left him. The wife's name was
Topazia.

VITTORIA: And why did she leave him?

GIULIANA: Because she was a restless, complicated woman, who got
tired of men immediately, and as soon as she had one, she immediately wanted a different one. That's what he told me. And he told
me that every now and then Topazia would turn up at his place,
tired, run down, in sad shape, make herself a couple of fried eggs,
take a bath, and then disappear again. She'd run off in the car. She
was a maniac for cars. She was always changing cars. And she
raced around in the car – like a crazy woman – and he was always
afraid she might kill herself.

VITTORIA: What strange people!

GIULIANA: On the other hand, he couldn't stand cars. He was very rich,
extremely rich, because his family had some land. But he didn't
like money, and he liked to live as though he was poor, in that
little apartment that he kept up all by himself. He wrote. He was a
writer. He'd published two novels and a book of verse. The book
of verse was entitled *The Useless Salamander*. One of the novels was
called *Springtime with the Sailor*. The other one was called *Jesus, Take
Me Away*.

VITTORIA: Jesus, take me away?

GIULIANA: I tried to read them. But I didn't understand one word.
I even gave them to Elena, and she didn't understand anything
either. And she was always telling me: 'No, no. I don't like that one!'
Elena has a long nose, big and long, and when something doesn't
sit right with her, her nose gets even longer, even bigger, and it
gets all scrunched up. But it doesn't get shorter when it's scrunched
up, it gets even bigger and even longer. It's very strange. She used
to say, 'No, no, I don't like him! I don't like that one! He doesn't
even make love to you, maybe he can't, maybe he's not a real man.
You've gotten yourself into quite a mess! Jesus, take me away!'

VITTORIA: And you?

GIULIANA: Because at first we weren't really even making love. For a
while we went along like that. I went to see him in the evening. I sat
there on the carpet while he petted the cat, listened to music, drank
tea. And he said how sad he was not being able to love me. I felt as
though I was being eaten up by sadness.

VITTORIA: And then?

GIULIANA: Then he told me to come live with him. And Elena was

beside herself. But I couldn't even imagine telling him no. So I went
to live with him and then, finally, we made love. And in the morning he told me not to get up, that there wasn't any point in getting
up, and so I stopped going to the store and I lost my job.

VITTORIA: But by then he was saying that he loved you?

GIULIANA: No. He always said he didn't love me. He was always telling
me about his wife Topazia. How intelligent she was, how beautiful, how stylish. Me, on the other hand, I had no style at all. And I
felt unhappy. I'd never been unhappy in my life. That was the first
time. When I lived with my mom, at Pieve di Montesecco, I wasn't
unhappy. I was sick and tired of being there, but I wasn't unhappy.
And instead, now I was miserable. And I'd lost all my friends – I
hardly ever saw Elena, and when I saw her she wasn't nice to me.
She told me I was destroying my life. And Paoluccio, the one from
the record store, I didn't see him anymore either. I stayed in bed all
day, or else I sat on the carpet, petting the cat, and thinking.... I had
learned to think. I'd become a different person.

VITTORIA: And him in the meantime?

GIULIANA: In the meantime he sat in front of the typewriter and typed,
every now and then, a word. Then he'd put on a record. This sad,
sad music.... At lunch, sometimes we made it to the trattoria downstairs, but sometimes he would cook. The housework, he did it all.
He was as good as a woman at housework.

VITTORIA: Did he even do the ironing?

GIULIANA: He ironed, he sewed buttons – everything, really. Being
alone, he'd learned how. Sometimes I thought, 'Who knows if he'll
marry me?' But it was a vague thought, confused, and I didn't dare
mention it. I put it right out of my mind. I gulped it down, the way
you'd gulp down some little bite of stolen food. He would have had
to get divorced in order to marry me. Out of the country.

VITTORIA: Did he have any children with Topazia?

GIULIANA: No. But can you imagine me asking him if he was going to
marry me? It wasn't something we discussed. He didn't love me,
I'm telling you. He considered me a person without style. And me,
because I felt so unhappy being a person without style, I suffered,
I ate my heart out. I became ugly, skinny, pale. And I was always
dreaming about bats and snakes. And I would ask him, in the
morning, why do I always dream about bats and snakes?

VITTORIA: And he'd say?

GIULIANA: Him? Nothing. He shrugged his shoulders. I wasn't impor-

tant to him. Nothing I said really ever sat all that well with him. He
thought I was always talking in banalities.

VITTORIA: But why did you stay with him, if he treated you like that?

GIULIANA: Because I couldn't detach myself from him. I couldn't move.
I was bewitched. Plus, it wasn't as though he mistreated me. Sometimes he was good to me, it was just that he had this indifference,
this indifference.... I'd been living with him for more than three
months when I realized I was expecting a baby.

VITTORIA: Oh! And so?

GIULIANA: And so I told him, and he told me I was wrong, that it was
impossible. He said it so convincingly that even I started to think
it was impossible and that I'd made a mistake. And one morning
I woke up and he wasn't there anymore. I looked for him everywhere. And he wasn't there. And I find, on the kitchen table, a
letter. He said he was going away for a while to visit his relatives.
He didn't leave an address. He said not to wait for him, because
he didn't know when he'd be back. He said I could go ahead and
stay in the apartment for a while if I wanted, but only until the end
of September, because after that he was subletting the apartment
to some Americans. I didn't know anything about any Americans.
He'd never said anything to me about them.

VITTORIA: And you? What did you do then?

GIULIANA: He'd left me a little money in a drawer in the credenza.
Hardly any. Thirty thousand lire.

VITTORIA: Not much.

GIULIANA: Right. I started to cry, and I cried for I don't know how long.
I must have cried for two or three days without eating or sleeping.
Every now and then I would go into the bathroom and wash my
face with cold water. Then I'd go back to bed and start to cry again.
By then, I was sure I was having a baby because every time I lit a
cigarette I got such an attack of nausea! I didn't have anyone to cry
with, I had to cry alone. Elena was away on vacation, because it was
summer. It was the end of July. Paoluccio, the one with the records,
I tried telephoning him, and he didn't answer. I didn't have anyone
except the cat. Manolo hadn't taken the cat with him. So I spent
hours petting the cat's tail, crying, while he meowed.... He was a
very affectionate cat. It seemed as though he wanted to console me
when he meowed.

VITTORIA: And then?

GIULIANA: Then nothing. One fine day I stopped crying and I went out to buy a little something to eat for me and the cat. A few more days passed and I was walking a lot, I was going out in the streets in the sun, because I was hoping if I walked and tired myself out, the baby would just disappear. But the days passed and I still had the baby. And one day, I was coming back home with a shopping bag full of peaches, because I didn't feel like eating anything else, just peaches. And in the courtyard I see this girl washing a car with a sponge. The car was very dirty and so was the girl, who was wearing some filthy white shorts and a sweaty T-shirt. And the girl looks at me and I look at her and that was it, and I went inside the house. And after a little, I hear the key turn and there's the filthy girl standing in front of me. And I ask her, 'Excuse me. Who are you?' And the girl says, 'Isn't Signor Manolo Pierfederici here?' And I say, 'No, why? Who are you?' And the girl says, 'I'm his wife.' And I say, 'Topazia!' totally dumbfounded.

VITTORIA: It was Topazia!

GIULIANA: Yes. If you knew how much I'd thought about her, about this Topazia – how many times I tried to imagine her. And there she was! A big, filthy girl with fat legs, blue eyes, blond hair falling over her neck, and wearing a very sweaty striped T-shirt. She said to me, 'Do you mind if I take a bath?'

VITTORIA: And so?

GIULIANA: So I told her, 'Wouldn't you like a couple of fried eggs, too?' And she started laughing and she said, 'Why not? But I'm going to take a bath first.' And she took a bath and she came out with Manolo's bathrobe, and she sat on the carpet in the living room, right next to me. And then I told her the whole story. To someone else – to the Topazia I'd imagined, so beautiful, disdainful, haughty – I wouldn't have said anything. But to the one there, to that great big ordinary girl, I felt the urge to tell her the whole story. The way I'm doing with you right now. And I asked her, 'Why did you dump him?' And she said, 'Me? Dump him? Like hell I dumped him. He dumped me!' Understand? That's how she talked. She had no style at all.

VITTORIA: She had no style?

GIULIANA: None at all. And she told me, 'He dumped me a little bit after we were married. He told me he wasn't capable of love. In the beginning I was desperate, but then I resigned myself to it and I found myself a job. I take photographs. I drive around in a car and I take photographs for a weekly magazine. Sometimes I turn

up here. I rest a little, take a bath, and if he's here we chat because
we've stayed friends. I don't hold a grudge against him. He's a man
who doesn't get along well with women.' That's what she said,
and I felt relieved, liberated, light, because in all those months I'd
felt such a terrible anguish growing inside me. I thought he didn't
love me because I was stupid, banal, vulgar, and because I had no
style. I told Topazia that and she started to laugh and she said, 'He
told you that you didn't have any style either? He always said the
same thing to me.' I had quite a laugh then! We had quite a laugh
together, the two of us!

VITTORIA: And then?

GIULIANA: Then we made ourselves some fried eggs and we ate all
the peaches and we went to sleep. And before she went to sleep,
Topazia said, 'Tomorrow, let's think about what you can do about
the baby. If you want to keep it, I'll help you raise him because I
have an inverted uterus and I can't have children.' And as I was falling asleep I thought to myself, 'Yes, yes, I'm keeping this baby. I'll
go to work. Topazia will help me find a job. I'll take photographs,
too!' But then I wake up in the morning and I start to cry, and I say,
'No, Topazia, no, I don't think I can have this baby! I don't have a
place to live. I don't have a job. I don't have any money. I don't have
anything.' And she said, 'Okay.' And she took me to a Hungarian
doctor, her friend, and he gave me an abortion.

VITTORIA: And then?

GIULIANA: Then I stayed in bed for a few days and Topazia took care
of me. When I was well, I went all around the city with her, and
I waited for her in the car while she went to her appointments
for work. She was very active, Topazia was. She was doing a ton
of things. In her free time she was taking Russian lessons, sight-
singing lessons, crew lessons. I couldn't even tell you all the things
she was doing. She went swimming at the pool, too. When I went
with her to the pool, I only went into the water up to my waist,
because I don't know how to swim and I get scared. Then I would
wait for her in the sun, on a deckchair. I had so much fun with her!
She made me feel so cheerful! I'd never had a girlfriend, apart from
Elena. The moments when I was by myself, on a deckchair at the
pool while Topazia was swimming, I would think of something and
I would say to myself, 'I need to remember what I was just thinking
because Topazia will be here soon and I want to tell her.' And then
here would come Topazia with her hair sopping because she always

swam without a cap, in her faded blue bikini and her fat legs. Apart from her legs, she had a good body. But she had no style.

VITTORIA: What does that mean, she had no style?

GIULIANA: It means she had no style. Life was simple to her. She took things however they came along. Anyway, I got along great with Topazia and I had more fun with her than I did with anyone else. With her, everything seemed easy. She didn't make a big fuss over things. She's someone who knows how not to make a fuss. On the other hand, when Elena came back and I told her the whole story, she started to cry. Elena doesn't know how not to make a fuss. She cries a lot, Elena does. She's one of those people who cries, and she has that long, long nose that's even longer when she cries, and it gets all wet and splotchy, and all that crying was getting on my nerves. She said, 'I knew it, I knew it! I knew it was going to turn out like this! And what are you going to do with a baby?' And I said, 'but I had an abortion.' And she said, 'Yes, you had an abortion, okay, but the next time this happens to you how are you going to manage? How are you going to manage? Jesus, take me away!' I wasn't having a good time with Elena. And I told her. I told her, 'I'm not having a good time with you anymore. Topazia's the only one I have a good time with!' She was very jealous of Topazia. And she said, 'You've turned mean. You've really turned mean!' Then Topazia left. She had to go to America for her magazine. So I went back to Elena's to stay. I wanted to take Manolo's cat with me, but Elena didn't want it because she said she didn't want anything in her house that belonged to Manolo, not even the cat, so I gave it to the doorman. And that was the beginning of a hideous period, because Topazia wasn't around anymore, and I didn't have a job, and Elena with her nose all long from crying over me, telling me that maybe it would be better if I went back to Pieve di Montesecco or else I'd fall into another ugly mess with some depraved guy, and I was wandering the streets waiting for something to happen to me. Topazia had left me a little money and even a letter for her friend in the antique store, but that guy didn't take me on in his shop because he already had a clerk, and Paoluccio had someone else in his record store, too. And meanwhile, little by little I was falling out of love with Manolo, but falling out of love is hideous – men all seem like idiots to you, and you wonder whether there are any left who are worth loving. So then one day I ran into a friend of Topazia's, a photographer, and he took me to a party. The party was at a house

on Via Margutta, a house with sloped ceilings that was nothing but
stairs and more stairs. There were a lot of people there, all sitting
around on those stairs, and eating cotechino[4] with lentils and drinking red wine, and they were dancing. And I was a little uncomfortable because except for the photographer, I didn't know anyone.
But after I drank a little wine, I wasn't uncomfortable anymore, and
I started to feel more cheerful. And there, at that party, that's where
I met Pietro. He was sitting on the first step and chatting with this
girl in orange slacks, who I later found out was his cousin. And by
the end I was completely drunk and I couldn't find the photographer anymore, and I was dancing by myself with my shoes in my
hand. And my head was spinning, and I fell down right by those
orange slacks. And I said, 'Something to remember: You can't wear
high heels with slacks! And another thing: having a pair of slacks
made in that colour was a terrible idea! You've got no style at all!'
And the girl laughed and laughed.… I fainted.

VITTORIA: You fainted?

GIULIANA: Not really fainted. Anyway, everything was kind of confused. It was the wine. And I found myself in the bedroom that
belonged to the owners of the house – a very kind painter and his
wife. And Pietro was holding my head and making me drink coffee.
The first thing I asked was if I had vomited. It would have upset me
to have vomited in front of such kind people. They told me I hadn't.
The girl with the orange slacks was fanning me with a newspaper.
And then Pietro walked me home. I wasn't drunk anymore, and I
was a little humiliated and sad. He went upstairs with me.

VITTORIA: To Elena's place?

GIULIANA: Yes, but Elena wasn't home then because she was with one
of her relatives who needed to have an operation on her stomach.
Pietro stayed with me. I told him the whole story. Then in the
morning he went to take a shower at his mother's house, because
the hot water heater was broken at our place. And I thought: He'll
never come back. But in fact he came back a few hours later with a
sack from the supermarket full of all kinds of things to eat. And we
lived together for ten days, until Elena came back. And in those ten
days, I asked him every now and then, 'Do you think I have style?'
And he would say, 'No.' Even he didn't think I had any style. But
with him there, I didn't care. I told him everything that came into
my head. I never shut up. And every now and then he'd say: 'You
never shut up for a minute. My head feels like it's about to explode.'

VITTORIA: You're certainly someone who could make a person feel like his head was about to explode.

GIULIANA: And then when Elena was due to come back, I told him, 'It's too bad you won't be able to stay here because that annoying Elena is coming back, plus the house is hers anyway.' And he said, 'Yes, that's too bad.' And I said to him, 'Marry me. Because if you don't marry me, who will?'

VITTORIA: What did he say?

GIULIANA: He said, 'That's true.' And he married me.

VITTORIA: But a person could say you've had incredible luck! Considering all that's happened, you've really had terrific luck!

GIULIANA: I still don't know if it was luck.

VITTORIA: It wasn't luck? To marry a young, handsome lawyer with lots of money – and you poor? You who didn't know how you were going to take care of yourself?

GIULIANA: Exactly. I didn't know. I was in debt up to here. I didn't have a job. And besides, it's not as though I have this great urge to work. I told him, I told Pietro – 'Yes, I'll marry you. But I'm afraid I don't love you, with you it isn't like it was with Manolo!' With Manolo, it was like I was bewitched. And he said, 'Never mind that.' And when Elena came back home, I told her, 'You know, I've found someone to marry me.' And she said, 'Someone to marry you?' Oh, so we're going to start all over again now with some new mess? Oh, poor me! Jesus, take me away!' She didn't want to believe it, that there was someone who was going to marry me. And when Pietro came, she stared at him with her beady little eyes and pointed her nose at him like she wanted to sting him. Then she said, 'Well, who knows, maybe this one isn't "Jesus, take me away." This one seems like a decent guy.' And I said, 'But I don't feel bewitched!' And she said, 'Go to hell.'

VITTORIA: She was right.

GIULIANA: Maybe so.

VITTORIA: God, but it's late. I need to get into the kitchen. The attorney will be back soon, and lunch isn't ready.

GIULIANA: You can tell him that it was my fault, that I made you stop and talk for a while.

VITTORIA: You made me talk? I never even opened my mouth. You did all the talking. Boy, do you talk! Do you always talk like that?

GIULIANA: Always.

VITTORIA: But when you talk that much, don't you get thirsty?

GIULIANA: Yes. Bring me a glass of milk.

VITTORIA: Now you want milk? It's noon!

GIULIANA: I'm very fond of milk.

Vittoria returns with a glass of milk, then leaves. Pietro enters.

PIETRO: (*Picking something up off the floor.*) What is this? My pajamas? How come Vittoria hasn't made the room up yet?

GIULIANA: How could she make the room up? Can't you see I'm still in bed?

PIETRO: And don't you think you ought to get up?

GIULIANA: I chatted a little with Vittoria. I told her my life story. She stayed to listen; she didn't miss a syllable. You on the other hand don't listen to me when I talk. This morning you left while I was still talking, even though I was saying something important.

PIETRO: Oh, really? What were you saying?

GIULIANA: I was saying that I don't see any serious reason for the two of us to live together.

PIETRO: That's what you were telling me?

GIULIANA: Yes.

PIETRO: We have no serious reason for living together? That's what you think?

GIULIANA: That's what I think. You strike me as a very lightweight person. You proved you weren't a serious person when you married me.

PIETRO: I am not a lightweight! I'm a person who always knows what he's doing.

GIULIANA: You've got quite a high opinion of yourself!

PIETRO: Maybe.

GIULIANA: Me, I never know what I'm doing. I make one blunder after another. Anyway, how can you say you always know what you're doing? Up to now you haven't done anything. Nothing important, I mean. Getting married was the first important thing in your life.

PIETRO: Before I met you, I was on the verge of getting married at least eighteen times. I always pulled myself back because I discovered something in those women that gave me chills. In the depths of their spirits, I discovered a stinger. They were wasps. When I found you, and I saw that you weren't a wasp, I married you.

GIULIANA: Something offends me in the way you say I'm not a wasp. Are you trying to say that I'm some domesticated little animal, innocuous, meek? A butterfly?

PIETRO: I said you weren't a wasp. I didn't say you were a butterfly.

You're always ready to pat yourself on the back for being so charm-ing.

GIULIANA: I don't think butterflies are charming. I think they're hate-ful. I almost prefer wasps. It offends me that you think I have no stinger. It's true, but it offends me.

PIETRO: The truth offends you? The truth should never be offensive. If you're offended by the truth, it means you haven't become an adult yet. It means you haven't yet learned to accept yourself. But here's my suggestion: Get out of bed, take a bath, and come eat. The soup must be ready by now.

GIULIANA: There is no soup. And I don't know if I'm going to take a bath. When I feel sad, I don't feel like bathing. You've made me depressed.

PIETRO: I made you depressed? Me?

GIULIANA: You came home from that funeral in such a holier-than-thou mood.

PIETRO: I'm not holier-than-thou.

GIULIANA: You are holier-than-thou. Sure of yourself, disdainful, and very unpleasant. You talk about me as if you knew me like the back of your hand.

PIETRO: In fact, I do know you like the back of my hand.

GIULIANA: It hasn't even been a month since we met each other and you know me like the back of your hand? But we don't even really know why we got married! We don't do anything but ask ourselves why, from morning to night!

PIETRO: You do. I don't. I don't ask myself anything. You're a person with a confused mind. I'm not. I see things clearly. I see far and wide.

GIULIANA: Listen to what a high opinion you have of yourself! An astonishing sense of security. 'I see far and wide.' I'm telling you we're in a fog. We're up to our necks in fog. We can't see a hand in front of our faces.

PIETRO: Shall I get the bath going for you?

GIULIANA: Huh?

PIETRO: Shall I get the bath going for you? If you take a bath maybe it'll clear your head. Baths are good for you. They get rid of toxins. They clear your head.

GIULIANA: You're not some kind of clean freak, are you? Tell me right now if you are, because I hate clean freaks.

PIETRO: Certainly. I'm a clean freak. Didn't you know?

GIULIANA: I don't think I will take a bath. I'm too depressed. You're so disagreeable, and it's scaring me! You're exactly the kind of man I can't stand! (*Goes into the bathroom. Water runs in the sink. She returns.*) In my opinion, marriage is a diabolical institution! To have to live together always, for your whole life! Why did I marry you? What have I done? What was I thinking when I chose you?

PIETRO: Did you decide to take a bath?

GIULIANA: Didn't you tell me I needed to take a bath?

PIETRO: It wasn't exactly an order. It was advice.

GIULIANA: Good thing. That's all we need, for you to start giving me orders!

PIETRO: So you find me disagreeable?

GIULIANA: Yes. I'm afraid so. You're so calm, so placid, so holier-than-thou. 'I know you like the back of my hand!' 'I see far and wide.' And what if you don't know anything about me? What if you made a blunder? What if you suddenly discover that I'm full of poison you can't see? Then? What'll you do then?

PIETRO: I'll dump you. It's only logical.

GIULIANA: Logical! (*Goes into the bathroom and comes back.*) Like hell it's logical. You're married now, and you'll keep me! You'll keep me as I am! Even if I'm completely different from what you thought I was, you have to keep me just the same, for your whole life! Wasn't I just telling you that marriage is a diabolical institution?

PIETRO: Careful. You're trampling all over my pajamas.

GIULIANA: I'm trampling on them because I want to trample on them! Because I can't stand you!

VITTORIA: (*Entering.*) Aren't you dressed yet? I've put the soup on the table.

GIULIANA: Soup? Didn't we say you weren't going to make soup?

VITTORIA: I made a little hot soup. I made it for me because I was cold and when I'm cold I like a little soup. Since I was already doing it, I made some for you, too. But if you don't eat it now, it'll get cold. It doesn't matter to me because I've already eaten two big bowls full and I feel great.

PIETRO: Come and eat. You'll take a bath later.

GIULIANA: There! If I take a bath after eating, I'll die. You want me dead? (*Goes into the bathroom.*)

ACT TWO

[*Same apartment, later that same day.*]

PIETRO: I've invited my mother and my sister to lunch tomorrow.

GIULIANA: But didn't your mother say she'd never set foot in this house?

PIETRO: That's what she said. But I convinced her to come to lunch tomorrow. After Lamberto Genova's funeral, I took her home and I convinced her. She let herself be convinced.

GIULIANA: Are you glad?

PIETRO: I am glad because I'm sick of being at war with my mother. I'd prefer to make peace with her, if such a thing is possible.

GIULIANA: Are you a mama's boy?

PIETRO: I'm not a mama's boy. But we won't be going to my mother's house anytime soon because Aunt Filippa is there, who is furious with me. Aunt Filippa is Catholic. She's even more Catholic than my mother. She wanted me to have a Catholic wedding, with lots of cardinals. Instead, they told her that I'd married a girl I'd met at a party, where she was dancing drunk with her sandals in her hand and her hair in her eyes. My cousin told her about it. Aunt Filippa nearly had a stroke.

GIULIANA: Your cousin? The one with the orange slacks?

PIETRO: Yes.

GIULIANA: It strikes me that you have a few too many relatives.

PIETRO: So Aunt Filippa hasn't even wanted to look at a photograph of you. My mother did. She looked at one for a second.

GIULIANA: Which photograph? The one where I'm wearing the raincoat?

PIETRO: Yes.

GIULIANA: It's not a good photo. I look like I've just been released from jail. And what did she say about my photograph, your mother?

PIETRO: Nothing. She sighed. She said you were pretty.

GIULIANA: She sighed?

PIETRO: She sighed.

GIULIANA: Just pretty?

PIETRO: Why? What do you think you are? Gorgeous? Enchanting?

GIULIANA: Yes, enchanting.

PIETRO: And yet I don't feel enchanted.

GIULIANA: You don't feel enchanted?

PIETRO: No.

GIULIANA: But I enchanted you!

PIETRO: You won't like my mother. And she won't like you. She won't like anything about this house. She'll disapprove of everything. She won't even like Vittoria.

GIULIANA: Why shouldn't she like Vittoria?

PIETRO: She has maids of a different kind. Old, silent, faithful women with flat feet who go around in slippers.

GIULIANA: If that's the problem, Vittoria has flat feet, too.

PIETRO: I'm just saying she won't like anything about the house. Nothing.

GIULIANA: So then if she won't like me and I won't like her and if she won't like anything about the house, why make her come here?

PIETRO: Because she's my mother.

GIULIANA: Good reason. And I'm hardly going to be bringing my mother here. You know what my mother is like? My mother saves all her old newspapers, she has a ton of them under her bed and underneath the armoires, and she cooks these soups, these concoctions of prunes and cooked apples, and she keeps all her saucepans on the windowsill. And in the evening she locks herself in the kitchen – locked in, you know – every evening until two in the morning. She stays locked up in there and no one knows what she's doing – if she's cooking more soup, if she's washing her feet, no one knows. No one's ever known. And if someone comes near the door to tell her to go to bed, she flies into a fit. She howls, she shouts, and she won't open the door. You understand?

PIETRO: Yes, okay. I know. That's your mother. But my mother isn't like that. My mother is a fairly normal woman.

GIULIANA: Why? Are you saying that my mother isn't a normal woman? Are you saying she's crazy?

PIETRO: I don't know. I've never seen her. From the way you describe her, I think she must be a little crazy.

GIULIANA: And does it seem nice to you not to have seen my mother yet?

PIETRO: You want us to visit your mother? Let's go. I've been a little busy lately, but as soon as I'm freed up, let's go visit your mother, given that she doesn't go anywhere, as you've been saying.

GIULIANA: Visit my mother? To see all the saucepans and the newspapers?

PIETRO: Sure, why not.

GIULIANA: My mother's not really crazy, poor thing. She's just an unfortunate old woman.

PIETRO: There. Exactly. And my mother's a poor, unfortunate old woman, too.

GIULIANA: Why? What happened to your mother?

PIETRO: My mother, poor thing, was a beauty in her youth, elegant, and she suffered a lot when she started to get old. She came down with a kind of neurasthenia. Then, during the war, when the city was being bombed, the house collapsed on top of her. Then she lost a little money, not a lot, but she got terrified, and she started thinking she was poor. And she often wakes up in the morning and cries. She feels hopeless because she's afraid of being poor. And then my sister has to go over and cheer her up. Besides, my father died some years ago and she suffered a lot because of that. And my sister isn't married yet and she feels hopeless about that, too. And now I've married you, a girl she knows almost nothing about, who she imagines is some kind of tiger.

GIULIANA: Those aren't true misfortunes. She's gotten old the way everyone gets old. Your father died when he was already elderly. They aren't true misfortunes, if you think about the unfortunate life my mother has had.

PIETRO: They may not be true misfortunes, but she suffers because of them as if they were. Anyway, we don't really need to decide which of us has the most unfortunate mother.

GIULIANA: Does your mother think that I married you for money?

PIETRO: She thinks you married me for money. She thinks you're some kind of tiger. She thinks you've had a heap of lovers. She thinks everything, and in the morning she wakes up and cries. That's why I told her to come here for lunch, so she'll at least look you in the eye, and she won't like you, but she'll be terrified of a person instead of being terrified of a shadow.

GIULIANA: It's a shame.

PIETRO: What's a shame?

GIULIANA: It's a shame I never had all those lovers, the way your mother thinks.

PIETRO: You still have time.

GIULIANA: I still have time? I could still have a few lovers yet, even though I'm your wife?

PIETRO: Not even in your dreams as long as you're my wife. But we can always get a divorce.

GIULIANA: There is no divorce in Italy.

PIETRO: Out of the country.

GIULIANA: Oh, right, out of the country. (*Silence.*) You've barely married me and you're already thinking of getting a divorce?

PIETRO: I'm not thinking of getting a divorce. I was just saying. In case you still wanted to have a few lovers.

GIULIANA: Some of the things your mother thinks are true. It's true that I married you for money. *Also* for money. I was ready to do anything. You know?

PIETRO: You mean you wouldn't have married me if I'd been poor?

GIULIANA: I don't know! Don't you understand that I don't know? I still don't understand it myself. I haven't had time to understand. Why did we get married in such a mad rush? What was the rush?

PIETRO: You told me 'Marry me, for God's sake. If you don't marry me, who will? If you don't, I'll end up throwing myself out the window.' Didn't you say that?

GIULIANA: Yes, that's what I said. But it was just a figure of speech. There wasn't really any need to marry me in such a mad rush. It's not like I was pregnant. Your mother must have believed you were marrying me because I was pregnant. You explained to her that I'm not really pregnant, didn't you?

PIETRO: Yes.

GIULIANA: What rush was there? We got married like the house was on fire. Why? Wouldn't it have been better to think it over a little?

PIETRO: I did think it over. Perhaps it was a reflection that lasted no more than a split second. But who says reflections have to go on for centuries? A lucid flash of reflection that lasts for a split second can be enough.

GIULIANA: No, a one-minute reflection is not a reflection. True reflections, useful, balanced reflections, are the ones that a person carries within himself for months and years.

PIETRO: You've had quite a few reflections, have you?

GIULIANA: Me? Never. Not one ever. I'm not capable of reflection. But I think it's fair to think things over before you do anything – before you do everything. And instead we didn't reflect at all and we got married like a couple of idiots – me *also* for the money, you *also* because you felt sorry for me. And that's why our marriage is rotten – rotten to the core! We may have made a frightening mistake. Maybe we'll be desperately unhappy together, even worse than your mother thinks.

PIETRO: It's possible.

GIULIANA: And so? So what are we going to do?

PIETRO: Let's get a divorce.

GIULIANA: Out of the country?

PIETRO: Out of the country.

GIULIANA: Good thing you have a little money, so at least we can leave the country for a divorce!

PIETRO: Good thing.

GIULIANA: So what should I make your mother for lunch?

PIETRO: I don't know. Broth. Boiled chicken. My mother has a delicate stomach. She has a gastric ulcer.

GIULIANA: Is broth good for a gastric ulcer? Is your mother very old?

PIETRO: Yes, old.

GIULIANA: How old is she, more or less?

PIETRO: Who knows? No one knows. She falsified the date of birth on her passport. She erased the date with ink remover and then she wrote in a new one. She probably took off about ten years.

GIULIANA: And who told you that?

PIETRO: My sister told me.

GIULIANA: Did she see her? Did your sister see her with the ink remover?

PIETRO: No. Aunt Filippa told her about it.

GIULIANA: This Aunt Filippa is quite a gossip. Isn't there some way to get her out of your hair?

PIETRO: No, because she's paralysed, and she goes around in a wheelchair.

GIULIANA: Maybe I'll get some ink remover and erase the birth date on my passport, too. When I'm old. But I don't have a passport. I've never had one. I just have a regular ID card from the post office. I should get myself a passport, otherwise how will I be able to leave the country when we want to get a divorce?

PIETRO: Right.

GIULIANA: When the day comes when we want to get a divorce, maybe it'll be enough if you leave the country by yourself. Though I can always use a passport because I'll be travelling a lot when I'm divorced. With Topazia. Will you pay me alimony?

PIETRO: Certainly.

GIULIANA: Thank you. I'll go travelling with Topazia, we'll see all kinds of places. We'll become investigative journalists and take photographs. We'll go to the desert and we'll photograph lions and tigers for that weekly magazine that Topazia works for. They pay well. Maybe I'll earn such a good living that I'll give up the alimony. I won't have any need for it.

PIETRO: Thanks.

GIULIANA: Not at all. It'll be lovely.

PIETRO: Lovely.

GIULIANA: And you? What will you do? Go back to living with your mother, your sister, and Aunt Filippa?

PIETRO: Maybe.

GIULIANA: I'm going to go travelling with Topazia instead. You know, I often ask myself what Topazia would think of you. But I don't think she'd like you. She'd say that your neck is too thick, your nose is too big, your ears are too long. Topazia is very difficult.

PIETRO: But she got married to that idiot.

GIULIANA: Manolo? But why do you say it like that, 'that idiot'? Why must you spit on everything in my life? You don't know Manolo. You've never met him.

PIETRO: I've read his books.

GIULIANA: You've read *Jesus, Take Me Away*?

PIETRO: Yes. And I've also read *Springtime with the Sailor*. And even *The Useless Salamander*.

GIULIANA: No! You have not read *Springtime with the Sailor*! You never even cut the pages!⁵

PIETRO: *You* never even cut the pages.

GIULIANA: I cut the first few pages. But I didn't get any further because I didn't understand it. I didn't understand because I was stupid, not because he was stupid. But it's certainly true that salamanders are useless creatures. What good are they? Doesn't get much more useless than that!

PIETRO: That's for sure.

GIULIANA: What are they? Aren't they the creatures that can walk through fire without getting burned? What's the use of throwing yourself in the fire?

PIETRO: But I think this Manolo of yours was stupid, a real idiot, and a coward. Didn't he run off when he found out you were having a baby?

GIULIANA: Yes, but it wasn't an act of cowardice. It was something else. He was afraid of life.

PIETRO: Being afraid of life is called cowardice. Getting a person in trouble and running out on her is called cowardice.

GIULIANA: I forbid you to spit like that on the things that belong to me!
(*Silence.*) So, for your mother, boiled chicken then?

PIETRO: Boiled chicken.

GIULIANA: Vittoria! Damn, she's not answering. She must be at the window gossiping with the girl who lives upstairs.

PIETRO: What do you want to tell her?

GIULIANA: That your mother is coming to lunch tomorrow.

PIETRO: And my sister.

GIULIANA: And your sister. This sister of yours, what's she like?

PIETRO: My sister is an absolute goose.

GIULIANA: Will she like me?

PIETRO: She'll like you very much.

GIULIANA: Because she's a goose? You think I'm a good match for geese?

PIETRO: Not because she's a goose. Because she's always content with everything. She has an optimistic temperament.

GIULIANA: And your mother is a pessimist. Someone who sees problems everywhere. She over-dramatizes. My friend Elena is like that, too, and so's my mother. My mother is quite a pessimist. I get along pretty well with optimists, on the other hand, with people who don't make a big fuss over things. I got along so well with Topazia because she knew how not to make a fuss.

PIETRO: And you get along with me?

GIULIANA: With you?

PIETRO: Yes?

GIULIANA: I don't know yet. I still don't understand what you're like.

PIETRO: But I understood you immediately, the minute I saw you.

GIULIANA: Immediately? The minute you saw me? At that party, on the stairs?

PIETRO: Not really immediately, the minute I saw you come in. After a little.

GIULIANA: Maybe when I was dancing, drunk, without my shoes? You understood I was someone you'd get along with perfectly?

PIETRO: Yes.

GIULIANA: How nice.

PIETRO: And you want to know something?

GIULIANA: What?

PIETRO: You never made me feel sorry for you. Not at all. Not even for an instant.

GIULIANA: No?

PIETRO: No.

GIULIANA: But why not? That night when I was crying, when I told you my whole life story, you didn't feel sorry for me?

PIETRO: No.

GIULIANA: But why not? I was alone – no money, no job, up to here in debt. I'd even had an abortion. I'd been abandoned, and you didn't feel sorry for me?

PIETRO: No.

GIULIANA: But then you're just heartless!

PIETRO: Don't be silly. You were alone, that's true. No money, no job, and you were feeling pretty hopeless, but I didn't feel sorry for you. When I looked at you, I never felt the slightest pity. I always felt very cheerful, when I looked at you. And I didn't marry you because I felt sorry for you. Anyway, if you ended up marrying all the women who made you feel sorry for them, what a mess that would be. You'd have to start a harem.

GIULIANA: Exactly. That's true. And why did you marry me, if you didn't marry me because you felt sorry for me?

PIETRO: I married you to cheer myself up. Didn't you know that I married you to cheer myself up? Come on. You do so know that.

GIULIANA: You married me because you had a good time with me but your mother, your sister, and your Aunt Filippa bored you?

PIETRO: They bored me to death.

GIULIANA: I believe it! Poor Pietro!

PIETRO: Now you're feeling sorry for me?

GIULIANA: But it wasn't as though you had to stay with them all the time, right? You went out, you travelled around, you had girlfriends?

PIETRO: Certainly. I travelled, I went out, and I had girlfriends.

GIULIANA: Boring girlfriends?

PIETRO: Girlfriends.

GIULIANA: And me? Why did I marry you?

PIETRO: For the money.

GIULIANA: *Also* for the money.

PIETRO: I believe that a person only gets married for one single reason. The 'alsos' have no real value. There's just one dominant reason, and that's the one that's important.

GIULIANA: Then I've yet to understand what that reason is for me.

PIETRO: Didn't you tell me, 'Marry me. Otherwise, who will?'

GIULIANA: Yes, and so?

PIETRO: So wasn't that the reason? That you wanted to have a husband? Whatever and whoever he was?

GIULIANA: Whoever. Yes.

VITTORIA: (*Entering.*) Did you call me?

GIULIANA: Not now. Earlier. Earlier I called you a bunch of times. Where were you?

VITTORIA: I was having a little chat with the girl upstairs.

GIULIANA: You're quite a talker. Don't you get thirsty, talking so much?

VITTORIA: I never get thirsty. I never drink anything. I don't sweat, and that's why I don't drink. Not even in the summer.

GIULIANA: You don't sweat?

VITTORIA: I never sweat. When I'm at home, working in the fields, doing the hoeing out in the sun in the middle of July, everyone's sweating and I'm not. I don't have so much as a drop of sweat on my skin.

GIULIANA: Strange.

PIETRO: Very strange.

GIULIANA: Maybe you're a salamander. A useless salamander.

VITTORIA: I'm what?

GIULIANA: I wanted to tell you that his mother and sister are coming to lunch tomorrow. You can make boiled chicken.

VITTORIA: Did you really need to tell me today? You could have told me tomorrow.

GIULIANA: You said you always go to Piazza Bologna to buy chickens, near your hairdresser, so that's why I'm telling you now, because when you go to the hairdresser, you can buy chicken, too.

VITTORIA: It's not easy to find free-range chickens these days. The chickens they sell in the stores aren't free-range. They're the ones that spend their lives getting fat under a lamp. If you want real free-range chicken, I can pop over to my house in Fara Sabina. I'd be back by tomorrow morning.

PIETRO: No. Let's not make things more complicated. Chicken from Piazza Bologna will do nicely. Tomorrow you can set the table with a tablecloth and make it look nice.

VITTORIA: With a tablecloth. Not with placemats?

PIETRO: No. My mother can't stand placemats.

VITTORIA: We have a tablecloth. But we don't have the table pad to put underneath.

PIETRO: Today you can buy a table pad in Piazza Bologna, too.

GIULIANA: You certainly wouldn't want your mother to stick her nose under the tablecloth to see if there's a table pad.

PIETRO: You don't know my mother. She'll be able to tell there's no table pad just by touching it.

VITTORIA: I need to leave soon if I'm going to get everything done. (*Exits.*)

PIETRO: Can it be true that she never sweats?

GIULIANA: I don't know. It seems to me she sweats like a horse.

PIETRO: She strikes one as such a nice girl. Did you check her references before you hired her?

GIULIANA: Yes. I telephoned Signora Giacchetta.

PIETRO: And who is Signora Giacchetta?

GIULIANA: She's Signora Giacchetta. Where she worked before. She sings Signora Giacchetta's praises all day long. She was a wonder around the house, Signora Giacchetta was. She did the wash, she ironed, she cooked, she did everything. She never even let Vittoria get her hands wet. I don't understand why she kept a maid.

PIETRO: Are you sure she exists, this Signora Giacchetta?

GIULIANA: She answered my telephone call!

PIETRO: You don't get references over the phone. You go there in person.

GIULIANA: You wanted me to go to Signora Giacchetta's?

PIETRO: Yes.

GIULIANA: You are so annoying! You are so, so annoying! Nothing sits right with you. Signora Giacchetta doesn't sit right with you. The placemats don't sit right with you. The chickens aren't free-range.

PIETRO: It was Vittoria who said they don't sell free-range chickens anymore! I don't give a damn about free-range chickens!

GIULIANA: What are we going to talk about with your mother tomorrow? After we've talked a little bit about Vittoria and about free-range chickens, what will be left to talk about?

PIETRO: Oh, I really don't know!

GIULIANA: Can we talk about Lamberto Genova?

PIETRO: Which one? Yours or mine?

GIULIANA: A little about the one and a little about the other, right? (*Silence.*) Shall I have Elena come, too?

PIETRO: Which one? Your Elena or my Elena?

GIULIANA: Why? Which one is your Elena? Is there an Elena for each of us, too?

PIETRO: My cousin, Elena? Or your friend, Elena?

GIULIANA: Your cousin, Elena? The one with the orange slacks? Oh no, I can't stand that one. No, I was talking about my friend, Elena.

PIETRO: The one who's a clerk in a stationery store?

GIULIANA: Yes. Why, is there something wrong with being a clerk in a stationery store?

PIETRO: I didn't say there was anything wrong with it. I said 'a clerk in a stationery store' to make clear whom I meant.

GIULIANA: So then if you wanted to make clear you were talking about my mother, you'd say 'the pants maker,' because that's what kind of work she does? Have you told your mother that my mother makes pants?

PIETRO: I think I told her that she was a seamstress.

GIULIANA: And why is that? Is it more socially acceptable to be a seamstress than a pants maker? Is it socially unacceptable to make pants? You're full of social prejudices, do you realize that?

PIETRO: You're imagining things. Making pants or being a seamstress – aren't they the same thing?

GIULIANA: Precisely. Isn't it the same thing?

PIETRO: Precisely.

GIULIANA: Want to know something?

PIETRO: What?

GIULIANA: You know that big bottle of ink that I spilled all over a customer when I was in the stationery store?

PIETRO: So?

GIULIANA: You know who the customer was?

PIETRO: Who was she?

GIULIANA: I'm afraid it was your mother.

PIETRO: My mother?

GIULIANA: Yes.

PIETRO: You spilled a bottle of ink on my mother's head?

GIULIANA: Not on her head. On her dress. All over her dress. And it's not like I did it on purpose.

PIETRO: But who says it was really my mother?

GIULIANA: I'm just afraid it was. It was your mother. I recognized her from the photograph you have on your desk. That customer's face stayed in my mind because I got fired after that. Things were going great in that stationery store. It wasn't a lot of work. They fired me because of your mother. Although also because I always came in late.

PIETRO: My mother has a good memory for faces. If it was her, she'll recognize you immediately.

GIULIANA: So let me get my Elena to come to lunch tomorrow. So she can see if your mother was really the one with the ink.

PIETRO: No, there's no need to have your Elena come. My mother won't be comfortable with your Elena.

GIULIANA: And who would your pig of a mother be comfortable with?

PIETRO: Could I ask you please not to insult my mother even before she gets here? You throw a big bottle of ink all over her and now you're insulting her?

GIULIANA: My mother won't like you at all. She hardly likes anyone. She's very pessimistic, my mother. She's very timid. She stays in her house, in a corner near the window, keeping watch over her saucepans. Terrified, timid, bitter, in her little Japanese housecoat, with her hair tied into a ponytail and twisted around on top of her head with a black elastic band, her hands shaking, looking around her with eyes like a rabbit that's got hunters on her trail. No. Better that we don't go.

PIETRO: So we won't go. (*Laughs.*)

GIULIANA: Why are you laughing? Surely you're not laughing at my mother?

PIETRO: No, I'm thinking about you spilling ink on that woman, who might be my mother, and I started to laugh.

GIULIANA: Why are we talking so much about mothers? We've been here for an hour talking about nothing but mothers. Are mothers so important?

PIETRO: They're pretty important.

GIULIANA: If I make you laugh, that means that you don't feel be-witched. It means I don't make you feel bewitched. You don't make me feel bewitched, either. When I was in love with Manolo, I didn't laugh. I never laughed. I didn't laugh, I didn't talk, I'd even stopped breathing. I was still as a statue. I was completely dazzled, be-witched. You know what I mean?

PIETRO: Yes.

GIULIANA: Why, have you been bewitched sometimes, too?

PIETRO: Sometimes. And I didn't like it. I would never marry a woman who had me bewitched. I want to live with a woman who can cheer me up.

GIULIANA: What do you see in me that's so cheerful?

PIETRO: I have to go out. Where's my hat?

GIULIANA: Have you got another funeral to go to?

PIETRO: No. It's raining. It's pouring. When it rains, I wear my hat.

GIULIANA: Oh, God. Now when Vittoria leaves the hairdresser, she'll get her permanent wet. She'll be furious when she gets back.

ACT THREE

[Same apartment, lunchtime the next day.]

GIULIANA: Pietro!

PIETRO: I'm right here.

GIULIANA: Vittoria isn't back yet.

PIETRO: What do you mean she isn't back.

GIULIANA: She hasn't come back. Since yesterday. She didn't come back after the hairdresser. You were out having supper. I drank a glass of milk and I went to sleep. This morning, after you went out, I ring the bell and she doesn't respond. I get up. I look for her all over the house, and she isn't here.

PIETRO: Should we call the police?

GIULIANA: No. The custodian's wife says she probably went to see Signora Giacchetta again. She really used to like living with Signora Giacchetta. She hardly had a thing to do. She liked it here, too, but she thought there was too much work.

PIETRO: What work is there here? There's just two of us, and the house is small.

GIULIANA: Yes, but you change your shirt twice a day. Vittoria doesn't like to iron. At Signora Giacchetta's there weren't any men's shirts. Signora Giacchetta is a widow.

PIETRO: That's too bad.

GIULIANA: It's too bad she's a widow?

PIETRO: It's too bad about Vittoria. We'll have to look for another maid. Call an agency.

GIULIANA: But you always say you can't trust agencies!

PIETRO: What did you manage to put together for lunch? My sister and my mother will be here in a little while.

GIULIANA: I have some spezzatino[6] in the house from yesterday. I warmed it up.

PIETRO: My mother can't eat spezzatino! I told you she has a gastric ulcer.

GIULIANA: Isn't spezzatino with potatoes good for a gastric ulcer?

PIETRO: No. Besides, there can't be much left!

GIULIANA: Sure there is. There's almost a kilo of meat. Plus I called the custodian's wife and asked her to lend me a table pad. Vittoria was supposed to buy a table pad in Piazza Bologna.

PIETRO: (*Examining the tablecloth.*) This isn't a table pad. This is a piece of oilcloth.

GIULIANA: Yes. The custodian's wife was using it to cover the baby's carriage. But it's clean. I cleaned it with a sponge.

PIETRO: For a first? What is there for a first?

GIULIANA: For a first? For a first course you mean?

PIETRO: Yes.

GIULIANA: Nothing. There's a little eggplant parmesan left over from yesterday.

PIETRO: You can't give my mother a lunch of nothing but leftovers! Sauté some rice in butter.

GIULIANA: Shall I sauté some rice in butter? Okay. I got up late this morning and I was hoping Vittoria would be back besides. I'm really sorry she's not coming back. I felt comfortable with her. I told her all about my life. (*Exits.*)

Pietro is alone. He looks under the tablecloth some more. He picks newspapers up off the carpet. He rearranges the cushions. The doorbell rings. Pietro goes to the door. Pietro's mother and sister enter.

GINESTRA: Oh, mom. Look how cute it is here! It's a lovely house!

PIETRO'S MOTHER: (*Sighing.*) Too many stairs. I suffer from a heart condition and stairs aren't good for me. I had to stop three times to catch my breath. Why didn't you take a house with an elevator?

PIETRO: We liked this house. And we were in a hurry besides. We weren't really attending all that closely to small details.

PIETRO'S MOTHER: Attending to small details? Noticing whether there's an elevator for when your mother, who suffers from a heart problem, visits – you call that 'attending to small details'?

PIETRO: But you said you'd never come to our house.

PIETRO'S MOTHER: And that's how you resigned yourself to the idea that I would never come?

GINESTRA: You don't suffer from a heart condition, mamma. Your heart couldn't be healthier. You had an electrocardiogram just a few days ago.

PIETRO'S MOTHER: Certain kinds of heart problems can't be seen on an electrocardiogram. Even poor Lamberto Genova had an electrocardiogram a few days before he died, and they didn't see anything. Poor Virginia told me about it.

PIETRO: Why are you calling her 'Poor Virginia'? She's not dead, too, is she?[7]

PIETRO'S MOTHER: Poor Virginia! She's not dead but she's been left alone. And not in good financial straits either. And her children give her no comfort. One lives in Persia. The other one has gotten himself involved with a terrible woman. Fortunately, however, he hasn't married her.

PIETRO: There's been a minor inconvenience. Our housekeeper Vittoria went to the hairdresser yesterday and she hasn't returned.

GIULIANA: (*Entering.*) It's almost ready. The rice is nearly cooked.

PIETRO'S MOTHER: Good afternoon, young lady.

GINESTRA: Good afternoon.

GIULIANA: Good afternoon.

GINESTRA: We were admiring your beautiful house.

PIETRO'S MOTHER: I've seen you before, young lady, somewhere. Where have I seen you?

GIULIANA: You've seen me in a photograph.

PIETRO'S MOTHER: No. That photograph doesn't look like you. Anyway, you must not be very photogenic. No, I've seen your face somewhere. I have an excellent memory for faces. I never forget people's faces. Where have I met you?

GIULIANA: May I ask you not to call me 'young lady'? Given that I married your son a week ago?

PIETRO'S MOTHER: Where did you get married? At city hall?

GIULIANA: Yes.

PIETRO'S MOTHER: I'm a devout Catholic. For me, only weddings that take place in church are valid. To me, civil weddings are not valid. In any case, I'll call you Signora if you like.

PIETRO: Don't you want to call her by her first name, mom?

PIETRO'S MOTHER: Her name is Giuliana?

PIETRO: Giuliana.

PIETRO'S MOTHER: A pretentious name. A simple 'Giulia' would have been much better. Why in the world did they give you such a pretentious name?

GIULIANA: And isn't your daughter named Ginestra? Ginestra isn't a pretentious name?

PIETRO'S MOTHER: No, Ginestra is not a pretentious name. My husband

loved the writer Leopardi. We called her Ginestra because of Leopardi.[8] And also because, when I was expecting, I found myself in
a place where the Scotch broom was in blossom. Absolutely beautiful. In Rossignano. We were on holiday that year in Rossignano.
Where are you from?

GIULIANA: I'm from Pieve di Montesecco.

PIETRO'S MOTHER: And where is Pieve di Montesecco?

GIULIANA: In Romagna.

PIETRO'S MOTHER: Oh, in Romagna. Rossignano is in Romagna, too.[9] Do
you know Rossignano?

GIULIANA: No.

PIETRO'S MOTHER: You don't know Rossignano? That's strange. Didn't
they take you to Rossignano on vacation when you were a little
girl? Where did they take you?

GIULIANA: They didn't take me on vacation.

PIETRO'S MOTHER: Oh, they didn't?

GIULIANA: No, my mother had other things on her mind.

PIETRO'S MOTHER: What did your mother have on her mind?

GIULIANA: That she didn't have any money. She and my father are
separated. My father left us when I was small.

PIETRO'S MOTHER: Yes. My son hinted at something like that. Your
mother is a woman who has been sorely tried by life?

GIULIANA: Yes.

PIETRO'S MOTHER: I, too, have been sorely tried by life. My children
haven't given me much comfort. I lost my husband. My sister Filippa is forced to live in a wheelchair. And now my son has chosen
to bring me this great sorrow as well. He's made a marriage I disapprove of. I have nothing against you, young lady, or Signora, or
Giuliana, or whatever you like. But I don't believe you're the right
person for my son or that he's the right person for you. Do you
know why my son chose you? Do you know why he wanted to get
married to you?

GIULIANA: No.

PIETRO'S MOTHER: To hurt me.

PIETRO: The rice is probably overcooked by now. Let's go sit down.

Ginestra and Pietro go into the kitchen to get the rice.

PIETRO'S MOTHER: I like rice to be very well cooked. This housekeeper
of yours, what was her name?

GIULIANA: Vittoria.

PIETRO'S MOTHER: She went to the hairdresser and she never came back? Servants are always doing that these days.

Ginestra and Pietro return from the kitchen with the rice.

GINESTRA: Mamma, if you only saw the kitchen! They have a tiny little kitchen. So pretty.

They are seated at the table.

PIETRO'S MOTHER: You'd better check to make sure she didn't take anything with her.
GIULIANA: Vittoria? Oh, no. Vittoria didn't touch anything. She couldn't be more honest.
PIETRO'S MOTHER: How long had you had her?
PIETRO: Four days.
PIETRO'S MOTHER: And how can you talk about honesty after four days? (*Laughs.*) You're naive. You're very naive! Life will teach you to be less naive! You've already been sorely tried by life yourself, isn't that true?
GIULIANA: A little.
PIETRO'S MOTHER: Did you check this Vittoria's references?
GIULIANA: Yes. From Signora Giacchetta.
PIETRO'S MOTHER: Giacchetta? The ones who have that household appliance store on Via del Tritone?
GIULIANA: I don't think they're the ones. Signora Giacchetta didn't have any appliances in her house. She didn't even have a washing machine. She washed all her sheets by hand. She washed them herself, Signora Giacchetta, not Vittoria. She never even let Vittoria get her hands wet.
PIETRO'S MOTHER: And why did she leave Signora Giacchetta?
GIULIANA: She left because there was a dog. An enormous hound, a mastiff. Vittoria didn't like the dog. So she left.
PIETRO'S MOTHER: Because of the dog?
GIULIANA: She was disgusted by that dog. He slobbered constantly. And he made a mess everywhere he went.
PIETRO'S MOTHER: Dogs, provided you train them properly, don't make a mess.

Vittoria enters.

GIULIANA: Oh, Vittoria! You're finally here! I was afraid you were never coming back!

VITTORIA: Yesterday evening, when I left the hairdresser, it was pouring. I didn't want to ruin my permanent. So I went up to see Signora Giacchetta for a minute, who's just right next to the hairdresser, to wait for the rain to stop. Signora Giacchetta asked me to stay and sleep over, because she was alone and she was afraid. The husband had gone to Rieti. So I stayed there to sleep over. Signora Giacchetta made panzarelle with ricotta. Maybe I ate a little too much because they were so good, and last night I felt sick and my stomach was giving me trouble. So this morning Signora Giacchetta wouldn't let me get up. Meanwhile, the husband came back and he brought four chickens, and they gave me two of them as a gift. They're free-range chickens. Signora Giacchetta cooked them, she roasted them because these aren't boiling chickens, they're roasting chickens. Good thing you haven't gotten to the main course yet. Signora Giacchetta brought me back in her car so I'd get home quicker. (*Exits.*)

PIETRO: Wasn't Signora Giacchetta a widow?

GIULIANA: Yes. It seems to me she was a widow.

PIETRO'S MOTHER: And the two of you aren't going to fire her? She stays out all night and you two aren't going to fire her?

GIULIANA: No, I wasn't thinking of firing her at all. I'm so glad she came back!

PIETRO'S MOTHER: You're not going to reprimand her? Aren't you going to say anything? She doesn't come home because she doesn't want to get her permanent wet. She's thinking about her permanent before her duties – and the two of you don't say anything to her? What world are we living in?

GIULIANA: I don't dare say anything to her. She brought me two chickens as a gift.

PIETRO'S MOTHER: The servant's usual means of extortion.

Vittoria returns with the roasted chickens.

VITTORIA: They're real free-range!

GIULIANA: Didn't you say Signora Giacchetta was a widow?

VITTORIA: Yes, she's widow. That guy who stays with her, he's not really her husband. He's a guy who comes over every now and then. He's married, married with five children. Even the dog is his.

PIETRO: And why is Signora Giacchetta afraid to be by herself? Doesn't she have that enormous dog?

VITTORIA: Ah, no. The husband took the dog to Rieti. Not the husband – but anyway, the guy who stays there with her.

PIETRO: Couldn't you have called last night to say you wouldn't be back?

VITTORIA: How could I call? Signora Giacchetta doesn't have a phone.

PIETRO: She doesn't even have a phone!

GIULIANA: She doesn't have a phone? But I called her when I checked your references.

VITTORIA: Yes. But she forgot to pay the bill and they cut off her service. (*Exits.*)

PIETRO'S MOTHER: Everywhere you turn, immorality is rampant. Even among the simple people, it's rampant. This girl talks as if it were nothing – a woman living with another woman's husband.

GINESTRA: This chicken is very good!

PIETRO: Definitely free-range.

PIETRO'S MOTHER: It's not free-range.

PIETRO: It's not free-range?

PIETRO'S MOTHER: No. It's a good chicken, well-cooked, but it's not free-range.

Vittoria returns with the fruit course.

VITTORIA: Next time you come, I'll make panzarelle with ricotta.

PIETRO'S MOTHER: I have an ulcer. I can't eat that.

VITTORIA: You have an ulcer? My mother had an operation for her ulcers two years ago. After the operation, she nearly died. They'd already given her the holy oil. The doctor told me – it's a perforated ulcer. She can't be saved. They took her to the general hospital. She was, you might say, already dead. And then you know what I did? I asked them to let me take her back home, and at home I put two kilos of chicory on to boil. I gave her chicory water to drink. That bitter water washed out her insides and that's how she was healed. A month later she was fine and eating everything. Now she even eats peppers.

PIETRO'S MOTHER: Even peppers?

VITTORIA: She eats everything. You'd never believe how strong my mother is! If you could see the way she works in the fields! One day I'd like to bring her here. She loves to come to Rome. She always goes to the hospital to say hello to the sisters who took care of her. You'd never believe how much the sisters love her! Everyone loves my mother. She's a saint. I'd walk through fire for my mother. (*Exits.*)

PIETRO: She really is a salamander.

GIULIANA: A useless salamander.

PIETRO'S MOTHER: What are the two of you talking about? She doesn't seem like a bad girl at all, this Vittoria of yours. Maybe she's just a little confused. It's very difficult these days to find capable girls. They don't want to go into housework anymore. They'd rather work in factories. And then, in the factories, they find Communists, and then when they're tired of working in the factory and they want to go into housework again, they've got subversive ideas and do their work unwillingly, chaotically, with all those ideas in their heads. The trouble that Virginia had with her servants this winter. She went through six of them. She's been reduced to hiring a fifteen-year-old girl. She couldn't find anyone else. They don't want to stay with Virginia. I don't know why.

GINESTRA: They say she doesn't give them enough to eat.

PIETRO'S MOTHER: Yes, that's true. Virginia has never cared all that much about food, not even for herself. She just doesn't care about it, it's not important to her. She says it's money thrown away. But servants want to eat. So, when she lost poor Lamberto, Virginia found herself alone, alone in the house with that fifteen-year-old child. And yet she hasn't lost her spirit. She's courageous. Poor Lamberto felt ill in the bathroom while he was shaving. In his pajamas, with his shaving brush in his hand, he collapsed. She carried him to bed in her arms. He drew his last breath. Poor Virginia now finds herself in financial straits that are far from good. She may be forced to sell the house. She says she'd like to find herself some work. She could give cello lessons. She's a wonderful cellist, Virginia is. She has a marvellous touch. She's a virtuous and courageous woman.

PIETRO: Too bad she's so unbearable.

PIETRO'S MOTHER: Why? The two of you always need to say something bad about everyone. Virginia is a virtuous and courageous woman. I see her everyday. I'm very close to her because she's alone. She doesn't get much comfort from her children. No. She spends the evenings alone, with that servant girl, and she's started teaching her needlepoint. But even that one says she wants to leave. She's afraid.

She's afraid to walk down the hallway at night when it's dark. Because there was a death in the house.

PIETRO: Maybe she's just found a new position, where she's hoping to get more to eat.

PIETRO'S MOTHER: Yes, it's possible. Even that's possible. Virginia is too frugal when it comes to food. Poor Lamberto. Sometimes he used to complain to me. He complained about the cooking in his house. Do you know what Virginia buys from the butcher? Lungs. Something you'd normally give to the cat. She browns them very slowly in a frying pan with rosemary and sage. She says they're good.

GIULIANA: But if Virginia was eating lungs when she was richer, what's she going to eat now that she's gotten poor?

PIETRO'S MOTHER: Ah, I don't know. I really don't know. She's already so skinny, poor Virginia. She's a skeleton.

PIETRO: She's the ugliest woman I know.

PIETRO'S MOTHER: You're wrong. Virginia isn't ugly. She has gorgeous hair. And she's very chic besides. She dresses well. She couldn't have more style.

GIULIANA: She has a lot of style?

PIETRO'S MOTHER: A very great deal. Virginia has a very great deal of style.

GIULIANA: But does she spend a lot on dressing herself?

PIETRO'S MOTHER: Not a cent. She makes everything herself. She makes gorgeous knit dresses. She makes dresses, hand bags, even coats.

GIULIANA: She knits coats? With knitting needles?

PIETRO'S MOTHER: She knits everything. She made one for Ginestra. Right, Ginestra? No, Virginia is really very industrious.

GINESTRA: But the one she made for me stretched all out of shape the first time I washed it, and ended up with these super-long sleeves. I had to give it away.

PIETRO'S MOTHER: Naturally. You washed it at home. I told you to send it to the cleaner. If you would like, Giuliana, my dear, I'll tell Virginia to make you a little coat. Or else a knitted jacket, if you prefer. Knitting is a welcome distraction for Virginia.

GIULIANA: I think Virginia must have other things on her mind now than making me a coat.

PIETRO'S MOTHER: No. She'd do it with great pleasure. It'll even seem to her as though she's paying me back a little. Because I've been a big help to her in these very sad days. I sent my gardener to her to be of whatever help she needed. I've always been very close to her. No, knitting is a distraction for her. She's alone in that empty, half-dark house. I don't know why she always keeps the shutters half-closed. In fact, I'm going to see her today, when I leave here. Lamberto Genova was a dear friend of our family's. To die like that, so suddenly, of a coronary thrombosis! God wanted to give me this great sorrow, too. Even though I was still so unsettled by the sorrow that my son had given me, getting married the way he did, all of a sudden, in such a hurry, without even stopping to explain to me clearly who he was marrying. And not in church. At city hall. I know, he's an atheist, okay, but that's not really a good reason for not having the wedding in church! Everyone has church weddings, even atheists! So poor Lamberto came to visit me a few evenings before he died. He found me in tears, and he consoled me. He told me: 'Were you expecting comfort from your children? No. You were wrong. Children provide no comfort at all.' And then he told me – 'Stay close to Virginia when I'm not here anymore.' Obviously he'd had a premonition. And besides, as a doctor, maybe he knew he was sick. I said to him, 'My dear Lamberto, with my heart in such a state and all this sorrow, I'll go long before you.' Then we started talking about the after-life. He was not a believer. Unfortunately, he was not a believer. He was a materialist. Maybe his studies brought him to materialism. And as he was leaving, he was still saying, 'Pay attention to your heart. It's a worn-out heart, one that has suffered. There's no need to worry yourself to death because of your children. Children follow their own path.' I said to him, 'My dear Lamberto, but to make such an unreasonable, unfortunate marriage! My only son!' He left, shaking his head. Even he never had much comfort from his children. It's not that I want to offend you, Signorina, because I have nothing against you. You have to understand me – I'm a mother. One day you'll be a mother, too. Mothers worry. Think about the fact that who you are was never fully explained to me. They told me that you two met each other at some party thrown by painters. One of those painters' parties. And you weren't feeling too well at that party, right?

GIULIANA: I'd had too much to drink.

PIETRO'S MOTHER: Wine? Liquor?

GIULIANA: Red wine.

PIETRO'S MOTHER: Apparently it was bad wine. Not wholesome, good-quality wine. When the wine is wholesome, it doesn't make you sick. People nowadays give parties with bad wine. They do it on purpose, so the girls who aren't used to drinking get sick, and the men take advantage. The next time you go to some party, don't drink. Drink only water. Did you know them well, those painters?

GIULIANA: No. I didn't know anyone. I happened to be there by chance with a photographer who was a friend of my friend, Topazia.

PIETRO'S MOTHER: Did you know them well, Pietro?

PIETRO: I didn't know them at all. I also happened to be there by chance.

PIETRO'S MOTHER: You drank, too?

PIETRO: I drank a little.

PIETRO'S MOTHER: Why do you drink in the houses of people you don't know? Who is this friend of yours, Topazia? A very, very pretentious name.

GIULIANA: Topazia is my dear friend. The dearest friend I have. Elena is another friend of mine. She's wonderful, but I don't feel as comfortable with her as I do with Topazia. She's too pessimistic. She sees trouble everywhere. I can't handle being around pessimists. I'm very susceptible to outside influences. I immediately get infected by their pessimism.

PIETRO'S MOTHER: And my son? Does he perhaps seem like an optimist to you, my son?

GIULIANA: He doesn't seem so pessimistic to me. If he were, I wouldn't have married him.

PIETRO'S MOTHER: You believe he's an optimist? You're mistaken. It's just that he's superficial. Even my daughter Ginestra is a little superficial. In their superficiality, my children have brought me pain and worry. Why didn't you reflect a little, my dear, before getting married? Why so much nonchalance, if you're someone who has been sorely tried by life? You're not a believer, are you, Signorina?

GIULIANA: According to what day it is. It depends on the day.

PIETRO'S MOTHER: What dreadful words I'm expected to bear. But that's what I had imagined. You're not a believer. If you had been a believer, you would have asked God to give you inspiration, and God would have led you away from my son. He would have directed you to a more suitable man. And yet the more I look at you, the more it seems to me I've seen you before. Where can I have seen you? Where?

GIULIANA: Maybe in some store....

PIETRO'S MOTHER: What kind of store? These girlfriends you were telling me about, what kind of people are they? This friend Patrizia – or what did you say her name was?

GIULIANA: Not Patrizia. Topazia.

GINESTRA: She wouldn't be Topazia Valcipriana, would she?

PIETRO'S MOTHER: Who Valcipriana? Oh, the Valcipriana girl. That's right, her name is Topazia! The one who got into such a terrible marriage. With that Pierfederici man? A writer!

PIETRO: Jesus, take me away!

PIETRO'S MOTHER: Yes, he wrote a novel called *Help Jesus* or something similar. But they're not really talking about Jesus. They put these titles on books to dirty Jesus's name. It's incomprehensible and full of dirty words. I never even finished cutting the pages. This Pierfederici was very handsome. Above all, he had a lot of style. Her – the Valcipriana girl – she wasn't ugly, but she had no style.

GIULIANA: You think she doesn't have any style?

PIETRO'S MOTHER: Not even a little. So this Pierfederici man married the Valcipriana girl and left her immediately – after two weeks of marriage. He's ill, a neurotic. Even poor Lamberto, who was treating him, said so. Seems to me he was throwing money away. And he led this girl astray, too. She doesn't want to live with her family anymore. She travels. She's got all kinds of men. Seems she may not be able to have children because she has an inverted uterus. She's your friend?

GIULIANA: Yes.

PIETRO'S MOTHER: Oh, but that's where I've seen you! I saw you getting gelato at the Café Aragno with the Valcipriana girl. With that Topazia. The Valcipriana girl was wearing these totally filthy white shorts – indecent – and a kerchief around her neck. She looked like some kind of street urchin. You had on a yellow terrycloth dress. The two of you weren't making the best impression, my dear, I must say. Neither one of you. Do you still have it, that terrycloth dress?

GIULIANA: Yes.

PIETRO'S MOTHER: Don't wear it anymore. Make a gift of it to Vittoria. It's not right for you, that dress. Yellow isn't right for you. And made out of terrycloth! You wear terrycloth at the seashore, not in the city. Is your friend Topazia planning to come to visit you here? When she comes, let me know. So I don't come the same day. I'd prefer not to run into her. I find her unpleasant. Yesterday at Lamberto Genova's funeral, Cecilia Valcipriana was there. The mother. Destroyed. A complete wreck.

PIETRO: Why?

PIETRO'S MOTHER: You're asking me why? Because she's worried about her daughter. And because of her sadness over Lamberto's death. They were good friends. He was her doctor. She was being psycho-analysed.

GIULIANA: Lamberto Genova was a psychoanalyst?

PIETRO'S MOTHER: Yes.

GIULIANA: Did he have an office somewhere around Circonvallazione Clodia?

PIETRO'S MOTHER: I don't know. He had two or three offices. I never went there. I've never been psychoanalysed. I don't need it. I have my faith.

GIULIANA: I knew this Lamberto Genova. I knew him very well. I was being psychoanalysed by him.

PIETRO: You were being psychoanalysed? This I didn't know. You never told me that.

PIETRO'S MOTHER: You married her and you didn't even know that she'd been psychoanalysed? And by our own poor Lamberto?

GIULIANA: Twice. I only went to see him twice. Topazia didn't take me there, but that Hungarian doctor that Topazia knew, he took me after she'd already left for America. He took me because he said I had a strong inferiority complex. I was identifying with my shadow.

PIETRO'S MOTHER: And Lamberto, what did he tell you to do?

GIULIANA: Nothing. He told me absolutely nothing. When I got there, he made me stretch out on the couch, and I was supposed to talk. He was in an armchair at his desk with his back to me. I talked – I like to talk. I really like telling people all about myself. But it was costing 8,000 lire per session. So the second time, I said to him, 'Do I really have to pay 8,000 lire per session just to talk? To someone who turns his back on me? I'm up to here in debt, I don't have a job, I don't have a home, I don't have anything, and I'm supposed to come here and spend 8,000 lire every time?'[10]

GINESTRA: He was making you pay 8,000 lire per session? And then the wife was feeding him lungs?

GIULIANA: I never paid him. I asked him to loan me a little money instead. He told me no. He said he never lent money to his patients because it interfered with the treatment. Good excuse, I told him. He laughed. He enjoyed himself so much with me. Those moments when he turned around to face me, when he quit doing analysis, he'd laugh with me. But after the second time, I didn't go back any-more. It cost too much. If it had been free, I'd have gone all the time because I liked it. It was restful to talk stretched out that way on

the couch, telling my story to those round shoulders, to that neck
covered with grey curls....

PIETRO'S MOTHER: Curls?

PIETRO: It wasn't Lamberto Genova. Lamberto Genova was a thin, tall,
upright man with a completely bald head.

PIETRO'S MOTHER: A smooth, bald, naked head. A perfect pear. There
wasn't a hair left on his head. He'd lost them all.

PIETRO: Don't you remember the name? The name written on the door?
This doctor of yours – surely he must have had a name?

GIULIANA: He had a name, which I don't remember. I don't have a good
memory for names.

GINESTRA: But now you've stopped identifying with your shadow?

PIETRO'S MOTHER: You're using '*tu*' with her, Ginestra? So soon?[11]

GINESTRA: Isn't she my brother's wife?

PIETRO'S MOTHER: But it was a civil wedding. And we barely know
her besides! All my son has seen fit to tell me is that he married a
woman who had been sorely tried by life.

GIULIANA: No, I haven't stopped identifying with my shadow. Perhaps
I never will.

PIETRO'S MOTHER: So you owed poor Lamberto Genova 16,000 lire? I'll
give it to Virginia. I'll give it to her right away. I'm going there now.

PIETRO: But what if it wasn't Lamberto Genova that she went to? What
if she went to someone else? To someone with curly hair.

PIETRO'S MOTHER: That's true. What a confusion. You've hardly spoken
today, and yet you've completely confused my thinking.

GIULIANA: Everyone says that. Everyone tells me that when I talk I confuse their thinking. Even Vittoria is always telling me that.

PIETRO'S MOTHER: *Always!* But you've only had Vittoria for four days!

GIULIANA: Pietro says so, too.

PIETRO'S MOTHER: Oh, Pietro. Confusion is his paradise. He loves
confusion. He always has, ever since he was a boy. He loves confusion and disorder. To think that my poor husband so loved order.
He was so meticulous, so accurate, so punctual. In his schedule,
in the way he dressed ... everything. Yesterday, at poor Lamberto
Genova's funeral, I was ashamed. Pietro had some dreadful hat on
his head that looked as though it had been pulled out of the garbage bin. Make him throw that hat away. There he was with that
disgraceful hat falling down over his eyes, a horrendous scarf tied
around his neck. He looked like a thief.

PIETRO: In your dreams, I'll throw it away. It's a great hat.

PIETRO'S MOTHER: You know why he wears that hat?

GIULIANA: Why?

PIETRO'S MOTHER: To humiliate me.

GINESTRA: It's not really such an ugly hat. It's a country gentleman's
    hat.

PIETRO'S MOTHER: You, Ginestra, are the eternal optimist. You say
    you like optimists? Here's my daughter – a true optimist. Not an
    optimist, no. She's accommodating. Accommodating because she's
    superficial. She doesn't seek perfection. My children don't seek
    perfection. I, on the other hand, aspire to perfection. Perfection or
    nothing. Why don't you give me your measurements? Tell Vittoria
    to bring a measuring tape. I'll take them to Virginia right away so
    she can get started on your coat.

GIULIANA: It's not enough that I owe money to poor Virginia, 16,000
    lire, but I'm forcing her to make me an entire coat, too?

PIETRO'S MOTHER: What money? Weren't we saying that you had gone
    to a different doctor?

GIULIANA: Oh, right. That's true.

PIETRO: Vittoria! The measuring tape.

VITTORIA: (*Entering.*) Did you call?

PIETRO: A measuring tape.

VITTORIA: We don't have a measuring tape. I was looking for it yes-
    terday myself, to measure the table when I was supposed to buy a
    table pad. There isn't one.

PIETRO'S MOTHER: Don't you even have a measuring tape in the house?

VITTORIA: No, we're still doing without a lot of things. I couldn't buy
    a table pad yesterday. But about that, I need to clear the table and
    take the oilcloth back to the custodian's wife. She's asking for it.

PIETRO'S MOTHER: I'll take your measurements another time. In the
    meantime, I'll buy the wool. I don't want poor Virginia to have to
    bear the expense. She's found herself in economic straits that really
    are not good. She has to sell her house. It's such a shame! A beauti-
    ful house in the Aventino.[12] They've been there for more than thirty
    years. For you, as an eyeball estimate, we'd need three kilos of yarn
    for a coat.

GINESTRA: Three kilos of yarn, Mama? You're crazy. You'll need two
    and a half at most.

PIETRO'S MOTHER: There are also the sleeves to think about. You're
    always an optimist. I'm saying we'll need at least three kilos. What
    colour do you want for your coat?

GIULIANA: Blue, maybe?

PIETRO'S MOTHER: Blue? But what shade of blue? Baby blue? I'm afraid that wouldn't go well with your complexion. Sea green is better. Or else a dead-leaf green. Let's go, Ginestra. Let's go to the House of Wool.

PIETRO: Shall I take you in the car?

PIETRO'S MOTHER: It's not necessary. Anyway, I'd be ashamed to go out in that car of yours. It's covered with dents and mud. It's indecent. (*She puts her hat on in front of the mirror.*)

PIETRO: What a fancy hat!

GINESTRA: As soon as Mama found out that you were getting married, she ran right out to buy herself that hat.

PIETRO'S MOTHER: Yes. Because I believed that the two of you would get married in church. I could hardly imagine you'd do things the way you did, in a mad rush, just to humiliate me. In a mad rush, in secret, like thieves.

PIETRO: Why? Thieves don't get married in church?

PIETRO'S MOTHER: Like thieves. You did things like thieves. To cause me sorrow. So you could seem like non-conformists. For chaos. For the love of chaos. The love of breaking the rules. Let's go, Ginestra. If it gets dark, we won't be able to see the colours of the wool.

GINESTRA: Goodbye. Thank you.

PIETRO: Goodbye.

GIULIANA: Goodbye.

PIETRO'S MOTHER: Goodbye. (*Pietro's mother and Ginestra exit. Giuliana and Pietro are left alone.*)

GIULIANA: I'm afraid there's no escaping poor Virginia's coat.

PIETRO: I'm afraid not.

GIULIANA: That mother of yours is a little loopy. You didn't tell me she was a little loopy. If she weren't loopy, she'd really be unbearable.

PIETRO: Yes, if she weren't loopy, she'd be exhausting.

GIULIANA: Good thing she's loopy instead. You didn't describe her to me right. Me, with my mother – I'm sure I described her to you right. The way she really is.

PIETRO: Let's go see your mother after all. Mothers are important.

GIULIANA: You don't really know how to describe people. You don't. Maybe you're a moron. At certain times I wonder whether I've married a moron.

PIETRO: Even though you were ready to marry anyone?

GIULIANA: Anyone, yes, but not a moron.

PIETRO: Why in the world didn't you ever tell me that you'd been psychoanalysed?

GIULIANA: Didn't I tell you? Who knows how many things I still haven't told you. There hasn't been time for it. All in all, we know so little about each other. We got married in such a mad rush. Like thieves.

Vittoria enters.

VITTORIA: What shall I make for supper this evening?

GIULIANA: Eggplant parmesan.

PIETRO: Again? Oh, no, enough with the eggplant parmesan. Let's find something else.

GIULIANA: Would you prefer lungs?

VITTORIA: I could make an onion frittata.

PIETRO: Good idea.

VITTORIA: I returned the oil cloth to the custodian's wife. But we still need to buy that table pad, if your mother comes over again. Because the custodian's wife needs the oil cloth.

GIULIANA: Was there a table pad in Signora Giacchetta's house?

VITTORIA: No, because we always ate in the kitchen, without a table cloth, on the kitchen table. Right on the marble.

GIULIANA: Right on the marble? Doesn't Signora Giacchetta even have a Formica kitchen? She's not very modern.

VITTORIA: It's not so much that she's not modern, it's that she finds herself in a bit of difficulty. If she wins a lawsuit against her poor husband's relatives, then she'll have the house all redone new.

GIULIANA: But she has a car? Didn't she bring you back in her car?

VITTORIA: It's not her car. It belongs to the company. Signora Giacchetta works for a company that's in the soap business. There's a loudspeaker in the car, with a recording in the back that plays advertising for soap. I'm a little embarrassed when I find myself in that car, travelling through the streets, shouting about soap. Signora Giacchetta said she was embarrassed at the beginning, too, but not anymore. She's gotten used to it. She'll come here one day with all her different soaps, Signora Giacchetta will. If the two of you want to buy soap, she'll give you an excellent discount. Do you need anything?

PIETRO: No, thanks, we have soap.

VITTORIA: No, I mean now, do you need anything? I'm going to visit the girl upstairs for a little while, to see if she can lend me some onions. We don't even have an onion in the house.

GIULIANA: Okay.

Vittoria exits.

PIETRO: Nice girl, that Vittoria.

GIULIANA: Very.

PIETRO: Did you tell her all about yourself? Even about the psychoanalysis? Did you tell her about that?

GIULIANA: No, I may not have told her about that yet. Your mother is so different from mine, though! We've got entirely different mothers. With mothers so different, and everything so different, are we going to be able to live together?

PIETRO: I don't know. We'll have to see.

GIULIANA: Your mother doesn't think I married you for money at all. She doesn't think anything, your mother. She's too loopy to think.

PIETRO: Right.

GIULIANA: If she thought much, it would be unbearable. She'd be thinking unbearable things. Instead, she doesn't think about anything, she runs around chasing useless details. In the end, it doesn't matter much to her to know what sky I dropped out of.

PIETRO: Yes, that's how it is.

GIULIANA: But why are mothers so important? Is that what psychoanalysis has discovered, how important they are? According to psychoanalysis, are they more important than anything else?

PIETRO: Yes, according to psychoanalysis, the origins of our behaviour are found in our relationships with our mothers.

GIULIANA: That's so strange! These mothers, curled up and hidden in the depths of our lives, at the very core of our lives, in the dark, so important, so influential over us! A person tends to forget about it in the course of living his life, or just doesn't give a damn. Or else you believe you don't give a damn, but you never stop giving a damn about any of it. That mother of yours – so loopy, and yet influential! It hardly seems she could influence anything, and yet she made you what you are – you!

PIETRO: She made me what I am.

GIULIANA: She's not really the one with the bottle of ink. It was someone else. Good thing I didn't spill ink all over your mother. Otherwise, it might have brought us bad luck. Seeing as how a mother is so important.

PIETRO: Spilling ink doesn't bring bad luck. It's bad luck to spill salt on Fridays.

GIULIANA: Not just on Fridays. All the time.

PIETRO: Only on Fridays.

GIULIANA: Vittoria says it's all the time.

PIETRO: Before long, poor Virginia is about to have three kilos of wool spilled on her, along with a commission to make you a sea-green coat.

GIULIANA: Not sea green. Dead-leaf green.

PIETRO: Poor Virginia.

GIULIANA: What a lot of random nonsense we talk. Always leaping from one branch to another.

PIETRO: Not from branch to branch. From leaf to branch.[13]

GIULIANA: From leaf to branch. We never have a logical conversation. All in all, we know so little about each other! We should be trying to understand who we are. Otherwise, what kind of marriage is this? We married each other in such a rush! What was the rush?

PIETRO: Oh, let's not start in again on the subject of our marriage. We're married and that's it.

GIULIANA: Like hell, that's it. Don't be so superficial. Why did I marry you? And what if I did marry you for money?

PIETRO: Forget about it.

GIULIANA: Forget about it like hell. That would be horrible.

PIETRO: Where's my hat?

GIULIANA: Do you have a funeral?

PIETRO: No, and it's not raining. But I want my hat. I need to go somewhere and I want my hat. I've decided I'm going to wear my hat whenever I go out.

GIULIANA: Maybe because your mother said she couldn't stand that hat?

PIETRO: Maybe.

GIULIANA: You see how important mothers are? You see how influential they are?

PIETRO: So? My hat?

GIULIANA: I'm afraid Vittoria may have put it back in mothballs.

PIETRO: Damn! This madness for mothballs! Tell her to get it out.

GIULIANA: Vittoria must still be with the girl upstairs. When she goes up there, she never comes back down. We could eat frittata without onions.

PIETRO: Fine, I'll go out without my hat.

GIULIANA: Where are you going?

PIETRO: To see a client. In the Quartiere Trionfale.

GIULIANA: In the Quartiere Trionfale? Maybe my psychoanalyst wasn't at the Circonvallazione Clodia. Maybe he was in the Quartiere Trionfale.

PIETRO: Bye. I'll be back in a little while.

GIULIANA: Bye. Are onions bad for an ulcer?

PIETRO: The worst. But you don't have an ulcer. My mother does.

GIULIANA: Is it true she has an ulcer?

PIETRO: No one knows. She says so. No one's ever known if it's true. Lamberto Genova said no. He said she was as healthy as a horse, that there was nothing wrong with her. No one knows.

GIULIANA: Mothers are so mysterious!

PIETRO: They couldn't be more mysterious!

GIULIANA: And so important!

PIETRO: Yes. So important!

GIULIANA: But at a certain point, it's fair to tell them to go to hell a little, right? You might still love them, but you tell them to go to hell a little. Isn't that true?

PIETRO: Certainly. And your mother? What's wrong with her?

GIULIANA: Oh, my mother's got every kind of health problem. Rheumatism, stomach problems, her liver – her bile ducts have got I don't know what wrong with them. She's got everything. Mothers are also so annoying!

PIETRO: They couldn't be more annoying.

GIULIANA: You know what I think?

PIETRO: What?

GIULIANA: I think maybe I never met this Lamberto Genova guy at all.

July 1965

Notes

1 The title of Ginzburg's first play, which comes from an Act II conversation between newlyweds Pietro and Giuliana, poses interesting problems in translation. By that point in the play, Giuliana has been interrogating Pietro for some time regarding his reasons for marrying her, and he finally responds, *'Ti ho sposato per allegria'* – literally, 'I married you for cheerfulness.' Such a translation obviously does not work, and what is needed is a

noun in English that can reasonably suggest what '*allegria*' does in Italian. For not a few who have worked with Ginzburg's best-known play, the solution has been the word 'fun,' such as *I Married You for Fun*, the title Henry Reed (1914–86) gave to his unpublished translation, which was produced as a BBC radio play in January 1980; or, in other English-language citations of the play, as 'I Married You for the Fun of It.' Reasonable people may disagree, but I find such translations unsatisfying. Pietro does not suggest that he married Giuliana 'on a lark' or as a joke (in other words, that he wasn't *serious* when he married her), which is what the 'for fun/for the fun of it' versions suggest. Instead, he cites the 'boredom' and gloom of his family home and his desire to escape from it. 'I always felt very cheerful, when I looked at you,' he tells Giuliana; and when he says he married her 'to cheer myself up,' she immediately reiterates, 'You married me because you had a good time with me but your mother, your sister, and your Aunt Filippa bored you?' There's every indication that Giuliana would have reacted badly had she understood, in Pietro's statement, some version of what we mean in English when we say we did something 'for the fun of it'; such a motivation would have been insulting. On the other hand, the idea that Pietro married her to lift his spirits or to find relief from an oppressive family situation strikes her as perfectly sensible.

2 Ginzburg's published scripts rarely provide much information about the physical settings of her plays or about time or scene changes between acts. Where it has seemed useful, I have provided such information, as here, between brackets. Except in the case of *The Interview*, which spans a decade, and *The Armchair*, which spans six years, the plays take place in the 'present day' – that is, more or less at the time they were written. Ginzburg's date appears at the end of each play.

3 A community some twenty-five miles northeast of Rome.

4 A northern Italian specialty, *cotechino* is a kind of sausage, usually rather large in diameter and made from pork rind and meat from the cheek, neck, and shoulder. It is often eaten with lentils at New Year's.

5 As in many parts of the world, books in Italy were once sold with the signatures unsevered. The reader was expected to have the binder or bookseller do the job or to have a proper paper knife on hand (a *tagliacarte*, in Italian). Here, the meaning is literal, but the sense is the same as 'You never even cracked the spine' or 'You never even opened it.'

6 A hearty meat stew prepared in an almost infinite array of variations. The basics of the method are that the meat is browned, then cooked slowly in Marsala or other wine, and combined with tomatoes and garlic. Olives,

onions, or potatoes, along with various herbs and spices, are added according to the preference of the chef. Spezzatino is served as a *secondo* or main course.

7 In *Lessico Famigliare* (Turin: Einaudi, 1963), Ginzburg wrote of her childhood experience with the death of a family friend, a certain Signor Galeotti: 'As soon as anyone died, my father immediately appended the word "poor" to his name, and he was furious with my mother who wouldn't do the same. This "poor" habit was greatly respected in my father's family … And so it was that Galeotti became "poor Galeotti" an hour after he was dead' (49–50).

8 Literally, *ginestra* is the Italian for Scotch broom (now scientifically identified as *Cytisus* but which formerly belonged to the genus *Genista*), a flowering shrub noted for its showy, bright-yellow flowers. 'La Ginestra,' meanwhile, is the name of a long and rather pessimistic poem by the Italian Romantic poet Count Giacomo Leopardi (1798–1837), written the year before he died and subtitled 'The Flower of the Desert.'

9 Though Ginzburg generally used the names of real towns and cities in her plays, neither Pieve di Montesecco nor Rossignano appears to exist in Romagna, though both have the 'sound' of small provincial towns.

10 Describing her own incomplete psychoanalysis, Ginzburg wrote: 'I found it enormously annoying that I had to pay him money. If my father had known not only about my analysis but also about all the money I was spending on Dr B., he would have let out a shout that would have brought down the house. But it wasn't just the idea of my father's shouting that made me uneasy. It was the thought that I was paying money for the attention that Dr B. dedicated to what I was saying. I was paying for his patience with me … I was paying for his irony, his smile, the silence and half-light of his office … nothing came to me for free, and that's what I found unbearable. I told him so, and he responded that he might have anticipated such a thing. He always anticipated everything; I never managed to catch him by surprise.' 'La Mia Psicanalisi,' in *Mai Devi Domandarmi* (Einaudi, 1991, 43–4; my translation).

11 Like French, Spanish, and related languages, Italian recognizes both formal and informal forms of second-person address. In several of the plays, Ginzburg marks the moment when the conversation turns more intimate and the characters switch from the formal '*lei*' to the informal '*tu.*' In an anglophone context, the rough equivalent would be a move to first names; if that strategy were to be adopted in performance, however, speeches that preceded this point would need to be modified to emphasize increased

'pre-*tu*' formality ('Sir/Ma'am' and 'Mr/Mrs/Ms,' for example).

12 The Aventine Hill, one of Rome's famous Seven Hills, is home to an elegant, architecturally rich residential area.

13 The saying in Italian is *'saltare di palo in frasca'* – literally, to jump from pole to branch, i.e., to jump from one conversational topic to another or to speak in non sequiturs. Giuliana quotes the saying accurately, but Pietro corrects her. He insists that the saying is *'di palo in foglia'* – from pole (or branch) to leaf. Though he is wrong, she accepts his version.

The Advertisement

A PLAY IN THREE ACTS

Cast:
Teresa
Elena
Boy
Lorenzo
Giovanna

ACT ONE

[*An apartment in the Trastevere District, Rome.*]

A bell rings. Teresa opens the door. Elena enters.

TERESA: Good afternoon.

ELENA: Good afternoon. I called this morning. I've come because of the advertisement in the *Messaggero*. My name is Elena Tesei.

TERESA: Which advertisement? I placed three.

ELENA: The room.

TERESA: Ah, the room. You need a room. Then I'll show you the room. It has a western exposure. It gets the full sun all afternoon. You can see St Peter's. Make yourself comfortable for a moment. Would you like a cup of coffee?

ELENA: No, thank you.

TERESA: The apartment has five rooms. It's too big, but I don't want to leave it because I don't like to move. Moving is sad. So I'd like to let a room out to a young female student who can do a little house-work for me. I hate housework. Do you?

ELENA: Not me. Certain kinds of housework I don't mind. And I don't
have money to pay for a room. That's why I answered your advertisement.

TERESA: As I was saying, I placed three. One for a buffet. Do you know
anyone who might like to buy an inlaid rosewood buffet, truly,
truly, truly nineteenth-century? It's that one there, see? I don't keep
dishes in it. All that's inside are some old magazines. I don't know
what to do with a buffet. I always eat in the kitchen. The other advertisement was for my villa at Rocca di Papa.[1] I want to sell it. It's
a ten-room villa, with an English garden. Garden. I'd say it's almost
a park. I never go there. The few times I've been there, I was dying
from the gloom. I can't bear the countryside. When I smell hay or
cows, I feel like crying. Maybe because, when I was little, I used
to live in the country. I started hating the countryside when I was
little. I had a brutal childhood.

ELENA: Has anyone responded?

TERESA: To the advertisements? For the buffet, one woman called me.
I didn't treat her very well. She said to me, 'How much are you
asking?' I said, 'Two million lire negotiable.' Negotiable means that
you're prepared to negotiate, right? She tells me, 'That's too much.'
How is that too much for a rosewood buffet, truly nineteenth-
century? And plus she'd never even seen it! For the villa at Rocca di
Papa, no one has responded yet.

ELENA: For the room?

TERESA: For the room, four people responded. You're one. Of the others, one was a young woman with a three-month-old baby. No.
The other was a violinist. No. I like music. I'm even fond of small
children. Unfortunately, I can't have children. But I've been suffering from headaches recently, and I need a little peace. Another one
came this morning, but she was an old woman. In the advertisement I put 'student.' But that one was a retiree. She must have been
at least sixty. I prefer a young person, and she was uncouth besides.
I'm looking for someone more refined, someone with a little culture. To be able to share a little conversation once in a while. Have a
cup of tea together. Listen to records. To have some company since
I live alone. What am I going to do with the company of an old
woman? Don't you think?

ELENA: Certainly.

TERESA: So would you like to see the room? (*She opens a door in the rear
and they look at the room.*) Today, you can't see St Peter's because of

the fog. Otherwise, you'd see it. The air is good, we're beneath the Gianicolo.[2] You're a student? What are you studying?

ELENA: Literature. I'm in my second year. Last year I lived with my aunt and uncle, but I don't want to live there anymore because of the noise. I sleep with two cousins and, when I have to stay up to study in the evenings, they complain about the light. My parents live in the country, near Pistoia. They have a little guest house there for foreigners. They don't give me much money because they haven't got much and they say I can stay with my aunt and uncle. I don't spend anything at my aunt and uncle's, but I don't like it. No, it's not that I don't like it, it's the noise.

TERESA: I don't want money for the room. Some company and a little bit of housework. I live alone.

ELENA: You're not married?

TERESA: I am married. I'm separated. We've maintained a fairly good relationship and he drops by often to visit. He even telephoned me a little while ago. He told me, 'Sure, it's a good idea to find yourself a young woman, a student, so you won't be alone in the house.' At night, all alone in this house, I get scared. I used to have a maid, but she stole and I got rid of her. But she was old besides. I don't get along with old people, maybe because I grew up in my grand-parents' house – my grandparents on my father's side. They didn't love me. They preferred my brother. What a terrible childhood! For example, I don't live with my mother because she's old. I can't stand her. It's not that we don't get along – it would be impossible not to get along with my mother anyway because she never says a word. I think in her entire life she must not have said more than a hundred words. But I can't tolerate her, I can't stand her. Do you get along with your mother?

ELENA: Oh, yes. My mother isn't old. She's so young. We seem like sisters. And she doesn't really do a thing to keep herself young. She washes her face with laundry soap. She's on her feet by six in the morning with her pleated plaid skirt and her work boots, and her thick red socks. She's always got her boots on – because she goes walking all around the countryside. She splashes through the streams of water running through the fields, she gets stuck in the mud. She's in the garden, she's in the chicken coop, she's in the woodshed, she goes into town to do her shopping with a sack over her shoulder. She never rests for a moment and she's always cheer-ful. My mother is an extraordinary woman.

TERESA: She runs a guest house, you say? What kind of guest house?

ELENA: For foreigners. A small guest house. Since we have a very large old house, with a lot of land around it, a few years ago my family thought of putting in a small guest house. It's a very beautiful house, but uncomfortable, cold, old-fashioned. Foreigners like it. It was my mother's idea, to tell the truth, because my father doesn't really have ideas. Poor mom, she's exhausting herself to death with that guest house. The servants don't want to stay because it's so lonely there. They're always short a maid or they're missing a cook. Often she has to light the stoves herself – they're all wood stoves. My father doesn't do a thing. All he does is play tennis with the guests. Then he has conversations in English. He speaks English very well, with an Oxford accent. Around the time I left, there were six guests there. Sometimes we even got up to eleven. But since my mother hardly makes them pay anything, in the end she and my father aren't earning a living. It's nothing more than a burden. A burden for my mother, because my father – he has a great time, he's chatting in English, he's playing tennis, he's playing Ping-Pong.

TERESA: Maybe I could run a guest house, too. At Rocca di Papa, in my villa. It's a ten-room villa. But then I'd have to be at Rocca di Papa. Which I hate.

ELENA: Why did you get a villa there if you hate the place?

TERESA: It was Lorenzo. My husband. Lorenzo loves the country. He wanted us to settle down in Rocca di Papa. So he had the villa built and we went there every day to supervise the work. We attended to the smallest particulars of that house, I can tell you. We spent so much money on it.... Then, when it was finished, we slept there one night. Just one night. In the morning my husband said he had things to do in Rome and that he'd be back that evening. He took his car and he left. I stayed behind. I stood staring out the window and I looked at the trees, at the fog on the hills, the fields, the city. My god the city was far away! And then I heard the sound of cow bells, and I could really smell the cows, too, and I smelled milk, and I started feeling depressed. So I took my car, the Seicento,[3] because I had a Seicento and Lorenzo had a Flavia, a car for each of us. I went down to Rome. We still had a house in Rome – not this one, another house on Via dei Banchi Nuovi. But empty because we'd taken all the furniture we had to Rocca di Papa. Not a stick of furniture. I bought two box springs, two mattresses, two blankets, four sheets, and we camped out in the house. My husband said, 'Okay, we'll sleep here tonight, but tomorrow we have to get settled in at Rocca di Papa. Instead, we never again set foot in Rocca di Papa. I went back, once or twice, to pick up some pillowcases or sheets. All those months we slept in the empty house – with just the beds in it. When we brought coffee up from the café, we set the cups on the floor. We ate in restaurants. All so we wouldn't have to stay at Rocca di Papa.

ELENA: But couldn't you tell your husband that you didn't like being at Rocca di Papa? Couldn't you have told him before he had the house built?

TERESA: What if I didn't know I wouldn't like being there? I thought I would like it. I thought we'd have lots of children – seven or eight babies. I saw myself watering the flowers. I thought I'd keep some chickens and rabbits. How does your mother do it? Your mother has a flower garden, right?

ELENA: She has flowers, yes.

TERESA: Does she have rabbits? Chickens?

ELENA: Yes.

TERESA: Well, I realized that I hate chickens, too. Not just cows. And that day in that big, beautiful deserted house, in the middle of all those trees, I began to feel terribly depressed. Because when I smelled that country smell, I remembered my childhood. I told you I had an awfully unhappy childhood. We lived with my grandparents on my father's side – mom, my brother, and me. Our grandparents were farmers. Poor farmers. My father was there at first, and I was afraid of my father. He used to beat my mother. He didn't beat me, but when he saw me playing in the kitchen, he'd grab me by the arm and shove me out the door. He said I wasn't his. He said my brother was his, but not me. I was Uncle Giacomo's child. Who knows if it was true that I was Uncle Giacomo's? I don't know. I've never known. Uncle Giacomo lived at the other end of town, and I would see him sometimes around the village. A little man, with his pipe in his mouth, wearing boots, with a great big dog that always followed him around. He would look at me, search around in his pocket, and give me two or three pieces of candy. Then he'd whistle for the dog and he'd go off on his way. And I thought: 'Why doesn't he take me away, if I'm his? Why doesn't he take me to his house?' He had a beautiful house with a huge front door and a balcony that wrapped all the way around. I was playing by the fire in the kitchen and my father came in and he grabbed me by the arm and he shoved me outside on the walk. I was crying and my grandmother

pulled me back inside the house. And she said to my father, 'What
are you, some kind of dog?' And he said, 'Keep your mouth shut
about things you don't understand. That one's not mine. That one
is Giacomo's.' Giacomo was my father's brother, but he'd quarrelled
with my grandparents over some forest land they had and they
didn't speak to each other anymore. And my grandmother said,
'Even if she is Giacomo's, it's not her fault.' And my father said,
'That's true, but I can't look at her, and one of these days I'm going
to take off for America so I don't have to see her anymore.' And that
night my father woke up and beat my mother. He beat her until her
nose and her mouth were bleeding. Then my father left for America
and we stayed with my grandparents. My grandparents were mean
to my mother, too. They were always yelling at her, and little by
little my mother became even more sullen, dishevelled, frightened,
bent over. My father used to write to my brother from America and
send him packages of clothes. My brother had a nice wardrobe. He
had some wool sweaters in different colours with zippers, some
big, warm leather gloves, leather jackets with fur lining inside.
Then when my brother was fourteen, my father sent him the money
so he could come to America. And so even my brother left.

ELENA: And your mother let him leave?

TERESA: Sure, she let him leave. We were living in misery! Then my
grandfather became paralysed and my mother took care of him.
She dressed him, she put food into his mouth, she carried him in
her arms like a baby so he could sit close to the fire. And he used
to insult her and scold her. And my grandmother scolded her, too,
and they were always yelling at her that it was her fault that my
father had gone away and that there wasn't anyone left to work
in the fields. My mother was killing herself working in the fields,
taking care of my grandfather, feeding the animals. My mother
never said anything. She always kept her mouth shut. One of her
legs swelled up on her and she walked around dragging that swollen leg, with her foot in an old slipper. I would still run into Uncle
Giacomo in town, but he didn't give me candy anymore. He'd look
at me and he'd go off on his way. And I thought, 'Why doesn't he
come to get me, if I'm his?' Little by little we sold all the land and
the animals and the house had to be mortgaged. When my grandparents died, we gave the house away, too, and we went to live
with my Aunt Amata, who had a dry goods store. So my mother
started being Aunt Amata's housekeeper, because it's in her nature

to be a servant. She's never done anything else her whole life. When I was twenty, I ran away from that village because I didn't want to stay in the dry goods store selling buttons. I didn't want to end up a servant like my mother.

ELENA: And you came to Rome?

TERESA: Yes, I came to Rome. And I worked in a shop that sold olive oil and wine. Since I was so attractive, I had lots of men after me, and one time one of them said to me, 'Come on, I'll take you to be an extra in a film.' He was somebody who had I don't know what to do with movies, and he took me to Cinecittà, and there they had me pose nude in a gold knit bra, with gold underwear, and a long veil all the way to my ankles. I was so beautiful! And I thought – I'm in the right place now. I'll become a movie star. I even wrote to my mother that I was in the right place, and that she should come to Rome to live with me. But my mother didn't budge, and the truth is that I was happy because I can't stand my mother. When I see her dragging that leg around, I feel rage and humiliation all at the same time. And I start thinking about those years when we lived with my grandparents in Reggiano Alto, when we were destitute in that house.

ELENA: And so then did you really become a movie actress?

TERESA: Not in my wildest dreams. They took me, but only as an extra. After that time with the gold bra, they took me for another film and that time I had a bra and underwear made of purple velvet. I had to stretch out on a tiger skin. I was a little more than an extra that time because at a certain point I was supposed to get up, take a bunch of grapes from a fruit bowl, eat the grapes while moving my hips and smiling at a sailor who came in and started eating grapes with me. I'm sure they saw that I didn't really know how to smile or move my hips. They were telling me, 'More voluptuous! Sexier! More voluptuous!' I had to repeat it over and over until, finally, I injured the muscles in my stomach from moving my hips. Then they took me to be a nun who escapes from a burning hospital. I was always at the gate at Cinecittà, waiting for them to take me, but I was earning practically nothing, though I always had high hopes. And there, in Cinecittà, I met Lorenzo. My husband. One day I was sitting down in the ruins of Troy, which were all these scorched-looking stones, and I was eating chicken and bread, because they were giving us sack lunches and that time I'd gotten a sack with chicken. I like chicken and I was enjoying my lunch. I was dressed

up as a Trojan, all wrapped in a sheet, and he – Lorenzo – sat down
nearby and he says, 'You're so beautiful! What are you eating? Are
you eating chicken? How about giving me a little.' I just shrugged
my shoulders. I didn't like him. He struck me as too short. I don't
like short men. And he had on a white raincoat that was all wrinkled and a black beret on his head, a turtleneck sweater with one
of those loose rolled collars, and his beard all long and unshaven.
He looked like some poor student. Then a huge wind came up, a
tramontana,[4] and his raincoat was blowing around him and snap-
ping in the wind, and my sheet was flying all over the place and I
had to hold it closed over my thighs. We were up on a little flat area
of sandy ground, and I was eating chicken and sand. I said to him,
'Who are you? Are you a student?' He said, 'No, I'm not a student.
I finished my studies a while back. I'm thirty years old. I'm an engineer.' And I say, 'And what did you come here for?' He told me that
he'd happened there by chance with a German friend of his who
was doing the music for a film. I looked at him and the only thing I
liked about him were his eyes, because Lorenzo has gorgeous eyes
– big, deep blue, smiling eyes with long lashes. Eyes too beautiful to be wasted on a man. I said to him, 'Why in the world don't
you shave?' And he rubbed his hand across his jaw and he said,
'You're right. I'll leave right now and go straight to the barbershop.
We'll see each other later.' And I did see him that evening in front
of the gate. He was leaning against a street light and smoking. We
went to supper – him, me, and that German musician friend of his,
whose name was Gunter. Then we snuck away from the German
guy and Lorenzo came to sleep at my place. I had a room on Via del
Lavatore, a terrible room where I was paying 12,000 lire a month.
We stayed together for three days. In those three days, we didn't
do anything but make love, sleep, smoke, and eat these little cans
of Simmenthal loaf[5] that I had on the windowsill. Lorenzo usually
rattles on like a machine gun when he talks, but in those three days
we hardly spoke because both of us were so sleepy. We wanted to
make love and sleep and that was it. Then he told me he was going
downstairs for a minute to buy some cigarettes. He never came
back. I didn't see him again for six months. Sometimes I thought,
'What could have happened to him? Maybe he was worried he was
supposed to pay me? Idiot.' But I felt mortified, and the desire to
go to Cinecittà faded, because I was thinking that you meet such
strange types there, who take you to bed and eat your Simmen-

thal loaf and then disappear without a word. I started working
in a hairdressing salon. I wanted to become a hairdressing artist.
They didn't let me do anything – only hand them hairpins and do
some shampoos, and they were barely paying me anything. It was
a beautiful shop in the Piazza di Spagna. And one day I saw him
come in – Lorenzo – together with a tall, gorgeous woman wearing
a mink coat. He was still the same, with the beret, the raincoat, and
his whiskers unshaven. He says to me, 'Oh! You're here?' as if we'd
just left each other the day before. The woman had come to have
them touch up her highlights. She was an American and she didn't
speak one syllable of Italian. Under my breath I asked him, 'What
are you doing with a lover like that?' And he tells me, 'She's hardly
my lover. She's Gunter's lover.' And I say, 'How is Gunter?' and he
says, 'Fine.' Am I boring you by telling you all this?

ELENA: Oh no. I'm enjoying hearing about it. Please go on.

TERESA: He introduced me to the American woman but she didn't
understand a damn thing and was just saying 'bad, bad' about her
highlights, which she thought had turned out all wrong. He was
talking to her really fast in English, I think explaining that her highlights weren't really all that bad after all, but in the end he must
have gotten sick of it because he left and I saw him walking out
toward Piazza di Spagna with his raincoat flying around him, and
I thought, 'There, I've lost him again.' The American girl left too,
after she'd worn everyone out about her highlights, but also after
buying a trainload of lotions and little soaps. That evening, he was
waiting for me at the door to the shop. He took me to supper.

ELENA: With the American girl again?

TERESA: Of course not, no. In fact, he told me that he didn't like the
American girl. He took her out for walks as a favour to Gunter
because she was a chore and noisy, and poor Gunter asked him for
a break now and then. I said to him, 'And the cigarettes?' And he
goes, 'What cigarettes?' I say, 'Yes, didn't you leave to buy some
cigarettes and then never showed your face again?' So he told me
that, that day, at the tobacco shop, he'd run into a friend of his, and
they started chatting, and he'd totally forgotten about me. When
he remembered that he had to come back to my place, it was late,
the middle of the night, and he thought I would be sleeping. The
next day, his mother wanted him to go take some of the dogs to the
country. Coming back with the dogs, he had an automobile accident, and he dislocated his shoulder. They put him in a cast. He

didn't remember the house number anymore on Via del Lavatore, so he didn't write me. Plus the fact that he never writes letters. He hasn't written a letter since he was eight years old. The last letter he wrote was to the Baby Jesus asking him to bring him a fireman's helmet for Christmas. He was eight. The fireman's helmet never came, and so after that he didn't write letters anymore. That's what he told me. He talked so much! He rattled on like a machine gun, but I was under some kind of spell, listening to him talk. I told him, 'I have the impression that you're telling me a pack of lies.' He said, 'No, I never tell lies, never. I really was in the hospital with my shoulder in a cast. But in my mind I had such a lovely memory of you during those months.' I told him, 'What an ugly way to say it. You talk as if I were a thing, not a person.' Then he told me, 'You're still not a person to me. You may become one, it may happen that you become one, but for now you still aren't. And I'm sure I'm still not a person for you either, only a confused, indistinct shadow.' And I say to him, 'No, no, no! When I make love with a man he isn't some shadow for me. I don't make love with shadows. I make love with people, and I want to be a person to you. I want you to be concerned about me and to think highly of me. Otherwise, it would be better if you took off and left me alone!' And I started to cry. He gave me his handkerchief. A filthy handkerchief. I threw it down and I said, 'I don't want some filthy handkerchief.' Am I boring you?

ELENA: No.

TERESA: I told him, 'I've already had a lot of men in my life. The first was when I was fifteen years old. He was the pharmacist at Reggiano Alto. Many of them have treated me badly, but not one of them has ever said something like that to me, that I wasn't a person to him, that I was something you could simply leave behind, a shadow. No one's ever dumped me. I've always dumped them when I got tired of them, and I get tired quickly!' And I was crying like an idiot. You know why? Because I was in love. It was the first time I'd been in love and I was thinking, 'There, I've fallen in love with this guy, this poor, dirty guy who doesn't shave, this nobody of an engineer who rattles on like a machine gun, and he's telling me who knows what kind of lies, and maybe in a little while he'll turn the corner and disappear again for six months.' While I was crying, he stood there watching, rubbing his jaw, then all of a sudden he got up, paid the bill, and left. I ran after him, and I caught up with him in the parking lot in the Piazza del Popolo, just as he was getting into his car. He had an Anglia then. I slipped into the car beside him, still crying, and I said, 'Don't leave me like that.' And he said, 'What do you expect from me? Why don't you find someone else, someone who can make you happy? What do you and I have to give to one another?' And I was saying, 'No, no. I want to be with you. I don't know why, but I want to be with you!' So he came with me to Via del Lavatore. I said to him, 'Why in the world do you have an Anglia. Aren't you poor?' And he said, 'Poor? No, I've got lots of money.' So that night, that's how I found out he had lots of money. He lived with his mother in a palazzo on Via Venti Settembre, and the whole palazzo was his. They even had a butler. We lived together a little while without getting married, first in Via del Lavatore and then in an apartment on Via dei Banchi Nuovi, and he would say sometimes, 'If it really matters to you, I'll even marry you, because I see how well we get along. Pretty well. All things considered.' And I said to him, 'Now am I a person to you?' And he said, 'I would almost say so.' He lived with me, but every now and then he went back to his mother's. He'd disappear for a few days, and I was always afraid he'd never come back. Because with him you never could tell. His mother had furious scenes with him about me whenever he went there, and she said if he married me she'd disinherit him, which she didn't wind up doing in the end. I don't know why. In the meantime, I had quit working and I stayed home and I read books because he said I was as illiterate as a kitchen maid. I read, but the books I was reading kept floating away from me like water. I forgot everything immediately, maybe because my mind was always flying back to him. He was a fixture in my life, whether he was at home sitting next to me in his sweater, sharpening his pencils and filling up these little notebooks with numbers, or whether he was out in the city chatting with his friends and waving his hands around. Then he married me because I thought I was expecting a baby. In fact, I wasn't expecting a baby at all, but in the meantime we got married in my village at Reggiano Alto. We spent our honeymoon in Reggiano Alto at the Albergo Italia, and in the evening we stayed in the back of my Aunt Amata's dry goods store playing tombola.[6] With Aunt Amata and my mother. My mother adored him. She was in a state of admiration when it came to him, and even my Aunt Amata adored him. Aunt Amata used to say, 'You don't deserve him, not a husband like that. Hold on to him tight, because you could lose him, stupid and crazy as you are, and with the terrible life you've always made for yourself.' Aunt Amata had never forgiven me because I ran away from our village and because she found out that I had boyfriends in Rome and appeared in movies practically nude. But at the time she was proud of me because I'd married an engineer, someone she realized was very well educated and even rich and who had an entire palazzo in Rome and who, even though he was rich, was a simple man who played tombola in the little room in the back of her shop and was so kind and attentive to my mother and to her.

ELENA: Is your husband the one here in the photograph?

TERESA: Yes. We'd just come back from Reggiano Alto there after getting married. He took me to his mother's house. She hated me without ever having seen me, and as soon as she saw me, she hated me worse, and I cordially hated her back. We gave each other a couple of little smiles, me with my arms crossed over my stomach and her as nervous as could be, always fiddling with these bangs that came down over her forehead and which she'd dyed blue. She was trying to be friendly, so she gave me a ring as a gift, but later, after I was gone, she told Lorenzo she didn't understand what he could have seen in someone like me, who wasn't the least bit refined, who looked older than my age, and who had hands and feet that looked like they belonged to a kitchen maid, and Lorenzo got a big kick out of repeating to me everything his mother had said, laughing like a crazy person. So I told him I never wanted to go back to his mother's again. But we went back anyway because he wanted us to go every now and then and I would obey. I always ended up doing whatever he wanted.

ELENA: But why?

TERESA: Why? Because he dominated me, and he dominated me because I loved him. He ordered me to read and I read. He ordered me to spend time with his friends, and I did. He told me not to eat pasta and beans all the time because I was getting fat and he didn't like me fat, and I obeyed. I made pasta and beans for him, and while he was eating I stared out the window, or else I nibbled at a salad. I obeyed him. I had no will of my own left. He ordered me to go with him to see his mother and I went. I forced myself to be nice to his mother and she forced herself to be nice to me. She'd start arguing with Lorenzo because she didn't want to let it all come out by arguing with me. They'd argue about the interest they had in some land in Puglia at a place called La Pavona. They'd get into fights. I ended up falling asleep in an armchair because I'd eaten too much. The only thing I liked at my mother-in-law's house was eating, and I always filled up as much as possible – and also because, when we were with his mother, he let me eat without bringing up how fat I was, maybe because he thought he was paying me back with food for the enormous bore those hours were for me. So my mother-in-law said that if a young woman falls asleep right after lunch, it means her liver isn't working properly. She, of course, had a perfect liver. She was always talking about her liver, about her kidneys, about her circulation, about her spleen. Hers were always in completely perfect condition. Her sister Paola, who was married and lived in Puglia, had marvellous health as well – the complexion of a newborn baby, intestinal tract like the workings of a clock, perfect teeth. Since Lorenzo had left the house, on the other hand, he'd ruined his perfect health – his complexion was yellow, his eyes were cloudy, he was losing his hair. Because he drank alcohol, stayed up all night in cafés chatting with his friends, ate bad oil. I said, 'No, I don't cook with bad oil. I have oil sent from Reggiano Alto!' But she didn't believe in the oil from Reggiano Alto. She only believed in her own oil, from her orchards. That was the only pure oil. But she never gave us any of that oil. She promised, but she never gave us any. In five years of marriage, I never had the benefit of so much as a cupful. When Lorenzo went to La Pavona, I always told him to pick up a few bottles and bring them to me, since the oil was his, too, but he'd forget, and I would get angry every time, and I'd get angry at his sister who lived on that farm and didn't have to spend money on anything, living there with her husband and their nine children, eating up all the olive oil and the wine and the cheese that were ours, too. But Lorenzo told me I had a vulgar way of thinking. In the beginning we lived as if we were poor, not precisely because we really meant to live that way, but because it didn't matter to us to have a better life and we were happy. He had just that one sweater, two shirts with the cuffs all frayed, and no tie. I had a three-year-old skirt and shoes with the heels all bent. Then we started throwing money out the window, since we had some. I had no idea how to spend money. I'd go out of the house and buy everything I laid eyes on. He was a maniac for paintings. He started buying up paintings, and little by little he'd assembled quite a few and he filled the house with them. All the walls were covered with paintings – we had paintings in the kitchen and in the bathroom, hanging on the wall or piled up on the floor. Plus he was spending money on motorcycles and cars. If a new model of motorcycle came out, he immediately gave the old one away and bought himself the new model, and he did the same thing with cars. He ran around on the motorcycle like the devil himself. He'd already had four motorcycle accidents and two serious car accidents, and he was constantly being fined for speeding, so whenever he went out in the car or the motorcycle I nearly died from the worry. He didn't pay the fines because he always left the house without any money. He told me I should go pay them, but I forgot about it and I would find the tickets everywhere – in drawers or in his pockets and under the seat in the car or on the floor, and I can't even tell you how much worry those tickets gave me, but I didn't pay them because it seemed to me that he was the one who should take care of them.

ELENA: He was a very disorganized man.

TERESA: Yes. And his lack of organization combined with mine, and the result was a truly terrifying level of disorder. He told me that he needed an organized wife who would keep his drawers tidy and pay his traffic tickets. He was always telling me how I ought to be, about the kind of wife he'd rather have had. And so I was always telling him about the kind of husband I'd have preferred. First of all, I would have wanted a husband who spent less money, who was sweet to me, simple, understanding, who didn't confuse my mind with difficult discussions, who brought me flowers occasionally, or a box of candy, some little gift, who at least had a little regard for me. He had no regard for me: If he met a friend on the street, he'd forget to come home for lunch and I'd wait hours and hours for him with lunch all cooked and ready, terribly worried that something had happened.

ELENA: Couldn't he have called you?

TERESA: But he didn't. He didn't call because he wasn't thinking about me. In those moments, when he was chatting with his friends, he was thinking about everything except me.

ELENA: What a strange person!

TERESA: So we started arguing – not just every now and then, but every day, and little by little things between us began to fall apart. We had some pretty terrible fights. He would slap me and I'd bite him and scratch him. A few times we stayed up arguing the whole night long, and at five in the morning he'd leave on his motorcycle so he didn't have to look at me anymore, and I'd stay in bed and cry.

ELENA: What were you fighting about?

TERESA: What about? I don't even know anymore. About his being late, about the traffic tickets, about money, about the paintings he bought, about his family, about a word. He would leap on some word I had said, half-distracted. He would dissect it, extracting every possible hidden meaning, until that word had become huge and turned into a monster. And at some point I couldn't understand anything anymore. My mind was all mixed up, and I'd just start sobbing. He'd smack me and I'd bite his wrists and his hands, and while I bit and scratched him I was thinking: 'Look how we ended up. Look how low we've fallen! What a shame. What a hell this is!'

ELENA: It really must have been hell.

TERESA: It was. But then, I don't know how, we made peace and the hell disappeared. After smacking me around and beating me, he started being so good to me. He said he loved me and that he wouldn't trade me for any woman. We'd make love and then he'd say he felt a little hungry and I'd get up and cook some pasta. And then we'd go to sleep and we'd sleep until it must have been three in the afternoon. Both of us used to like to sleep. We had some sleeps that practically never ended.

ELENA: But wasn't he working?

TERESA: He wasn't working. He had that engineering degree, but he didn't do anything with it. He didn't want to hear anything about getting a job, or a position of any kind. He said he'd feel discouraged by a regular job, and he was studying for another degree in pure physics. Pure physics was his passion. He had these notebooks with graph paper and he filled them with calculations, then he got sick of them and tore them up, and I would find little pieces of paper covered with numbers all over the place, along with the bills and traffic tickets. Of course he didn't need to get a job because we had plenty of money to live on. In fact, he used to say we even had too much money. We were tossing it out the window, the two of us were. Some evenings we went out dancing with friends at nightclubs. There would be eight or ten people and he would pay for everyone. Then he got the idea of the villa at Rocca di Papa. I can't tell you how much money we threw away on that. He'd work out a particular layout of the rooms, then he wouldn't like it anymore, and he'd have them tear the walls down. He went back and forth from Rome to Rocca di Papa on his motorcycle or in the car, tearing around like the devil, then he'd go to the antiques market and buy antique furniture. We had some really valuable furniture there. And paintings.

ELENA: And no one lives in the villa now?

TERESA: No one. Who do you think would want to live there? Just going in the door is unsettling. Uninhabited houses are unsettling. It smells all closed up, it smells damp – because it is damp, in the middle of all those trees. I could certainly rent it out, but see, it's unsettling for me to think about other people going there, where we were supposed to be. I'd rather sell it, maybe even with all the furniture inside. That way it's closed, finished – not mine anymore. I wouldn't see it again. It's in my name. Lorenzo put it in my name.

ELENA: Won't burglars get in, if the house is deserted?

TERESA: I don't know. And, in the end, what do I care? Sure, there are some valuable paintings there. I'm always telling him to go take them out, but he never does. He puts it off and he puts it off. He's a man who always puts everything off, as if he didn't have anything but time. Besides, those paintings don't really mean a thing to him. The painting mania is long gone. At the time, as soon as the villa was finished, he spent entire days hanging paintings. He hung all the paintings we had, plus others that he bought just so he could hang them there. Little by little we stripped the house on Via dei Banchi Nuovi and left it empty. He wasn't talking about anything but that villa and about the life we were going to have there, with lots of friends, and animals, and children. I wanted children, too, and it was so lovely to think about the children we'd have, and the names we'd give them, and the clothes and the toys we'd buy for them. Some doctors had told me I couldn't have children. But I thought they were wrong. That instead I'd have a flock of children. As I said, we stayed in the villa at Rocca di Papa one night. Just one night.

ELENA: And afterwards?

TERESA: And afterwards, as I said, we continued living in the house on Via dei Banchi Nuovi, all emptied out, and it wasn't very comfortable there because we didn't have so much as a side table to set a glass on. Since we'd spent so much on the villa at Rocca di Papa, we were a little short on money and we argued – maybe because of money or maybe because we were so uncomfortable, but in our peaceful moments we said that it was all temporary and that we'd get settled in at Rocca di Papa before long. To tell the truth, neither

one of us had any desire to go there, but each of us pretended it
was the other one who didn't want to go. He said I was the one
who didn't want to because I liked spending the evenings with my
friends in nightclubs too much. And then he started saying that I'd
ruined him because I'd taken away all desire he had to read and to
study, and that the instant he sat down to study, I'd call him because I wanted him to keep me company or make love, so he never
managed to have a moment of concentration. Since we were so
uncomfortable in that house, he started spending the afternoons at
his mother's place.

ELENA: Did he study at his mother's place?

TERESA: Of course not. He wasn't doing a thing either. He'd sequester
himself with his books, and his friends would come to visit and
he'd get caught up in chatting with them. He talked so much! My
God, the way he talked with his friends! They were my friends,
too, and sometimes they'd come to see me and explain that I wasn't
treating him right, that he was unhappy with me because I didn't
understand him. I tormented him and weighed him down with
my worrying and my jealousy, and it's true that I was very jealous.
When he came back home, I'd make huge scenes accusing him of
being out with other women. They were telling me that I should let
him work because he was in the middle of a very important course
of study and that I needed to concern myself with giving him a
tranquil, orderly life and a house that was truly a home, and not
with anything else. I was furious with them because it seemed to
me they were the ones who were causing him to waste time with
their endless chatting and all those long discussions. But I was
pretty unhappy myself and I felt all alone. And then something
happened. I cheated on him. I had never cheated on him. Lots of
times I was on the verge of cheating on him, but I'd always pulled
myself back.

ELENA: You cheated on him with who?

TERESA: With a friend of his, a guy named Mario, a journalist who used
to come to the house all the time. They were close friends and had
been since they were children. I cheated on him with this Mario
guy.

ELENA: And he found out?

TERESA: Yes. He found us together. He'd left for La Pavona. He was
away for two weeks and he came back unexpectedly at night. I was
in bed with Mario. I heard the key turning in the lock. Mario was

sleeping. I shook him. And there was Lorenzo, on his way in with
his bag, his beret, his wrinkled raincoat, his whiskers unshaven. He
stood in the doorway for a moment – tiny, pale, no expression on
his face, so colourless, so cold.... Mario woke up and they looked
at each other. Lorenzo left again. I heard the thud of the door. I
had slipped my robe on, and I was shaking and crying. I ran down
the stairs after him and I saw him getting into his car, the Flavia.
He slammed the door and took off. There I was, in my robe, in the
street at night, freezing, in tears, desperate – because I understood
that was the end.... I went back upstairs. Mario had gotten dressed.
He said, 'I'm going to look for him.' He was frantic, too. He left as
well, because I hardly meant anything to him and it had been a stupid thing to do – one of those things that no one even knows how
they happen. There's a little curiosity in them, and a little misery....
I had attached myself to Mario because I thought I could get free of
my misery for a moment. I had grabbed at him the way you hide
under a tree when it's cold and the wind is blowing. But he didn't
mean anything to me, not a thing, and so I started writing letters
to Lorenzo. I wrote floods of letters to him at his mother's house,
and I tried to call constantly but the butler answered and said he
wasn't in. I went to his mother's. I didn't see him. His mother was
in the living room in an armchair, with that fringe of blue hair and
a feather boa. The sister was there, too. I had never been able to
stand his sister, but we'd always been polite. I used to send Christmas presents for her nine kids and she'd send me these bed jackets
that she had crocheted. They told me Lorenzo wasn't in, that they
didn't know where he was. They told me we should start legal
proceedings for a separation, because we certainly couldn't live
together anymore, we were destroying one another. And I started
to cry, and I said that we were actually very happy together, that we
couldn't live without each other, and that they couldn't understand
how much we loved each other. And little by little all the hate I
had for them burst out, and I started shouting that they'd been the
ones who'd turned Lorenzo against me, that they had it in for me
because I was poor, and that I'd wipe my ass with all their filthy
money, and then my mother-in-law fainted. Or at least she pretended to faint, and my sister-in-law shoved me to the door, all the
while saying that I was killing her mother: 'You're killing mama!
You're killing her!' And I went downstairs crying and shouting
with the butler right behind me, completely expressionless, and he

helped me put on my overcoat and gave me my scarf.

ELENA: And you never saw Lorenzo again?

TERESA: Of course I saw him. I saw him a few days later. I told you I see him all the time, he comes here all the time, he may even come by in a little bit today. You'll run into him if you stay for a while.

ELENA: No, it's late and I should be going. I should get to the university. I have a class.

A doorbell rings. Teresa opens the door. A boy enters with a box.

TERESA: Oh yes. The grocer.

BOY: Right. Shall I put it here?

TERESA: Yes, there. (*To Elena.*) I ordered some canned goods. Simmenthal loaf. Fruit in syrup. I always eat canned goods since I've been by myself. I'm quite a cook, but I don't feel much like cooking just for me.

BOY: About the cat, my dad said he'd send it over a little later. He doesn't have it at the store. It's at home. My dad will go pick it up a little later and he'll bring it over. You should see what a beauty of a kitten it is. Plus it's a purebred. A pedigree.

TERESA: Yes, okay. (*To Elena.*) They're giving me a Siamese kitten as a gift.

BOY: My father also said, if you could pay the bill....

TERESA: But of course I'll pay it.

BOY: My father is very sorry, but he said, if you could pay it this evening.... He needs to close the accounts.

TERESA: I will pay it. Don't bother me about it now. You can very well see I'm busy. (*The boy exits.*) So do you want the room?

ELENA: Sure, thank you, I think I do. Would tomorrow be too soon for me to move in?

TERESA: Come tomorrow. I'll be expecting you. I won't disturb you when you're studying. But when you stop studying for a few minutes, we could keep each other company a little. I need company. I'm very much alone. I've been left by myself like a dog. And I don't know how to live by myself, that's the horrible thing. I feel so miserable.

ELENA: Don't you have any girlfriends?

TERESA: No. I had girlfriends when I was young. But then I lost touch with them because I was always with Lorenzo and I didn't need anybody else when I had him. We had both male and female

friends in common, people to spend the evening with, but I don't
see them anymore. I haven't had the desire, because they remind
me of when I was with Lorenzo and I was his wife and everything
was going so well. We were carefree, as happy as two young people
can be, and with so many dreams.

ELENA: But didn't you say your life with him was hell?

TERESA: It was hell, yes. But I was happy in that hell, and I'd give
anything to be able to go back. To be like it was a year ago, all
over again. We've only been separated for a year. We agreed on a
separation. His mother didn't want us to get a no-fault divorce. She
didn't want him to have to pay me alimony. He wanted to. After we
separated, he helped me find this house and he gave me money so I
could furnish it. I bought some furniture. The buffet.

ELENA: The rosewood buffet? The one you want to sell?

TERESA: Yes. What am I going to do with a buffet? I don't have dishes.
I hardly ever invite anyone to lunch. I eat in the kitchen. I'm by
myself.

ELENA: Why did you buy it then?

TERESA: I don't know. I think I bought it because I had the idea that
Lorenzo might come back to live with me. And then, if he did, that I
should offer him a real home.

ELENA: But he didn't come back.

TERESA: He's never coming back. It's over. He says that since we've
been apart he's regained his tranquillity, his equilibrium. He says I
always made him live as if we were in the middle of a sandstorm.
He says it used to seem to him, with me, as though he were sinking
into a well full of black water – muddy, putrid water – as though he
were losing himself a little at a time. He has quite a lot to say! He
has a way with words. He says he left me because, if he'd stayed
with me, the day would have come when he'd start hitting me and
wouldn't stop until he'd killed me. Or I'd end up killing him. He
says he's doing fine without me. I don't know if it's true. He doesn't
seem all that happy to me. He doesn't have a girlfriend, a real
woman. He goes with whores. He spends his evenings in nightclubs
with his friends, just exactly the way he did when he was with me.
I don't believe he's studying. He says he is, he says he's studying,
but I don't believe it. He's just chattering, chattering, chattering with
his friends. The other day I ran into him on the street. He was with
Mario. I never saw Mario again after that infamous night, and my
heart nearly stopped when I saw them together. They were chatting.

I went up to them and the three of us went to get some ice cream. Mario was a little embarrassed. Not Lorenzo. He went on chatting as if it were nothing. He was talking about Spinoza. A philosopher.

ELENA: I'm actually studying Spinoza now for my exams. I have exams in February.

TERESA: Oh, right, you have exams in February. Okay. I'll let you study. I won't disturb you. Once in a while I'll bring you coffee or maybe even a zabaglione[7] to keep your strength up. I'll be like a mom to you. You're so much younger than me. How old are you? Eighteen?

ELENA: Oh, no. I'm twenty-two.

TERESA: And how old would you say I am?

ELENA: I don't know....

TERESA: There's no point in telling you my age. I'm a little run down these days, because I can't sleep. I'm run down and I'm getting fat. Ugly, isn't it? Because I'm sad about getting fat. I eat to make myself feel better. Do I seem fat to you?

ELENA: No. Just right.

TERESA: Do I seem run down to you?

ELENA: A little bit pale.

TERESA: Because I have insomnia. I take sleeping pills, but they don't do any good. When I was with Lorenzo, boy did I sleep! I slept so soundly. Now I sleep a little and I wake up. I fall asleep and I wake up – all night long like that. Often I have a dream, a horrible dream. I wake up covered in sweat.

ELENA: What do you dream?

TERESA: Horrible. If I were to tell you about it, it wouldn't seem horrible to you, and I don't even know why it's so horrible. I know that I wake up in a cold sweat, barely breathing. Anyway, I'm in a courtyard, and at the end of the courtyard there's a wall, a dead end, as high as it can be.... And I know what's on the other side of that wall.

ELENA: What's there?

The phone rings. Teresa answers it.

TERESA: Hello? Who is it? Oh, about the ad? About the buffet? Well, it's a rosewood buffet, truly, truly nineteenth-century. Come and see it. Two million negotiable! What? Negotiable. Negotiable, I said! (*Elena gives a signal that she's leaving.*) Just a minute! (*Puts down the phone.*)

ELENA: I need to go. I'll be back tomorrow.

TERESA: I'll expect you. You'll see how well you get along here. There's sun all afternoon in the room. Because it's on the west. It has a western exposure. I'll really give you no bother. I won't ever disturb you. I'll bring you coffee, tea, zabaglione … as if I were your mother.

ELENA: Thank you. I'll see you later.

TERESA: Goodbye. (*Returns to the phone.*) I was saying two million negotiable. Come see the buffet. Come today. I'll be home all day. What do you mean too much? But I said negotiable. You haven't even seen it! Because how much did you want to spend? What do you mean a buffet couldn't cost two million? An antique buffet? Where are you from? Do you really think I'm going to give it away for nothing? An antique buffet of inlaid rosewood? With four winged putti holding up grapevines? But come see it. I'm saying you should come see it – never mind about the price because it's negotiable. You understand? It's negotiable!

ACT TWO

[*The same apartment, about a month later.*]

The doorbell rings. Elena opens the door. Lorenzo enters.

LORENZO: Excuse me. The Signora isn't in?

ELENA: She's gone out. She should be back before long.

LORENZO: Where did she go?

ELENA: Are you Lorenzo?

LORENZO: I'm Lorenzo, yes. You must be the student.

ELENA: Yes, that's me, the student. My name is Elena Tesei.

LORENZO: Lorenzo Dal Monte. A pleasure.

ELENA: A pleasure.

LORENZO: Where did she go?

ELENA: She went to Rocca di Papa with some people who might buy the villa. She put an ad in the *Messaggero*. These people called early this morning. They seemed pretty ready to buy. Teresa was very happy.

LORENZO: Have you seen it, the villa I mean?

ELENA: No.

LORENZO: Too bad. It's gorgeous. We spent a pile of money on it. I designed it myself. Sometimes I think I'm in the wrong profession. I should have been an architect. My problem is this: I'm good at all kinds of things, but none of them in depth. So I oscillate between the pure and the applied sciences. I don't know how to choose between them. I'm attracted to both at the same time. Do you understand?

ELENA: Yes.

LORENZO: The truth is that I'm a dilettante. There are dilettantes and there are professionals in this world. Unfortunately, I'm a dilettante. Okay, goodbye, I'm going to go. Tell Teresa that I'll be back.

ELENA: No, don't go. Teresa will certainly be home in a little bit. She's been so hoping to see you recently, and you never stop by! I've been here more than a month and Teresa expects to see you every day. She never wants to leave the house. A few times I wanted to take her to the movies and she wouldn't budge from the house for fear that you'd come by and find no one here. She's called you quite a few times, but the phone doesn't answer.

LORENZO: I was in Puglia. I've been in Puglia all month. My phone doesn't answer because I'm living alone now. I was living with my mother before, but I took a little apartment below her. I was in Puglia. On my property.

ELENA: Maybe you could drop Teresa a line.

LORENZO: Write to her? I never write letters. I don't believe I've written a letter since I was eight years old.

ELENA: I know. You don't write letters since the one to the Baby Jesus, telling him he should bring you an infantryman's helmet, though he never did bring you one.

LORENZO: Not an infantryman's helmet, a fireman's helmet.

ELENA: A fireman's helmet. Sorry.

LORENZO: He didn't bring me one. Instead, he brought me some stupid kaleidoscope that got broken immediately. Does that seem to you the kind of joke you should play on a kid?

ELENA: It really isn't.

LORENZO: I see Teresa has told you a lot about me.

ELENA: Teresa talks about you all the time. She never talks about anything else.

LORENZO: How is she?

ELENA: Fine. She says she's sleeping better now that I'm here. She isn't afraid at night anymore. She isn't still having those nightmares that she used to have.

LORENZO: And you? How are you fitting in here?

ELENA: Oh, I'm fitting in quite well. Teresa and I keep each other company. In the evening, when I've had enough of studying, we play
cards, listen to records. Then we go off to bed, and in the morning,
while Teresa is still sleeping, I get up, I go out and do the shopping,
straighten up the house, and then I go to the university. We almost
always eat together. We've become good friends. A week ago I had
a touch of the flu, and Teresa took care of me – she wouldn't let me
get up, and she brought me breakfast in bed on a tray.

LORENZO: I'm pleased you've become friends. Teresa is by herself a lot.
A month ago, the day before I left to go down to my property in
Puglia, she called me and she said, 'I'm so glad – a very nice girl is
coming to live with me, a literature student.' I said, 'Yes? Good, I'll
come meet her.' But then I had to leave.

ELENA: We've become friends. And to think that I came here by chance,
because of an ad in the newspaper. If I hadn't read the newspaper
that day, I'd never have met Teresa.

LORENZO: But why does that seem strange to you? All human relationships are a question of chance. We go where the wind takes us. I
met Teresa because one day a friend took me to Cinecittà, a place I'd
never been before then and where I doubt I'll ever go again. It was
one of those days with a tramontana wind. Teresa was sitting in the
middle of the ruins of Troy. A dry, sandy wind was blowing. The
ruins of Troy had been set up on a clearing covered with sand. The
wind was picking up the sand and blowing it into your eyes, into
your mouth. You could barely stand on your feet. I've always had
the impression that I met Teresa in a sandstorm.

ELENA: I know. Teresa has told me the story. She told me the whole
story.

LORENZO: Teresa still hopes I'll come back to live with her. But I can't. It
will never happen.

ELENA: No, she doesn't hope that. She doesn't hope that anymore.

LORENZO: She told you that she doesn't hope that anymore? It isn't
true. She still hopes. I remain a permanent fixture in her thoughts.
I'd like it if she could find another man and make her life over
again.

ELENA: She never sees anyone.

LORENZO: Yes, she never sees anyone because she has no desire to see
anyone because she's still thinking about me. She's pinned all her
hopes on me. She thinks that if I left her, it was because of that thing

that happened. But it wasn't. I didn't leave her because of that. That was a simple pretext. But I would have left her all the same, maybe no more than a few days later. The truth is that I left her because I'd stopped loving her. I never felt any jealousy. When that thing happened, I had already detached myself from her. I was thousands of light years away. I didn't love her any more. I've tried to explain that to her over and over. But she doesn't understand. She doesn't want to understand.

ELENA: Poor Teresa!

LORENZO: In the end, I think I stopped loving her early on, shortly after we got together. But I didn't tell myself that clearly, not right away. The feelings I had for her were complex, indecipherable. Deciphering them took me some time. We got together because I felt sorry for her. She was suffering – nightmares, fears, anxieties. I got together with her because of a disagreement with my mother. I wanted to be with some poor girl who was alone, disoriented, who came from a world entirely different from ours, from my family's world, I mean. I got together with her so I could be with a girl who was crazy, mixed-up, confused. I wanted to heal her misery, bring light to her confusion. The truth is, I was confused and miserable, too, not really capable of giving security and health to someone who, in many respects, was just like me. That was the mistake I made – I got together with an individual who was just like me. Really, we're happiest with people who aren't just like us. We're happy with individuals who are our opposites, who possess something we lack. Instead of healing her misery, I felt myself being swept away in her anguish. It seemed to me I was sinking little by little in swirling black water, that I was losing my reason and my ability to breathe. A horrible sensation.

ELENA: But why?

LORENZO: What do you mean why? Why was I feeling that way? Don't you understand? You may be too young to understand. I felt as though I were drowning. Have you ever felt as though you were drowning?

ELENA: I was close to drowning once, when I was a child.

LORENZO: You're still a child. I shouldn't talk to you about my life. Certainly Teresa is telling you all our business, too. You need some clean air. It's suffocating here.

ELENA: Oh, no. I'm doing great here.

LORENZO: In this house? You're doing great here? Poor little thing.

Who knows how Teresa is oppressing you, with the story of all our misfortunes. See, Teresa has the need, as much as I do, to pour our troubles out onto someone else. But neither one of us pays attention to whether the one who is listening is in a position to bear the weight.

ELENA: I don't know if I'm of any help to Teresa. When she talks, I'm there to listen. I don't give her lots of advice. What advice could I give her? I tell her not to think about you anymore.

LORENZO: Good advice. But useless. Advice is always useless anyway. The only real help we give to our fellow human beings is to listen in silence.

ELENA: But you're so different from what I imagined!

LORENZO: Yes? Why? How did you imagine me? Teresa never paints me the way I am. She's never understood me. I'm just like her, and yet she's never understood me.

The doorbell rings. Elena goes to open it. Teresa enters.

TERESA: Oh, hello. Anyone who gets to see you should feel lucky. It's been a month since I've had any idea where you were.

LORENZO: I was in Puglia. So? I heard there's someone who wants to buy our house.

TERESA: Our house? It's not ours. It's mine. If I sell it, the money is mine. Didn't you put it in my name?

LORENZO: Have I ever said that I wanted the money?

TERESA: There was someone who was thinking of buying it. I'm just coming back from Rocca di Papa now. I was there with him. He's the director of a bank.

LORENZO: Which bank?

TERESA: I don't know. I didn't ask him.

LORENZO: That was the first thing you should have asked him.

TERESA: So why don't you take care of it then? Seeing as how I don't ask good questions.

LORENZO: Why should I take care of it, given that the house is yours?

TERESA: And yet you're saying that I don't ask good questions.

LORENZO: I don't have time.

TERESA: I don't have time either.

LORENZO: Why? What do you have to do?

TERESA: And you? What have you got to do?

LORENZO: More than you.

TERESA: I have things to do.

LORENZO: What?

TERESA: It doesn't concern you.

LORENZO: So is he buying it, the bank director? Does he like it?

TERESA: No. He said that the layout of the rooms is absurd. That you have to walk down three kilometres of hallway in order to go to the bathroom. That the terrace has a midnight exposure. The kitchen is dark. I said to him, 'I'm not responsible for the layout of the rooms. The plan for the villa was designed by my ex.'

LORENZO: Oh yeah? You said that? 'By my ex'? (*Laughs.*)

TERESA: Yes. When you talk about me, you say 'my ex,' too.

LORENZO: No, I never say 'my ex.'

TERESA: And if I've heard you do it?

LORENZO: When?

TERESA: Anyway. He isn't going to buy it in his wildest dreams.

LORENZO: He's an idiot. The terrace has a midnight exposure so you can enjoy the cool night air in the summer. And the bathroom isn't all that far from the bedrooms.

TERESA: He may be an idiot, but he doesn't want to buy it.

LORENZO: (*To Elena.*) You should see it. Go see it one day. If you want I can take you. It's really a gorgeous house.

TERESA: What's the point of Elena's seeing it? You don't want her to buy it, do you?

LORENZO: Why not?

TERESA: Because she doesn't have a cent.

LORENZO: In any case, I'd be happy for her to see it. To show her I know how to build a house.

TERESA: Why don't you go live there, if you like it so much?

LORENZO: Me? At Rocca di Papa?

TERESA: Yes.

LORENZO: But I like it where I am.

TERESA: With your mother?

LORENZO: I told you I'm not at my mother's anymore. I have a tiny little apartment all my own.

TERESA: So you can take your whores home at night.

LORENZO: Since you and I are separated, I bring whomever I want there.

ELENA: Listen, Teresa, I've put the chicken on. We're making chicken and rice soup, right?

TERESA: Yes, dear.

LORENZO: Are you going to invite me to lunch?

ELENA: With pleasure, right Teresa?

TERESA: He doesn't like chicken and rice soup.

LORENZO: That's not true. I love it.

TERESA: Have your tastes changed in a year?

LORENZO: My mother makes it for me all the time.

TERESA: So. You were in Puglia?

LORENZO: I was in Puglia, yes. (*To Elena.*) I have some land there. It produces quite well. We've got olives, wheat, vineyards – about thirty hectares. My sister and her husband live there. They have nine children. I envy them. They love each other so much, they never get tired of each other. My brother-in-law takes care of the fields and, in his spare time, he paints. To tell the truth, his paintings are hideous. My sister sometimes rides horses. They send the kids to school in Torcia, which is the closest town. My brother-in-law goes hunting. It's a lovely life.

ELENA: I grew up in the country. I like the country. It makes Teresa depressed. But not me. My parents have a little guest house for foreigners in the countryside near Pistoia. We've also got olives and vineyards. No wheat. They don't have that.

LORENZO: Right. Teresa gets depressed in the country. It reminds her of her childhood. She didn't have a nice childhood. She must have told you about it.

ELENA: Yes. She told me the whole story. I know everything about her. And I've told her all about myself. Though it's true there wasn't much to tell about me. Until I was twenty years old, I lived in the country. Nothing ever happened there. Toward the end, I was getting a little bored. A sweet boredom, because I read a lot, I daydreamed, I thought. When I left, I cried so much because I was sad to leave my mother and my little sisters. It may have been the first big sadness of my life.

LORENZO: And here? Has anything happened here?

ELENA: In Rome? Not much. Last year I was with my aunt and uncle. But it was noisy. Then I read an ad in the newspaper, I responded, and I came here. With Teresa, the two of us felt close to each other right away. Now she's my dearest friend. I even wrote my mother about her. We get along great together, right Teresa?

TERESA: Yes, dear.

LORENZO: You women make friends fast. A month's enough for you to become friends. With men, friendship proceeds slowly, in stages. In my experience, I've only known one feeling to be that sudden, only one that strikes like a bolt of lightning. Love.

TERESA: That's not true. After you met me, you disappeared for six months without showing the slightest sign that you were alive. So you weren't all that struck by lightning.

LORENZO: When I met you? In the ruins of Troy?

TERESA: Yes.

LORENZO: Who says I haven't been struck by lightning other times? Maybe you think there's been no one in my life other than you?

TERESA: And who else was there? That girl you had when you were twenty-two who didn't love you back?

LORENZO: So is the chicken and rice soup ready?

ELENA: In a little bit. The chicken should cook a little longer. I'll go grate the parmesan while we wait. Are you in a bad mood, Teresa?

TERESA: No, I have a headache.

Elena exits.

LORENZO: You have a headache.

TERESA: A little.

LORENZO: Are you in a bad mood?

TERESA: Could be.

LORENZO: She's very sweet, that girl. Very friendly, simple.

TERESA: Yeah.

LORENZO: The advertisement was a good idea. Now I feel better, too. I didn't like knowing you were alone in the house, especially at night. Are you sleeping better now? The girl was saying that you're sleeping better.

TERESA: What does the girl know about it?

LORENZO: Are you still having nightmares?

TERESA: I still have that horrendous dream.

LORENZO: Which dream?

TERESA: I've told you about it a bunch of times. You don't have a good memory. No, it's not that you don't have a good memory. You don't have a good memory when it comes to me. Like that time when you went downstairs to buy cigarettes and you didn't come back because you'd forgotten that I existed.

LORENZO: Oh, don't start digging through ancient history. What's the point of being separated if we have to keep rummaging around in all that old business?

TERESA: It was a hideous beginning. I should have understood. You met a friend at the tobacco shop, you started chatting, and you forgot about me. As if I were a common whore.

LORENZO: Oh come on. I hardly knew you.

TERESA: No. We'd been together for three days. We'd been making love for three days. For me, those three days, they counted for something. I wouldn't have been able to forget about you if I'd gone downstairs to the tobacco shop. Which friend was it that you met at the tobacco shop? Mario? Gunter?

LORENZO: I don't remember? And what does it matter anyway?

TERESA: Maybe it was Mario.

LORENZO: Maybe.

TERESA: You see him often?

LORENZO: Who?

TERESA: Mario.

LORENZO: I see him every day.

TERESA: And you never remember that you found him in bed with me that night? When you look at him, don't you think about it? That he betrayed you? He was your dearest friend and he betrayed you. Don't you think about it?

LORENZO: Let it go. I'm begging you to let it go. It's something I've overcome. My friendship with Mario is a very delicate thing, straightforward, deep. Don't poison it with that memory. I've cleansed our friendship of that memory and now it's the way it was before. I'm begging you to keep your hands off it. There are some things you can't understand.

TERESA: Oh, you've cleansed your friendship of that memory. Because that memory was filthy? It was a filthy memory?

LORENZO: Surely you understand that it wasn't so nice finding your wife in bed with your dearest childhood friend. But I'm begging you – let it drop. Let's talk about something else.

TERESA: And me? I betrayed you, too. You've cleansed your friendship with Mario, gave it a good wash, rinsed it off, and now it's the way it was before. That's what you said. And your feelings for me? Those can't be cleansed, washed, and rinsed off? Those feelings are defiled for good and so you've tossed them out? You forgave Mario – you're with him from morning to night – but me, on the other hand, you can't forgive? Maybe because your feelings for me weren't all that delicate and deep?

LORENZO: Teresa, you stubbornly insist on believing that I left you because you betrayed me. No. I would have left you anyway. I left that evening because I said, 'She's with Mario. I'd better leave.' But I was not, as you believe, deranged with jealousy. I felt nothing more than a slight bitterness, a vague sense of astonishment. But it was over, do you understand? It was already over. I was millions of light years away from you. I'd seen my sister in Puglia and I'd told her that I was going to leave you because I couldn't live with you anymore. Because I was destroying myself and I was destroying you.

TERESA: You were in love with someone else?

LORENZO: No, no, no! Love isn't the only thing in this world! I don't live only for love! At the moment I'm not in love and I'm alive all the same. I talk with my friends, I continue with my studies, I buy paintings. In your world, the only thing is sex! That's why, in your world, I can't breathe. I'm sick of sex! I've had it up to here with sex!

ELENA: (*Entering.*) It's almost ready. The chicken is almost cooked.

TERESA: You're sick of sex, are you?

LORENZO: Sick to death.

TERESA: You're quite a liar, you are! I know you so well by now. You say you've never told a lie in your life and the truth is that you're covered in lies – from head to toe! Do you really believe I don't see how you look at women? Do you really believe I don't see that the minute you're close to a woman you change colour? You light up. You switch yourself on like a light bulb.

LORENZO: And I'm telling you that I do just fine without women. For me, it's the ideal condition.

ELENA: I made a little bit of mashed potatoes, too.

LORENZO: You shouldn't eat so many potatoes, Teresa. They're making you fat.

TERESA: And what difference does it make to you if I get fat? I have no need to please you any longer. We're separated. I can eat all the potatoes I want.

ELENA: But I only made a little bit of mashed potatoes. They turned out good – no lumps. I whipped them in the blender.

TERESA: Is the blender working? Yesterday it seemed not to be working.

ELENA: It's working, yes.

LORENZO: This is the first time I've eaten here.

TERESA: Yes, this is the first time he's eaten here. He's never deigned to eat with me since we've been separated. He comes, stays for fifteen minutes, and makes his escape.

LORENZO: You're in the mood to argue. I'm not. I've got no desire to argue today. (*To Elena.*) I was telling you earlier about my sister, who has quite an enviable life. I stayed with them for a month. What peace. My sister's house is a gorgeous place. It's on a small hill and you can see the sea off in the distance. I went swimming every day. I would go to the beach on my motorcycle, first thing in the morning. You couldn't see a living soul on the beach. It was so peaceful, and I got my nerves back to normal. That's why Teresa can't manage to get me to argue with her today.

TERESA: I don't envy your sister. That husband of hers is an idiot.

LORENZO: Yes, he's not exactly a genius. But he's a nice guy. And he's an honest person.

TERESA: One time when we went to visit him he caught me in the hallway and he kissed me on the mouth.

LORENZO: My brother-in-law?

TERESA: Your brother-in-law, yes.

LORENZO: This is the first I'm hearing of this.

TERESA: Well, I didn't tell you because I didn't want to upset you. He must be cheating on your sister constantly. It's a fact that she's as dull as olive oil.

LORENZO: Why is olive oil dull?

TERESA: You could at least have brought me some bottles of olive oil from there. (*To Elena.*) They've got plenty of it. If you remembered even once to do something useful for me. I was talking about your sister. The one who's up to her eyeballs in her husband's affairs. Poor little thing. I hardly envy her. I feel sorry for her. She's twenty-nine years old and she looks forty. That's a fact. She has an ass that goes on forever.

LORENZO: (*To Elena.*) The truth is that my sister-in-law is a beautiful woman. She's like a Botticelli.

TERESA: Yes, she's a real bottle of something.[8] She looks like a barrel. You didn't even bring me a little wine? They have all that wine that they're just giving away. Your sister has never seen fit to bless me with so much as a drop – the only thing she ever thought to give me are those horrendous bed jackets. I, on the other hand, always used to send down boxes of gorgeous gifts for all those children.

LORENZO: Come on, let's go eat. Where shall we eat? Are we eating in the kitchen?

TERESA: In the kitchen, yes. I don't have dishes. I don't even have a silver service. If I had dishes and silver, I would set a nice table here in the dining room, with a tablecloth. Since I don't have anything except these ceramic plates, I eat in the kitchen. Your fault, because in five years of marriage you were never kind enough to buy me a nice set of dishes. When I wanted to buy a set, you always said it wasn't worth the trouble. Your mother was always promising me a silver service, but I'll be damned if I ever saw one. Your sister, on the other hand, has a lovely silver service. Your mother gave it to her.

LORENZO: Why don't you buy plates and silverware for yourself?

TERESA: Now? Now I've hardly got money to throw away. You think you're giving me so much money, but in fact you're hardly giving me any. It's barely enough. I want to put an ad in for the buffet again. I'm selling it. What am I going to do with a buffet? All that's inside are some old magazines. Plus another ad – I want to put one in for the kitten.

LORENZO: The kitten?

TERESA: My Siamese kitten. Haven't you seen her? She must be on the balcony. They gave her to me a week ago. I want to mate her with a purebred Siamese. I don't want to cross her with bastards. She's in heat. She meows all night long.

LORENZO: Who gave her to you?

TERESA: She was given to me. You don't need to know by whom.

ELENA: The grocer gave her the cat as a gift. She turned up at his place by chance after she jumped out of someone's window.

LORENZO: My sister has six dogs and five cats.

ELENA: And nine children.

LORENZO: Nine children.

ELENA: My mother has three dogs. No cats. She doesn't like cats.

LORENZO: Your folks have a place in the country, near Pistoia? I really like the Tuscan countryside. Do you visit them often?

ELENA: Certainly. I go there all the time. I'm very close to my mother.

LORENZO: Could I go with you some time to see the countryside? I love the Tuscan countryside. It settles my nerves. It calms me down.

ELENA: Certainly.

TERESA: No. Don't take him there. Your mother, when she sees him, will take him for a gangster. Doesn't he give you the impression that he's some kind of gangster – unshaven, that sweater, that filthy air he has about him? You know he never washes. They're not much in the habit of washing in his family. His sister stinks of sweat from a metre away.

LORENZO: Can we leave my sister out of it, please? Can we go eat?

ELENA: Let's go eat, yes.

TERESA: And the kitten? Has the kitten eaten?

ELENA: I gave her a chicken bone.

TERESA: Are you crazy? You must never give bones to cats. Bones are bad for them. They're cats – it's not like they're dogs.

ACT THREE

[*The same apartment, some weeks later.*]

TERESA: (*Yawning.*) What time is it? Eleven? Is it eleven already? Shall we make some coffee?

ELENA: I've already made coffee. I'll bring you some. (*Exits. Returns with coffee.*)

TERESA: You came in again very late last night. I heard you. I couldn't sleep because of that damned cat. It did nothing but meow the entire night long.

ELENA: I went to the movies.

TERESA: With Lorenzo?

ELENA: Yes, with him and some others.

TERESA: With which others? Mario and Gunter?

ELENA: Yes, those two. Then we went to have some ice cream. So I was out late.

TERESA: Yesterday I put the ads in again. For the cat, for the buffet, and for the room. I didn't put in an ad for the villa at Rocca di Papa. I don't want to sell it anymore. I thought I'd put in a guest house there, like your mother. Maybe make some money. I could live here and leave the guest house in someone else's hands to manage. The important thing is to make some money. The coffee is bad this morning. It tastes like hazelnuts.

ELENA: It seems good to me. Just think, this is the last time we'll have coffee together. Tomorrow morning I'll be at my aunt and uncle's. I'm so sorry to be leaving. I was so fond of this house.

TERESA: Only of the house?

ELENA: Oh, hush. You know how sorry I am to be leaving you. But you understand I have to study. Here, with you, I wind up not studying, you know? We don't do anything but sit and talk. It's very noisy at my aunt and uncle's, but in the end I get more accomplished.

TERESA: Lorenzo always used to say he couldn't manage to study or concentrate when he lived with me. There must be something in me that prevents other people from concentrating. But with Lorenzo it was a lie, because even now when he's not with me anymore, he still isn't getting anything done. He chats. He roams the streets. My god does he talk!

ELENA: But he's about to publish a book.

TERESA: A book? A book about what?

ELENA: On atoms. Gunter says it's very good.

TERESA: And what does Gunter know about atoms? Isn't he a composer?

ELENA: The other reason I was late getting back yesterday is that we also went out for a walk around the city after ice cream. I walked forever. My legs still hurt.

TERESA: Just the two of you with the others?

ELENA: No. Lorenzo and me.

TERESA: With me, he never wanted to walk. He always went in the car, when he was with me. He used to go walking with his friends and never with me. He said I was exasperating because I couldn't keep up with him. He said I took short steps.

ELENA: I need to tell you something, Teresa.

TERESA: Tell me.

ELENA: It's difficult.

TERESA: Oh, what in the world could it be? I never closed my eyes last night. I have a huge headache. If I don't find a Siamese, I'm going to mate that damned beast with the doorman's cat.

ELENA: You used to love that kitten and now you're calling it 'damned beast'?

TERESA: Because it won't let me sleep.

ELENA: Teresa. This is the thing I need to tell you. Lorenzo and I love each other. We're in love. That's why I'm leaving. It isn't because I need to study. It's because I love him. So, you understand, I can't live here anymore.

TERESA: I figured that out on my own.

ELENA: You figured it out? Really? You figured it out? Is it so obvious?

TERESA: Yes.

ELENA: You figured it out and yet you kept calm about it? No crying, no shouting? Completely cold, silent, calm?

TERESA: Why should I cry? Anyway, he doesn't love me anymore – whether he's with you or someone else, it's the same thing.

ELENA: And you and I can still be friends? Can I still come visit you?

You'll still care about me, the way you did before?

TERESA: Why wouldn't I, my dear?

ELENA: You're so wonderful. You're such a wonderful woman, so generous. I know you still love him.

TERESA: That's true. I still love him. I'll always love him. That's my bad luck. If he gave me a sign from the opposite end of the earth, I'd come running to him. I'd come running back on all fours. I would always take him back, even if he were old, starving like a stray dog, covered with bedbugs, riddled with syphilis, and with patches on his pants. It's true – being with him was hell, but I would give my life – my life, I'm telling you – to go back to the time when we were together. But none of that matters now. It has nothing to do with you. Are you thinking of marrying him?

ELENA: How could I marry him when he's married to you?

TERESA: I could give him an annulment.

ELENA: You're so wonderful! I'm so happy! He's such an extraordinary man! I fell in love with him immediately, as soon as I saw him. And him with me.

TERESA: Yes. I figured that out.

ELENA: Fate is so strange! To think that I happened here by chance, purely by chance, all because of a newspaper ad. I might not have read the newspaper that day, and wouldn't have come here at all. And I wouldn't have met you or him!

TERESA: When you're happy, you never stop marvelling at how intelligent chance has been to have brought you to happiness. But when you're unhappy, you're not at all amazed to see how stupid chance has been. Stupid and blind. It seems natural to you that fate is just that stupid. So obviously unhappiness is natural for people and no one finds it astonishing.

ELENA: You're so strange today! The way you're thinking seems so calm, so unequivocal, so cold.

TERESA: About the advertisement – I told you that I put in an ad for the room. Just like the one I put in for you.

ELENA: Just like it?

TERESA: Yes. Two or three people have called me. So you need to straighten up. Pick your clothes up off the chairs. That way the room looks orderly if anyone comes to see it.

ELENA: I've already packed my suitcase. I'll leave at noon. The room is all straightened up.

TERESA: Is Lorenzo coming to pick you up in his car?

ELENA: Yes. Plus you put in another ad for the kitten? And another one for the buffet?

TERESA: Yes, but I don't know, maybe I'll keep the kitten. You wouldn't want her, would you?

ELENA: I can't keep her at my aunt and uncle's house. They won't want her. My mother wouldn't want her, either. She doesn't like cats. Why don't you want her anymore? You used to love her so much! When you give her a husband, she'll stop crying.

TERESA: That's true. Last night she wouldn't let me close my eyes. I didn't fall asleep until it was morning. I had that horrible dream again.

ELENA: The one about the wall?

TERESA: Yes, a wall, a courtyard, some old furniture, trash, broken glass. I'm walking in the middle of all that, rummaging around in all that trash. Then I beat against the wall, and I want to call out, to shout, but my voice won't come out. I know there's something terrible on the other side of the wall.

ELENA: And what is it?

TERESA: Someone. A person who is very dear to me. I can't reach him because of the wall.

ELENA: I have bad dreams, too, when I'm tired, when I have to take exams. It's exhaustion. Why don't you get out of the city for a while? Go visit your mother?

TERESA: Yes, perhaps I should go back to my village for a bit. It's been a while since I've seen my mother. And I never write to her either. Living with Lorenzo, he infected me with that horrible habit of his of never writing letters. Before, I used to write to my mother every once in a while. It was better before. How a man can ruin you! He ruins you, and then he just leaves you sitting there.

ELENA: Forgive him. It's not his fault if he hurt you. Even you – though through no fault of your own – hurt him.

TERESA: That's true. He was better before, too. He was less frivolous, less cynical. Before that cursed day when we found ourselves on the same path.

ELENA: He's neither frivolous nor cynical, and you know it.

TERESA: I could have married someone else, if I hadn't met him that day. I was so young and pretty. I had lots of guys around who wanted me. I could have picked a simple, calm, kind man. I could have had a normal, orderly life. Instead, I ran into him! What rotten luck! He ruined me. He destroyed me. Then he took off, like someone who tromps all over your lawn and takes off. 'You're nothing,' he told me. 'To me, you aren't a person. You cheated on me, but it doesn't matter a thing to me. I'm millions of light years away from you.' What shall I do? You tell me, what shall I do now? What's left to me other than to shoot myself in the heart? I have a pistol, you know? I've had it since we got the villa at Rocca di Papa because I thought I'd be afraid to be alone there at night when he was away. Then we only stayed up there that one night. A horrible night. We fought – I don't remember why anymore. Over something ridiculous. Over a key that no one could find. Or maybe over some word. One simple word between the two of us could turn into a monster. He would pull its guts out. He would dissect it. He drew out each tiny, hidden meaning. I bit his hand. He slapped me. My ears were ringing, blood was coming out of my nose. He had my tooth marks on his wrist. He had a cut on his forehead that I gave him with a pair of scissors. I threw the scissors at him. He had to put a bandage on the cut. And I thought, 'I'm going to kill him, now that I have that pistol.'

ELENA: Where do you have the pistol now?

TERESA: What do you care where I have it? I have it. I have it in my purse. One of these days, I'll shoot myself. So the two of you won't need an annulment. I'll make him a widower.

ELENA: Give me the pistol.

TERESA: Like hell.

ELENA: Give me your purse.

TERESA: Like hell.

ELENA: Get rid of the pistol! I'm begging you, Teresa, I'm begging you! Get rid of it!

TERESA: Okay, I'll get rid of it.

ELENA: I have to get dressed. It's late. I have to finish packing. He'll be downstairs in a little while. You won't be alone, Teresa! I'll come visit you all the time! He'll come all the time. The two of us still love you so much. (*She hugs Teresa.*)

TERESA: Okay.

ELENA: I have to get dressed. (*Exits.*)

Teresa walks through the room. Then into Elena's room. The stage is left empty. The sound of a pistol shot is heard. Teresa runs to the phone and dials a number.

TERESA: Hello, Lorenzo! Lorenzo, come over! For God's sake, come over! I've killed her. I didn't mean to, I didn't mean to, but I killed her. She's dead. She died instantly. For God's sake, Lorenzo, come over, come over!

She bursts into tears. The doorbell wrings. Teresa dries her eyes with her hand. She opens the door. Giovanna enters.

GIOVANNA: Good morning. I called a few hours ago. I'm here for the ad in the newspaper. My name is Giovanna Ricciardi.
TERESA: Which ad? I placed three ads.
GIOVANNA: The room.

November 1965

Notes

1 The medieval town of Rocca di Papa is in Lazio, about thirty kilometres southeast of Rome. As its name suggests, it was named for a pope – Eugene III (1145–53), organizer of the Second Crusade.
2 Located on the far 'right bank' of the Tiber and just south of Vatican City, the Gianicolo is the only one of Rome's famous hills to be found west of the river. Not traditionally counted as one of the Seven Hills, the Gianicolo is nonetheless sometimes referred to as 'The Eighth Hill.'
3 A small, economical model of Fiat, manufactured and widely distributed from 1955 to 1969 as the ideal 'city car.'
4 A dry north wind that brings frigid air from the Alps, popularly associated with disorientation and loss of self-control.
5 Cured beef in gelatin.
6 A raffle-type game, somewhat similar to Bingo.
7 A dessert in which egg yolks, sugar, liqueur (usually marsala or the like), and sometimes spices are combined, whipped, and slowly heated over a *bain marie* or double boiler until they form a soft custard.
8 Here, Teresa makes an unkind pun: Lorenzo says his sister is a Botticelli; Teresa says, 'Yes, she's a *botticella*' – a form of the word *botte*, a wooden barrel used for aging balsamic vinegar, wine, etc.

Strawberry and Cream

A PLAY IN THREE ACTS

Cast:
Barbara
Tosca, a maid
Flaminia
Letizia, Flaminia's sister
Cesare, Flaminia's husband

The action unfolds in the modern day, in a villa in the Tuscan country-side, not far from Rome.

ACT ONE

The doorbell rings. Tosca opens the door. In the doorway is Barbara, with a suitcase. She is wearing a black leather jacket and blue jeans.

BARBARA: Good morning.

TOSCA: We're not buying anything.

BARBARA: But I'm not selling anything. I wanted to speak with the attorney.

TOSCA: The attorney isn't here. He's out. And his wife has gone into town to do the shopping. Who might you be?

BARBARA: A cousin.

TOSCA: Oh, a cousin? Make yourself comfortable. The Signora won't be long. You're so wet!

BARBARA: Yes. It's snowing.

TOSCA: It's snowing. The weather's horrible. But did you come from the train station on foot?

BARBARA: Yes.

TOSCA: On foot? With your suitcase? Couldn't you have taken a taxi?

BARBARA: I didn't know it was so far.

TOSCA: You didn't know? So you've never been here before? You're a cousin, but you've never been here before?

BARBARA: Never.

TOSCA: Strange. Go ahead and wait. The Signora won't be long.

BARBARA: (*Taking out a cigarette.*) Could you give me a match, Signora?

TOSCA: I'm no signora. I'm a maid. I've been a maid my entire life. Here are the matches. I've only been here for eight days, but I'm not staying. I already told the Signora that I'm not staying, that I'm going to leave. I don't fit in here.

BARBARA: You don't fit in?

TOSCA: No. I don't fit in. I've already told the Signora that I don't fit in, so she can start looking for another maid. I'll stay until they find another one. Ersilia, the maid they had before, did you know her?

BARBARA: No.

TOSCA: No? Though that one was here for eight months.... She left because she had varicose veins. She couldn't do it. The house is much too big – two floors, a ton of rooms. But I'm not leaving because of the work. I've leaving because we're too isolated. Today when it's snowing, it's like being in a tomb here. All that silence – like being in a tomb. I don't like the countryside. I like the city. The noise. I'm sorry to be leaving, because they're not bad people. But it's not as though they give you a great deal of satisfaction either. They eat, and they don't say it's good, it's bad, nothing. They never tell you anything. So you never know whether they're happy or not. And all that silence besides! The attorney, I saw him for a moment the day I got here, I ironed a few of his shirts, and he left immediately. The Signora – the Signora doesn't talk. She doesn't talk to me. All day long she reads or plays the piano. But it's not any kind of music a person could enjoy. I'm there in the kitchen with the cat, and hearing the sound of it just makes me sleepy. Luckily, there's the cat. He keeps me good company. I talk to the cat, if I want to talk to someone. Sometimes Signora Letizia comes, the Signora's sister. She doesn't live far away. Do you know her?

BARBARA: No.

TOSCA: You're the cousin of the attorney or of the Signora?

BARBARA: Of the attorney.

TOSCA: Luckily, as I was saying, Signora Letizia comes sometimes.

With Signora Letizia, or else with Ortensia, the woman who comes
to do the ironing, I can have a little conversation. With the Signora
on the other hand, it's impossible. Part of the time she doesn't feel
well, part of the time she sleeps, part of the time she plays the
piano. We have a television, but the Signora never turns it on. She's
told me I'm welcome to turn it on myself, but then she goes up to
bed. She's not going to want me sitting there in the living room, all
alone, with the television, is she? The living room isn't my place.
We all need to stay in our places. At the other house where I used
to live, we had a television in the kitchen. Everyone would get
together in the kitchen in the evenings to watch television, and
the neighbours would come, too. We'd roast some chestnuts, and
the time passed very pleasantly. I made a mistake when I left that
other house. I left because they were paying me so little. But I made
a mistake. Here, the Signora even gave me a cashmere sweater.
But I'm not fitting in. It's not the work. I'm just telling you, it's not
the work. Me, I've worked my entire life. I've been a maid since
I was eleven years old. No, it's the place. When I left on Sunday,
I went to the movies in town – it was a thriller – and I came back
here, it must have been around nine. I almost took a taxi, because
it's a fairly long walk from town to here. But they wanted a thousand lire, so I came on foot. Outside, it was dark like you wouldn't
believe, there wasn't a soul on the road, and I can't tell you how
frightened I felt, partly because the film was full of dead people,
and partly because you also have to pass along the wall of a cem-
etery on the way, and when I got back here I was covered in a cold
sweat. I found the Signora in the living room playing the piano and
I told her, 'I shouldn't have to worry about winding up murdered
as I'm walking home.' She said to me, 'If you're afraid of the dark,
you can take the flashlight the next time.' I told her, 'I don't know
if there will be a next time. I don't know if I'll be staying another
Sunday, because I'm not fitting in here.' She said, 'Stay at least until
we have another maid. Don't leave me with my husband away so
often. What am I going to do here by myself?' I felt sorry for her.
But tell the truth, would you live here? In the countryside, with all
these trees? Would you live here?

BARBARA: I'd live anywhere. Except for my own house.

TOSCA: You say that. You say that, but it's not true. You wouldn't live
here. You'd run away. The Signora, she lives here, but she's a special case. A solitary type. Why don't you like staying at your own
house? Where is it, your house?

BARBARA: In Rome. On Via delle Procellarie.

TOSCA: Ah, on Via delle Procellarie. Pretty close to where I was before. I used to go to the market in Piazza Garibaldi. You know Piazza Garibaldi? Don't you like it on Via delle Procellarie? It's a lovely street. Very centrally located. At least it's Rome. It's not Rome here. Here, it's the country. The attorney, when he hired me, he told me I could go to Rome when I wanted. You catch the commuter train and it takes twenty minutes. But am I supposed to catch the train for Rome on Sundays after I'm done washing the dishes? I finish washing the dishes at four. By the time I'm dressed, it's going on five. What time am I going to get to Rome? I have a daughter in Rome, you know? She works for a hairstylist – Pino. Pino, the hairstylist. On Piazza Quadrata. You know where Piazza Quadrata is? There. My daughter is more or less your age. You even look a little bit like her. If you want to have your hair done, I'll give you a coupon and they'll give you a discount. Here, let me give you a coupon. I have a book of them in my pocket.

BARBARA: Thanks.

TOSCA: Not at all. Ask for Camilla. My daughter is Camilla. And why don't you like staying on Via delle Procellarie?

BARBARA: Because of my husband.

TOSCA: You have a husband? You? So young?

BARBARA: I'm eighteen years old. I have a baby who's a year and a half.

TOSCA: So young! You're like my daughter. She's eighteen, too, my daughter is. She just turned eighteen in April. But my daughter isn't married. Not even engaged. How is it that you got married so young?

BARBARA: I made a mistake.

TOSCA: Yes. A mistake. Young people make mistakes. And with a baby! And so now you're not getting along with each other?

BARBARA: I've left him.

TOSCA: You left him. You left your husband! And the baby?

BARBARA: My mother-in-law is there to look after him.

TOSCA: At least your mother-in-law is there. Because he's small, the baby is. And so you left the house? This morning? With your suitcase?

BARBARA: I jumped out of the bathroom window. Everyone was sleeping. I threw the suitcase down first. Then I jumped. No one woke up.

TOSCA: But what floor are you on?

BARBARA: The second floor.

TOSCA: That's a pretty good jump. You couldn't leave through the
door?

BARBARA: My mother-in-law sleeps in the room off the front hall. The
soles of my feet still hurt.

TOSCA: I believe it. That's a pretty good jump. You could have broken a
leg. And so you came to the attorney to get advice? You're putting
yourself in his hands? Partly because he's your cousin and partly
because he's an attorney?

BARBARA: Yes.

TOSCA: The attorney will tell you to go back home, you'll see. Maybe it
was just a moment of anger. It's a shame the attorney isn't here. It
seems to me they said he was in London. But I think he's just about
to come back because the Signora told me to wax the floor in his
room. They don't really sleep together.

BARBARA: He's in London?

TOSCA: Yes. Seems to me they said he was in London.

BARBARA: I'm going to go then.

TOSCA: And where do you think you're going to go? In this weather?
With that suitcase? Wait for the Signora. If you're the husband's
cousin, you're the wife's cousin, too. Maybe the Signora can give
you some advice as well. (*The doorbell rings. Tosca opens the door.
Flaminia enters.*) Here's the Signora. There's a cousin of the attorney's
here. One of his cousins. She's been waiting quite a while.

FLAMINIA: A cousin?

BARBARA: I'm Barbara.

FLAMINIA: Barbara!

TOSCA: She's been waiting quite a while. We chatted a little bit just to
pass the time. Otherwise, the time would never go by. What shall I
make for supper?

FLAMINIA: Go into the kitchen, Tosca. I'll talk to you shortly.

TOSCA: Go into the kitchen. What am I going to do in the kitchen if I
don't know what to make for supper? Clean out the storage room?

FLAMINIA: Yes.

TOSCA: Shall I throw out all those crates? But where shall I throw
them?

FLAMINIA: Yes.

TOSCA: You told me to clean out the storage room, but I held off because I didn't know where to throw the crates. And then I was just
talking here with the young lady, your cousin. Well, she's a Signora,
too. She's married. With a baby. So young! Young people make mis-

takes. So where shall I throw them? The crates, I mean? Shall I give them to the gardener?

FLAMINIA: Yes.

TOSCA: It's full of ants out there where the crates are. It needs to be cleaned with bleach. Did you bring me any bleach?

FLAMINIA: Yes, in that bag.

TOSCA: I'll give the floor a good cleaning with the bleach, then I'll put down some insect powder so the ants will go. They stink, those crates. It's been years since anybody cleaned in there. (*Exits.*)

FLAMINIA: What brings you here?

BARBARA: I thought I would find Cesare. I need to talk to him.

FLAMINIA: Couldn't you have called instead of coming all the way here?

BARBARA: It didn't occur to me.

FLAMINIA: Cesare is in London.

BARBARA: When will he be back?

FLAMINIA: I don't know.

BARBARA: I've left my husband. I ran away. I jumped out the bathroom window. Everyone was asleep. Last night he almost killed me. Look. (*She shows her neck.*) He was about to strangle me. My mother-in-law called the doorman. The two of them took him by the arms – the doorman and a neighbour, who's a pharmacist. They were thinking of calling the police. My mother-in-law didn't want them to. So the pharmacist gave him an injection and he fell asleep almost immediately. He fell into bed like a log. I can't even tell you what the room looked like. He'd thrown everything all over the place. He pulled all the linens out of the closet. A coffee service that we had – beautiful, Japanese – he smashed it to pieces. At dawn I packed my suitcase and I ran away. He didn't budge. Even the baby was sleeping, luckily, since he never sleeps.

FLAMINIA: And why did you come here? What in the world were you thinking?

BARBARA: Where else was I going to go? I don't have anyone. And I haven't got a cent to my name. I didn't know Cesare was in London. The last time we spoke was Wednesday. I called him at his office. I was crying. I told him, 'Help me. I can't stay with my husband anymore.' He told me, 'Calm down, sweetie.' He always talks to me that way. We had an appointment Thursday at five at Café Stella. He didn't come. I waited a long time, but then I had to leave. I'd left the baby in the park with a friend of mine, and it was getting

cold. I had to take the baby back home. Maybe he came later. I don't
know. The next day I called the office, but no one answered.

FLAMINIA: What do you want from Cesare?

BARBARA: What do I want? I want him to tell me what I should do. I
don't have anyone. I've only got him. If I can't live with my husband anymore, it's because of him. If I hadn't met him, I'd stay with
my husband, maybe until the end of time. And once, a little while
back, he told me: 'If you can't stay with your husband anymore, if
you don't have anywhere to go, come to me. As far as my wife is
concerned, don't give it a thought. There's no jealousy between me
and my wife. Ours is a relationship of a somewhat special nature.
As if we were no longer husband and wife, as if we were brother
and sister. It's not a marriage anymore; it's something else. My wife
knows about you, and it doesn't matter to her. She's an exceptional
person anyway, my wife is. A superior woman. So very good.' He
told me I could come here any time.

FLAMINIA: In fact, it doesn't matter to me in the slightest the girlfriends
he has. But I don't want you here. You need to leave, because you
can't stay here.

BARBARA: Okay. I'll go then. It's just that I don't know where to go.

FLAMINIA: Don't you have any family?

BARBARA: No, I don't have anyone. I had a grandmother, but she's
dead. My grandmother raised me. I don't know how to do anything
because she never taught me to do anything. She only sent me to
school a little. She used to drink. She destroyed herself with drink.
She drank her soul out. In the beginning, she was rich. We had a
lovely house. But little by little she sold everything – furniture,
carpets, everything. When she died, there was nothing left. I was
sixteen years old. I had met Paolo, my husband. He was already
my boyfriend. I was expecting a baby. He married me. His mother
didn't want him to, but he married me anyway. I was sixteen years
old, he was twenty. When he married me, he didn't have a real
job, but then he found a position on the Socialist party newspaper. That's his party. In the beginning, except that we didn't have
money, everything went the way it's supposed to. I was happy, the
baby was born. We'd inherited a small vineyard near Teramo. Even
a little bit of money. And we'd bought a refrigerator, and a carriage
for the baby. Then at five months the baby caught whooping cough,
and they sent me to Soriano del Cimino for a better climate. I met
Cesare there. I knew him because we had been to his office once,

my husband and I, about the mortgage on the vineyard. Cesare came to Soriano on an excursion with some friends. He recognized me. He smiled at me. I was in the park with the baby in my arms so he could get a little fresh air underneath the trees. The baby had dropped his pacifier and Cesare picked it up and went to wash it off in the drinking fountain. So we started talking. He offered me an ice cream at the stand, an enormous ice cream – strawberry and cream. He'd forgotten about those friends of his. They'd gone off somewhere on their own. We ate supper together at a restaurant – Tre Camosci. That's how everything started. Then I went back to the city and we saw each other again. I was leaving the baby with my mother-in-law, and I would go out with one excuse or another. But my husband had started to seem little and stupid, and everything about him bothered me – when he laughed for no reason in the movie theatre, when he would go out with his raincoat all buttoned up crooked. When he tried to explain politics to the doorman, when he'd get frightened because his throat hurt and he'd start downing formalin lozenges....[1] I came to know every one of his defects, I thought he was pretentious and grumpy, I noticed that his teeth protruded, that his ears stuck out on the sides. And the house seemed tiny to me, ugly, dirty. I'd go out and I'd find myself with Cesare. And my mother-in-law started to suspect something. She said to me, 'Where are you going? Have you got a lover?' And I'd laugh and say, 'No, I don't have any lover. I'm going here, I'm going there, I'm going to the yard goods store to see if they have any remnants so I can make myself a skirt, I'm going to see my friend Marcella' – that's my friend who's a clerk at Standa.[2]

FLAMINIA: And now you can't go stay with this friend of yours?

BARBARA: With Marcella? No, no. Marcella has seven little brothers and sisters. They've got a house with mattresses all over the floor. So as I was telling you, my mother-in-law started to suspect something little by little, also because when I came home from being with Cesare, I was so happy. I was happy in a way I couldn't hide and she, my mother-in-law, would look at me and say, 'When you come back home, your face looks like you just won the Merano lottery.'[3]

FLAMINIA: And then?

BARBARA: Then one time my mother-in-law left for Teramo with the baby for ten days to visit some relatives. My husband was in Vicenza for work. I told Cesare to come to my house. He didn't want to. He said it wasn't wise. That the doorman might see him. But it

was so important to me, and I insisted. And he came. He stayed
there with me the whole night. And in the morning, I hear the key
turn in the lock, and I see my mother-in-law standing there with
the baby wrapped up in a blanket. The baby had gotten a fever and
she thought she should come back home because it was so damp at
Teramo. Cesare was ready to leave – he was all ready, with his raincoat, his briefcase under his arm. But I was still in my nightgown.
We were in the kitchen and I was making coffee. I say to my mother-in-law, 'Mother Caterina, this is the attorney, Signor Rolandi,
who's come to have me sign a receipt for the vineyard. I'm making
him a little coffee.' But you have to understand, it was seven in
the morning. My mother-in-law's not exactly an idiot. So there she
was, silent, with her lips all tight and the baby asleep around her
neck. Cesare left. My mother-in-law put the baby to bed and started
washing up some of the baby's things in the bathtub, still pale, still
not saying a word, her lips still tight. And I said, 'Leave that alone.
I'll do it.' Her? Nothing. She hasn't addressed a word to me since
that morning. And when Paolo returned from Vicenza, he already
knew everything because she'd written to him in Vicenza. I went to
pick him up at the station and I saw him get down from the train,
tiny, with his raincoat all rumpled looking, his beard unshaven.
And then all of a sudden I felt such terrible remorse for the way I'd
hurt him. I felt such sorrow for him, such sorrow.… He slapped me
in the face. People gathered around immediately. He said to them,
'It's my wife. I can hit her when I want because she's my wife.' Back
at home he didn't hit me anymore that time. He started to cry. And
I started to cry, too, and we cried together, holding on to each other,
all afternoon long. I told him the whole story. And little by little,
as I was telling the story, I felt myself freed of a weight, and all the
lies I'd told in those months began to lift like a fog, and I felt light,
empty, I felt that everything had become clear, and he stroked my
hair. He dried my tears, almost as if he felt sorry for me. Then, in
the evening, we went out and he bought me a ring – this ring here,
see? Because he'd earned a little money and he remembered that
since we'd been married he'd never given me a single gift. So the
next day I went to see Cesare at his office and I told him, 'Enough.
It's over. We won't be seeing each other anymore.' And he said to
me, 'Okay, if that's how you want it. That's fair. You're right. We
won't see each other anymore.' And I told him – 'We'll see each
other tomorrow, just to say goodbye for the last time. We'll meet at

Café Stella at five for the very last time.' And the next day we met at the café, and then we went walking for a little beside the Tiber. I was crying and he said to me, 'Don't cry, sweetie. What can we do? I can't exactly marry you. You have a husband. I have a wife. I'm forty years old. You're eighteen. We'll break up. You'll feel better. You'll have lots and lots of babies yet. So many beautiful things are going to happen to you.' Okay, I tried. For a little while I tried not to think about it, to not go looking for him anymore. I didn't call him for two weeks. I went out, I'd go walking around the city by myself. I went to see Marcella. I went to sit on the benches at the Villa Borghese. Without the baby – I left the baby with my mother-in-law. I was too distraught to be with the baby. I bought myself an ice cream. I watched people passing by. And I was thinking: 'Yes, but how am I going to manage the rest of my life? Will my whole life be like this?' So then I called Cesare again. I only wanted to know if he was doing okay. And we started to see each other again. He didn't want to. He tried to find excuses. He said he was busy. But I begged him so much that he finally came. I was over in a corner of Café Stella, in the back, close to the window, and I saw him coming from a long way off. Tall, serious serious, walking fast the way he does, looking so severe. He came in and sat down with a sigh, shaking his head. He ordered a rhubarb liqueur. Me, ice cream. We sat there without saying anything. We didn't have very much left to say to each other. He was smoking. I was looking at him. He was looking at his watch. I said, 'Another minute more.' He said, 'What's the point?' I said, 'There's no point.' I started to cry. He didn't like it at all that I was crying in the café. He said, 'Blow your nose! Come on, try to pull yourself together. You're behaving like a child.' I went home. At that point, my husband was always at home because he wasn't going to the newspaper anymore. He'd gone out on disability. He said he was having an attack of exhaustion. He said to me, 'Did you see him?' and I said, 'Yes.' I had no more desire for lies. So my husband hit me. At first, just slaps. Then it kept getting worse. One time he even went to Cesare's office. But it's not like he hit him. He sat down and he started to cry. And all of a sudden he fainted. He fell on the floor. Cesare called the guard, and they loaded him into the car and took him to the emergency room, because he'd injured his lip when he fell. There – and that's the whole story, up to today.

FLAMINIA: I'm sorry. It's a sad story. But I don't know why you came here to tell it to me. I have nothing to do with it. As Cesare told you, the two of us have lived together like brother and sister for years. Ours is no longer a marriage. So all the things you're telling me about, the dramas, the jealousies, the tears, are so far removed from my life that it's as if they took place in another universe. I don't feel one way or the other about what you've told me. Besides which, I don't see what I can do for you.

BARBARA: It's true. You can't do anything.

FLAMINIA: So why don't you pick up your bag now and go wait for Cesare in the café at the station?

BARBARA: He's coming back tonight?

FLAMINIA: I don't know.

BARBARA: And what am I going to do if he doesn't come back tonight? Where am I going to go, when it gets dark?

FLAMINIA: I don't know. Go back to your own house.

BARBARA: No. I'm afraid. I'm afraid of Paolo, that he's going to kill me.

FLAMINIA: Go to a hotel.

BARBARA: And if I don't have a cent?

FLAMINIA: You want money from me? I could even give you some. Giving money to my husband's girlfriend strikes me as slightly funny. My husband might have taken care of that himself. He left without giving it a thought. He never thinks that other people might need some money. He never thinks of other people at all. He thinks of himself.

BARBARA: If you gave me a little money, you'd be doing me a favour. Look what I have in my pocket. Five hundred lire. That's all I've got. I could sell my ring, or pawn it, but it's not worth much. It's fake. We only paid 5,000 lire for it.

FLAMINIA: But what were you thinking, when you ran away from home?

BARBARA: Would you rather I let him kill me?

FLAMINIA: Okay. I'll give you some money. I'll give you 40,000 lire. That's all I have in the house. Go to the café at the station, go to a hotel, go wherever you like. As long as you get out of here.

BARBARA: Thank you very much. You're very kind. But you see, it's not just a question of money. If I go sit in the café now, as you say, or I go off to a hotel, I'm afraid that, little by little, I'll start to feel hopeless. I'm afraid I'll start to feel like dying. Because I'll start thinking about my life, and where my life is going to end up, where I'll go tomorrow, how I'll manage. And I'll also start thinking about all the bad things I've done, and I'll regret them, because I don't even know how I could have done things differently, and I'll start feeling sad for everyone, for my husband, for the baby, for Cesare. It seems to me that they're all so unhappy, so terribly terribly unhappy.

FLAMINIA: Yes, but I don't know what I'm supposed to do about it if you start feeling hopeless. And do you want me to tell you the truth? My thinking is that not even Cesare can do anything about it. My thinking is that he won't be able to do anything for you, or he won't want to. My thinking is that he's tired of you. When he gets tired of a woman, he cuts the cord, he goes to Paris, he goes to London, he stays away for as long as he can.

BARBARA: That's what you think? You think he went to London to get away from me?

FLAMINIA: I think he went to London to attend to business, but also because he was tired of having you underfoot. Because he feels sorry for you. Because he feels sorry for your husband. And because you make him afraid, and so does your husband. And when he comes back from London, today or tomorrow, he'll take care to make sure he doesn't see you and he won't help you, and you'll go looking for him and you won't find him. You'll wait for him and he won't come. Because he's not in love with you anymore. And maybe he never was very much in love with you. Do you understand?

BARBARA: He told you that?

FLAMINIA: Yes. He told me that. He doesn't have secrets from me. If he wants to live with you, he could go right ahead because it doesn't matter to me. I get along beautifully, even by myself. For all the company he provides. He's never here. We don't have any children. He's free. Free as the air. As for money, both of us have all we need. If he doesn't come to live with you, it's because he doesn't love you. Do you understand?

BARBARA: So I could always go jump in the Tiber.

FLAMINIA: Yes. But it would be stupid. You're young. You'd do better to go back to your baby. I never had any children. If I had, I'd never leave them. I'd rather kill myself.

BARBARA: I was good with the baby when I was happy. When I still hadn't met Cesare. And then even after, at the beginning, when I'd come home after being with Cesare. I wanted to sing, make jokes, even play with the baby. Now instead, I'm so very unhappy. Since you've never had any children, you don't know that children are like a lead weight when a person is this unhappy.

FLAMINIA: It seems to me you haven't got the slightest sense of duty.

BARBARA: Is that how it seems to you? It seems that way to me, too. Maybe because no one taught me anything. My father – I don't even know who he might have been. I'm the child of 'father unknown.'[4] My mother died when I was small. I had my grandmother, but my grandmother couldn't teach me much of a sense of duty because she didn't have one herself. She was always leaving the house to go sell things. Then she came back and hid so she could drink. She locked herself in the bedroom. I knocked, called out, and she wouldn't answer. I fell asleep curled up on the carpet so many times. But then she even sold the carpets. My grandmother didn't even teach me to wash my face. It's a miracle that I learned to wash my face in the morning. Could I have something to eat? I'm hungry and I feel faint. I haven't eaten since noon yesterday.

FLAMINIA: Yes, eat and then be on your way.

BARBARA: All right.

FLAMINIA: I can't carry your fate on my shoulders. I haven't had such a cheerful life either. Now Cesare doesn't matter at all to me anymore, but before I managed to arrive at this level of detachment, I suffered. I tore myself apart, I tormented myself. He has always betrayed me. At a certain point I told myself: Never mind about that. We'll be together like friends. I've betrayed him myself, to see if it would matter at all to him. Well, you know, he didn't feel one way or the other about it. On the contrary, maybe he was even glad. Why did we stay together? I don't know. Out of indifference. Out of inertia. Nowadays, I don't have affairs. I'm not good-looking anymore. I live in the country. I take care of the flowers. I read. I get bored. I play the piano. I wait for Cesare. When he comes I listen to him tell me stories about his girlfriends. Do you call that a cheerful life? No. It's a disgusting life. If I wanted to find one fine hour in my life, I'd have to go far back in my memory, years and years into the past. What do you expect me to do for you? In all honesty, I can't do anything. The only thing I can give you is a little something to eat, if you're hungry. (*She rings a bell.*)

TOSCA: Yes?

FLAMINIA: Bring the young woman something to eat.

TOSCA: What?

FLAMINIA: Whatever she wants.

TOSCA: Cheese? Some prosciutto?

FLAMINIA: Yes.

TOSCA: Is the young woman staying for lunch, too? The young woman
     – your cousin, that is?
FLAMINIA: She's not staying for lunch. She's not my cousin.
TOSCA: She said she was your cousin. (*Exits.*)

A doorbell rings. Flaminia opens the door. Letizia enters.

FLAMINIA: Letizia. This is Barbara. Cesare's girlfriend.
LETIZIA: Oh, I know you. I saw you once, this winter, at the movie the-
     atre with Cesare. You were sitting in the row behind me.
BARBARA: They were showing *Bikini Vacation*.
LETIZIA: Awful film.
BARBARA: Awful.

Tosca enters.

TOSCA: Here. I even toasted some bread. There's prosciutto, cheese.
     Poor woman. She arrived completely soaked! She's like my daugh-
     ter. My daughter always goes out without her umbrella, too. Young
     people! Young people make mistakes. Good morning, Signorina
     Letizia. Are you staying for lunch with us? I have some pork chops.
     They've been sitting around for a while, and so I thought I'd make
     pizzaiola.[5] It's the only thing to do with them. I don't know if you'll
     be satisfied with that. I still don't know if you're happy with me.
LETIZIA: I'm staying for lunch, yes. Since there's pizzaiola.
TOSCA: The Signora didn't tell me what I should prepare, so I made
     pizzaiola. Do you like it with lots of garlic, pizzaiola, I mean?
LETIZIA: If there's no garlic, it's not pizzaiola.
TOSCA: Exactly. You're right. Well said. If there's no garlic, it's not piz-
     zaiola. But there are those who only put in a little and those who
     put in a lot, according to the way they do things in their household.
     The Signora hasn't given me any instructions. She doesn't tell me
     anything, so I've no way of knowing if people here like garlic or
     not.

Barbara has finished eating. She rises and pulls on her jacket.

LETIZIA: You're leaving already?
TOSCA: You're leaving? It's still snowing, you know. At least wait until
     it stops snowing. (*Barbara lifts her suitcase, which falls open. Tosca and*

Barbara force the suitcase closed.) The lock is broken. It won't close anymore. It'll need to be tied. I'll go get a piece of rope. (*Exits.*)

LETIZIA: Where are you going with that suitcase?

BARBARA: I've left my husband. I don't know where to go.

LETIZIA: You're not really putting her out on the street, are you?

FLAMINIA: I gave her a little money. But she can't stay here.

LETIZIA: Why not?

FLAMINIA: Because she's Cesare's girlfriend.

LETIZIA: Of course. If people found out, they'd consider it strange. Better if she goes to a hotel.

FLAMINIA: It's not because of people. It's because of me. I have no desire to have her in the house, not even for one night.

BARBARA: I'm afraid. I'm afraid my husband wants to kill me. I'm afraid he's going to come looking for me and kill me. Where am I going to go? I don't know where to go.

LETIZIA: Of course not. Husbands never kill you.

FLAMINIA: Actually, if the issue is husbands who kill their wives, the newspapers are full of them.

LETIZIA: Is he the violent type, her husband?

FLAMINIA: As I understand it, he's pretty timid. But timid people, when they lose control, they're frightening.

BARBARA: It wouldn't really take much to kill someone like me. It wouldn't take anything at all.

LETIZIA: I'd drive her to my house, but I can't. My husband and my mother-in-law, they're old-fashioned types. Conformists. But something's coming to mind. Right nearby, at Roccapriora, there's a hostel run by nuns. I know the Mother Superior very well, Mother Anastasia. She's a wonderful woman. You could stay there. Your husband will certainly never find you.

Tosca returns with a piece of rope.

TOSCA: There wasn't even a piece of rope in the house. I had to go out to the gardener's. It's still snowing. I went out in slippers and now my feet are soaked. I said to the gardener, 'The snow needs to be shovelled from the walk.' He told me, 'It's not up to me to shovel the snow. They always call a boy for that, the son of the guy who delivers the coal.' I said, 'So go call the boy.' He told me, 'Go call him yourself.' 'Me? I'm wearing slippers.' He told me, 'You should put on your shoes.' You understand how he spoke to me? 'You should put on your shoes.' (*She ties the suitcase.*)

LETIZIA: So it's all set? Shall we go to Roccapriora?

BARBARA: Let's go.

LETIZIA: (*To Tosca.*) Take the bag out to my car.

TOSCA: You'll be taking her then, in your car? Not a bad idea if you take her, because it's still snowing and the wind out there is enough to blow you away. (*She exits with the suitcase.*)

LETIZIA: (*To Barbara.*) You'll see how well you get along with Mother Anastasia. And it's a beautiful place besides, high on a hill in the middle of the woods. There's a gorgeous view.

FLAMINIA: You can imagine how important it is to her to have a nice view.

LETIZIA: Let's go then, Barbara.

BARBARA: All right. But I don't really have much patience with nuns. I'm afraid I'll start feeling hopeless again tonight.

LETIZIA: But at least your husband won't find you there.

BARBARA: Yes.

FLAMINIA: Goodbye.

BARBARA: Goodbye. Thank you for the money. And thank you for giving me something to eat.

FLAMINIA: Not at all.

BARBARA: As soon as Cesare arrives, tell him to come find me at the Roccapriora convent. Will there be a phone there?

LETIZIA: Listen, your husband isn't going to get it into his head to kill Cesare is he?

BARBARA: I'm afraid of that, too.

TOSCA: (*Returning.*) This rope won't hold. It's half-rotten.

BARBARA: (*To Tosca.*) Thank you. Goodbye, Signora.

TOSCA: Don't call me signora. I'm not a signora. I'm a maid. I've been a maid since I was eleven years old. And I don't have a husband. That's how I had my daughter, by a good-for-nothing who's never shown his face since.

ACT TWO

The doorbell rings. Flaminia opens the door. Letizia enters.

LETIZIA: All done. I've delivered her to Mother Anastasia. I dropped a few hints – that she had found herself in a delicate situation, that her husband was the violent type. They got her situated in a room with two retirees. Two elderly women, cultured people. One of them is the widow of a colonel. A lovely little room, very clean. It was hot. The radiators were set to scalding. For lunch they had chickpea stew. You could smell such a wonderful fragrance in the air! Tomorrow, I want to make chickpea stew. With oil and rosemary, it's delicious! I'm completely frozen. It's rotten weather out. The snow's coming down in great big flakes.

FLAMINIA: Now what's she going to do?

LETIZIA: Who? Barbara? Nothing. They'll take her to the church for services. In those nun hostels, time passes in one manner or another. They take you to services. They make you walk up and down those endless hallways. A bell rings, and you go to the dining hall. You eat pasta and chickpeas. Everything's regulated by the sound of the bell. They make you go to sleep at seven in the evening. What in the world did Cesare see in that girl? She's not at all pretty.

FLAMINIA: Cesare has arrived. He telephoned from the airport. He'll be here in a little while.

LETIZIA: Oh! And did you tell him about Barbara?

FLAMINIA: Yes.

LETIZIA: And he said?

FLAMINIA: He didn't say anything.

LETIZIA: Poor Barbara!

FLAMINIA: What's going to become of her? She'll be with the nuns for a while. And then?

LETIZIA: She can put herself to work.

FLAMINIA: Doing what, if she doesn't know how to do anything?

LETIZIA: She'll go back to the husband.

FLAMINIA: You believe that? No, I don't believe she'll ever go back to the husband.

LETIZIA: Cesare will get her an apartment.

FLAMINIA: Cesare? He doesn't give a damn. He's tired of her. He won't be getting her any apartment, not Cesare.

LETIZIA: She'll start working as a whore. What do you expect? We can't exactly nursemaid her for the rest of her life. Today, we gave her a hand. Tomorrow, God will provide.

FLAMINIA: Like hell God will provide.

LETIZIA: Don't swear.

FLAMINIA: I'm not swearing. I'm telling you that God doesn't provide. What does He provide? I believe that God, if He exists, expects us to take care of ourselves.

LETIZIA: And so why is it they say He's omnipotent?

FLAMINIA: Who knows? I don't know. That's something they never explain.

LETIZIA: Well, now's not the time for a theological discussion. Look, we did what it was possible to do.

FLAMINIA: For that girl? Is that the way it seems to you? To me it seems we haven't really done a great deal.

LETIZIA: How have we not done a great deal? You gave her money. I drove her to Roccapriora. I left her in the nuns' hands. I even carried her suitcase for her through quite a maze of hallways because at one point she felt she was having an anxiety attack. And you say we haven't done a great deal? What do you expect anyway? I don't understand you, Flaminia. When I got here this morning, it looked like you were about to put her out on the street.

FLAMINIA: That's true.

LETIZIA: The brilliant idea of the Sisters of Roccapriora – I was the one who thought of that. You didn't want her in the house. But that's fair. She's your husband's lover. Enough, out. Let's talk about something else. I almost tore my hand off lifting that damn suitcase. It was heavy as hell. She's a woman who doesn't know how to live. If you really intend to run away from home, all you take with you is a toothbrush. And she isn't so pretty, either. But what did Cesare see in her? (*Cesare enters.*) Oh, hello, Cesare.

CESARE: Where is she?

LETIZIA: With the sisters. At Roccapriora. Wasn't that a brilliant idea? A gorgeous place. High up in the hills, in the woods. All those dear little sisters, nice and clean and awfully kind besides. Such tranquillity, such peace. The idea just came to me.

TOSCA: (*Entering.*) They want Signora Letizia on the phone. Welcome home, Signore. I'll set the table for you right away.

CESARE: I'm not eating. I ate on the plane. I'm exhausted.

FLAMINIA: I'm not hungry either.

TOSCA: You must want to eat something. I made pizzaiola. And I also stewed a couple of potatoes. I didn't know. The Signora didn't give me any instructions for a side dish.

LETIZIA: (*Re-entering.*) That was Mother Anastasia from the Roccapriora convent. They say she ran away. She jumped out of the window. With her suitcase. As soon as services were over.

CESARE: Where did she go?

LETIZIA: And who knows?

TOSCA: The young woman? That poor young woman. So young! A

baby! But I heard you were taking her to the sisters and I thought, 'She won't stay there. She's not the type. She's too unhappy.' When a person has that much sadness and disappointment weighing down on her, she can't really stay with nuns. It's useless. You run away. There's too much silence with the nuns. Silence is good for someone who's calm, someone who doesn't need anything. You know how the nuns are. They put you there. They tell you to pray to the Madonna. They stick a rosary in your hand. They tell you to resign yourself to your fate. I know because I stayed with the Ursuline Sisters for an entire month. I couldn't take it. Time simply refused to pass. And what a silence! And then the sound of the bell every now and then. When one has that much sadness and disappointment to mull over, then all that silence, time refuses to pass. I can still hear the sound of the bell in my ears. I couldn't bear that bell. I was ready to set fire to it. Shall I serve?

FLAMINIA: Yes.

Tosca exits.

LETIZIA: Where can she have gone?

CESARE: And who knows? She might have gone to see a friend of hers. Some Marcella person.

FLAMINIA: The one who has mattresses all over the floor?

LETIZIA: Do you think she might have gone back to her own house, to the husband? No, she was afraid he might kill her. She wouldn't really jump into the Tiber, would she?

TOSCA: (*Entering with the meal.*) If I'd thought of it, I could have taken her to my aunt's house, where my daughter sleeps. There's room. They'd have set a little bed up for her near my daughter. My aunt always has room for everyone. During the war, she kept some Jews hidden. They awarded her a gold watch. (*Exits.*)

CESARE: My God, I'm tired. I'm exhausted.

LETIZIA: I'll taste a little of this pizzaiola. It should be good. You guys eat something, too. It's not as though something tragic has happened. Maybe she's gone back to her own house and to her baby. Or perhaps she'll turn up here again in a little while.

FLAMINIA: No, no. I don't want her here.

LETIZIA: The Signora wouldn't be jealous, would she? You're strange. I find you very strange, Flaminia. In part you're consumed by the thought that you haven't done enough for her. In part you're terri-

fied by the thought of having her underfoot. I understand you don't
want her in the house. That's more than legitimate. But then why
are you still thinking about what she's doing and where she might
be? Do you really think I don't recognize the fact that you're still
thinking about her? When all is said and done, what does she matter to either one of us?

FLAMINIA: Nothing.

LETIZIA: Go look at yourself in the mirror. Your face looks like someone you know has died. You're pale, you look green. Look at your
husband. He's calm. He doesn't let things upset him. All this has
nothing to do with him.

CESARE: But none of you understands. That girl is in no danger. Not of
killing herself or of being killed. They're all fantasies. She's a little
crazy.

LETIZIA: I'm going to lie down on the sofa upstairs. I'm tired. It's been a
difficult morning. Call me if you need me. (*Exits.*)

CESARE: (*To Flaminia.*) You don't want her to come back here. But I
don't want her here, either.

FLAMINIA: 'So where do I go? I don't know where to go.' She kept
repeating that.

CESARE: God, I'm so tired. I'm exhausted. I have a headache. My head
is splitting. I was never in love with that girl, Flaminia, I've already
told you. You know that. She was never very important to me. In
the beginning, she was just something to make my life more cheerful. But little by little, everything fell apart. Now she's become a
nightmare for me, an obsession. I hate all the places I used to go
with her. I hate her jeans, her hair, and all the trouble she brings
with her. I hate her husband, her mother-in-law, her house, her
front door, her street. There are times when I'm afraid I'm never
going to get free of her. That I'll always have her underfoot, always.
I don't know how she got it into her head to come here. I'm afraid
now she'll always come here, that she'll keep coming back. We'll
never have a moment's peace again.

FLAMINIA: You told her she could come to you, to your house, if she
didn't know where to go. Did you tell her that or didn't you?

CESARE: A lot of things get said.

FLAMINIA: You told her your wife was such a good woman. Noble.
Superior. Extraordinary. That I would have taken her in, consoled
her, looked after her. She believed you. She believes you. She
believes everything you say to her. But in reality, I'm neither noble

nor good. I'm heartless. My heart feels small, dried up, like a small, dried prune. And it's not even true that I'm not jealous of her. I'm ferociously jealous of her. But not out of love for you. My jealousy is more wicked than that. It's a jealousy made up of envy, of shame, of humiliation. I'm jealous of her because she's young and I'm not so young anymore. Because she has a baby and I don't. Because she has a jealous husband who wants to kill her, and I, on the other hand, have a husband who doesn't give a damn about me. Because she's in love with you. Who knows what she sees in you, while I, on the other hand, know exactly what you are. You're nothing. A nothing man. And I don't love you anymore. I don't love you even the slightest bit anymore. You're not a husband to me, and you're no friend or brother, either. Nothing. I don't love anyone. I don't feel like protecting or consoling anyone. I want to stay here alone, here in this house, with the door closed, and die like that. Understand?

CESARE: Could you spare me your insults, Flaminia? I've told you that I'm very tired. Couldn't you have chosen a better moment? Do you think I don't realize that you're putting on this particularly vulgar little fit of jealousy for my benefit?

FLAMINIA: A nothing man. Cold. Cynical. Limited. Maybe even very stupid. I've thought so for quite some time. But my thinking was confused. Now, I'm thinking clearly – in fact, intensely so. I don't love you anymore. I haven't loved you for quite a number of years. But now I detest you, I despise you. So much so that it's nearly impossible for me to tolerate your presence.

CESARE: You want us to separate?

FLAMINIA: Yes.

CESARE: Flaminia. You're very tired. We're both very tired. Our nerves are shot. That damn girl. If we only knew where she ended up.

TOSCA: (*Entering.*) Signora! My daughter just called. You know that girl – she went to see her, to see my daughter, to have her hair done. I gave her a discount coupon. In Piazza Quadrata. My daughter works for the hairdresser Pino, in Piazza Quadrata. Camilla, that is. My daughter is Camilla. So that girl, that woman, ran away from the sisters and went right to Piazza Quadrata to get her hair done. My daughter says she really needed it. She gave her a cute hairdo. She left just a moment ago. Young people! The ideas young people get into their heads! When they don't know what to do anymore, they go to the hairdresser. It's a way to pass the time.

LETIZIA: (*Entering.*) What's happened?

TOSCA: To my daughter's! She went to my daughter's! To the hair-dresser Pino, where my daughter is. She just left! My daughter says she still had her suitcase, but they gave her a new rope because the other one was completely rotten. She's so wonderful – my daughter, I mean. She really knows how to style hair. If you want, I can give all of you a discount coupon, too. Here they are. I always keep them in my pocket.

LETIZIA: Yes, and before that she went to see that friend of hers, Mar-cella, who's a sales clerk at Standa. She gave me Marcella's first and last name this morning in the car because she wanted me to tell her to come and visit her at the convent. So I phoned Standa a little while ago, and I asked them to call Marcella. She told me that Barbara had been there not an hour before, still with her suitcase, and that she bought a pair of stockings. Then she left again. From Roccapriora she got to Rome in ten minutes. She hitchhiked.

CESARE: Didn't I tell you all there was no reason to worry about that girl? She's a girl with plenty of resources. Crazy as she is, she certainly doesn't lose sight of what's important. Even in all her craziness, she maintains a reserve of good, healthy sense.

LETIZIA: After she left the hairdresser's, where did she go?

TOSCA: And who knows?

LETIZIA: Well, but when someone buys herself stockings, hitchhikes, goes to the hairdresser's, it means she's not quite so hopeless after all.

CESARE: Exactly. That's what I've been saying.

FLAMINIA: You people have very strange ideas about despair. When a person is hopeless, she might not do things any differently from the way she usually does. She might do what she's done her entire life.

TOSCA: With those jeans! With that suitcase! And where might she be now?

LETIZIA: I had a very nice meal, Tosca. Your pizzaiola was delicious.

TOSCA: Did you like it? I'm so glad. I do my best. But they don't tell me anything here, and I don't know if they're happy with me or not.

FLAMINIA: What difference does it make if we're happy, seeing as how you've given me your two weeks' notice and you're leaving?

CESARE: She's leaving?

TOSCA: Well, yes. I'm leaving. I'm not fitting in here. I can't do anything about it. I'm not fitting in.

CESARE: You're not fitting in?

TOSCA: I'm not fitting in. I'm not fitting in here. There's too much

silence. There's too much countryside around here. I look out the
window and there's not a soul to be seen. Just trees. Trees, snow,
clouds, more trees. So the time, you understand, never passes. I
clean the kitchen, I wash the windows, I polish the silver, I do all
the things that need to be done. But the time, you understand –
time doesn't pass.

CESARE: Okay, but for now, go into the kitchen, Tosca. Go, go on. Go
polish the silverware.

TOSCA: I'll go into the kitchen, but what's there to do in the kitchen?
Since I've already polished the silverware? (*Exits.*)

LETIZIA: With those jeans! With that hair! With that suitcase! Who
knows where she might be?

FLAMINIA: And where shall I go? I don't know where to go.

CESARE: You're tired, Flaminia. Your nerves are tired. I'm very tired
myself. We should give ourselves a little break. Take a cruise. You
know, when a person really wants to rest, he takes a cruise. It's
good for your health. You come back fresh, detoxified.

LETIZIA: That might not be a bad idea. And what if I come along?

CESARE: We could even leave soon, in a few days. We could close the
house up. Our new housekeeper says she doesn't want to stay anyway. Let's close up the house. I'll leave all my business in the hands
of an associate. We'll stay away a few months. What do you have to
say about the idea, Flaminia? Where would you like to go?

FLAMINIA: And where shall I go? I don't know where to go.

CESARE: Flaminia! Don't make me lose my patience. Answer me! I
asked you a question! Are you delirious!

FLAMINIA: I answered you.

CESARE: Damn that girl! Damn, damn her!

LETIZIA: If we only knew where she ended up. Can she possibly have
gone back home to her husband and her own house?

CESARE: Of course she went back to her own house. I'd bet my right
arm on it.

LETIZIA: And what if her husband kills her? If we open up the newspaper tomorrow and read that he's killed her?

CESARE: No, no, I'm begging you both. Let's not imagine the worst.
Let's come back to reality. The two of you have never seen the
husband. I've seen him. He's a puppy dog. A puppy dog with
damp fur. He couldn't hurt a fly. You two did more than enough for
that girl. I thank you and I'm grateful to you. It was a frightening
episode, and I regret it. I would have preferred to spare you having

to see my mistakes, my weaknesses. But that's how it happened. Let it go. Now let's try to get back to ourselves. Let's talk to each other like adults. Let's talk about something else. Let's talk about our cruise. I need sunshine, the ocean, some fresh air.

LETIZIA: Of course. I agree – we did what we could. Flaminia talked to her a long time and very kindly. She tried to reason with her. She gave her some money. What else was one to do?

CESARE: Oh, really? You gave her some money, Flaminia? How much did you give her?

FLAMINIA: I don't remember.

CESARE: Do the two of you know what she's doing right now? She's touring the city, going from one café to another, eating gelato. Her passion is strawberry and cream. She's capable of eating ten of them in a single afternoon. She doesn't get sick. She's got the stomach of a rhinoceros.

LETIZIA: She's a child.

FLAMINIA: A nothing. A nothing man. How have I managed to live with him for so many years? What have I done? My God, what have I done?

CESARE: Flaminia, what are you saying? Are you delirious?

LETIZIA: She's a little shaken up. I'm a little shaken up myself. Come on, Flaminia. Let's take a walk. See, it's not snowing anymore. Put on your fur coat and your overshoes.

FLAMINIA: And where shall I go? Since I don't know where to go....

LETIZIA: She's shaken up. She's a little shaken up. You know, she upset you, that girl did. And me, too. Young people nowadays don't know what road to take. They get married the way they eat ice cream. They have children. They fall into the hands of the first un- scrupulous person who comes along. No, I'm sorry, Cesare, I didn't mean you.

CESARE: No, please, insult me. Go right ahead and insult me. Your in- sults don't offend me. I don't feel one way or the other about them. I've decided to take all of this in good humour. Come on. I'll go out with you.

FLAMINIA: I'm not going out. I have no desire to go out.

LETIZIA: Flaminia. Dear Flaminia. Poor little thing. Don't let yourself get discouraged like that. Look what a face you're making. And you're cold as an ice cube. And yet nothing has really happened. Everything's just the way it's always been. In life, it's very rare that anything new happens.

FLAMINIA: Right. It couldn't be more rare. And even when something
new does happen, life doesn't change. It stays the way it is. Disgusting.

LETIZIA: My god. I only hope that girl hasn't jumped into the Tiber!

CESARE: No, no, of course she hasn't. None of you understands what's
going on. She'll wander around the city eating gelato. Strawberry
and cream. I've spent an inheritance on her in strawberry and
cream gelato. You've no idea how much gelato she can eat in a single afternoon, even in the middle of winter. You have no idea. But
she's not going to jump into the Tiber. She wouldn't even consider
it. You don't understand at all. This is hardly a tragedy; it's a joke.
Life is very sparing with tragedy, and instead it hands us jokes by
the fistful. You know what else I'd tell you? If by some chance she
did throw herself into the Tiber, that's it, I'm fed up. I don't want to
hear her name again. She's jumped into the Tiber? Forget about it.

October 1966

Notes

1 It is likely that Ginzburg is referring here to Formitrol, at one time a popular and widely used over-the-counter remedy in Italy, sold as lozenges and
recommended for sore throats, hoarseness, etc. Formitrol lozenges were
apparently quite delicious, and children ate them as candy. Among Formitrol's active ingredients was formalin – that is, *formalina* – the aqueous
solution of formaldehyde. The product was evidently taken off the market
in the late 1970s and more recently repackaged as 'NeoFormitrol,' which
now contains dextromethorphan instead, a rather addictive antitussive. Of
interest is the fact that weak solutions of formalin are still recommended
today by at least a few allopathic and homeopathic practitioners for throat
and mouth infections.

2 A large Italian grocery-store chain.

3 Italy's oldest and largest national lottery.

4 Barbara says she's the daughter of 'N.N.,' the Italian abbreviation for '*non
noto*,' which was once used on birth certificates to indicate that the identity
of the father was unknown.

5 The term *pizzaiola* indicates a sauce made with tomatoes, garlic, and oreg-
ano, and a cooking method that requires any number of different meats

and even fish to simmer slowly in the sauce. Traditionally, the *pizzaiola* treatment was reserved for poorer cuts of meat, or meat that was not fresh, but the popularity of Italian cuisine has changed that, and cookbooks now often call for fine cuts of beef or veal – or even duck – to be prepared in this way.

The Secretary

A PLAY IN THREE ACTS

Cast:
Sofia
Nino, Sofia's brother
Titina, Nino's wife
Enrico
Perfetta, a maid
Silvana

The action takes place in a country house on the outskirts of Rome.

ACT ONE

SOFIA: Hello, Luisa? Hi, Luisa. I'm coming to Rome tomorrow to have
lunch with you. Don't make me tripe. I know you love it, but I
don't. And, please, no kidneys either, if you don't mind. Kidneys
remind me of my husband. It was the very last meal I made for him
before I left. They don't cost much in England. I slept so badly last
night! There was a tremendous wind. And the baby wouldn't stop
crying. Right, because my sister-in-law isn't producing enough
milk. The dogs were howling, too, and I really had the urge to take
them a little dish of poisoned meatballs. I came down to the kitchen
to make myself a cup of coffee and – forget that! – the coffee maker
wasn't working. Plus I have a cold that's killing me. It's been giving
me a pain in my back whenever I breathe. I don't know if I have a
fever; I couldn't find the thermometer. Sure, I'll call Enrico. He's
right nearby; it takes five minutes to get here. Plus there's barely

any heat in this house. I'm in bed. I'm just about done with my translation. It's a mystery novel. They find this girl dead in a laundry basket. A coloured girl with a yellow plastic raincoat. Oh you're right, I do have a raincoat just like it, but I don't wear it anymore. The murderer is the caretaker's stepson. With a hoe. He dumped her for another woman. There's even a little drug traffic involved. Edoardo is expecting to make a bundle with his mystery novels. Poor Edoardo. It's another of his illusions. They won't sell. Edoardo's mysteries never sell. Poor Edoardo! I mean, you tell me: What kind of life does he have? He spends all day long in that huge bed of his, under that pink satin comforter, while Isabellita mani-cures her fingernails! And then those guys they know from their hometown come over to read his Tarot. They're just some guys, really dark, short little guys who dress entirely in black. Nino calls them the Beagle Boys.[1] Or else he gets visits from the Conocchias, those two cretins, whom Isabellita adores. She met them last summer in Rimini. They cook. They have some regular blowouts. And believe me, no one's washing any of those dishes. The house-keeper comes whenever she remembers. Does that seem like any kind of life for a cultured man? An editor? Who does he have to talk ideas over with? With those hicks from his hometown? They're a bunch of brown-nosers, that's the only thing they're good for. Edoardo still owes me 100,000 lire for some other books I translated for him. This time he's really got to pay me. I don't have a cent. My husband? He seems to have fallen off the face of the earth. It's been a year since he last put in an appearance. I heard he got a job somewhere in Venezuela and that they're paying him pretty well, not that he's sending me anything. Yes, I do know that Edoardo owes you money, too. But I've got to get paid first. You have an apartment; I haven't got a thing. This house? The house where I'm staying? It's not really mine; it belongs to my brother. I know we don't pay rent, but there's always something to spend money on because this place is crumbling around us! Anyway, I'm sick of the country. And I'm sick of living with my brother and my sister-in-law. I envy you that cute little apartment in Rome, no relatives crawling all over you – everything's there just for you to enjoy. And you've got that delicious tenant. Don't you think Gildo is delicious? Remember: I found him for you. You owe me. Edoardo and me. We found him for you together. And you're picking up 15,000 lire extra every month. Fifteen thousand for that little hole of a room. Oh, really? He hasn't been paying his rent? Well, but what's a couple of months? Don't be a bitch about it. Gildo is a delightful person. You should marry him. He'd be an ideal husband. Well, sure, women haven't been his strong point up to now. But lots of people like that get married. At least you'd have a husband. Me? I should marry him? I already have a husband. Granted, he's been a little distant lately. No, I haven't asked him about giving me alimony. Because what if he decides to go after me for abandoning our marriage? Well, because I was the one who left him. I'd made him kidneys for supper. They're really cheap in London. Kidneys and onions. It was for him, not for me: I hate all that stuff. Then I packed a bag and took the train for Italy. Okay, Luisa, so I'll be there tomorrow. Not on the train. In my Seicento. If I can get it to run. Maybe I'll even spend the night. You don't have room? How can you not have room? Oh. Gildo's two aunts are there. You put them up in the dining room? What are they like? A couple of old tightwads, I'll bet. I understand. Put Gildo on for a minute, will you? Gildo? Hi, Gildo. I'm thinking of coming up to Rome tomorrow. If I've recovered, I mean. Yes, it's a pretty bad cold and it's been giving me a lot of back pain. Oh, forget aspirin. I never take aspirin. Gildo, listen, how come you're not paying the rent? Don't make me look bad in front of Luisa. Edoardo? Edoardo owes you money? And who doesn't Edoardo owe money to? He owes me an astronomical sum. I've almost finished the latest translation. Yeah, I'm taking it to him tomorrow. It's a novel called *The Hyena*. The hyena is an old colonel. They call him that because he has really long teeth. No, he's not the murderer. The murderer is the caretaker's stepson. There's a coloured girl in the dirty-clothes basket. Dead. With a yellow raincoat. Poor Edoardo! He's never going to get anywhere this way. His books don't sell! Edoardo's mysteries never sell! If he were at least making some money, it might be understandable. But instead he does these disasters and never scratches a cent out of them. He used to be an exquisite editor. Do you remember Le Cicerchie? What was that, four years ago? Those beautiful, elegant little books – tiny, tiny books with some sort of little animal on the outside in black … what was that? A gecko? Oh, sure, he was taking a loss. What kind of money do you expect him to make with a stable full of poets? But at least he had something of a name as an editor. Now, with these terrible books he isn't making money and he's discredited. What do you expect? He buys the rights at random without ever having read the books. Read them how? He doesn't know French or English. He reads them after they've been translated and that's when he feels like puking. But by then he's already bought the rights and he's obligated to publish them. Besides, who does he have to toss ideas around with? Sure, of course, he tosses them around with you, but that has its limits. It's not like you're this fountain of ideas, and I'm not saying that to offend you, but even you've gotten a little dull. Poor Edoardo. He spends the entire day in that great big bed. At night he goes out and wanders around the city. With that procession of young guys dressed in black who follow him around. The Beagle Boys. Plus he drinks. He drinks much too much. Yes, I know you drink, too. It's not good for you. Within a few years you'll both have atrophied livers. Did Edoardo tell you about the magazine? Yes! He wants to do a monthly magazine. How in the world could he not have told you? Oh, really? You haven't seen him for a week? Haven't you been feeling well? It's a magazine called *The Wigeon*.[2] That Princess Farina is giving him the money for it, the one who lives in that tower, at the Lido dei Pini. He's hoping to get back on his feet again with *The Wigeon*, but I don't see it working. Okay, bye Gildo. Give my regards to your aunts. How are they? Two sweet little old ladies? Luisa told me they're a couple of tightwads. Bye Gildo. (*She dials another number.*) Hello? Enrico? You need to stop by and see me for a minute. I'm in rotten shape. I have a terrible cough, plus I've got a pain in my back, on the right side, whenever I take a breath. I don't know about a fever; I can't find the thermometer. Do you think I might have pneumonia? I slept terribly last night. Who says it's quiet in the countryside? There was quite a wind, all the shutters were banging, and the dogs were howling. Yours got started and all the rest answered. Of course, yours is the mother of ours, so ours heard its mother and answered. I really felt like taking some meatballs out to them.… Listen, Enrico, I'm out of cigarettes. I'd love some Kents. I shouldn't smoke? Come on, if I didn't smoke I'd go crazy. And I'm also out of Kleenex. Get your mom to give you a box, she's always got some. Yes, I'm in bed, translating the last few pages of that novel. The caretaker's stepson. With a hoe. No, it doesn't frighten me. It's so idiotic that it isn't frightening at all. I hope he's going to pay me. He has to pay me. Poor Edoardo. You know he's putting together a magazine? *The Wigeon*. It's the name of a restaurant where he goes to eat in the evening with all those guys.

I don't know what he sees in them. They're just brown-nosers. No, in the evenings Isabellita doesn't set foot out of the house. Isabellita gets sleepy at nine at night. You know Isabellita, she's such a mess. She doesn't do a thing all day long, but at nine at night she's ready to collapse from exhaustion. Edoardo goes out to eat in the restaurant with those guys – he eats, but especially he drinks. Then he wanders around the city with his entourage. He talks and he talks. My god, how he talks! Just this small man – with all that long hair falling across the nape of his neck, a worn-out overcoat, his socks unravelling – back and forth all night through the streets. Poor Edoardo. Listen, Enrico, could you also bring me a coffee maker? Ours isn't working. The washer must have fallen apart. No, I don't need anything else, Enrico, thanks for everything. (*She hangs up the receiver.*)

Nino enters.

NINO: Were you talking to Enrico?
SOFIA: Uh-huh. I told him to stop by. I don't feel very well.
NINO: So I can get him to look at my horse. It won't eat and it's shitting blood. I'm afraid it might have swallowed a nail.
SOFIA: Enrico isn't exactly a veterinarian, you know.
NINO: It doesn't matter. I think he knows something about horses. Besides, I want him to take me to the vet in his car. Mine's not working. I think the carburetor's dirty.
SOFIA: Well, go ahead and take the Seicento. I'll lend it to you.
NINO: You can't really lend it to me since it's as much mine as it is yours. We bought it together, remember? Fifty-fifty?
SOFIA: But you've never put in your half!
NINO: That's only because my assets aren't liquid. I'll reimburse you as soon as Edoardo pays me for my translation.
SOFIA: You can lead a horse to water....[3]
NINO: Don't talk to me about horses. Look, it doesn't matter. I don't want to take the Seicento anyway. It stalls every ten metres.
SOFIA: We have bad luck with machines. Even the coffee maker's broken. The coffee won't come out. We're unlucky with horses – and with machines.
NINO: No, the horse was just fine up until yesterday. I'm not sure what happened. He must have swallowed a nail. Last night, I took a blanket out there and moved into the stall. I didn't sleep a wink. I

kept an eye on the horse. The horse kept an eye on me, too. He was looking at me like he pitied me. He kept staring at me with his big, sad eyes. I swear, I almost felt like crying.

The telephone rings.

SOFIA: Hello? Oh, hi, Isabellita. What? My slacks? Yes, I got them at a clearance sale at Nordio's. Eight thousand lire. The very last 8,000 lire I had. But don't think about buying yourself slacks like these. What? No, listen, it's just not a good idea. You've got a behind the size of a kettle drum. No, it won't do you any good to go to Nordio's. The only thing they've got are slacks and sweaters. Besides, I'm begging you: Don't go around spending money when your husband has so many debts. He owes money to me, to Nino, to Gildo, to everyone. No, I am not being mean to you. Isabellita, don't get all upset. Would you just do me a favour and call Edoardo to the phone? He's asleep? How is he supposed to be making it as an editor when he's asleep all the time? What did you guys do yesterday? You had your cards read, right? You had your cards read with the Carrochias? That must have been fun. Poor Edoardo. What? You've got a bone to pick with me? With me? I said you were petit bourgeois? When? Who did I say that to? Of course not. I might have said that you were a bit of a mess. Okay, Isabellita. I'm going to let you go because I've got a ton of things to do. Edoardo's up now? Sure, put him on. Hello, Edoardo. I'm coming to Via degli Incappuciati tomorrow. I'm bringing you the translation. I can't even tell you about that book. It'll make you puke. Yes, I know you already bought the rights, but what I'm wondering is why you bought them! Edoardo, I want the money you owe me. This time I really mean it. I don't have a cent. I bought myself a pair of slacks at Nordio's and there went my last 8,000 lire. My husband? He doesn't send me money anymore. I don't allow myself to expect it. I don't even know where he is. He's fallen off the face of the earth. Edoardo, listen, these mysteries that you're trying to put together are pitiful. You can't go on like this. It's grotesque. You know, I've was thinking a lot about *The Wigeon* last night. You might be able to get back on top of things with that one. I'll stop by tomorrow and we can talk about it. You'll only be at home in the morning? And after that? Where are you going after that? To see Princess Farina? I could come to see the Princess, too. I could take the two of you in my Seicento.

NINO: (*Grabbing the receiver.*) Keep in mind that her Seicento stalls every ten metres.

SOFIA: (*Taking back the receiver.*) Yeah, but all it needs is a little push. Oh, the Conocchias are taking you? No. Not with them. I can't stand them.

NINO: (*Grabbing the receiver again.*) Edoardo, do you know anything about horses? No? One of my horses isn't doing too well. I'm pretty worried. Sure, I'd love to come down one of these evenings, as soon as the horse is better. Is your magazine going well? Any chance you might be interested in a photo essay on Paestum? No? You don't use photographs at all? Oh, well. No, photography's the only thing I'm really good at. Never mind. (*He hangs up the phone.*)

Titina enters.

TITINA: My milk is running out. Last night I expressed seventy grams. This morning eighty.

SOFIA: That's not really so little.

TITINA: It's practically nothing. And you should see it. It's grey. I'm sure it can't possibly have any nutrition in it.

SOFIA: Why don't you feed him formula?

TITINA: Because Enrico doesn't want me to. He's obsessed with the idea of mother's milk and he doesn't want formula. But the baby's hungry. He cried the entire night last night. I was desperate for a little sleep so I called Perfetta and asked her to rock him for a while. She came in wearing two coats, one on top of the other, and her head all wrapped up in a wool shawl. And she tells me, 'I came this time, but next time don't start calling me in the middle of the night because I need my rest.'

NINO: Sure.

TITINA: But I need my rest too! If I don't get a good night's sleep, I'll never produce any milk. Oh, sure, it's no problem for you. The minute a baby starts crying, you take off.

NINO: Okay, so I went to the stable last night. But not to sleep; it was because the horse needed looking after. Anyway, if the kids are crying it's your fault. You've spoiled them.

TITINA: I have not spoiled them! He's crying because he's hungry. Damn Enrico and his obsession with mother's milk. But I'm tired. I'm exhausted. I'm anemic. When I looked at myself in the mirror this morning I was shocked to see how pale I've gotten.

NINO: You've always been pale.

TITINA: Not true. When I was a girl I was a flower. I had a complexion like a flower. Everyone told me so. Skin like a camellia. Now look at my skin; it's coarse – I look like a farmer.

NINO: I don't remember any camellias.

TITINA: And I'm afraid I might be pregnant again. My period is really late.

SOFIA: Don't tell me that!

NINO: You must have counted wrong.

TITINA: No, I never make that kind of mistake. What a thought. It really isn't fair. I have so much weight on my shoulders – the house, the kids, all of it. One of these days I'm going to take off and hail to the king.[4]

NINO: What king? We live in a republic.

TITINA: Hail to the king. I'm getting out of here. I'll go back to my mom's house, back to my home town.

NINO: Except that you and your mother have never gotten along. You don't do anything but argue.

TITINA: My mother said, if I ever wanted to come back home, that my little room would always be waiting for me.

NINO: I'm going down to take a look at the horse for a minute. (*Exits.*)

TITINA: Horses are all he thinks about.

SOFIA: You've had two children in three years. Now you're about to have your third. How many kids do you want?

TITINA: What does it matter to you? You're not the one who has to worry about it, are you? You don't give a damn about me anyway. At night, when they're crying, there's never any real risk that you might get up and see if I need anything. You keep yourself closed up in here with the typewriter and the telephone, and meanwhile the house could be falling down around you.

SOFIA: It's not as though I'm amusing myself. I'm working.

TITINA: Great job. Translating books for an editor who never pays you a cent.

SOFIA: He'll pay me.

TITINA: He is never going to pay you. You only keep working for him because you're in love with him. That's the truth.

SOFIA: Me? In love with Edoardo? Me?

TITINA: Yes. And don't think I hadn't figured it out. I've seen that one coming for quite a while now.

SOFIA: Let's not talk nonsense.

TITINA: See, just now my head is starting to spin like crazy. It must be some kind of fatigue. What am I going to do, if I'm pregnant again, and I'm already sick?

SOFIA: Why don't you use the birth control pill?

TITINA: I'm against it. The Church is against it.

SOFIA: You're not exactly some big churchgoer.

TITINA: You're wrong. I have a very deep religious sense. I don't go to church, but I pray all the time. I pray everywhere. In the bathtub. In the kitchen. Wherever I am.

SOFIA: I never go to Mass. But I pray to Jesus a lot.

TITINA: Where did you get those slacks?

SOFIA: At Nordio's.

TITINA: I'd love to buy myself a nice new pair of slacks, but I don't have the money.

SOFIA: If you're pregnant, what are you going to do with slacks?

TITINA: Yeah, that's true.

SOFIA: Anyway, the Church isn't against the pill. They're in the process of discussing it.

TITINA: Well, until they've finished discussing, I'm not taking anything like that. Besides, I read an article about how some women, when they take the Pill, they start growing moustaches.

SOFIA: Better a little moustache than ten children.

TITINA: No! I don't want to wind up with a moustache!

SOFIA: I'm still thinking about what you said. How could you possibly imagine that I was in love with Edoardo? Me?

Perfetta enters with Silvana.

PERFETTA: This young lady is looking for a job. I also wanted to say that the coffee maker isn't working.

SOFIA: I know. The washer is worn out.

PERFETTA: No, the washer is still okay. The filter is completely plugged up. I tried to unplug it with a hairpin, but it didn't work. I spent the entire night on my feet, rocking the baby, and now my stomach feels like a rock. I could use a sip of coffee.

Perfetta exits.

TITINA: Perfetta can be so unpleasant at times.

SOFIA: What is it that we can do for you, Signorina?

SILVANA: Signora Coltellacci sent me. She said you were looking for a
    secretary.

SOFIA: A secretary? Us? No, I wouldn't think so.

TITINA: And who's Signora Coltellacci?

SOFIA: There must be some mistake. I'm really sorry. We need all kinds
    of things here, but a secretary isn't one of them.

SILVANA: But Signora Coltellacci told me to come here. She gave me
    this address. She even wrote it down for me on a piece of paper.

SOFIA: Show me the paper. (*She reads.*) Nino Azzarita, Tolfa, Vicolo del
    Moro 23. Well, it's very clearly written. Signora Coltellacci has such
    beautiful penmanship.

TITINA: Nino Azzarita is my husband. But he doesn't need a secretary.

SOFIA: Right. He's this woman's husband and my brother. But he's out
    of work. He's chronically unemployed. He doesn't need a secretary.

TITINA: My husband is not chronically unemployed. He works. He
    works very hard. He takes care of the grounds and the estate. He
    has a lot of interests – music, philosophy, photography, horses. But
    at least for now, he doesn't need a secretary.

SOFIA: Look, we need all kinds of things. We need a coffee maker.
    We need a veterinarian. We need a medical doctor. We need a wet
    nurse. In fact, we need just about everything – except a secretary.

SILVANA: I understand. Never mind.

SOFIA: And you came all the way out from Rome for this? Did you
    come on the train?

SILVANA: On my Vespa.

SOFIA: Oh, a Vespa. I used to have one, too, but I sold it. Now, I have
    a Seicento. But it tends to die every ten metres. Don't go. Stay and
    rest for a while. Would you like some coffee? We're expecting En-
    rico to stop by in a little while – he's our doctor – and he'll bring us
    a new coffee maker.

SILVANA: Thanks. I will sit down for a few minutes. My name is Silvana
    Scotti.

SOFIA: We're rather isolated here. It's a welcome distraction for us to
    see a new face!

SILVANA: Actually, I can learn how to do almost any kind of work. I'm
    from Viterbo. A few months ago I came to Rome and enrolled in
    the Academy of Dramatic Arts, but I'm afraid I don't have any real
    talent for the theatre. My family doesn't send me any money. It's
    a tense situation. They wanted me to stay in Viterbo. But I can't
    go back there now. In Rome I did some work as a babysitter, I did

some tutoring, I helped Signora Coltellacci out at her store. But I couldn't make ends meet that way. Yesterday, I was this close to selling my Vespa. And then Signora Coltellacci told me to try coming here.

TITINA: But who is Signora Coltellacci?

SOFIA: Isn't she the one who has the store on Via del Babuino where they sell those art nouveau lamps? I'm pretty sure she's a friend of Gildo's.

SILVANA: Right. She owns a lighting store. She's always been incredibly kind to me. I've been staying at her house. On my sleeping bag.

SOFIA: I have a friend who might be able to give you a job. He's an editor. He might need a secretary. He does have one little problem, though. He doesn't pay. He never pays you.

SILVANA: I don't think that would work so well for me.

TITINA: Of course it wouldn't work for you. It isn't working for anybody!

SOFIA: Poor Edoardo!

SILVANA: Edoardo?

SOFIA: Yes. Edoardo Sequi. Do you know him?

SILVANA: Yes. I translated a book for him. A mystery.

SOFIA: Did he pay you?

SILVANA: No.

SOFIA: He doesn't pay. He never pays.

TITINA: You've worked as a babysitter? Do you like children?

SILVANA: No, I don't. I don't have the patience. In my house, back in Viterbo, I had four younger brothers and sisters. I had to take care of them because my mother got headaches all the time, and she closed herself up in her room in the dark. It was hell. They were little pests. So I wound up with a very strong dislike for children. But I would even look after children, if that's what came my way. I'd do anything. Whatever I could find.

TITINA: And now that you've left, what is your mother going to do? Who's looking after the children?

SILVANA: I don't know. The maid's going to have to deal with them. But she's always without a maid, my mother is. She has a very pessimistic personality and not many maids can put up with it. She's suffered for years with these headaches. She has a neurosis.

TITINA: And when your mother doesn't have a maid, who takes care of the children?

SILVANA: Exactly. I don't know. My father is always away. And when he's home, he doesn't bother with the children. He's a huge egotist, my father is. He might have become that way because he found so many things annoying. In order not to be tormented all the time, he got used to thinking only of himself. His books, his clothes, his collection. He has a collection of antique porcelains.

TITINA: I feel terrible for your mother. You shouldn't leave her by herself.

SILVANA: And what should I do? If I hadn't left, I'd have wound up with a neurosis, too. The air in my house is unbreathable. My mother stays in bed all the time, in the dark. She moans, she cries, she rings the bell. She's afraid she has cancer. She's afraid my father has another family somewhere. She's afraid the household is going to fall apart. That my brothers go to school in the morning without drinking their milk. She doesn't have cancer, but she's right to be afraid about all the rest. My father does have another family and my brothers don't drink their milk. Sometimes they don't even go to school. They go out and play in the streets. My father comes to the house very little. He travels. He's in business. When he is home, he keeps to himself in his studio. With his collection of antique porcelains. He's crazy about them. He takes them out of the display case and looks at them through a magnifying glass. He dusts them. Every once in a while, my mother howls, a long, high-pitched sound, like a factory siren. Hearing her scream that way used to drive me crazy. He, on the other hand, didn't notice. I think they've never put her in a clinic because it would have cost too much. So I couldn't stay at home anymore. I couldn't.

Nino enters.

NINO: Wasn't Enrico supposed to be coming by?

SOFIA: No one's seen him yet. This young lady came, however. She's here by mistake. Signora Coltellacci sent her. The one who has the store where they sell art nouveau lamps. She thought we needed a secretary.

NINO: I do need a secretary.

TITINA: You need a secretary? You?

NINO: Yes. I mentioned exactly that to Signora Coltellacci.

SOFIA: What are you going to do with a secretary?

NINO: I can use the help. I have a lot of unanswered correspondence.

TITINA: You have unanswered correspondence?

SOFIA: Even though there's not a living soul who writes to you?

NINO: Plus I ought to reorganize my photography archive. My papers. My notebooks. I need to put some order into my life. Signora Coltellacci sent her? Fine. She promised me she'd send somebody.

SILVANA: I really need a job.

NINO: And I really need a secretary. You'll live here. We have a big house with lots of rooms. Come along with me. I'll show you the house. And the garden. I'll even show you my horse. Do you know anything about horses?

Nino and Silvana exit.

ACT TWO

[The same house, a few hours later.]

TITINA: Sofia, listen. I think Nino's lost his mind.

SOFIA: You think?

TITINA: You want to stop typing and come over here and listen to me?

SOFIA: Go right ahead and talk. I'm listening.

TITINA: No. If you're typing, you can't listen to me. I need someone to listen to me. Otherwise, I'm going to wind up talking to the walls.

SOFIA: You can have a pretty good conversation with the walls. Every once in a while I talk to Enrico. Talking to Enrico is like talking to the wall. Every now and then, he gives you a little nod.

TITINA: Better than the wall, then.

SOFIA: A little better. Not much different.

TITINA: What I'm saying is, I'm afraid Nino's lost his mind. I'm fed up. Fed up. I asked him for 30,000 lire so I could buy myself a coat. I'm embarrassed to wear the coat I have. He told me no – he didn't have it. And so now he's hired a secretary? What money is he paying her with?

SOFIA: I don't know.

TITINA: She's not even someone who could actually help me with the kids. You heard her, she said she hates children. She's this eccentric young girl, a drifter, a runaway. One of these young girls you see running around nowadays. No heart, no feelings, no attachments – one of those rootless girls. Did you see the way she was dressed? Did you see her hair?

SOFIA: Like a little mouse fished out of the water.

TITINA: I don't want her here. I can't even imagine having her here. But what am I supposed to do? He's crazy. Nino is crazy. I don't really want to be with a guy who's crazy. I'm going back home, back to my mom's house.

Perfetta enters with Enrico.

PERFETTA: The doctor is here. I heard he was bringing a coffee maker, but he says he forgot. I had coffee with the farmer's wife. How are you going to manage?

SOFIA: Don't worry about it.

PERFETTA: The baby is crying.

TITINA: Go rock him.

PERFETTA: I don't have time. I have to wash the dishes.

TITINA: Why didn't you wash them last night?

PERFETTA: Don't you remember? I went back home in the afternoon. They were holding the annual festival in my village. You told me I could go. Don't you remember? (*She exits.*)

TITINA: She's so unpleasant, that Perfetta. Enrico, I have no more milk. Last night, seventy grams. This morning, eighty. The baby's constantly crying. Have you decided yet whether I can give him some formula?

ENRICO: Give him formula.

TITINA: Finally! What should I give him? Nestogen with half cream?

ENRICO: No. Give him Pelargon.[5]

TITINA: They told me that Nestogen with half cream is best of all. The lady next door told me so.

ENRICO: Well, if you already know, why are you asking me?

TITINA: Enrico, I'm afraid I might be pregnant again. I'm ten days late. What do you think?

ENRICO: What do you want me to think?

TITINA: I'm anemic, Enrico. I'm tired. I'm exhausted. Look how anemic I am. Look at my lips. I can't have another baby!

ENRICO: You're not anemic. You're just fine. You're as healthy as a horse.

TITINA: Don't talk to me about horses. The horse is sick. Yesterday evening he was shitting blood.

SOFIA: Did you know that Nino has hired a secretary?

ENRICO: A secretary?

TITINA: Yes. As if we didn't have enough to worry about. As if we were some kind of millionaires. I have a winter coat that's pitiful to look at. All of our sheets are falling apart, and he's hired a secretary.

SOFIA: Sent by Signora Coltellacci.

ENRICO: And who is Signora Coltellacci?

SOFIA: It doesn't matter who she is. She's this woman who has a lighting shop. A little while ago, this girl arrived wearing black tights and a big black hat made out of some kind of animal fur, in this completely wrinkled dress, her hair flying all over the place. She looked like a mouse fished out of the water. And he says, 'Great! I need a secretary. I'm really behind in my correspondence.'

ENRICO: He's behind in his correspondence? Who writes to him?

TITINA: No one, Enrico, no one. Every once in a while, my mother writes to him, asking him to pay back the 300,000 lire he borrowed from her. My poor mom, it's not like she's rich. She has a little dry goods store back in our village. And then there's my dad's pension. He died. He was a railroad worker. She's not rich. When I got married, she was overjoyed, because she thought I was marrying a rich guy. Instead, we haven't done anything but ask her for money. And whenever my mom comes to visit, she leaves in despair because she sees that we need so many things, that I'm exhausting myself, that we don't even have the sheets and towels we need. We aren't getting anything out of the land. We have to live! Us, the kids, Sofia – all of us are dependent on the land. Take Sofia – her husband hasn't given her a cent in years. She works doing translations for Edoardo. Edoardo doesn't pay her.

SOFIA: Poor Edoardo.

TITINA: To hell with poor Edoardo! Anyway, does this strike you as a good time to hire a secretary?

SOFIA: Don't forget that you guys also owe money to Enrico.

TITINA: *You* guys? *We* owe money to Enrico – including you. You're living with us. We're all in the same boat. The other day you went out and bought yourself a new pair of slacks. Just because we're talking about it, I'll tell you that it's been quite a while since I bought myself anything new to wear.

SOFIA: Eight thousand lire. The last 8,000 lire I had. I have nothing left. I'm afraid you're going to have to give me a loan, Enrico, at least until Edoardo pays me.

TITINA: She's in love with Edoardo. That's why she's working for him, even though he never pays her.

SOFIA: Please don't talk nonsense. Me in love with Edoardo! Can you imagine such a thing! Get out of here, Titina. I need Enrico to take a look at me, because I don't feel well. That's why he's here, after all.

TITINA: I'm not doing so well either. I'm worse than you. I'm completely exhausted. I'm at my wits' end. And Enrico, you have a lot of nerve saying that I'm just fine. I know that I have a serious case of anemia. My uncle, Gaetano, saw me. He's a doctor. He doesn't practise anymore because he helps my mom out in the store, but he has a medical degree. He saw me last Christmas when I went home. As soon as he saw me, he said, 'Good God! You've barely got a drop of blood left in you. It's terrible, terrible anemia.'

Perfetta enters.

PERFETTA: The baby is crying. He's hungry. He's chewing his hands. It's completely pitiful. If you aren't going to come and feed him, I'll do it myself. You know what I'm going to give him? Bread soaked in broth. My sister brought all of her children up on bread soaked in broth, and they've all done better than certain other children I could mention.

Perfetta and Titina exit.

ENRICO: So?
SOFIA: My back hurts. Here. Every time I take a breath.
ENRICO: Where?
SOFIA: Here.
ENRICO: It's nothing. It's just a pulled muscle.
SOFIA: A pulled muscle, you're telling me? Are you sure it's not pneumonia?
ENRICO: No, you don't have pneumonia. You're healthy as a horse.
SOFIA: Please don't talk to me about horses.
ENRICO: Take some aspirin. It'll go away.
SOFIA: And just what are aspirin going to do for a pulled muscle? I don't believe in aspirin. They were prescribing aspirin back before the Flood. No one takes aspirin anymore. Look, Enrico, I've got to get out of this house. You've got to fix me up with something.
ENRICO: Fix you up how?
SOFIA: Don't you need a secretary?
ENRICO: Me? No.

SOFIA: I want to get out of this house! I'm not doing well here. You know, it's not so great, at my age, living with your brother and your sister-in-law. When all is said and done, they're supporting me. I'm a weight. And I always feel like someone who has no business being here. Really, it's my house, too, because my poor daddy left it to both of us – to my brother and to me. But when I'm here, I always feel as though I'm in the way. I always feel they'd be happier – Nino and Titina – if I weren't here. And it's terrible being someone like me, a woman separated from her husband. I don't feel like an old maid, but I'm not a widow either. Take me out of this house, Enrico. Marry me! Why don't you marry me?

ENRICO: How am I supposed to marry you? You're already married.

SOFIA: My husband has dropped off the face of the earth. He hasn't written me for quite a while. They say he's in Venezuela. But he could be dead. Maybe I'm a widow. Anyway, you don't really need to marry me. We could just live together. We can let your mother think I'm a widow and that we got married, since she probably cares about such things.

ENRICO: I can't imagine where you got such an idea.

SOFIA: Why not? I could get your house in order. I'll water the plants. I could keep your mom company. We could play rummy together. Your mom likes me. I'd just be there in your house – peacefully cultivating the roses, reading books.

ENRICO: Why don't you give the roses a little water here at your own house? They look pretty dry.

SOFIA: Because here I don't feel like it. Every once in a while, we could invite someone to have supper with us. It wouldn't be such a bad life.

ENRICO: You and I grew up together. We've been friends since child-hood. We were schoolmates. We see each other constantly. After all this time – seeing each other, talking the way we do together – it's become a habit. We can't transform the friendship habit into a con-jugal habit. It would be a mistake.

SOFIA: Don't you want me? I understand. You don't want me. Never mind. You used to be so in love with me, when we were nineteen. Remember?

ENRICO: Yes.

SOFIA: But in those days, I wasn't interested in you. Then, a little bit later, we spent those few days together in Carnia.[6]

ENRICO: Right.

SOFIA: It was terrible.

ENRICO: Yes.

SOFIA: But maybe that's just because I was feeling so bad. And the cooking in that hotel was a horror. It's strange – I remember so little from those days. I remember that I didn't feel well and I was terribly cold. And there was a stuffed rabbit in our room. How I cried that morning. Why was I crying so hard?

ENRICO: Because you weren't in love with me.

SOFIA: That was it. You were consoling me, but you were so sad at the same time. Because you weren't in love with me either. Because there we were, together, without love. And then I ran away, remember?

ENRICO: Sure. You left me a letter.

SOFIA: Right. When was that? Eight years ago? Ten? And then I went and enrolled in the university and had that ridiculous affair with that Greek actor. And a little after that I got a job with that newspaper, and they sent me to London. And in London I met Filippo, and I married him. And things went wrong pretty fast after that. But we kept on going for quite a few years. I used to get up in the mornings and hide my head under the sheet so I couldn't see his face, on the pillow right next to me. But the moment always came when I had to look at him. He had a face like a Roman emperor. Grand. Well proportioned, with that aquiline nose and olive complexion. He was a beautiful man, but it was precisely the kind of beauty I detested. Why did I marry him? Do you know that I've never stopped asking myself that, in all these years? I would get up and do the laundry on the balcony, where there was a wash basin. You could see a tiny little courtyard from there, with black gutters all around. Do you know why they paint the gutters black in England?

ENRICO: I don't.

SOFIA: I made our meals on a broken-down electric hot plate because the woman who owned the house didn't want a stove. Filippo would get up, get dressed, slip into his camel-hair overcoat, smooth down his collar and the sleeves, smooth down his black hair, and walk out like an emperor. He made publicity posters for a cookie factory. They paid him very badly. We didn't have a cent. I stayed home, cooking on my knees on the floor, and as soon as I heard the old woman go out, I ran and carried the frying pan to the balcony. I spent hours looking out over the balcony, contemplating the walls and the gutters. My husband would come back home, settle himself on the bed, and stare out into space. He was despondent. But not because of money. He was despondent because he had to live with me. I was despondent, too, but we didn't say anything. Between the two of us we built up a huge silence, a swollen, black silence that stretched for endless distances. In all that silence, neither of us did anything but ask ourselves why we were together there, in that room, with that balcony, that wash tub and those gutters. One morning I just took off. I left him a letter. A letter and a plate of food, already cooked, that just needed to be heated up. Kidneys. Kidneys and onions. I took the train and I came back to Italy. I never saw him again. You know something? When I used to stand there looking out over the balcony, I felt this enormous sense of homesickness for Italy. Faced with all those black gutters, the stuffed rabbit, and that hotel in Carnia where I stayed with you, it was almost a delightful memory.

ENRICO: Because it was a memory.

SOFIA: That's right. Time has a way of making things seem less unpleasant than they were, and so we think we must have loved them. But the truth is, it was horrible – even the stuffed rabbit. My entire life has been a series of horrors. And now, if I were to come to live with you, with your mom – playing rummy, taking care of the flowers – after a while I'd find something – even there, in your house – like here, like London, like everywhere, something that would make me want to run away.

ENRICO: Yes.

SOFIA: So. Now what do I do? Where do I go, Enrico? Maybe what really horrifies me are real things. Maybe I'm one of those people who hates reality. Do you think I'm like that?

ENRICO: It's possible.

SOFIA: It's possible! You say it's possible? That's your way of telling me something so frightening, as if it were nothing? You're my friend, you're fond of me, we even used to be lovers, and you tell me such a dreadful thing?

ENRICO: Why shouldn't I tell you the truth? Isn't the truth what you want?

SOFIA: Where am I going to go, Enrico? Where can I go?

ENRICO: I don't know.

SOFIA: Talking to you is really like talking to the wall.

Nino enters.

NINO: Hi, Enrico. I need you to take me to the veterinarian. If we just
    call, he won't come. We have to go get him and bring him here.
ENRICO: I hear you have a secretary.
NINO: Yeah, she's upstairs. Taking a bath. She was feeling sweaty. She
    came all the way from Rome on her Vespa.

Titina enters.

TITINA: Did you tell Perfetta to get the guest room ready?
NINO: Yeah.
TITINA: For that girl? You're thinking of letting her sleep here?
NINO: Certainly. Where do you expect her to sleep? She's my secretary.
TITINA: But I don't want some girl I don't know in the house!
NINO: You'll get to know her. She's a very nice girl.
TITINA: You're out of your mind. Enrico, are you listening to this? He's
    crazy. Call a doctor!
NINO: Don't we already have Enrico here?
TITINA: A doctor for crazy people. He hired a secretary! Enrico, you
    understand our situation: We don't have a cent, we're drowning in
    debt, we've got troubles up to here, and he allows himself to hire a
    secretary.
NINO: None of you understands what's going on here. I don't have to
    pay this girl because Signora Coltellacci is going to pay her. I'm
    doing a favour for Signora Coltellacci. Signora Coltellacci wanted
    to help her out. She met her casually, through friends. She asked
    me to do her a favour and let Silvana work here and she would pay
    her at the end of the month. Actually, she's going to give me the
    money and I'm going to pay her. Signora Coltellacci has a big heart,
    and she felt sorry for the girl. But she can't keep her in her house
    because there isn't room.
TITINA: And why is it that you need to do favours for Signora Coltel-
    lacci? Who the hell is this Signora Coltellacci anyway? Is she one of
    your mistresses?
NINO: No. She's a little old lady. A little old lady with her hair dyed
    red. Very big-hearted. And the girl can help us with the kids. She'll
    help Perfetta in the kitchen. She's ready to do anything. She doesn't
    have a cent. She had to run away from her own house because her
    parents are such frightening creatures. Her mother's half-mad. She
    needs the warmth of a real home.
TITINA: This house doesn't actually give off any heat. It's as cold as the
    bottom of a well in here.

NINO: How do you mean that?

TITINA: In every way it's possible to mean it. The radiators barely work.

NINO: You have no idea what it means to be truly alone in the world, without a home. Forced to sleep in Signora Coltellacci's bathroom.

TITINA: Why? Doesn't Signora Coltellacci have a guest room? I thought she was a rich old lady.

NINO: She is a rich old lady, but she doesn't have a guest room. She has a tiny little apartment, all done in Venetian tiles. Very cute. But it's like the inside of an egg – packed with furniture up to the ceiling. Plus she has a bunch of little dogs.

TITINA: I'm getting out of here. I'm going back to my mom. My little room is always waiting for me there, at home with my mom. Peaceful and sunny, with geraniums in the window. I'm tired. I need a little peace and quiet.

ENRICO: Maybe the girl really will help you with the kids.

TITINA: No. She said she detests children. She ran away from her own house. She's a vagabond. For all we know, she's also a whore and a thief. I'm tired. This house is nothing but a seaport – people come in, they leave, they eat, they sleep.

NINO: Even though no one ever visits and you complain that we never see a living soul?

TITINA: I'm tired, Enrico. I'm pregnant. I'm afraid I'm pregnant. I'm severely anemic. I can barely stand. You know I'm Catholic, Enrico. I am profoundly, deeply Catholic, and that's why I'm against abortion. But I don't want this child. Paolo is only two years old. Furietto is three months old, and I'm still breastfeeding. I need something to get rid of this baby.

ENRICO: Like what?

TITINA: I don't know. Find something. Aren't you a doctor? I have a husband who's crazy. He thinks about nothing but Signora Coltellacci's problems, even as far in over our heads as we are. Help me, Enrico.

NINO: Let's go, Enrico. Drive me to the veterinarian.

TITINA: Sure. The horse is the only thing he thinks about. About that girl, about Signora Coltellacci, and about his horse.

Enrico and Nino exit. Perfetta enters.

PERFETTA: The girl took a bath and flooded everything. Of course it was up to me to bail the water out with a bucket. Meanwhile, I had the potatoes on the stove and they wound up burning.

SOFIA: Couldn't she take a bath at Signora Coltellacci's house?

PERFETTA: She asked me for an extra towel. She said the one Signor Nino gave her was too small. But we seem to be fresh out of big bath towels here. So I gave her Signora Sofia's bathrobe. She said it was damp, but she took it.

SOFIA: How could it be damp? I didn't take a shower this morning and I never used it.

TITINA: I used it.

SOFIA: Why didn't you use your own this morning?

TITINA: Mine's in the dirty-laundry basket.

PERFETTA: Is that girl eating here? Because there won't be much.

TITINA: It'll do.

PERFETTA: Sure, it'll do. It'll do for all of you. I'll put everything on the table and end up with nothing to eat.

TITINA: I'll make you an egg.

PERFETTA: No, you know eggs make me sick.

TITINA: But she's a mouse. She must eat like a mouse.

PERFETTA: She's a mouse? That young woman? Get set for a surprise. Some of these skinny young girls, they eat like there's no tomorrow.

TITINA: I wonder if Signora Coltellacci is also planning on covering her room and board.

Perfetta exits. Silvana enters.

SILVANA: I like this house.

SOFIA: Isn't that nice.

SILVANA: And I really like all the countryside around. The country air does me good. It gives me an appetite.

SOFIA: Today I believe we'll be having potatoes. Our noon menu is usually rabbit with potatoes. Our menu in the evening is caffe latte and braised broccoli. Do you like caffe latte?

SILVANA: Not all that much. But it doesn't matter. A little piece of cheese is enough for me.

SOFIA: A genuine mouse.

SILVANA: Sorry?

SOFIA: Nothing.

TITINA: Signorina, you know, you really can't stay here very long. We're not at all accustomed to having guests.

SILVANA: But I'm not a guest! I'm here to work. All I ask is to make myself useful.

TITINA: Do you know how to sew? Iron? Cook? Do the mending?

SILVANA: I've never done it. But I can try.

TITINA: Didn't your mom teach you anything?

SILVANA: No. I told you what my mother is like. She's neurotic. She spends all her time in bed, in the dark, and rings a little bell. It was three rings for me, two for the maid, four for my father. If nobody came, she'd start making this howling sound, very high-pitched, like a factory siren. She was an ill woman. She had to be treated like one. But I could never really bring myself to do that. I was always trying to reason with her. We fought constantly, and that only made her more despondent. Believe me, nobody was giving much thought to getting the mending done. I couldn't stand my mother anymore, so I packed a bag and I ran away.

TITINA: And how do you think you're going to get along? How did you imagine that someone who doesn't know how to do anything would earn a living?

SILVANA: I enrolled in the Academy of Dramatic Arts. Though I don't think I'm really cut out for a career in acting.

TITINA: And so?

SILVANA: So nothing. For now, it's enough not to be living at home anymore. I'll do whatever I'll have to do.

TITINA: Go into the kitchen. Have you seen where the kitchen is? Have you seen Perfetta? Tell Perfetta to give you the basket of ironing. Do you know how to iron?

SILVANA: No, but I'll try. It can't be all that difficult.

TITINA: On the contrary, it's extremely difficult.

SILVANA: Perfetta will teach me.

TITINA: Perfetta doesn't know how to iron. No one in this house knows how to iron. I'm the only one.

SILVANA: Then you can teach me.

TITINA: Listen, missy. I won't be teaching you anything. I don't have time. I have to tend to the baby. It's already past his feeding time. I need to get the Pelargon ready. Look, you can't stay here. Go back home. Think about your mom. Your mother obviously needs you.

SILVANA: I can't go back to my house, I'm telling you. I'd rather sleep under a bridge or on a park bench. I have a sleeping bag. If you have a sleeping bag, you can sleep anywhere. I could make the Pelargon for him while you do the ironing. I know how to make

Pelargon. I used to do it for my brother.

TITINA: While I do the ironing! So now you're giving the orders? And how come you're so interested in making the Pelargon all of a sudden? Didn't you say that you don't like children much?

SILVANA: You don't really need to love children in order to make a little baby formula.

Titina and Silvana exit. Enrico and Nino enter.

NINO: No veterinarian. He wasn't there. Enrico says maybe I should give him an enema.

SOFIA: Give the horse an enema? Do they give enemas to horses?

NINO: Why not? They give enemas to everyone else. But I have to say I don't have a lot of faith in Enrico's opinion. It seems to me he doesn't really understand that much about horses. He tries to guess. For now, I think I won't do anything. I'll just wait. Where's the secretary?

SOFIA: She went to get the baby's Pelargon ready.

NINO: Good for her. She's pitching right in.

ENRICO: Wasn't Titina giving him Nestogen?

SOFIA: She changed. Now she gives him Pelargon.

NINO: That girl's going to be a big help around here. She's going to solve all of our problems. She'll take care of the children and the house. She can go to town to do the shopping on her Vespa. She's a very simple girl, not at all fussy. She can retype all my notes. I have all these notes scattered all over. Observations, travel diaries, random thoughts. She can put a little bit of order in our lives. She's going to be a great secretary.

SOFIA: Are you sure she knows how to type?

NINO: Of course. If not, she wouldn't be a secretary.

ENRICO: You're going to have to thank Signora Coltellacci. I'd love to meet her in person someday, this Signora Coltellacci. I've heard so much about her.

NINO: Oh, she's just a little old lady with her hair dyed red. With a lot of tiny dogs. But you guys want to know the truth? It's not really true that I brought this girl into the house as a favour to Signora Coltellacci. I told Titina that, but it isn't true. You know who that girl is?

ENRICO: Who is she?

NINO: She's Edoardo's girlfriend.

SOFIA: Edoardo's girlfriend!

ENRICO: Edoardo has a girlfriend? And his wife knows?

NINO: No, she doesn't know anything about it. He says he's in love. He says he's going to leave his wife and go live with that girl. He doesn't know when. He's planning to break the news to Isabellita a little at a time.

ENRICO: And he's the one who asked you to bring her into the house?

NINO: Yes. He begged me. Just for a little while. At least until he leaves his wife. The girl was living with Signora Coltellacci, but Signora Coltellacci couldn't put her up any longer. So I called Signora Coltellacci and told her to send her here. But the two of you can't say anything to Titina. If Titina finds out this is Edoardo's girlfriend, she'll kick her out of the house just like that. She can't stand Edoardo. Besides, she'd accuse me of being immoral, of protecting an adulterer. The truth is, I think Edoardo's never going to decide to leave his wife. Meanwhile, here's this unfortunate girl who doesn't know where to go.

SOFIA: That's Edoardo's girlfriend? A girl like that? A mouse?

NINO: He says he's in love with her. You try to figure it out. I think the whole thing is just a stunt. He's bored, and every once in a while he invents some great love for himself. This has happened a couple of times before.

ENRICO: And the girl? Is she in love with him?

NINO: The girl? Yes. He says she is. But you see how she acts. She's a little lizard. One of these girls you see around nowadays. They have no real thoughts of their own. They have no future.

SOFIA: A mouse.

ENRICO: Exactly. Mice and lizards have no future. What they have instead are sad little eyes that look straight at you. They scamper here and they scamper there. They hide under rocks. They never ask for anything and they don't have anything to give anyone.

SOFIA: Edoardo has never spoken a word to me about this girl. And yet he's more my friend than he is yours.

NINO: Maybe he and I aren't so close, but the other night he confided in me. We went for a walk for a couple of hours, the two of us. Up and down along the Muro Torto.[7] He was right there next to me. He's a small guy, you know. With all that long, grey curly hair, the collar of his overcoat all worn out, his little bow tie. When he talks, he's always waving his hands around under his chin, under his nose. Delicate, white hands, always a little bit dirty, because he never bathes. But he said he was thinking of leaving his wife. That his relationship with his wife is over and done with. They've nothing left to say to each other. But what he ever found to say to his wife, I don't know. He met this girl several months ago, I think in Signora Coltellacci's store, and he fell in love. But of course he had to fall in love with her, because she's a kind of lizard, elusive, melancholy, indecipherable. When he has her figured out, he'll stop loving her. He must like Isabellita for the same reason, because in her own way, she's another indecipherable being.

SOFIA: I don't know what makes you say Isabellita is indecipherable. She's a polenta. Not much mystery in polenta.

NINO: That's your opinion. Isabellita is a being who is full of mystery. She's grand, motionless, dense as a mountain. As an ox. Oxen, mountains – they're full of mystery.

ENRICO: So now he wants to leave his wife?

NINO: Yes. He told me he wants to leave her. To be with that girl. He wants to give up the publishing house, the mystery novels, that magazine that he hasn't even started yet, and do something else with himself. What, exactly, he doesn't know yet. He's thinking – study astrology or mathematics. But he's fed up with everything he's been doing up to now.

SOFIA: And Isabellita? What's she supposed to do if he leaves her?

NINO: But he won't leave her. I don't believe it. It's all talk. He'll go back home in the evening, after he walks around for a while and amuses himself talking about it. He'll slide into bed, where Isabellita will already be sleeping. Right away he'll find Isabellita's big, fat rump, and he'll warm himself against it as though he were leaning against the stove. He has a little bottle of wine on the floor next to the bed, and before he falls asleep he'll toss back a couple of good belts. In the morning he won't get up. He'll stay there in bed with the pink comforter, and meanwhile Isabellita will be going back and forth in that light blue dressing gown she has, with her bleach-blond hair, still all sleepy. Then he'll dictate a few letters, and she'll start typing real slow, with just one finger. Then those guys they know from their hometown will show up, all dressed in black – because they're always dressed in black – and they'll sit around on the bed, discussing politics. Edoardo doesn't understand a damn thing about politics, but he'll have his say. Then Gildo will drop by, and they'll continue the discussion – him, Edoardo, the guys. Politics, finances, the magazine, the mystery novels. Isabellita, as always, will keep her mouth shut, towering over everyone like a mountain. Then the Conocchias will come over, and by then conversation will pretty much have dried up. So they'll all sit down to have their Tarot cards read. And then, all of them together, they'll make themselves something for lunch, they'll eat, they'll drink wine. That's Edoardo's life. It's never going to change. He's not going to run off with that girl. Of course he isn't.

ENRICO: You talk about it so cheerfully. The picture you paint of Edoardo is one of a happy man. But I believe him to be, in fact, a man who is profoundly unhappy. I don't believe either his wife or his girlfriend matter to him at all. I think he's one of those guys who studies and analyses his life down to the tiniest detail. His life, his intelligence, his relationships. Day after day. They grind him up, they tear at him, they toss him around. He's mincemeat.

SOFIA: Poor Edoardo.

ENRICO: Poor Edoardo. Right.

Titina enters.

TITINA: I've just had a telegram from my Uncle Gaetano. My mom has pleural pneumonia. It's very serious. I have to go right away. What shall I do? Who am I going to leave the babies with?

SOFIA: I'm here. Perfetta's here. Even the secretary's here.

TITINA: Nobody who really loves children. You couldn't give a damn. You have absolutely no feeling for children. Perfetta – you know what she's like. Unpleasant. Anyway, about the secretary: I fired her.

NINO: You fired her?

TITINA: Yes. I told her to prepare the baby's Nestogen. You have to mix it up really well with a fork. But she didn't mix it right and it turned out all full of lumps. She must have gotten the measurements wrong.

SOFIA: Weren't you giving him Pelargon?

TITINA: I changed my mind. I decided to give him Nestogen.

NINO: What right do you have to fire my secretary? I won't let her leave. She's staying right here. You know, it's not exactly a crime to make a mistake mixing powdered milk.

TITINA: That's what you say: It's not a crime. And if the baby comes down with gastroenteritis? I grabbed the bottle out of her hands and I poured the milk down the sink. I told her to get out of my

way. She told me I was an old fool. I called her a viper. Then I
  slapped her.

SOFIA: She's not a viper. She's a lizard. A mouse.

TITINA: I don't have any idea what I'm supposed to do with mice. You
  have to give me some money, Nino. And I also need the train schedule. My mom is very, very ill. I don't even know if I'll find her alive.

NINO: I don't keep any money in the house. Maybe Enrico can loan
  you some.

TITINA: Call Enrico. Tell him to bring us some money. And the train
  schedule. And a suitcase. The zipper is broken on mine. Who's
  going to watch the children?

NINO: What do you mean call Enrico? Can't you see that Enrico is right
  here?

TITINA: Oh, right, Enrico. I didn't see you. I'm all upset. Well, get a
  move on. Go on home and bring me back the things I need.

NINO: You get a move on, too, Sofia. Go find the girl and see if you can
  calm her down. Make her stay.

Silvana enters.

SILVANA: I think I'd better go. The Signora doesn't want me here. She
  called me a viper. I called her an old fool. Then she slapped me –
  just a little. I wasn't actually offended. I seem to be someone whom
  other people like to slap. My mom used to do it too. I don't really
  feel one way or another about it. But I do think I should leave.
  The Signora doesn't like me. Though I don't like her all that much
  either. So that's why I'm going. I feel bad about it because I liked it
  here. Anyway, I can always sleep outdoors. I have my sleeping bag.

TITINA: Look, you. I don't know you. I don't know who you are or how
  you wound up here. I don't want you underfoot. I don't have time
  to concern myself with your problems. I have to leave because my
  mother is ill. What are you still doing here, Enrico? Get moving!
  I need you to get me those things! I'm going to have to travel the
  entire night. This is too much of a strain. After the train there's the
  bus that jerks and rattles the entire way. I'm afraid this trip is going
  to make me lose the baby.

SOFIA: Isn't that what you want?

TITINA: Shut up. This could kill me. What am I going to do if as soon
  as I get there I've got to go straight to bed? Who's going to help me?
  Who's going to help my mother?

Perfetta enters.

PERFETTA: The horse is dead.

NINO: No!

PERFETTA: Oh, yes. He's dead.

NINO: And that's how you choose to tell me about it?

PERFETTA: How should I tell you about it?

ACT THREE

[*The same house, not quite a year later.*]

SOFIA: Hello, Luisa? Hi Luisa. I'm coming to Rome tomorrow to have
lunch with you. Don't make me tripe. I have a ton of things to tell
you about. Since you got back from Paris we haven't seen each
other even for a minute. It's been a while since we've chatted. How
long were you gone? Eight months. That's a while. Yes, I'm in bed.
I'm finishing my translation. It's a mystery novel. They find a body
on an airplane, in the airplane lavatory, a man, and nobody knows
who he is because his name doesn't appear on the passenger list.
He's got a playing card in his wallet with the address of a motel
scribbled on it. They go to the motel and they find another dead
body in the elevator, and he's also got a playing card in his pocket.
And they go on like that, from body to body, until they get to the
Ace of Spades, and that's in the pocket of a girl – but she's still alive,
serving soup in a homeless shelter. Drugs are involved. Has he paid
me? Of course not. But you know what? Now Signora Coltellacci
may take over the publishing house. Gildo's going to be in charge
of it. Yes, Gildo. Your former tenant. Now Gildo's got a gorgeous
penthouse with wall-to-wall carpet. He's not coming back to your
place, so don't even think about it. The penthouse belongs to the
Conocchias, and they aren't making him pay any rent. You, on the
other hand, were making him pay 15,000 lire every month for that
hole of a room. He never paid you? Well of course he couldn't, poor
Gildo. Edoardo owes him a pile of money. But he'll never see it.
Maybe you ran into my husband when you were in Paris? Someone
told me that he's in Paris now. I can't recall who, maybe Gildo. Did
you know that Edoardo and Isabellita aren't together anymore? No.
No, they're not together anymore. If you only knew how many

things went on while you were gone. Isabellita is staying with the
Conocchias. She's looking for an apartment. What? You mean that
room you've got? But it's a hole. No, she's looking for a full-sized
apartment of her own. Yeah, she broke up with Edoardo. It's a
pretty definite breakup. She says he wanted to adopt an orphan. It
happened a little while after you left. You remember that girl who
came by here? The secretary? Well, she was Edoardo's girlfriend.
Yes. And just think that I wound up staying here alone with her,
after Nino and Titina left. Titina's mother had died. It was just us,
alone with the babies and with Perfetta and we were getting along
fine. We almost wound up becoming friends. Enrico would come
by in the evenings and the girl would play the guitar. Well, so then
one day she tried to kill herself. I go in her room and I see that she's
sleeping. After a little while I go back and she's still sleeping. I got
scared and called Enrico, but he wasn't there. I found a little tube of
sleeping pills on the floor. I call Edoardo. He isn't in. Only Isabellita
is there. I tell her, 'Get Edoardo over here right away because his
girlfriend has committed suicide.' Just like that. I lost my head. I
call an ambulance. Meanwhile, Enrico arrives. He leaves with the
girlfriend in the ambulance. After a little bit, Edoardo and Isabellita
arrive. He's pale, her hair's a mess, and she's wearing her fur coat
on top of her night shirt. I went into a crying jag and just started
insulting everyone, Edoardo, Isabellita, everyone. Up until that
moment Isabellita had no idea the girlfriend even existed. So she
went into a crying jag, too. What a night. The babies woke up and
started howling and Perfetta was going around like a ghost with
her eyes as wide as saucers. Isabellita was sobbing and Edoardo
threw himself onto the sofa like a dead man. Finally, in the morning, Enrico comes back. He says the girl is better. Edoardo and
Isabellita take off. I go to their house in the afternoon and find
Isabellita packing her bags. She says: 'I'm not going to tolerate
infidelity. Not even a little. I'm an old-fashioned woman. I can take
a lot of things, but infidelity isn't one of them.' Edoardo? Edoardo
was stretched out on the daybed with a down comforter on top of
him. Silent. Pale. A corpse. The Conocchias show up, and Isabellita
takes off with them. So I'm alone with Edoardo, trying to drag a
word or two out of him. Nothing. I go to see the girlfriend. She
hasn't got a word to say either. I say to her, 'Why did you want to
kill yourself.' Silence. I don't know what was up with her. Right up
until the night before she was happy and playing the guitar. Then,

she takes a bottle of sleeping pills. Why? Why not? No way to drag an explanation out of her. Enrico called her father in Viterbo. The father comes, a tall, handsome man with black eyeglasses. Not at all impressed. He says it's a family habit. That all of them have bad cases of nerves. So as soon as she's on her feet again, he brings her back home to Viterbo. But she doesn't stay at home for even a month. She goes back to Rome again. She goes to stay with Edoardo. So Edoardo and the girlfriend live together for a while. A few weeks. Meanwhile, Isabellita is having fits and crying all day long at the Conocchias' house. They're giving her Sedobrol and trying to console her. Well, so then the girlfriend comes back here. Yes, here! She's back with us again. The evening when she showed up here again, Titina started screaming that she didn't want her in the house. She'd just come back from visiting her family. She was still in mourning, pregnant, nauseous, in absolutely the worst mood. You bet she didn't want that girl there. She never really liked her much, and of course now she's jealous. After the whole story of Edoardo came out, she decided that girl had some kind of power over men – a public menace in that little mouse! Nino and I tried to get her to calm down. We called Enrico. Enrico explained that they couldn't just throw her out of the house, because who knew if she might try to kill herself again. Anyway, bottom line: the girl is still here with us. 'Til when? Who knows? Edoardo? Poor Edoardo. He's still there. In his house on Via degli Incappucciati. His place has turned into a real cave. No one ever opens a window. The Conocchias sent one of their old housekeepers two or three times, but then she insisted she wasn't going to go back there, that Edoardo was nice enough but he had made it clear that he found her annoying. So there he is, stretched out on his daybed, smoking one cigarette after another. He doesn't eat, he just drinks. My God, how he drinks. Remember that magazine he was starting? *The Wigeon*? Well, they put out one single issue. One of those strange guys Edoardo always had around gave him an article that was rather pro-Chinese, and Edoardo published it in *The Wigeon* without reading it. You know how he is, it's difficult to get him to actually read anything. Anyway, that was right when the whole drama of that girl was starting up. So Princess Farina was absolutely furious about the article and cut off his funding. So bye-bye *Wigeon*. Nighty-night. No one would ever dream that Edoardo was pro-Chinese. He barely understands the first thing about politics. Of course, out of spite, he immediately became pro-Chinese. He tore a picture of Mao out of some magazine and tacked it to the head of his bed. Poor Edoardo. He's so alone. Whatever became of that girl, I'm sure I don't know. As for her, she doesn't want to hear a word about Edoardo. She said she left him because, if she hadn't, she'd have started feeling the urge to commit suicide again. What do you expect? Edoardo is a sadist. A sado-masochist. All you need to do is see what he's made of his own life. He's an intelligent man. So full of life. So fascinating. Everyone wanted to hear what he had to say. So he took up with Isabellita, who's a cretin. Then he fell in love with that girl, who's a lizard. He's taken his life and broken it into pieces. He's thrown it all away. He's made mincemeat out of it. (*She begins to cry.*) What? No, no, I'm not really crying. None of this matters to me. It's none of my business. Maybe Isabellita would get back together with him, but now he's the one who doesn't want her anymore. He doesn't want the girl either. He doesn't want anyone. Not a thing. I'm going to say goodbye, Luisa. Okay? Bye-bye. (*She cries. She blows her nose. She dials another number.*) Hello, Gildo? Hi, Gildo. You need to go see Edoardo and find out if he needs anything. You need to take him a little something to eat. I don't know if the guys are going to stop over today, but even if they do, they never bring him anything to eat. They don't have a cent among them. Yes, I know you don't have a cent either, but you can always get the Conocchias to give you a loan. What would the Conocchias have to keep themselves busy if people didn't ask them for money? I'll be in Rome tomorrow and I'll go see Edoardo. The girl? The girl is fine. I don't know where she is. I think Titina may have palmed the kids off on her. Good with children? You must be kidding. She detests kids. She has to look after them, but I don't know if she really keeps an eye on them. She sits on the swing and reads Freud while they play. Gildo, did you know that Luisa was back? Who is she? What do you mean who is she? She's my friend who rented you the room. I say 'rented' just as a figure of speech because you never paid her. You brought your aunts, your cousins, your grandmothers all to stay there, without ever bothering to shell out so much as five cents in rent. You've made me look completely horrid in front of her. Yes, horrid. Let's not talk about it. Couldn't you at least take her a bunch of roses? You don't have any money? I know you don't have any money. But you can go cut the roses in Enrico's garden. Okay, fine. When I go tomorrow I'll bring you some of Enrico's roses and you wrap them up in some lovely tissue paper and take them to Luisa. You also need me to bring tissue paper? You can buy some at the store for ten lire. You're so annoying, Gildo. (*She hangs up the phone.*)

Titina enters.

TITINA: You do nothing but talk on the telephone. That explains why we pay a truly frightening figure for the phone each month.

SOFIA: The telephone is my only comfort.

TITINA: Aren't you lucky to have such a comfort. I have none at all.

SOFIA: You have a husband and children. That means you don't need comfort. You have the essentials.

TITINA: I'm tired. Everything is weighing on me.

SOFIA: The essentials are always heavy.

TITINA: I'd be happy to do without the essentials. I'm tired. I'm exhausted. At night, I tumble into bed like a dead woman. All day long I slog along like a workhorse.

SOFIA: Let's not talk about horses.

TITINA: When my poor mamma was alive, I always used to think that at least I could go back to her if I needed to rest. To my house, my village, my little room. There were geraniums on the windowsill. What peace. Now my mamma's house has been sold and I don't have a home anymore. This should be my home, but I never have a moment of peace here. Everything's always so dull. You type and you make telephone calls, you make telephone calls and you type. Nino comes and goes in his muddy boots, fixated on his own affairs, his record albums, then the girl, the veterinarian, and the horses. I'm the one who carries the weight of the entire household, and no one addresses a word to me. Nino doesn't even remember I exist. He doesn't see me anymore.

SOFIA: Are you jealous of that girl?

TITINA: No. I'm not jealous. I don't have time to be jealous. But I am sick of having her here. I don't know why we have to be responsible for a girl who is nothing to us, who means nothing to anyone. Once upon a time, families were what was important.

SOFIA: What do you mean, families?

TITINA: That's right, families. Each family was a kind of enclosed shell. Now that families don't exist anymore ... people come, people go, the door is always open to anyone, you get yourself involved with the first person who comes along as if he were your dearest relative. Strangers show up in your house and start making a nest. Can you explain to me why that girl is here? Nino says it's not a good time to tell her to be on her way. Because who knows, if we put her out on the street she might try to kill herself again. What a lovely gift he's given us, your friend Edoardo.

SOFIA: Poor Edoardo.

TITINA: Not only is he taking advantage of you by making you trans-late those novels and then never paying you, we also have to keep his stupid mistress in the house. The secretary. What a wonderful secretary! She doesn't even know how to type. She can't fry an egg. Want me to tell you something, Sofia? We are never going to be rid of her. She's stuck to us like glue. She's like a sickness. Like cancer.

SOFIA: Oh come on. She'll go. One fine day, she'll just up and leave.

TITINA: She's never going to leave. Actually, she did leave, then she came back. We're going to have her forever.

SOFIA: But what trouble is she really? She helps around the house a little. Yesterday she cleaned the staircases.

TITINA: Yes – cleaned them so well that I had to do it all over again. You shush, Sofia. You don't like that girl, either. She's caused us a lot of trouble. It bothers you, too, to have her here. Because she was Edoardo's girlfriend. You suffer when you have to see her around, because you're always thinking that she went to bed with him and you didn't.

SOFIA: You know how little I care? Who Edoardo goes to bed with doesn't matter to me a bit. I don't feel one way or the other about it.

TITINA: You're in love with Edoardo, Sofia.

SOFIA: I'm not in love with anyone.

Enrico enters.

SOFIA: Hi, Enrico.

TITINA: Oh, Enrico. You're just who I wanted to see. I was wondering if I could increase the amount of Guigoz I give the baby. Right now I'm giving him seven and a half scoops in three parts water. He just turned ten months yesterday.

ENRICO: Weren't you giving him Pelargon?

SOFIA: She changed. Now she gives him Guigoz.

ENRICO: By now you could be giving him cow's milk.

TITINA: Cow's milk? No, I don't really trust cow's milk.

ENRICO: Why do you ask my advice if you don't have any intention of following it?

TITINA: That kid never lets me sleep. Before long, the new baby will be here and he'll be crying too. I'll never get any sleep. Sometimes I think I'll never be able to sleep again.

SOFIA: You should have the new baby sleep with the secretary.

TITINA: Why don't we quit calling her the secretary? She's not a secretary. She's not even a maid. Actually, I haven't figured out what she's doing here.

ENRICO: She's only going to be here with you for a little while longer.

TITINA: Really? And why is that?

ENRICO: Because we're going to get married soon. That's actually what I came to tell you. We're getting married in September.

SOFIA: You've decided to marry her? You're marrying the mouse?

ENRICO: Yes. I'm going to marry the mouse.

TITINA: I'm stunned, Enrico. I didn't have any idea you'd set your cap for her.

ENRICO: I didn't set my cap for her. I don't set my cap for people, as you quaintly put it. Very simply, a little while ago I started to think that I might like to be able to marry her. I told her as much, yesterday when we took a walk together. She said yes.

TITINA: I'm sure. It would have been amazing if she'd told you no. Marrying you, a wealthy doctor, a landowner. Her, a little lizard with no place to live. Not even a half-slip to her name. You're so naive, Enrico. Naive and old-fashioned. You go to her to ask for her hand in marriage. No one does that anymore.

Nino enters.

NINO: I need a screwdriver. The switch on the electric pump is broken. There's no water for the horses.

TITINA: Horses are the only thing he has any compassion for. Inside, we could all be dying of thirst – he wouldn't go to any trouble. For his horses he can be bothered to stir himself.

SOFIA: Enrico's going to marry the mouse.

NINO: What mouse?

SOFIA: Silvana. The girl. Our secretary.

NINO: I know. He told me. It may not be a bad idea.

TITINA: It's a terrible idea. Once upon a time there was one balanced person here, someone with his head firmly on his shoulders – and that was Enrico. I used to find that comforting. Now even he's lost his bearings. Getting married to that little loser. We should get ready for a shock. Hail to the king. I thank God because at least He's getting her out from under our feet. But I'm sorry for you, Enrico. And for your mother. What is your mother going to say?

ENRICO: I don't know. I still haven't told her.

NINO: Enrico must have fallen in love with her when he went with her to the hospital. He's used to falling in love with sick people. But I'm glad you're marrying her, Enrico. She's a fine young woman. And she needs affection – a simple, calm, steady affection. Edoardo's emotional life was too complicated for her. She's just a girl. A poor little lizard on the run, a pitiful mouse. She needs someone who'll protect her. And maybe you need someone to protect, Enrico.

TITINA: As far as I'm concerned, Enrico, you couldn't possibly sink any lower. But of course it doesn't matter to me. It's your business. I'm just happy you're getting her out from under our feet. I can hardly wait until she's not underfoot anymore, with her Vespa, her backpack, her guitar. And us with the eternal nightmare that she's going to get it into her head to kill herself. I've become selfish, Enrico. The first thing I think of is whether something is to my advantage. I've become selfish and cynical. I didn't used to be. When I was a little girl I was romantic, sentimental. But you see what I've become. I don't give a damn about anyone else, Enrico. Marry whomever you want.

NINO: Of course he's going to marry whomever he wants. That's all we need – for him to have to ask your permission before marrying someone.

SOFIA: And Silvana? Is she happy to marry you? Has she already forgotten Edoardo?

TITINA: You're so naive, Sofia. She hasn't 'forgotten' Edoardo simply because he has never actually existed in her mind. This is what young women are like nowadays – odd, ridiculous, heartless, no emotions, no memories. Little mice. Wherever they happen to find themselves, they make a nest. They eat whatever crumbs they can find. Edoardo forgotten? You make me laugh! You make the mistake of thinking you and she come from the same species. You're the one who needs to forget Edoardo, not her. That's right, you, Sofia. You're in love with Edoardo. Everyone knows it.

SOFIA: If I were in love with Edoardo, I'd go be with him, now that he's alone.

TITINA: Naturally. But you don't go because he doesn't want you. He
doesn't want to have a thing to do with you. It's obvious.

NINO: Nothing's obvious when it comes to Edoardo. It's very hard to
understand him. The only thing that is certain is that he no longer
has any desire to live.

ENRICO: True, he doesn't want to live anymore.

NINO: So have you got that screwdriver, Enrico?

ENRICO: Me? Why would I be running around with a screwdriver? I
have one at home.

NINO: So let's go get it. Meanwhile, I'll show you the horse. I have a
new horse, an absolute beauty. The Connocchias sold it to me. I'm
paying them in instalments. But I'm not quite as fond of this horse
as I was of the other one who died on me a few months back. Now
that I think of it, it died the day the secretary arrived. That was a
special horse. Unique. I loved him the way you'd love your father.

ENRICO: Or a son?

NINO: No. Not a son. Like a father. I could tell by the way he looked at
me. I could feel a kind of paternal protectiveness.

Perfetta enters.

PERFETTA: Do any of you need anything? Because I thought I would go
down to the village for a bit. I want to watch television at the bar.

NINO: Give me a hand first carrying the couch out to the stable. I don't
have any place to sit when I go out there to listen to music: I put the
record player out there. The horse is crazy about music. You should
see how attentively he listens, Enrico.

TITINA: What couch? You can't mean the one in the hallway?

NINO: Yes. That's the one.

TITINA: No. That one belonged to my poor mother. I don't want it to
wind up in the stable.

PERFETTA: Take the couch down there? Couldn't you have told me
earlier? My sister is waiting for me. And I really don't think I
can manage the strain. I had to have my appendix removed. The
wound gets irritated for the slightest reason. Really, it would be
better if you carried the couch down there yourselves. You and the
doctor. You're men. Excuse me, Signora Sofia, can you lend me your
raincoat? It's raining, and I'm not supposed to get my head wet. It'll
make me sick.

SOFIA: Take it.

PERFETTA: Thank you. (*She leaves.*)

TITINA: I promise you trouble if you touch that couch.

NINO: We'll talk about it later. Come on, Enrico. You know, I don't know what we're going to do without our secretary. She did so much. She cleaned out the stables. She cleaned out the rabbit coops. She looked after the children. A darling person.

TITINA: Darling. Really darling. She doesn't know how to sew on a button. Poor Enrico. He couldn't have made a worse choice. But it doesn't matter. I'm just glad that she's not going to be underfoot anymore.

Nino and Titina exit. Silvana enters.

SILVANA: I helped Perfetta peel the potatoes. I cut my finger. Do you have a bandage, Sofia?

SOFIA: No. Enrico might.

SILVANA: I'll see if he can give me one.

SOFIA: So you're getting married.

SILVANA: Yes. I'm getting married.

SOFIA: Are you happy?

SILVANA: Not happy or unhappy. I don't know.

SOFIA: Do you love Enrico?

SILVANA: I don't know. He seems to me to be a very reasonable, fair person. If he wants to marry me, maybe that means it would be for the best.

SOFIA: And Edoardo? You're not in love with him any more?

SILVANA: He tormented me. He made me feel terrible. He made me want to die.

SOFIA: Why?

SILVANA: I don't know why. He would talk and talk and I never understood anything. It was agonizing. Or else he would go mute and I couldn't drag a syllable out of him. He was like this vast darkness. A nightmare. Anguish itself. I was dying. I wanted to die. I wanted to try being with a fair man, a calm man. I wanted to see if I could manage not to think about dying all the time.

SOFIA: And Edoardo? Did you ever stop to think that maybe he also suffered when you left him?

SILVANA: We were together for just those two weeks. He was always stretched out on that daybed of his, with a comforter. Apricot-coloured. One morning Isabellita comes to take back the comforter.

She snatches it off him and stuffs it into her bag. She looks at me.
I look at her. She hauls off and slaps me. I'm used to slaps. My
mother used to give me quite a few of them. I burst out laughing. Edoardo started laughing, too. He was drunk. I was drunk,
too, because whenever he was drinking he used to make me drink
with him. Isabellita takes off with the comforter. The two of us
start laughing all over again. The best times with Edoardo were
the laughs we had now and again. But that was the last time we
laughed. That morning, when we quit laughing, he turned mute. I
looked at him and saw his face was grey, hollowed out, his mouth
looked bitter. And suddenly I was gripped by the most terrible
sense of hopelessness. There he was in bed, without the comforter
anymore, his feet in wool socks all full of holes. I said to him, 'Did
you love Isabellita?' And he said, 'Yes, I loved her. She was my
wife.' I said, 'And me.' 'What about you?' 'What am I?' He turned
and held out his hand – he has long, thin hands, always filthy – and
he tugged on my hair a little. A few more days passed with him in
complete silence. Then one day he told me that I needed to leave
because he wanted to be alone for a while. I asked him, 'Do you
want me to call Isabellita.' And he said, 'No.' He wanted to be alone.
Not with Isabellita and not with me. Alone. He told me, 'Do you
know what you've been for me? A way to break free of Isabellita.
Nothing else. I wanted her to get out of here and I made use of you.
Completely unconsciously, you know. Unconsciously. But that's
what I wanted, in my unconscious. To be alone.' I said to him, 'You
understand that words like that are enough to make me kill myself.'
And he said, 'The worst thing is that nothing matters to me anymore. Who kills himself, who doesn't kill himself. I don't feel one
way or the other about it. I'm far away from you, so very far away.
I've broken the sound barrier. Go on, get out of here, stupid little
girl, leave me alone. I'm dead.' So I took my guitar, my backpack,
my windbreaker. I said, 'Bye.' He turned his head toward the wall
and said, 'Bye.' I left. I called Signora Coltellacci. She wasn't there.
I called Enrico. He came. We went to pick up my Vespa, which I'd
left in Signora Coltellacci's garage. And then I came back here.

SOFIA: And you decided to marry Enrico.

SILVANA: Right. Because I don't know what else to do. I don't know
where to go.

SOFIA: I'm glad. So you'll stay close by. I've started to be very fond of
you.

SILVANA: Maybe I'll be all right with Enrico.

SOFIA: Do you want to have children?

SILVANA: No. You know I detest children. And you? Do you want to have children, Sofia?

SOFIA: With whom?

SILVANA: I don't know.

SOFIA: I wouldn't know who to have children with. My husband has dropped off the face of the earth.

SILVANA: Is it true that you're in love with Edoardo, Sofia?

SOFIA: Who told you that?

SILVANA: Enrico told me.

SOFIA: It's true. Only he doesn't love me. He was probably the only man I could have gotten along with, and I was the only woman he could have gotten along with, but he didn't understand that ... he didn't want me. So ... that's that.

SILVANA: Life is such an ugly thing. Miserable. Filthy. It really makes you feel like dying.

Enrico, Titina, and Nino enter.

TITINA: The sooner you get married the better, Enrico. I admit I'm saying that for personal reasons. I can't wait for you to take that girl out of here. I've never been able to stand her. The only thing I'm sorry about is that afterwards we may not see each other much anymore. Since you're marrying a woman I find unpleasant, I won't be able to have you over to the house as often. I'll just call you when I need you.

NINO: You need Enrico seven times a day. Every time one of the children bats an eyelash or yawns, or rubs his ear, you immediately send someone to call Enrico.

TITINA: Okay. I have a very apprehensive nature. But from now on, I'm going to use Enrico as a doctor and nothing else. As a friend – perhaps not any longer, because he's marrying a woman I don't like.

ENRICO: Maybe you'll get to know her and you'll love her.

TITINA: I already know her too well. I've had her in the house for quite a while. I have always said to her, with complete frankness, that I didn't like her. She stayed anyway. She has no pride. That's how these modern young women are. They're without pride, without dignity. Young women who never, ever blush. Youth today can take all the humiliation the world has to offer without blushing or going pale. Just like that one there. She's looking at me, giggling. I can say anything I want about her, right to her face. She's good for nothing. She doesn't make the bed. She just pulls the sheets up without really making the bed again, ever. She doesn't wash her hair. That's the wife you chose, Enrico.

ENRICO: She'll change.

TITINA: No. You're mistaken. She won't change. Instead, she's only going to get worse. I'd like to see the expression on your mother's face when she shows up at her house.

ENRICO: My mother very much wants me to get married.

TITINA: I went to have tea with your mother a few days ago. She said to me, 'That crazy girl with a guitar, what is she still doing in your house? Hasn't she managed to cause enough trouble already?' If she'd only been able to imagine, poor woman, that the guitar was about to become her daughter-in-law.

The telephone rings.

SOFIA: Hello? Isabellita? Hello. What do you want? Nino? Yes, he's here. What's happened, Isabellita? Edoardo? What happened to Edoardo. Out with it, you idiot. What?

Nino takes the receiver.

NINO: Hello? Yes? What? Oh! Yes, right away. I'm on my way. (*He hangs up.*)

ENRICO: Is Edoardo ill?

NINO: He shot himself.

ENRICO: Is he dead?

NINO: Yes.

SILVANA: Dead? Edoardo is dead?

TITINA: He killed himself, yes. He shot himself. Do you understand? And it's your fault. Because you fooled around with him for a while and then you got tired of it and you dumped him. People like you, they don't kill themselves, they only pretend they're going to kill themselves, in order to attract attention, in order to be on centre stage. But there are also real people, who kill themselves and who die for real. Poor Edoardo.

NINO: Come on, Enrico. We've got to get to Rome right away. Poor Isabellita.

Enrico and Nino exit.

TITINA: To hell with poor Isabellita. She shouldn't have left him either. For a few infidelities. I wouldn't leave Nino for a few infidelities. I'd stand by him. Marriage is a serious thing. Today people have gotten into the habit of tossing it out the window. Life, too – you don't just throw it away. Life isn't something you should toss out like a bucket of water. Does that make you cry, Sofia? Are you crying? You have good reason to cry. He was your love. But take a look at this girl here. She isn't crying. There's not a tear on her face. She takes, she grabs, she goes, she comes back, she takes one man, she takes another one, throws the first one away, throws the other one away. Without a tear. Without a shiver. Without a twitch. Just like that.

SILVANA: Leave me alone. Please, please, leave me alone.

TITINA: Leave me alone! How convenient. You live in my house for month after month. You eat, drink, sleep in my house. At least I have the right to tell you what I think of you. And what I think is that you're a little whore. A viper, with poison in your teeth. When you finally get out of here, I'll be able to breathe again. Every morning I used to wake up and say to Nino, 'When is she going to leave?' And he would say, 'Be patient. She'll go, as soon as she gets herself situated.' But I was afraid. For myself, for Nino, for the children. I'm afraid of vipers. I'm afraid of mice.

Enrico enters.

ENRICO: My car won't start. And Nino's is in the shop for repairs. Sofia, give me the keys to your Seicento.

TITINA: Her Seicento stops every ten metres.

SOFIA: No. Not any more. I had it fixed. I'm coming with you, Enrico.

ENRICO: No, Sofia. Maybe it's better if you don't come.

Perfetta enters.

PERFETTA: The baby is awake and he's crying.

TITINA: Go pick him up.

PERFETTA: No. I can't look after the baby, too. I've got a meal to prepare. It's not like I have twenty arms.

TITINA: Enrico!

ENRICO: Hmm?

TITINA: I don't feel very well, Enrico. It's close to my time. I felt a contraction. What am I going to do if I go into labour tonight? Someone better stay here. Either you or Nino. To take me to the clinic, if I start having labour pains.

ENRICO: There's Sofia. If that happens, Sofia will take you to the clinic.

TITINA: No. Don't you see what condition Sofia is in? Anyway, how is she supposed to take me to the clinic, on foot? What do the two of you have to do in the city? Especially now that Edoardo is dead. There's nothing more to be done for him. We need to think of the living, not of the dead. I don't want to stay here alone in the house tonight.

Nino enters.

NINO: Are we going, Enrico?

ENRICO: Your wife is afraid to stay here alone in the house tonight.

TITINA: Without a man. Without a car. I am afraid. I'm close to my time. Have you forgotten that I'm close to my time? You're going to leave me like this?

SILVANA: There's my Vespa. If you feel bad tonight.

TITINA: Right. I'll go to the clinic on your Vespa. In labour.

PERFETTA: Your stomach is still high. The baby hasn't dropped yet. He's not coming tonight, this baby. It'll be another month. When the moon changes. When the moon changes, you'll have him. You hear that the other one is crying? One of you needs to go get his bottle ready.

TITINA: I feel terrible. You, girl, go get the baby's bottle ready. Do something. Try to make yourself useful. Eight parts Pelargon. Three parts water.

SILVANA: Weren't you giving him Guigoz?

TITINA: I changed. Now I'm giving him Pelargon.

NINO: How about those keys? The keys to the Seicento?

SOFIA: I had them in the pocket of my slacks. Where are my slacks?

PERFETTA: Your slacks? They must have gotten left out in the stall. The Signore was wearing them yesterday because his were full of mud.

Perfetta, Titina, Silvana, Nino exit.

SOFIA: Poor Edoardo, Enrico. Poor Edoardo. (*She cries.*) I was so in love with him. But I never told him. I was sure he didn't want me. Maybe he didn't want me, but who knows whether it might have helped him to know how much I loved him? And now, how am I going to go on living? What do I have to live for? I'm stuck here, in my room, translating those idiotic novels for him. It was the only thing I could do for him. I was happy, because I knew he existed. Drunk, dirty, full of debts – he didn't have a thing; he didn't even have a wife. But he existed. I complained so many times, but I was happy. But what's the use now? What am I going to do? What should I do? I don't want to stay here anymore. There's no point. Where am I going to go, Enrico? Answer me. I'm talking to you and you've got nothing to say to me? Talking to you is like talking to the wall.

Nino enters.

NINO: Apparently Titina has started to go into labour after all. I'm taking her to the clinic in the Seicento. You come with us, Enrico. On the way, I'll drop you at Isabellita's. Somebody really ought to be with her, poor woman.
SOFIA: Yes, you go, Enrico.

Enrico and Nino exit.

SILVANA: May I sleep here, Sofia? I'm afraid to sleep alone tonight.
SOFIA: Here? In this room? But there isn't another bed here.
SILVANA: I don't need a bed. I have my sleeping bag. I'll just stretch out on the floor in my sleeping bag. When I was staying with Signora Coltellacci, that's how I slept.
SOFIA: All right. Go get your sleeping bag.
SILVANA: Thank you. Do you want me to make you a cup of tea?
SOFIA: No. Thank you.
SILVANA: Tea is something I do know how to make. I used to make it for my mother, too. I'm afraid, Sofia. I'm terribly afraid. If I close my eyes, I see Edoardo in front of me.
SOFIA: So don't close your eyes. I don't need to close my eyes in order to see him. I have nothing else in front of my eyes. He's been in front of my eyes for years.
SILVANA: Sofia, I don't believe I will marry Enrico. What sense does it make? I'm afraid if I get married, if I have children, I'll end up just

like my mother. With a neurosis. (*Pause.*) Tomorrow morning I'm
going to go. I've decided that I'm going to get out of here.

SOFIA: You're going to leave? Where will you go?

SILVANA: Because I just don't feel like staying here anymore.

SOFIA: I'm sorry that you're leaving. I feel terrible about it.

SILVANA: Tomorrow, I'll get on my Vespa, with the road in front of me.
I won't think about anything. I'll forget Edoardo. I'll forget you,
too, Sofia, all of you. Do you care about me, Sofia? I do. I care about
you very much. You're the only person here who's been good to me.
Here? In the whole world. But you have to understand that I don't
like caring about people. I find that it hurts your heart.

SOFIA: Go get your sleeping bag. Go make tea. Bring me some tea, and
then get into your sleeping bag. But be quiet, because I don't feel
like hearing you talk.

SILVANA: Okay. (*She exits.*)

Sofia dials a number.

SOFIA: Hello, Luisa? Luisa, Edoardo is dead. He shot himself. He's
dead. Luisa? Yes, it was bound to happen. But we've all behaved
like dogs. We let him die there all alone. We're a pack of dogs, all
of us – me, Nino, Enrico, Isabellita, Gildo. Dogs. The girl? The girl
doesn't have anything to do with it. She's not a dog because she's
just a mouse. Yes, she's here. She's gone to get her sleeping bag. I'm
not coming to Rome tomorrow, Luisa. I won't be coming to Rome
ever again. I came for Edoardo, to see Edoardo, not for anything
else. The funeral? I don't know. What do I care about the funeral?
People throw life away as if it were a bucket of dirty water. Not
just Edoardo. Everyone, Luisa. As if it were a bucket of dirty water.
We're a bunch of dogs with our lives. Life is a bitch with us and
we're bastards with life. Do you have any idea why, Luisa? Answer
me. Damn you, answer me! Talking to you is like talking to the
wall.

April 1967

Notes

1 The Beagle Boys (the Banda Bassotti in Italy) were a gang of cartoon crimi-
nals created for Walt Disney comics in the early 1950s. They were loosely
based on Ma Barker and the Barker crime family.

2 Though the 'wigeon' is fairly unknown in English, the *fischione* is not in Italian. The wigeon (*Anas penelope*) is a species of duck, commonly hunted. Its Italian name refers to its loud, distinctive whistle.

3 Sofia cites the proverb *'campa cavallo che l'erba cresce,'* which is either of Neopolitan or Sicilian origin, depending upon which source one credits. In a literal sense, the proverb tells of a starving horse (*cavallo*) that must somehow find a way to survive until the grass (*l'erba*) grows enough to be eaten, but the metaphorical meaning is close to 'fat chance' or 'that'll be the day' – a reference to a protracted wait and an uncertain outcome. Nino's next line, however, demands a reference to horses.

4 Titina's expression, which she repeats in Act III, is *'salute al Re'* – literally, 'to the king's health.' The obvious sense of it is something like, 'and to hell with it.' *'Salute al Re!'* is also a line from the very beginning of the Italian version of Act II, Scene V of *Lohengrin*, one of Ginzburg's two favourite operas (the other was *Don Carlos*). Perhaps coincidentally, it is from *Lohengrin* that Ginzburg took the title for her 1991 collection of essays, *Mai devi domandarmi* – in Italian, Lohengrin's warning to Elsa: 'Never must you ask me [my name].'

5 Obviously, Pelargon and Nestogen are brand names of baby formula; both are produced today by Nestlé. Guigoz, which is mentioned later, is another.

6 Carnia is found in the Carnic Alps, in the province of Udine, not far from Italy's border with Austria.

7 The Muro Torto ('crooked wall') is part of the Aurelian Walls – Roman city walls whose construction began in the third century CE. One of the best-preserved sections of the Aurelian Walls can be seen today along Viale Muro Torto, which roughly traces the lower half of the Villa Borghese.

A Town by the Sea

A PLAY IN THREE ACTS

Cast:
Marco
Debora
Betta
Gianni

The words 'All the wild boars said yes' are the first lines of a poem written not by me, but by a person called Andrea Levi. He wrote the poem when he was a child. N.G.

ACT ONE

[*The main room of a slightly rundown, badly furnished summer cottage in a town near Ancona, an important port city on Italy's Adriatic coast.*]

MARCO: Okay. Here we are. All set. Not too bad, eh? It's a pretty big place. Clean. More or less clean. There's a little dust. You can't see all that much from the window. Just courtyards. But you can see the bottom edge of the hills. The sea must be over in that direction, toward the west. And Alvise's house must be up there, on the hill. I don't know which one it is. Maybe that red one, with the arches. Pull the sheets out; we'll make up the bed. We can have a little rest and then we'll go out and buy some groceries. Let's eat here tonight. Unless Alvise and Bianca invite us to supper. But I don't think they will tonight. We should make a list of all the things we're going to need. Salt. Matches. Oil. Things like that.

DEBORA: Where do you wash the dishes? There's no sink.

MARCO: It must be in the kitchen, right?

DEBORA: Except that there's no kitchen.

MARCO: What do you mean there's no kitchen?

DEBORA: There's this hot plate. Here's where you cook.

MARCO: Alvise wrote me that it was a room plus amenities. I would have thought that amenities meant a kitchen. What about that door? What's behind the door?

DEBORA: A shower. But the water isn't running.

MARCO: There must be an air bubble. In the pipes. Sometimes, air bubbles get formed in there. At least the water's running in the bathroom sink. Look, you can wash the dishes in the washstand. Does the hot plate work? Yes. That's the most important thing, that the hot plate works. Why don't you get started on the refrigerator? You can put that bottle of beer in it, the one in my bag.

DEBORA: The refrigerator won't come on. It's not working.

MARCO: It's not working?

DEBORA: No.

MARCO: It's on a gas tank. The tank must have run out. I'll let the landlady know.

DEBORA: The landlady would be that immensely fat woman who gave us the keys?

MARCO: No, the landlady is the pharmacist's wife. At least, that's what Alvise wrote me. The fat woman must be the housekeeper. She didn't seem the type to be a pharmacist's wife. Not with that filthy apron. Oh look, I can see the fat woman down in the courtyard, washing clothes at the fountain. She's definitely got to be the housekeeper.

DEBORA: Marco?

MARCO: Hmm?

DEBORA: I think this is a terrible house.

MARCO: Well, it's not the Reggia di Caserta.[1] But it's a house. The first real house we've had in two years of marriage.

DEBORA: It looks to me like one of those houses where they find people who've been murdered.

MARCO: Calm down. No one's going to kill us. We don't have a cent.

DEBORA: Even people without money can wind up murdered.

MARCO: But nobody's going to kill us. No one wants to do us any harm.

DEBORA: True. No one wants to do us any harm. But no one particularly wants to do us any good, either.

MARCO: That's not exactly right. We know a lot of people who want the best for us.

DEBORA: Who, for example?

MARCO: Our relatives. Your sister. My mother.

DEBORA: My sister can't bear to be in the same room with you.

MARCO: Right, that's true. I'd forgotten.

DEBORA: She says you're pretentious. That you think of yourself as some kind of genius, when really you've only got an average mind. And she says you're not reliable at holding down a job. She says I'll never have an easy life with you – no money, no furniture, and no children, either. She says I made a huge mistake when I married you.

MARCO: Who cares what she has to say? Your sister is a bourgeois princess, rolling in money, children, *and* furniture. On the other hand, of course, she's stupid as a mole.

DEBORA: Moles aren't stupid.

MARCO: There's no animal more stupid. What's more, all her furniture is hideous. And her children are ugly to boot.

DEBORA: No, the children are darling, and it's not as if your mother is all that fond of me.

MARCO: Of course she's fond of you, poor woman.

DEBORA: Your mother thinks I'm just some girl from a rich family and so I'm not right for you. She thinks I'm spoiled and capricious. She thinks I'm a good-for-nothing.

MARCO: You are spoiled. Pretty much good-for-nothing, too.

DEBORA: How am I spoiled?

MARCO: You never get out of bed in the morning. You won't take a bath if there's no hot water. You won't smoke Italian cigarettes – it's Stuyvesants or nothing. If you need to buy a sweater, it's cashmere or nothing.

DEBORA: Of course it's cashmere or nothing. But that doesn't prove I'm spoiled. Most of the time I choose nothing.

MARCO: Please don't start sounding like you're some victim. And don't try to tell me you don't have any sweaters. You've got tons of them. And all of them are cashmere.

DEBORA: Because they were gifts from my sister.

MARCO: But you have them. You must have seven or eight.

DEBORA: No, only five. I used to have six, but I forgot one in Vicenza. In that hotel. It was called Pensione Patria. We've moved in and out of so many towns in the last two years! We've moved five times!

The same as the number of sweaters I have left. And we've changed hotels twenty times in every city. It's been torture.

MARCO: I had to change jobs a lot. It's not my fault. I've never been able to find a job that was really suited for me.

DEBORA: Marco, you're the one who isn't suited for the jobs. The first few days in a new job, you're totally happy. Then you start to find some little thing you don't like. You start talking about how this one's an idiot, and then that other one is, too. Between the two of us, the one who's truly spoiled is you.

MARCO: There's nothing in the world worse than a tedious, complaining wife. (*Singing.*) 'All the wild boars said yes!' Do you know that song?

DEBORA: No. And about the hotels. You've never found one that you liked. Either it's too hot. Or there's too much noise. Or the mattress is lumpy. You're the princess and the pea.

MARCO: Sure. I see the fat woman. In fact, now she's sitting and shelling peas. Speaking of mattresses, how's the one we have? It seems pretty okay.

DEBORA: No. It's full of lumps, if that's the issue. But in the first few days you're naturally going to insist on being happy here. Later on you'll start in with all your little complaints. The same thing happens with your jobs. Soon enough, when you decide the job isn't working out, you'll start saying that the city isn't working out for you either. It's cold. It's noisy. There are nasty smells. People's faces are unpleasant. And we'll have to move. You find all the rope you need to hang yourself, but never the one that's good enough to tie you down. That's what my sister says. But it's true.

MARCO: (*Singing.*) 'All the wild boars said yes!'

DEBORA: That's the reason we don't have any friends. We never stay long enough in one place to make friends. How long are we going to be here?

MARCO: I don't know. It depends. It depends on a lot of things. Alvise is coming at six, with his wife. His wife's name is Bianca.

DEBORA: You must have told me twenty times already that he's coming at six and that his wife's name is Bianca. Maybe you do have a friend here. You've got Alvise.

MARCO: We were very close at one time. But all these years have gone by. No less than nine years. We don't see each other anymore. I can't say how much he might have changed in all those years. I'm curious to find out. I don't know what his wife is like. I've never met her.

Once he sent me a photo of him and his wife, and another one a few
years later, with the wife and their son. His wife is very pretty. She
has curly blond hair, and her face is a little like a sheep. The baby is
cute. They've got him in a boarding school in Switzerland.

DEBORA: Why in Switzerland?

MARCO: I don't know. How do you expect me to know that? I don't
know anything about them. I know they've got piles of money.
Bianca is rolling in it.

DEBORA: Like me. I used to be rich, too. Apparently you and Alvise
have a weakness for wealthy women.

MARCO: You used to be rich. Once upon a time. Back before I met you.
But when I married you, you barely had the shirt on your back.
And your sweaters.

DEBORA: Of cashmere.

MARCO: Of cashmere.

DEBORA: So now you're criticizing me because I don't have money?
Were you hoping for a dowry?

MARCO: I wasn't hoping for anything. I'm just saying that I didn't
marry a wealthy woman. Your father had done a good job of fritter-
ing it all away before you and I met.

DEBORA: He used to play the stock market. He was crazy for it. That's
how he lost the money he had. Poor man. He was so kind. I'm sorry
you never got to meet him.

MARCO: Now Alvise, on the other hand, married a woman who truly is
rich. With property. And citrus orchards. And who the hell knows
what all else. Plus now they have that factory that's doing very
well.

DEBORA: Who told you that it's doing so well?

MARCO: I imagine it is.

DEBORA: And where is their factory? Can you see it from the window?

MARCO: I don't know where it is. The only thing I see from the window
are courtyards.

DEBORA: Marco?

MARCO: Huh?

DEBORA: Do you think Alvise is going to give you a job in his factory?

MARCO: I have no idea. I don't know what he's like now. Once upon a
time he'd have handed me the Turkish empire if he'd had it to give.
Now, who knows? People change.

DEBORA: Oh, really? He'd have handed you the Turkish empire? So he
thought highly of you?

MARCO: Yes, he thought very highly of me. He once held a very high opinion of me.

DEBORA: Though I don't believe Turkey had an empire. Persia is an empire, but not Turkey. You don't know your geography. You weren't very good in school.

MARCO: I did great in school. I was at the top of my class.

DEBORA: Whereas I was the dumbest ox in the school. It's an Eternit factory. What is Eternit?

MARCO: I don't know. Must be some kind of cement.[2]

DEBORA: How are you going to work in a factory where you don't even know what it is they do?

MARCO: I'll find out when I start working there.

DEBORA: And what are you going to find to do in an Eternit factory?

MARCO: All kinds of things. Lots of jobs. There are all kinds of jobs in a factory. I could do something in public relations.

DEBORA: And you'd like that? You'd be happy?

MARCO: Maybe. It would be a job. Something to get by on. I don't expect anymore to find a job that I'd really be happy doing.

DEBORA: What kind of job would you be happy doing?

MARCO: I'd like to be a scholar and write a book. A book about history. But, since we're broke and we have to live, I've bid farewell forever to the idea of being a scholar. I don't think I've got much of a vocation for scholarship anyway. So a job in the Eternit factory will suit me fine. Assuming Alvise wants to give me one.

DEBORA: And you'd like living here permanently? In this town?

MARCO: I don't mind this town. You've got the sea. You can go swimming. It's a big, old, peaceful town. I think we could get along pretty well here, even permanently. Naturally, if we're going to settle down, we'll look for a nice house. The nearest city is Ancona. I could go to Ancona all the time, to the library in my free time. You can get there pretty quickly in the car.

DEBORA: And me? What am I supposed to do here all day long, if we settle down here?

MARCO: You? I don't know. You could look for a job, too. Maybe substitute teach. You have your degree in literature.

DEBORA: I don't like teaching. I've never done it. I'm not cut out for it.

MARCO: Learn. A person gets used to things. A person can get used to doing anything.

DEBORA: Look who's talking. You, who never get used to anything. You, who are always so intolerant of everything.

MARCO: And you could make friends with Bianca. Spend a lot of time with her. You two could become close friends. She'd introduce you to people. You and Bianca could go to Ancona all the time – to go shopping, for concerts.

DEBORA: The idea doesn't grab me much.

MARCO: It doesn't grab you?

DEBORA: No. Concerts bore me. And the idea of that sheep-faced woman doesn't grab me either.

MARCO: If it doesn't grab you, I don't know what to do about it. Never mind, then.

DEBORA: Marco?

MARCO: Huh?

DEBORA: What are we going to do if Alvise doesn't give you a job? We've used up all our money. We've got practically nothing left.

MARCO: I don't know. I'll write some articles. I don't want to think about it right now. I'm tired. I drove the entire morning. Don't make me think. I'd love to take a shower. It's infuriating that there's no water. Maybe I could shave. (*Sings.*) 'All the wild boars said yes!' Do you know that song?

DEBORA: No. What is it?

MARCO: It's a song Alvise always used to sing. I don't remember what comes next. All the wild boars agree to the idea of becoming domesticated pigs. All except one, who chooses to stay wild. You know what we should buy when we go out? We should buy a few yards of plastic and put up a nice curtain to hide the hot plate, the refrigerator, and the wash basin. This room would turn into a totally different place.

DEBORA: And where are we supposed to hang this curtain?

MARCO: Oh, God. I don't know. I'll put up a metal bar with some rings. Or else a wooden rod. It's no big deal to put up a curtain.

DEBORA: It would be a better idea if we knew we'd be staying here a while.

MARCO: Certainly. But, assuming the worst, we'll be staying here at least a month. By 'assuming the worst' I mean if Alvise tells me he doesn't have a job for me. I sent the landlady a money order for 70,000 lire. That's a month's rent.

DEBORA: Doesn't that seem an enormous sum to you, 70,000 lire a month, for this room? Couldn't your friend Alvise have looked for something a little better?

MARCO: Yes, in fact, maybe it's a little expensive. But you know, in seaside towns the rates go up in the summer.

DEBORA: Do you think Alvise knows you want to ask him for a job?

MARCO: I don't know. In my letters I hinted at my situation. But always in a rather vague way. He knows I don't have much money.

DEBORA: He knows you don't have much money and he sets you up in this pit that costs 70,000 lire a month?

MARCO: Drop it, Debora. I wrote him to find me a simple little house for the summer. He must have taken the first one he came across. He wouldn't have spent much time looking. He's always very busy. He probably even had his secretary do the looking. But this house isn't so bad in the end. Let's not exaggerate. I like it. I was sick of hotels. And that time we ended up with your sister – what a torture.

DEBORA: You really have the nerve to complain to me about my sister? She put us up for three months. She finally even lent us the money to come here.

MARCO: I'm not complaining about your sister. She's been an angel. I'm just saying that I couldn't stand staying with them any longer. Those endless evenings. Those lunches. All their guests. All those ridiculous conversations.

DEBORA: Oh, nice. It was their house. They could invite whomever they felt like.

MARCO: Plus there was that obnoxious butler. When he picked my socks up off the rug in the mornings, he used to make this disgusted face, as if he were picking up dead mice.

DEBORA: You're not going to try to tell me the time we spent with your mother was more comfortable?

MARCO: I was more comfortable.

DEBORA: But not me. It was too hot. And there was never enough to eat.

MARCO: My mother, poor thing, she doesn't eat much. She's old. She doesn't realize. She's afraid of spending money.

DEBORA: Where in the world did I put that?

MARCO: What?

DEBORA: My dress. My dress with the little blue flowers. Oh god, I can't have left it.... I forgot it in that hotel. Where we slept last night. In Ancona.

MARCO: You're so absent-minded. You're always leaving something in the hotel. We'll write and have them return the dress. Antico Giappone. The hotel was called Antico Giappone.

DEBORA: You must be joking, Marco. It was the prettiest dress I had. It fit me so well. Those people at the Antico Giappone will keep it

for themselves. What am I going to wear when Alvise and Bianca
invite us to lunch? I can't exactly go out in slacks.

MARCO: You'll wear another dress. The red one.

DEBORA: It doesn't fit me very well. It's too long.

MARCO: So you'll hem it up.

DEBORA: But I don't know how to hem a dress.

MARCO: Oh my God. Figure it out. Learn how to sew a hem. Learn not
to leave your things in hotels all the time.

DEBORA: Maybe Bianca's housekeeper will fix the hem for me, hmm?

MARCO: I don't know if they have a housekeeper. I don't know anything.

DEBORA: How can they not have a housekeeper? They're rolling in
money, they've got that enormous villa, and you don't think they
even have a housekeeper?

MARCO: I've never seen the villa. I don't know if it's enormous.

DEBORA: Didn't you say that it's that red one up there?

MARCO: I guess so. But I don't know.

DEBORA: Well, imagine them not having a housekeeper. I'll give her a
little something if she fixes my dress. I'll give her a thousand lire.

MARCO: A thousand is too much. Five hundred would do.

DEBORA: You're stingy. You're stingy like your mother.

MARCO: My mother isn't stingy. She's poor. I'm poor, too.

DEBORA: We really aren't poor. We don't have any money – but that's
something else entirely. Truly poor people are different.

MARCO: I haven't had any money since I was born. That makes me
poor.

DEBORA: No. You're not truly poor. You're rolling in words. You talk
and talk and you get lost in words. Poor people, the truly poor,
don't lose themselves in words. Poor people have their feet firmly
planted on the ground. You and me, on the other hand, have our
heads in the clouds.

MARCO: You have very conventional ideas about poor people. There
are all different kinds of poor people. Some of them even have their
heads in the clouds. Listen, it's four o'clock. If we want to go out,
we need to get going. We'll buy some chocolates or some cookies.
We'll need to offer something to Alvise and Bianca. I'll make them
some tea. See if there are any cups.

DEBORA: There are cups, but there's no teapot.

MARCO: We'll need to get a teapot. And really those are coffee mugs,
not tea cups.

DEBORA: I don't see why we have to offer them tea. Nobody drinks tea anymore. It's gone out of style.

MARCO: Before we go out we should straighten up. You could dust a little.

DEBORA: Where do I find a dust rag?

MARCO: Oh for God's sake. I don't know. Figure it out. Use a Kleenex. Or use my dirty underwear. You'll find them in my bag. You're such a nuisance.

DEBORA: I wonder what this Bianca is like. A sheep, you said? A face like a sheep? And Alvise? Tell me what Alvise looks like.

MARCO: I can tell you what he was like once. We haven't seen each other for more than nine years. The two of us were around twenty then. The way I remember him, he was chubby, pale, flabby, with eyeglasses, and he had hanks of his hair that were always falling down over his forehead. And he always used to wear these shapeless, droopy overcoats that were so big they were practically falling off him.

DEBORA: Sounds like everything was falling. He must have been quite a dreadful sight.

MARCO: In the past nine years we've written to each other five or six times. I was out of the country when he wrote to tell me he was in love and that he was getting married. A beautiful young girl. Wealthy. Athletic. A swimming champion. He didn't play sports then. He hated fresh air and he suffered from the cold. He always stayed closed up inside, with all the lights turned down, like an owl, reading his German philosophers. He didn't have any money. He had a degree in economics and he knew all kinds of things. He was living off his translations and from the theses he was writing for students who didn't know how. The girlfriend was in love with him, too. Her name was Bianca. Filthy rich. Gorgeous. With blond curls. He sent me a photograph. Beautiful, just beautiful. With a face a little like a sheep.

DEBORA: I can't imagine it. I couldn't imagine a swimming champion with a face like a sheep. And him, given how you described him, I certainly don't understand how he managed to become the director of a factory.

MARCO: That's because you don't have any imagination. In any case, we'll see them soon. When I came back from being out of the country, he wrote me to come and see him here. I never came. I was depressed. I wondered about asking him whether he had a job to give me. But I didn't really feel like asking. Some time passed like that. Finally, a month ago, I wrote him to see if he would find me a house for the summer. As if you and I are the type to go on summer vacation. But it was a first step in asking him for a job later. We were the best of friends, when we were younger. We lived together without a cent, in Rome, in an ugly room on Via Panisperna. I didn't make any other friends after him. I didn't have time for it. Besides, the only people I met were imbeciles.

DEBORA: Thanks.

MARCO: I'm not talking about you. You're not a friend, you're my wife. It's different. Sometimes I do find you very stupid, but it doesn't matter. What we had then, Alvise and me, in Rome, on Via Panisperna, was time. We had so much time to waste. We used our time up in rivers of words. Who knows, when we see each other again, whether all those words will keep flowing between us? I'm afraid they won't. I'm afraid we'll have just a few forced, broken words, the kind of words you can only drag out of yourself with difficulty, painful for the one who's saying them and painful for the one who's listening. I'll ask him for a job. He won't like it that I asked, but maybe he'll give me one. I'll have to explain what I've been doing all these years. All the idiotic jobs I've done. All the imbeciles I've met. I haven't been very lucky. I'm already thirty years old. Here we are, you and me. We don't have any money. That doesn't matter, obviously. Everyone knows that doesn't matter. But we don't have a thing, we don't have a house, we don't have friends, we don't even have a city.

DEBORA: Oh, don't make me depressed. I'm usually the one talking like that, not you. Now maybe you wish I were one of those women who console their husbands and raise their spirits. It was your bad luck to get me. I'm feeling miserable enough now to throw myself out the window.

MARCO: You wouldn't hurt yourself. We're on the ground floor. You'd end up in the courtyard. You'd end up in the arms of that fat woman who's still shelling peas. Now there's a young girl crossing the courtyard. How funny. What a funny dress she's wearing. She's stopping to talk with the fat woman. Uh-oh. Now it looks like she's coming up here.

A knock at the door.

MARCO: Damn. Go put on a blouse. (*Opens the door.*)

Betta enters.

BETTA: Good morning. My name is Betta. I'm Bianca's cousin. Bianca and Alvise sent me to see if you needed anything. They were supposed to come by at six, but they aren't coming because they had to go to Ancona. They ask you to please forgive them. It was something that came up unexpectedly.

MARCO: I'm pleased to meet you, Miss. So you're Bianca's cousin? This is my wife. We're still a little disorganized here. Everything's a bit up in the air. We only arrived a little while ago. I'm sorry, we don't have anything to offer you, not even any chocolates. Would you enjoy a beer? Unfortunately, it's not cold. The refrigerator isn't working. The gas tank must have run out.

BETTA: I don't drink beer. And it isn't the gas tank. That refrigerator has never worked. I know because a guy I knew was staying in this house up until a little while ago. An English guy. When Alvise said that the two of you wanted a house for the summer, I remembered and I came to reserve it for you.

DEBORA: You found this house?

BETTA: Yeah, I did.

MARCO: You're using '*tu*' with her?[3]

DEBORA: Of course I'm using '*tu*' with her. Can't you see she's a child? She may have put on green eye shadow, but she's still a child. How old are you, Betta? Fourteen?

BETTA: I'm seventeen. You can get ice at the market. But there's really nothing to be done for that refrigerator.

MARCO: I appreciate your having found this house for us, Miss. You were very kind to go to the trouble. It's a charming house, clean. More or less clean.

BETTA: There are mosquitoes. You'll have to light a mosquito coil at night.

MARCO: Yes, of course. A mosquito coil is the only thing for mosquitoes.

BETTA: I brought you some.

MARCO: You even brought us mosquito coils? You're an angel. Thank you. I'm so sorry not to see Alvise and Bianca. I was anxious to see him again and to meet Bianca. Something unexpected, is that what you said, Miss? I hope nothing unpleasant has happened.

BETTA: No. Nothing special.

MARCO: Never mind. We'll see them tomorrow.

BETTA: I don't know when they'll be back.

DEBORA: If I knew they were going to Ancona, I would have told them to stop by the Antico Giappone hotel. I left a dress there.

MARCO: Debora is absent-minded. She's always forgetting things in hotels. Alvise and Bianca's house is that red one with the arches, up on the hill?

BETTA: No. That's Gianni's house.

DEBORA: Who's Gianni?

BETTA: A guy. A friend of the family.

MARCO: And which one is their house?

BETTA: You can't see it. It's covered up by trees.

MARCO: Listen, Debora. I'm going downstairs for a minute to buy something for supper. Bread, eggs, some matches. Things like that. I'll be right back. Please don't go, Miss. Keep my wife company. (*Exits.*)

DEBORA: Do you live here all year round? In summer and in the winter?

BETTA: Yes. All the time.

DEBORA: Where do you live?

BETTA: With Alvise and Bianca. I've lived with them since my mother died. Three years ago.

DEBORA: You're an orphan? Poor thing. So young. So you found this house for us? Did that acquaintance of yours manage all right here? The English guy?

BETTA: Yes. But then he got into an argument with the landlady and she threw him out.

DEBORA: Oh, really? She threw him out?

BETTA: Because he was bringing guys here. He was queer. At night, they would dress up like women and dance.

DEBORA: Queer! What a word! A child like you shouldn't know words like that. To tell you the truth, I find it a little expensive here, as houses go.

BETTA: You don't find a lot of rental houses here. The town isn't really set up for it.

DEBORA: Listen, why do you put all that green shadow on your eyes? It doesn't suit you. It makes you look old. You seem like an old child. Plus you're wearing your hair too short. Why so short? You'd be so cute if you didn't wear makeup on your eyes and if you let your hair grow a bit longer.

BETTA: I know I'm not cute. It doesn't matter to me.

DEBORA: And your dress looks as though you slept in the dog house. Doesn't your cousin tell you these things? Bianca?

BETTA: Bianca doesn't notice.

DEBORA: She doesn't notice? What do you mean she doesn't notice?

BETTA: She doesn't notice. She only remembers I'm around when she's really sick. Then sometimes she calls me. Or else when she wants me to go do an errand. I do errands for her. The shopping, everything.

DEBORA: Isn't there a housekeeper to do the shopping?

BETTA: They never have a housekeeper. They all run away. There's too much work. Too much of a mess and too much work.

DEBORA: Oh, really? Why in the world is everything such a mess?

BETTA: There's no regular schedule. People are always showing up for lunch.

DEBORA: They've got that many friends?

BETTA: Yes, Gianni comes, other friends of Bianca's come.

DEBORA: And who washes the dishes? Bianca?

BETTA: Not Bianca. Sometimes I wash them. Sometimes the custodian's wife.

DEBORA: So you have to wash all those dishes? You have to take care of everything? That's a lot of trouble. Poor girl. And you're an orphan? I'm an orphan, too. No father or mother. All I have is a sister, in Milan. Married with four children. I don't have any children. I don't have a house. I've been married two years and we've done nothing but move from one city to another. And I'm sick of moving all the time. The first few days when we're in a new place, I'm frightened. I suffer because I'm so afraid. Then I get used to it. As soon as I'm used to it, Marco decides we need to leave. We pack our bags, we load them into our Seicento. Streets, dust, trees, hotels. Always hotels. This is the first house we've had. I don't like it. I'll tell you the truth, I don't like it at all. But I'll even wind up getting used to this house. A person can get used to anything.

BETTA: I'd be happy if I could travel. You know that English guy who used to live here? I told him to see if he could find me a job in London. Any kind of job. He still hasn't written to me. But as soon as he writes to me, I'll pick up and leave.

DEBORA: And your family? Do you think your family is going to let you go?

BETTA: My family? Who's my family? I'm all by myself.

DEBORA: I was talking about your cousins. Alvise and Bianca. You don't want to live with Alvise and Bianca anymore? I understand. If you're the one who has to wash all those dishes.

BETTA: That's not why. It's not my house. I don't feel comfortable.

DEBORA: You don't feel comfortable?

BETTA: No. At night, when she screams a lot, I get scared.

DEBORA: Who screams at night?

BETTA: Bianca.

DEBORA: She screams?

BETTA: Last night. If you only knew what went on last night.

DEBORA: What happened?

BETTA: She was screaming. He was trying to calm her down. At one point he didn't know what to do anymore and he slapped her. Then she ran into my room and crawled into my bed. Her lip was swollen, the strap of her nightgown was torn. She was crying. She said she couldn't take it anymore. She was clinging to me. She was trembling. When she starts feeling desperate like that, she attaches herself to me. Alvise wanted to come in but she didn't want him in the room. I called Gianni.

DEBORA: Who's Gianni?

BETTA: A guy. Bianca's boyfriend. He came over. He stayed with her for a while, stroking her hand. He was her boyfriend, but that's all over now. He says it was never anything serious. But she's obsessed with him. She'd like to go away with him, but that's the last thing on his mind. He has things to do here. He doesn't know what to do with Bianca. He has his orchids. Gianni grows orchids.

DEBORA: And Alvise? Alvise let him into the house, this Gianni guy?

BETTA: Yes, of course. They're very good friends. They usually try to figure out together what to do about Bianca. Even last night, they closed themselves up in the study to talk. Gianni thinks Bianca should get a different analyst. He has one that could work for her, a Freudian. But Alvise says no, that an analyst would be pointless for her. Because she's a psychopath. When a person is a psychopath, analysis doesn't work.

DEBORA: And Bianca meanwhile? While they were talking?

BETTA: She fell asleep. I was sitting next to her and holding her hand. Later Alvise and Gianni called me because they wanted some tea. So I went down to the kitchen and when I came back up again, Bianca wasn't in my bed anymore. I found her in her own room. She was packing her suitcase. She was dressed, she'd put on a suit and her pearls, and she'd powdered her face. She'd put cocoa butter on her lips. I speak to her, she doesn't answer. She doesn't look at me, she doesn't see me. I run to call Alvise. And meanwhile she goes in the garage and jumps into her car, the Mercedes, and she's gone.

For a while we chased her in Gianni's car. But then we lost her. We
went back and spent the morning calling everyone in any place
where she might possibly have gone. We didn't find her. No one
can figure out where she might be. Now Alvise and Gianni have
gone to search along the highway for her, in all the motels. I think
she went to Rome. She has a friend in Rome, plus another analyst.
Also a Jungian. Gianni says it would take a Freudian, for her.
DEBORA: Does it seem to you that a young girl like you should find
herself mixed up in an affair like this?
BETTA: Is it my fault, if I'm mixed up in it?

Marco enters.

MARCO: Okay. I bought eggs, cheese, and bread. If you would like,
Miss, you can stay and have supper with us. We can set up here,
on this little end table. I was also at the general store and I bought
ten metres of plastic sheeting. Tomorrow I want to put up a curtain.
What do you think, Miss? I want to put up a nice curtain so you
won't see the washbasin and the hot plate anymore. The room will
be a lot more charming. Look what a nice design there is on this
plastic. They're roses.
DEBORA: We've come at a very bad time, Marco. Bianca had some sort
of a crisis last night. She left the house and they don't know where
she is.
MARCO: But weren't they in Ancona?
DEBORA: No one went to Ancona. Alvise and Gianni are looking for
Bianca in all the highway motels.
MARCO: Who's Gianni?
DEBORA: He's Bianca's lover.
MARCO: Bianca has a lover?
BETTA: As a matter of fact, she has several. But now she's obsessed with
Gianni. Every now and then she gets obsessed with someone.
MARCO: Good lord. I'm sorry for Alvise. I thought he was so happy. We
really have arrived at a terrible moment.
BETTA: Oh, but it's not a moment. It's been going on like this for years.
On top of everything, they don't have any money. They have their
son in boarding school in Switzerland, but now they're going to
have to take him out because it costs too much and they can't pay
for it anymore. Things at the factory are going badly. They're in a
lot of debt. They fight over money, although in the end they don't

care about money, neither one of them. He does just fine without
it. She runs up debts. They don't fight about Bianca's men, because
Alvise isn't the jealous type. He's gotten used to the idea.

DEBORA: Things are going badly at the factory? The Eternit factory?

MARCO: Yes, didn't you hear? Things are going badly.

A knock at the door. Gianni enters.

GIANNI: Good evening. My name is Gianni.

BETTA: Any news about Bianca?

GIANNI: Yes. She's in Rome. At the Residence Hotel. She called. She
wants some clothes. But the post office is closed now. Tomorrow
morning we'll need to send her this box of clothes.

BETTA: And where's Alvise?

GIANNI: At home. He's tired and depressed. He asks you to excuse him,
but he can't come out to see anyone this evening. Let's go, Betta. I'll
take you back home.

BETTA: Let's go.

GIANNI: Let me catch my breath for a minute. I'm dead tired myself.

MARCO: Make yourself comfortable, Gianni. Come sit here on this
deckchair. Would you like a beer? It's not cold, though.

GIANNI: Why not? Give me a beer. I see some bread. May I eat a piece?
I'm starving. I wouldn't mind a little cheese either. Beer certainly
is bad when it's warm. It tastes like soup. Soup is good, but when
something that isn't soup tastes like soup, it's disgusting. Strange.

DEBORA: No one's forcing you to drink the beer. Leave it there. I want
to leave, Marco. I want to leave right this instant. I don't want to
spend the night here.

GIANNI: Leave? Where do you want to go? It's raining. It's dark. You'd
be well advised not to try going out on the streets now.

DEBORA: I said I want to leave. You mind your own damn business.

MARCO: Debora!

GIANNI: Don't get angry. I just wanted to give you some advice.
Women are so tedious.

DEBORA: I wouldn't know what to do with your advice. Get up from
that chair and get out of here!

MARCO: Debora! Don't pay any attention to her, Gianni. Don't mind
her. She's just a little irritable.

DEBORA: Marco, we have no reason to stay here!

GIANNI: And so why did you come?

DEBORA: Mind your own damn business!

MARCO: Debora!

BETTA: Gianni and I are used to things like this. We're used to living in stormy weather. So it doesn't make much of an impression on us. Nothing really shakes us up. Because a person gets used to it. A person can get used to anything.

ACT TWO

[*The same summer cottage, the next morning.*]

MARCO: Here, Debora. I bought milk and some croissants. And I was also at the general store and bought a hammer, some nails, some wooden rings, and a ball of string.

DEBORA: Did you find enough rope to hang yourself with?

MARCO: I want to put the curtain up.

DEBORA: What are you messing with a curtain for if we're leaving?

MARCO: We're not leaving right away. I've decided that we'll leave in a few days. And meanwhile, even if it's only for a few days, I'd find it pleasant to live in an attractive room.

DEBORA: I don't want to stay here anymore. I want to leave.

MARCO: Yes, but not right away. In a few days. Meanwhile, let's make some breakfast now. Get up. I'm hungry. We didn't have any supper last night. I'll make some coffee. (*Sings.*) All the wild boars said yes!

DEBORA: He devoured our entire supper, that jerk. That Gianni. All I ate was an egg.

MARCO: You ate an egg – me, nothing. You pitched your little fit, then you ate an egg, then you started crying, then you went off to bed. Afterward I went out for a walk in town with Betta and Gianni. We walked around and chatted until almost dawn.

DEBORA: Yes, I heard you come back in. I didn't sleep well. There were lots of mosquitoes. I put out the mosquito coil. It was making me cough.

MARCO: Betta and Gianni told me Alvise's story. God, poor Alvise. What a disaster. It's an agonizing story. That crazy wife of his.

DEBORA: What do I care about Alvise? I've never seen him; I don't know him. You said that you used to be close friends. But what kind of a friend is he? Not exactly rushing to visit you, even after we came quite a distance to see him. He was tired, he was de-

pressed. One rushes to a friend even if he's tired. Even if he's having a hard time. Hard times are shared with friends. You know, he'd
never have given you any job. Not even if he could, if everything
was going well. He still wouldn't have given you anything. Because
he doesn't care about you.

MARCO: Hard times are not always shared with friends. Sometimes you
prefer to share them with people who are distant and uninvolved.

DEBORA: He shares his hard times with Gianni. With his wife's lover.
Strange, isn't it? We've fallen into a nest of strange people. A nest
full of crazies. Let's get out of here, Marco. Let's think about the
two of us. Because I don't know what we're going to do. How we're
going to live. You do realize that we don't have any more money?

MARCO: In the meantime, you should get up. Have some coffee. Then
we'll go out for a walk, we'll go down by the sea. It's lovely here.
The town's full of porticos and little stairways. And cats. With the
rooftops all covered in lichens.

DEBORA: I don't find it lovely. I find it horrible.

MARCO: You haven't seen it.

DEBORA: I've seen it from the window.

MARCO: You can't see anything from the window. Just courtyards.

DEBORA: I still haven't managed to figure out what we're doing here.

MARCO: I want to stay at least a few days. We've spent 70,000 lire on
the rent. We can't just throw that much money away. I don't exactly
find money lying around in the street.

DEBORA: Of course you don't find money lying around in the street. My
sister gave you that money.

MARCO: Exactly. That's why I want to stay here a while. I enjoyed
myself last night with Betta and Gianni. They're very pleasant to be
around. Gianni is quite a refined man. He knows a ton of things. He
has a degree in botany and he grows orchids.

DEBORA: I don't like him.

MARCO: You don't know him. You don't know anything about him.

DEBORA: I know as much as I need to know. I know that he's a guy
named Gianni, who is lovers with a crazy woman named Bianca,
whom we, however, have never seen and never will see. I know
that he's a guy with black sweaters and a long gold chain hanging
around his neck, with dirty black feet and filthy sandals, who lives
here in a seaside town and grows orchids.

A knock at the door. Betta and Gianni enter.

MARCO: Hello. Any news about Bianca?

BETTA: Yes. She tried to kill herself with sleeping pills. But they got to her in time. They pumped her stomach. The maid at the Residence Hotel found her. Alvise has gone to Rome.

MARCO: He left by himself?

BETTA: By himself, yes. With the driver.

DEBORA: And Gianni? Why are you still here, Gianni?

GIANNI: Alvise asked you to forgive him. When he comes back, when everything has calmed down, he'll come and spend some time with you. He really wants that immensely.

DEBORA: You haven't answered my question, Gianni. Why are you still here? Maybe Bianca needs you.

GIANNI: I can't do anything for Bianca. Seeing me only exasperates her, and that's that.

DEBORA: No, that's not that. It's that you're afraid. You're a coward, Gianni.

MARCO: Debora!

BETTA: He's not a coward. Gianni couldn't be braver. Once, when I was about to drown, he saved my life.

GIANNI: Bianca wants something from me that I can't give her. She wants to join her destiny with mine. She wants to live with me. She wants a child with me. She wants it all. And I, on the other hand, want none of those things with her. Nothing.

DEBORA: And yet she's your mistress.

GIANNI: My mistress? What a word. No one uses that word anymore. You're so nineteenth-century, Debora. You're not from our time. I was making love with Bianca for a while. Now that's all over.

DEBORA: I don't want to be of our time, if our time doesn't suit me. And I don't want you using 'tu' with me, buster. It's not as though we shared the same wet nurse, you know.

GIANNI: True. Anyway, I never had a wet nurse. My mother nursed me. She nursed me until I was twenty months old. That's what she says. She still talks about it. I'm her only child. She's in Brazil, and she comes to see me once a year. I live the entire year with the nightmare of her impending visits. I can't stand her. When she arrives, it's like an attack of hives. My analyst says that my aversion to my mother is a form of resentment. Because I was in love with my mother's breast and she cut me off. At twenty months.

DEBORA: Don't change the subject. We were talking about Bianca.

MARCO: Debora, maybe he doesn't want to talk about his business with you. Basically, we've just met. We've only known each other since yesterday.

GIANNI: No, I'll gladly talk about myself. It's the only subject I am glad to talk about. So, according to my analyst, it's because I feel such nostalgia for my mother's breast that I've had difficulty becoming an adult. That's the point.

DEBORA: All this chatter about analysts nauseates me. I'd burn every last one of them at the stake. What does all this have to do with Bianca?

GIANNI: I have difficulties in my relationships with women. There are complications. I wasn't in love with Bianca, but I was happy to make love with her. At first. But then not after that. After that I couldn't stand her anymore. I felt sorry for her. But for me, being with her was a terrible weight. I tried to talk to her about it, but she'd gotten attached to me. It's terrible when a woman gets attached to you. You don't really know how to get rid of her again. You have the sensation of being dragged to the bottom of a pond. And the water is dark, dense, muddy. I've never had a genuine, free, or happy relationship with a woman. Never.

DEBORA: I don't feel nostalgic for my mother's breast. I forgot about my mother's breast quite a while ago. You know what I do feel nostalgic for? I feel nostalgic for people who are healthy, normal, and calm. Because I get the impression that wherever you look there are nothing but unfortunate, desperate, crazy people. I'd prefer the other kind. Where are the other kind of people?

GIANNI: The other kind of people? The other kind of people, if they exist, don't seem to be stopping on your street corner. They keep right on going when they run into you. You know why? Because they have nothing to say to you. They don't recognize themselves in you. They run away. Because if we're making a list of crazy and desperate people, you're on it.

DEBORA: Making a list of desperate people! You said it exactly right, my boy. Marco and I don't feel nostalgic for our mothers' breasts. We don't go to analysts. But we are definitely desperate. We don't have a cent, and within a month we won't know where our next meal is coming from. That's the point.

GIANNI: You two don't have any money?

DEBORA: No. And do you know why we came here, Gianni? Because Marco was hoping that Alvise might have a job for him. We'd set Alvise up in our minds as some kind of hero. A guy who was

happy. As rich as he could be. As satisfied as he could be. As peaceful as he could be. We wanted to roost in Alvise's shadow. Absorb
his peace. We wanted to put down roots here. And instead we arrive and we find this disaster. The wife's crazy. The factory's about
to fall into the ocean. A nest of crazies.

GIANNI: The two of you were thinking of Alvise as a father figure. Obviously the two of you are in need of a father.

DEBORA: Oh, go to hell with your psychoanalysis! I have no need of
a father. Mine is dead. I loved him very much, but I'm doing just
fine without him. I don't need a father. I need some money. Understand?

MARCO: I'm sorry that you put it that way, Debora. Now they're going
to think I came here for selfish reasons, driven by some calculated
coldness. But that's not true. I had a desire to see Alvise, indepen-
dently of any use such a meeting might have been. Purely out of
fondness.

DEBORA: A fondness that has suddenly reawakened after nine years.
You've been away from him for nine years, and you were getting
along without him just fine. Why don't you tell the truth? Why
don't you say that we came here for one quite specific purpose?

MARCO: Don't be nasty, Debora. Don't be vulgar. I've found myself in
a difficult situation, and I thought of asking Alvise if he could help
me. But the true reason, the deep reason that drove me to come
here was our old fondness for each other, the memory of a friendship, so many memories that I share with Alvise and that touch me
very much.

DEBORA: In Rome. Nine years ago. On Via Panisperna. (*Sings*.) 'All the
pigs said no!'

MARCO: You're so unpleasant today, Debora. You're so nasty. One thing
I really hate is to hear a song that I like to sing mangled. And you
know that sweet little song is very special to me.

BETTA: You sing it, Marco.

MARCO: (*Sings*.) 'All the wild boars said yes!' In Rome, on Via Panisperna, Alvise used to sing that song. I only remember one line.
I don't know the rest of it anymore. Actually, I came here just to
ask him how the rest of it goes. All the wild boars agree to become
domesticated pigs. All except for one.

DEBORA: It occurs to me that Alvise may have other things on his mind.
It occurs to me that he may be as far as he can be from pigs and
wild boars.

MARCO: All except for one. One chose to remain a wild boar. He chose
to remain in his wild, free state.

DEBORA: For you, freedom consists of changing jobs, hotels, and cities
every three months. That's what being free as a wild boar would
mean for you.

MARCO: You keep getting more hateful.

GIANNI: Yes. When you say things like that, or when you talk about
money, your face gets sharp, evil. It's not your real face.

DEBORA: You've known me for one day. How do you know what my
real face is?

GIANNI: I've looked at you. I know your true face.

MARCO: Forgive us. We're in a difficult situation. Debora often gets
irritable.

GIANNI: I'm sorry. I can't come to you as any kind of help. I don't have
a job for either of you. I don't have any money either. I'm barely
managing to get by. I grow orchids.

BETTA: At first it was lemons. But his lemons died. Not the orchids,
though. They're beautiful.

GIANNI: They're gorgeous.

DEBORA: I hate the way orchids smell.

MARCO: We've arrived here at a bad moment. We've had some bad
luck.

BETTA: It's not a moment. It's been going on like this for quite a few
years. Alvise has never gotten along with Bianca. They've been talking about splitting up for years. For years things at the factory have
been going badly and they've been in debt. Bianca runs up a lot of
debts. She lives as if she were a millionaire. She's always got a lot of
men around, lots of affairs. And she's sick. She takes pills.

DEBORA: What does she take?

BETTA: She takes pills. It doesn't matter to him if she has other men.
He's used to it. He's resigned to it. He feels bad that she takes pills.
He hides them from her. She finds them anyway. He hides money
from her. She finds it. She used to be beautiful, rosy-cheeked,
healthy. She was a swimming champion. Now, if she walks two
steps she's tired immediately. She doesn't eat anymore. She can't eat
anymore. Up until five or six years ago, I remember she was gorgeous. Now she's ruined. Her teeth are ruined, her hair is ruined. I
think Alvise has stopped loving her. But just as he's about to leave
her, he doesn't have the heart because he feels sorry for her. He
wants to help her when he sees her so sick and so unhappy. He's

not jealous. He lets her have all the men she wants. Now she's obsessed with Gianni. Then, when she's in love, she becomes even more unhappy – she trembles, she cries, she wants a child, she spends the night next to the telephone or else she runs off in the Mercedes at 180 kilometres an hour along the freeway. She stays in a motel, and they find her the next morning like a dead woman because she's taken pills.

DEBORA: I feel bad to think that this young girl is mixed up in this terrible mess.

GIANNI: She's not so young anymore, Betta isn't. She's seventeen years old. Nowadays no one grows up. We stay children. Children look at the world with cold eyes. That's how I look at the world, too. It's not that they don't feel anxiety. On the contrary, they feel it in a frightening way. But their eyes stay cold. Cold as a stone. No tears.

DEBORA: Alvise must be completely thoughtless. How can he keep this girl in the house in a situation like that?

BETTA: I keep him company. I'm a comfort to him. I'm a presence in the house.

GIANNI: It isn't true that Alvise has stopped loving Bianca. He still loves her. Aside from her, he doesn't see anyone or anything. He's indifferent to the rest of the world.

DEBORA: Marco, I'm begging you, let's get out of here. Let's leave. I'm suffering having to stay here. I feel as though I've fallen into some spot in the world where the only stories anyone can tell are stories about something terrible happening. I'm not very strong. I'm no wild boar. If I stay here, I'm going to end up like Bianca.

GIANNI: Of course not. Don't leave. Betta and I need some company. We could use cheering up. It's a beautiful day today. We could go down to the water.

BETTA: In Gianni's boat. Gianni has a motorboat. There's a very lovely place where no one goes, with rocky cliffs along the shore and a sandy beach. I went there all the time with the English guy who used to live here. I even went swimming in the nude. Not that it meant anything to him – he was queer. We could buy some sandwiches and have lunch there. Gianni, you and I could go out and buy some sandwiches.

MARCO: Yes, that's a good idea.

GIANNI: You go buy sandwiches. Or else you and Marco. We'll wait for the two of you here.

BETTA: Let's go. Come on, Marco.

Betta and Marco exit.

DEBORA: That little girl is in love with you, Gianni. You could marry
    her, after all. Why don't you marry her?

GIANNI: Ah, no. I'm not going to do anything of the kind. It'd be like
    marrying my cat.

DEBORA: You're not making love with her?

GIANNI: No. Nothing of the kind. It would only make me anxious. Be-
    sides, it wouldn't make any sense. Women often make me anxious.

DEBORA: Not Bianca?

GIANNI: Bianca used to give me terrible anxiety. The relationship
    didn't last long. She stopped being my mistress, as you put it,
    very quickly. I stopped calling her. Before, I used to call her in the
    middle of the night. She'd come over. Do you see my house? It's
    that one up there, the red one with the arches. It's a beautiful house
    but it's falling apart. I'd like to sell it, but no one wants it because
    it's got a mortgage and also because it's so big, and you'd have to
    spend a lot of money on it.

DEBORA: We were talking about Bianca.

GIANNI: Why do you want to know so much about Bianca? Maybe
    because you identify with her?

DEBORA: You're such a bore with your psychoanalysis, Gianni.

GIANNI: I don't have much else to tell you about Bianca. When she took
    off, I felt as if I'd been liberated. I was alone again. It was a breath of
    fresh air.

DEBORA: You were alone with your orchids.

GIANNI: Yes. With my orchids.

DEBORA: I hate that smell.

GIANNI: You've told me. But I'm sure it isn't true. When you come to
    see my house, I'll give you some orchids.

DEBORA: I won't be coming. There isn't time. I want to leave. I'm sick of
    this place.

GIANNI: You always repeat the same phrases. You're like a broken re-
    cord. I don't have any money. I want to leave. I hate orchids. You're
    boring.

DEBORA: I don't care if you think I'm boring.

GIANNI: Yes, you do care. You don't want me to think you're boring. You
    want me to think you're pretty. I do find you very pretty, and also
    boring. But you're boring in a way that I like. I feel touched by it. It's
    strange, you know, I feel as though I've known you for years. You're

so pretty, so petite and sweet. You have moments in which your face turns sharp, bitter. You say nasty things. I even feel touched by that. But all women make me anxious. I'm better off alone.

DEBORA: No one is better off alone.

Marco enters.

MARCO: Okay. We've bought some bread, prosciutto, cheese, and wine. Betta went to get the boat. You're wanted on the phone, Gianni. You got a call at the pharmacist's house. It's long distance. (*Gianni exits.*) What were the two of you talking about when I came in?

DEBORA: Nothing.

MARCO: What do you mean nothing? You were talking about something. You seem in a strange mood, Debora. Aren't you feeling well?

DEBORA: My mind is confused. Where's my bathing suit? I can't seem to find it. What a mess.

MARCO: You must have left it at the Antico Giappone. If you don't find your bathing suit, what are you going to do?

DEBORA: I'll buy another one.

MARCO: Where? I haven't seen a shop that sells bathing suits. There's just the general store. They sell rope, plastic, nails. No bathing suits.

Gianni enters.

GIANNI: Alvise called. Bianca is dead.

DEBORA: Oh! She's dead?

GIANNI: Yes. Her heart failed and she's dead.

ACT THREE

[*The same cottage, a few days later.*]

Debora is alone. Marco and Gianni enter.

MARCO: Okay, Debora. I replaced all the dishes we broke. In just these past few days, we've broken quite a pile of dishes.

DEBORA: You could have done without replacing the dishes. That hateful pharmacist took all that money. And the refrigerator has never worked.

MARCO: But the wife gave me back 20,000 lire. Gianni came with me to see her. He convinced her.

DEBORA: Thanks a lot. It's cost 50,000 lire to stay here for a few days. It wasn't even some deluxe hotel.

GIANNI: Stop talking about money. You turn ugly when you talk about money. If you stop talking about it, maybe at some point money will start raining down on your head.

DEBORA: No, the only thing that rains down on us is rain. Our Seicento has a hole in the roof.

MARCO: It's not raining today. It's sunny.

DEBORA: That's not counting the other expenses. The plastic curtain that you never put up.

MARCO: A plastic curtain always comes in handy. We'll put it up in the next house we have. One day we'll definitely have a house.

DEBORA: Where?

MARCO: I don't know. Wherever I find a job. I wrote to some acquaintances of my mother's in Florence. They have a factory that manufactures ballpoint pens.

DEBORA: In Florence?

MARCO: Yes, in Florence. But we won't go there immediately. We could go to your sister's for a while, if you'd like.

DEBORA: I won't like anything. I'm unhappy.

MARCO: You said you wanted to be around peaceful people. Your sister is peaceful. Stupid, but peaceful.

DEBORA: She's not that stupid. But I've no desire to see my sister now. I've no desire to be around peaceful people. I know I said that, but it's not true. All kinds of things get said. I don't feel like leaving. I've gotten used to it here. I get used to things quickly.

GIANNI: Don't leave, you two. Stay here a while. A few more days. I'm asking you.

DEBORA: Marco wants to leave. That's what he's decided. I never argue with his decisions. I'm docile.

GIANNI: Docile and nasty.

DEBORA: Why nasty? Am I nasty?

GIANNI: You're sometimes nasty to Marco. You're cruel to him.

DEBORA: Is my face nasty today? Is my face sharp?

GIANNI: Today your face is unhappy.

DEBORA: I wouldn't want you to remember me with a sharp, nasty face.

GIANNI: No, that's not how I'll remember you. I'll remember your true face.

MARCO: You know, Debora, Alvise got home yesterday. Bianca was buried in Rome. Betta says he doesn't feel like seeing me. He's too despondent. I don't feel like it either. I haven't seen him for too many years. I wouldn't know what to say. Fate is so strange. To have come here just as Bianca was about to die. If I thought I might be able to help, that I might manage to raise his spirits, I'd drop everything and go see him. I'd force myself on him. But I'm a mess. I'm beside myself. What would I say? What words would I use?

A knock at the door. Betta enters.

BETTA: I've brought a thermos of coffee for you two. It's boiling hot. You can drink it on the road. And I also brought an electric razor for you, Marco. Alvise sent it to you as a gift. He says he remembers that when you shave with a blade you scratch your face all up.

DEBORA: In Rome. On Via Panisperna. When the two of you used to sing that song about the wild boars.

MARCO: Thank you. It's a beautiful razor. Tell him that I'm so grateful.

BETTA: Plus he gave me this portrait of Bianca for you both. She was still beautiful. It was a few years ago. She's with the baby. Before they put him in boarding school.

MARCO: She was so beautiful.

BETTA: Alvise asks the two of you to forgive him. He's sorry you're leaving. He'll write to you. Right now, he doesn't want anyone around. Just me and Gianni. We were with him last night until late. He and Gianni played chess.

DEBORA: Don't you feel any sense of guilt, Gianni? Don't you have any regrets when you're with Alvise? When you're playing chess with him? Maybe Bianca wouldn't be dead if she weren't in love with you.

GIANNI: She wasn't in love with me. She'd be dead all the same. She was looking for reasons to suffer.

DEBORA: All of us are looking for reasons to suffer. I'm looking, too. I find them, because you can always find them. It's the only thing in the world you can find immediately.

GIANNI: I brought back your jacket. It got left behind at my house yesterday.

MARCO: You were at Gianni's house yesterday, Debora?

DEBORA: Yes. While you were in Ancona. But that's not a jacket, Gianni, it's a sweater. It's one of my cashmere sweaters.

MARCO: Deborah says: cashmere or nothing. Wherever she goes she
  forgets something. I went to Ancona to retrieve her dress from the
  Antico Giappone hotel. It seemed like she would die if she didn't
  get back her dress with the little blue flowers.
DEBORA: It wasn't because of the dress. I wanted to be free of you for a
  few hours, Marco. All of a sudden I couldn't stand you anymore. I
  made up a reason for you to go.
MARCO: A reason to suffer?
DEBORA: Yes. So now you know.
BETTA: Have you been to Gianni's house a lot, Debora?
DEBORA: Not a lot. It's a beautiful, big house, but it's falling apart. He
  gave me some orchids. Those there. There aren't any flower vases
  here, so I put them in that soup tureen. I'll take them with me.
BETTA: But you don't like the way orchids smell.
DEBORA: No, I hate it. But now, having been forced to smell them in
  this room, I've gotten used to the smell. I've gotten used to this
  room and I would stay here forever.
BETTA: When the two of you come back next time, I'll find a more comfortable house for you.
DEBORA: There will never be a next time. We'll never be back here
  again.
GIANNI: Yes, you'll be back. You have to come back. Or else we'll come
  to Florence. We'll run into each other again, somewhere in the
  world. It's a small world.
DEBORA: No, it's big. Ugly and big. Noisy. Crowded. Crowded and
  empty. With lots of roads that lead nowhere.
GIANNI: But your road brought you here.
DEBORA: Yes, but only for a little while. The space of a few days. There
  wasn't time to think, to have a look around, to get acquainted, to
  breathe. There's only been time to suffer.
MARCO: Let's go, Debora. Close up your bags. Take a good look around
  to make sure you haven't forgotten anything. It's getting late.
DEBORA: What difference does it make if it's late? No one is expecting
  us.
MARCO: But no one is holding us here, either. Betta and Gianni have
  their own lives. Of course they're sorry that we're leaving, but
  they'll forget about us quickly enough. They're young. Now they'll
  go down to the beach, perhaps. They'll want to go to that little
  beach, the one with the rocky cliffs along the shore and the sand,
  where they like to go in Gianni's boat. I regret never having been

there. I imagine it's marvellous. I liked this town. I like the sea. And
I've very much liked being with the two of you. But I can't bring
myself to stay in one place for long. I don't believe I could have
settled down here, not even if we'd had a job. Oh God, the day will
surely come when I'll learn. I'll choose some place and I'll hang
on there. I'll get used to it. Because one gets used to anything. It's
incredible how a person gets used to things. It's incredible what a
person can bear. What he can swallow. Considering the quality of
the food that's put before him. Humiliations. Cruel tricks. Betrayals.
Farewells. It's incredible the bitterness and the sorrow that we push
down our throats, along with our saliva, every day. Some people
die of it, but not very many. An immense number of us get used to
it. You live and you breathe as if it were nothing. Goodbye, Betta,
goodbye Gianni. It's a huge shame that we arrived in such a terrible
moment. Such an ugly moment.

DEBORA: Moments are never all that ugly. What's ugly are the years.

MARCO: Oh, yes, the years are horrible. But we swallow those, too. We
get them down. We think of ourselves as so fragile, but in fact we
couldn't be stronger. We've got hides like rhinos. Like wild boars.

BETTA: I asked Alvise if he still remembers that song about the wild
boars. He doesn't remember it anymore.

GIANNI: It's not our hides that are so strong, Marco, it's our hearts.
Our hearts are unbreakable. They're strong because they're always
waiting for something. What they're waiting for, no one knows. But
they're equipped with infinite patience. Everything else about us is
so fragile. We have delicate stomachs, delicate skin, sensitive pal-
ates, fragile nerves. We suffer from insomnia, tremors, bad dreams,
night sweats. But the heart is never ill. It's utterly healthy. It swal-
lows everything, gets everything down – separations, loneliness,
poisons, the agonizing thoughts, the horrible years. It's the heart
that's strong, Marco, it's the heart.

June 1968

Notes

1 The immense and sumptuous royal residence and gardens built in the last
half of the eighteenth century by the Bourbon kings of Naples; at the time
it was likely the largest building in Europe. The Reggia di Caserta became
a World Heritage site in 1996.

2 Eternit was one of Italy's largest manufacturers of *fibrocemento*, an asbestos-cement amalgam used widely in roofing, plumbing, and other products. Though the dangers of asbestos began to be known in the 1970s, Eternit continued to manufacture asbestos products until the mid-1990s in its main plant in Casale Monferrato, some one hundred kilometres east of Turin. In recent years, the city of Casale Monferrato has spent millions of Euros in asbestos-remediation efforts in the area.

3 An adult would normally speak to a child with the informal '*tu*,' as Debora does. Marco either does not recognize how young Betta is at first or prefers to maintain an exaggerated social distance from the stranger at the door, an affectation an Italian audience would note. In short, he is criticizing Debora's manners.

The Wrong Door

A PLAY IN THREE ACTS

Cast:
Stefano
Angelica
Giorgio
Tecla
Raniero

ACT ONE

[*A country house outside Rome, 1968.*]

*Giorgio and Raniero are in a room, playing chess. The telephone rings.
Stefano enters and goes to the phone.*

STEFANO: Hello? Who is it? Oh, Signora Carafa. Good morning. You're
up, I see. No, nothing new, nothing special. Your daughter is still
sleeping. We had a pretty quiet night. All things considered, Angelica slept fairly well. No, Signora Carafa, don't come today. The
weather's terrible. You should stay inside on the couch where it's
warm, with your embroidery. Sure, excellent, make another pillow.
With a tiger's head? Excellent. Good boy, Istanbul. Yes, Istanbul
has already had his breakfast. The cats, too. No, no one's seen the
housekeeper today either. I don't know, I don't have her telephone
number and I don't remember where she's living anymore. Maybe
she's ill. But I'm managing just fine. As soon as Angelica wakes up,
I'll take her breakfast in to her. I've already got the tray prepared.
A poached egg, a grilled steak, a baked pear. Yes, rare. A great big

fillet, very rare. On a hot grill. Over an open flame. A couple of
turns. I know. Yes, Angelica is anemic, I know, I know. The egg is
very fresh. I get them at the dairy. They come in every morning
from the country. I know, you don't have to tell me. I'm a maniac
for fresh eggs. I examine them one by one over a light bulb. Some
friends are here with us. Tecla. Giorgio. Giorgio Zena, yes, the one
with the socks. And also Raniero. No, you don't know Raniero.
You wouldn't know him. I don't know him well myself. I laid eyes
on him last night for the very first time. Giorgio brought him over.
His last name? Tell me your last name, Raniero. Yes, he told me but
I didn't catch his last name. Camerana. Raniero Camerana. From
Siena? Are all the Cameranas from Siena? No, he's from Perugia.
All three of us slept here. Tecla in the guest room and the other two
in the dining room. We have lots of room. No, they're not leaving.
I told them to stay until Tuesday. Everyone is still on vacation until
Tuesday. You say what? Who'll make the beds? I don't know. No
one. Beds don't really have to be made every single day. No, really,
Signora Carafa, it's kind of an old-fashioned habit. You say what?
Who's going to wash all those sheets? I don't know. The housekeeper will reappear sooner or later. No, the washing machine is
broken. It's leaking water. I'm afraid they ripped you off with that
washing machine. But really, we're so grateful to you for giving it
to us. A washing machine is a huge convenience. Thank you so, so
much. We'll call the repairman. There is a warranty, but Angelica
put it somewhere and doesn't remember where. Yes, it might be the
anemia. Your memory gets weaker when you're anemic. No, please,
don't send your housekeeper. I don't find her pleasant to be around.
She has a very critical nature, your housekeeper does. Angelica and
I don't get along with people who are overly critical. We're pretty
easygoing here and we appreciate a little self-indulgence. Signora
Carafa, I've got to let you go because I have a few things I need to
get done. No, don't come. No, I'm telling you, don't come. Come
on, I don't say that to offend you, but Angelica gets even more
tense when you're here. Yes. She is like that. She requires a lot of
patience. Go take a walk. Put on that lovely red hat of yours. Oh,
of course, it's raining. But Angelica will call you when she gets up,
sure. Goodbye, Signora Carafa. (*He hangs up the phone.*)

GIORGIO: Was that Angelica's mother?

STEFANO: Yes. Why don't you go down to the cellar and get me a
bucket of coal? This damn stove has gone out.

GIORGIO: Let me finish this game. I'm winning. He's no great chess player, our Raniero. Why don't you go down to the cellar yourself? I'm a guest. Guests are sacred.

STEFANO: I need to be here when Angelica wakes up. I have to give her her medicine. Besides, I have to cook her steak.

GIORGIO: She isn't going to eat all that.

STEFANO: Who knows?

GIORGIO: The stove went out because you threw all those newspapers in there. How come the two of you don't have a radiator?

STEFANO: It's an old house.

GIORGIO: It's Cencio's?

STEFANO: Yes.

GIORGIO: Are you paying him rent or is he giving it to you for free?

STEFANO: We pay him rent.

RANIERO: Who's this Cencio?

GIORGIO: He's Angelica's husband. Ex-husband. Quite a guy. They were divorced three years ago. They went to Switzerland to get a divorce. They've got a daughter and he's got custody of her. (*A bell rings.*) There's Angelica. Good luck with the steak.

Stefano exits. Giorgio exits with the coal bucket. Tecla enters.

TECLA: Has anyone called over to the bakery? There's not a trace of bread in this house. Not even dry bread. At least with dry bread you can make food for the dog. Or for the cats. The cats are all in the kitchen sleeping, looking blissful and well fed. When I get up in the morning I need to eat a piece of bread. It's a habit I've had since I was a baby. I found a box of cookies and I ate one. It was revolting. But I saw on the box that there was protein for the dogs. Stay, Istanbul.

RANIERO: Doesn't seem to me that anyone has called the bakery.

Tecla exits. The telephone rings. Stefano comes back into the room.

STEFANO: (*Goes to the phone.*) Hello? Mama? Hello! Terrible, terrible. It was an awful night. Angelica never once closed her eyes. We were just lying there with the light on. No, don't come over. It's pouring. Stay home, where it's warm, and visit with Signora Borbona. You're polishing the silver? But everything at your house is already gleaming. What's the point of doing more polishing? You're obsessed,

Mama. No, don't come over. Don't even think about it. When she sees you, Angelica turns into a snake. What can I do? She can't stand the sight of you. I know you're always friendly to everyone. I know you didn't do anything to her. You even gave her your brooch with the silver pendant. I know, I know. As far as that goes, she doesn't want to see her own mother either. No, she's not eating. She can't keep anything down. Yesterday all she had was half a glass of milk with some cognac. I fed it to her with a coffee spoon. No, she's not pregnant. The doctor? He didn't say anything. It has something to do with her nerves. It'll pass. She doesn't want any other doctor. She only wants Dr Vlad. Yes, he's a psychoanalyst, but he's also a doctor. He used to work in a hospital in Berlin many years ago, before the war. Oh yes, he's very kind. Really an exquisitely kind man. Sure, I'm great. Yes, I ate. We have people here. Giorgio and some others. Giorgio Zena, yes, the one with the socks. What? I don't know. Do you carry support hose in your store, Giorgio? He's not here. He's gone down to get coal. But I doubt they carry support hose. They only stock those in medical supply stores. But what do you need with support hose? You don't have varicose veins. Oh, for Signora Borbona. Mom, I'm going to let you go because I've got things to do. Bye-bye.

RANIERO: That was your mother?

STEFANO: Yes. My mother.

RANIERO: What's wrong with your wife? Is she sick?

STEFANO: She can't manage to eat or sleep. She's in a state of mental anguish. It's been like that for a while, but she's been worse over the last few days. She's in the care of a psychoanalyst. Dr Vlad.

RANIERO: He's a good analyst?

STEFANO: Tactful. But you know, I don't know much about it. I've never been to a psychoanalyst. Angelica says that I'm neurotic, too, and I need psychoanalysis the way I need to eat to stay alive. Has anyone called the bakery?

RANIERO: I don't think so.

STEFANO: I'll go then. I could use a breath of fresh air. I have a bit of a headache. All night long with the light on. Me, you know, I've never been sick. I have an iron constitution. You haven't met Angelica yet. You'll see her, when she gets up. Last night when she realized that people were here she wanted to get up but I didn't let her. She was very tired. We took a walk, and, since she's not getting any nutrition, she gets tired out quickly. But she was curious to meet you. She's always curious to see new faces. She complains that she sees the same faces all the time. You're from Perugia?

RANIERO: Yes, I'm from Perugia.

STEFANO: I've never been to Perugia. (*Exits.*)

Giorgio and Tecla enter.

GIORGIO: Here's the coal. I found some old issues of *Annabella* in the cellar. I read myself a story: 'The Stars at Pontassieve.' Two sisters love the same man. They think he's an industrialist but he's a thief instead. He invites them to be guests at his villa. But the villa is stolen.

TECLA: How does an entire villa get stolen?

GIORGIO: He's staying there with an old, senile woman, and he says she's his mother. At night, he breaks into her dresser and robs her. The old woman's real son comes back and has the guy thrown in jail. The good sister marries the real son. The bad sister goes to jail because she helped him break into the old woman's dresser. The old woman comes to her senses for a bit and becomes enchanted when she looks up at the stars. She recovers her memory and remembers that the thief is the illegitimate son she had with a workman. Then she dies, but first she forgives her son and gives the baby her blessing.

TECLA: What baby?

GIORGIO: The thief's baby. Born in jail.

RANIERO: You're a terrible storyteller.

TECLA: You're a terrible storyteller and it's an idiotic story besides.

GIORGIO: Magazines must pay gobs of cash for stories like that. And it can't really be that difficult to write them. All you need is an idea. Any old idea. People will swallow anything.

TECLA: But you don't need money. You live with your family and they're all rich.

GIORGIO: Yes, I do. I'm always having to ask my father for money, and I'm sick of it. I know how to write, and I can write without ever getting tired of it. I would have made a great journalist. Instead, at twenty years of age they stuck me in that store. Men's socks. Women's socks. Men's sweaters. Women's sweaters. They're all there – my father, my aunt and uncle, my sister. Not my mother. She stops by for a moment at noon, in her beaver coat. She criticizes everything. She has a very critical nature, my mother does. Very authoritarian. She scolds my father because he gets caught up in long conversations with the customers. She scolds the shop girls because their smocks are wrinkled. She scolds my sister because she goes out of the house without drinking her caffe latte. That's her religion, caffe latte.

TECLA: But you're never at the shop. You're never there when I go in to buy a pair of socks. Your father's there, and he starts talking to me about Freud.

GIORGIO: Yes, that's my father's fixation, Freud. He knows him by heart. Dr Vlad gave him Freud to read. Dr Vlad is his big friend. My father wakes him up at night to tell him about the dreams he's having. I go to the store in the late afternoon. In the morning I'm at home. I wake up and I feel happy. Too happy to go into the store. I feel the urge to accomplish something in the morning – work, study, something I haven't figured out yet. I feel on pins and needles, all the way down to my bones. I sing while I'm shaving. I sing out of the desire to work, I sing out of joy. I go into the living room. We have a very large house, but I don't have a real room of my own, just a dark hole behind the dressing room. My mother says that if I want to write or study, there's the living room. The living room looks out onto the terrace. There's a glass door, and the terrace wraps all the way around. I see my mother on the terrace with her oversized eyeglasses and her quilted dressing gown. It's light blue. She's cutting the new shoots off the plants. Meanwhile she's talking to the dog and to the butler. The dog is black and sad-looking, with long ears. He's called Doctor. Since my mother wants the butler to call me doctor, I hear her say 'doctor' and I can't tell if they're talking to me or to the dog. The butler is also dark and sad-looking. He brings me a caffe latte. I drink the caffe latte, and I start to feel very warm because the heat in our living room is intense. And the desire to work just flows out of me. My mother goes on cutting the shoots, and every once in a while she glances my way. She's happy with me. I please her. To her, I seem like an intellectual. She thinks I must be Proust. She read somewhere that Proust wrote his book when he was around forty. Since I'm only twenty-three, my mother isn't worried about me. When she takes off her dressing gown, she puts on her fur coat and goes to the store, or to have cof-fee downstairs. She's happy. She thinks she's the mother of Proust.

TECLA: Why don't you get out of that house?

GIORGIO: I should. I've been thinking about it for years.

TECLA: Your mother's clipped your wings with her garden shears.

GIORGIO: I'm not sure I ever had wings. Maybe I have neither wings nor a sky to fly in. Maybe I'm just a barnyard animal. Every once in a while the suspicion crosses my mind.

TECLA: So go look for a barnyard. Make that your living room. Right now, you're a lap dog.

GIORGIO: Don't insult me. Everything is very difficult. Don't be unpleasant. I am going to leave. I'm going to leave this winter.

TECLA: I come from a poor family. I was raised in the building where my parents were caretakers.[1] The odours in that apartment we lived in were horrible – I can still smell them. There was the odour of varnish, of being closed up, of soup, of dust. My father made picture frames. There were jars of varnish and glue everywhere. There weren't any windows and it was suffocating in the summer. When my mother came to pick me up at school, she didn't have a coat. All she had to cover herself with was a sweater. It was a black sweater with purple stripes and long, long fur. Horrible. The other mothers had coats, veils, handbags. She planted herself in the doorway in her slippers and her sweater. I was so ashamed of her. At eighteen I won a stenography competition. I found a job in Rome. That's how I left Milan and my mother. My father had been dead for some years. In Rome I stayed at a boarding house with my aunt, but then I took a room with some girlfriends. It was a room in Montesacro,[2] on the very top floor. I faced the balcony and I could see the sky, the clouds, the city. I could breathe. How lovely the air smelled. It seemed to me I was queen of the city. I'd come so far. I started earning enough to live on and I bought myself a fur – a fake one – velvet worked so that it looked like leopard. But when I went to see my mother in Rome, because I had the fake leopard and a fake pearl necklace, and I had bleached my hair, she was convinced that I was working as a whore. She didn't want my money. Then she did take it, but with a look on her face like it was something disgusting. She didn't want to go out with me. She was ashamed to be seen with me on the street. I explained to her that I worked in a sewing machine factory. But she didn't believe there were any sewing machines. She shrugged her shoulders. She was convinced I was a whore, and she died believing that. That's the way it always is with parents. Either they're ashamed of us or we're ashamed of them. Or they're disappointed in us or we're disappointed in them. Or else they force their dreams on us until we're exasperated and ashamed of ourselves because those dreams are so distant from what we really are. Until they die and then we discover how badly we'd always treated them, and the regret eats our hearts out. What a beautiful life. When my mother died, I took it hard. I'd also just been through a situation with a man that ended badly, and I would have given anything to have my mother back, and the smells and the warmth of that apartment that they let the caretakers live in. I was full of guilt and remorse. I was anxious and terrified, and I was riddled with a sense of frustration, of castration. I really went through it all. I wasn't going to work anymore. I went out on sick leave, and I stopped getting out of bed entirely. Then I went to see a psychoanalyst. Dr Vlad. A friend of mine sent me to see him. More than anything, I was suffering from a caretaker complex.

RANIERO: And he cured you?

TECLA: More or less. Maybe you're never completely cured. But he helped me. Meanwhile, I'd found myself another job. Ballpoint pens. I'm still there. Dr Vlad is a very kind person. He'd go out of his way to help one of his patients. They pay me very well at my job. Sometimes I travel. I see places. I hardly seem like a care-taker's daughter. Do I seem like one to you? No. I have everything. I have a small apartment all to myself. I travel. I even take trips on airplanes. I've been out of the country. But it doesn't matter to me anymore to hide the fact that I'm a caretaker's daughter. I tell ev-eryone about it. I'm telling you the whole story even though I only met you yesterday and I don't know you. Giorgio knows. Giorgio and I know each other quite well. We're always running into each other here. Once upon a time I wouldn't have been able to tell any-one. That man who left me? I let him think that my father was the head of the Court of Appeals. My poor father. Him and his picture frames. That's psychoanalysis. Psychoanalysis teaches you to be what you are. But it's not as though you stop feeling bad. You have all your old wounds, and they stay with you. You feel them burn-ing. You made this mistake, you made that mistake. You offended this person, you offended that person. In the mornings you open your eyes and all your little toads are waiting there to jump into bed with you. They eat your heart out.

GIORGIO: Why don't you get married?

TECLA: Because I haven't been lucky. My relationships with men are always very complicated and entangled.

GIORGIO: You could marry Dr Vlad.

TECLA: Don't talk nonsense. He's too old. Besides, I'm in analysis with him. Analysis is something very special. You can't marry your psychoanalyst. You can't.

GIORGIO: Lots of women marry their psychoanalysts.

TECLA: But not me. I couldn't.

GIORGIO: We don't know anything about you, Raniero. Tell us something about yourself. The only thing we know is that you're from Perugia.

TECLA: Aren't the two of you friends? I thought you were. You brought him with you yesterday evening.

GIORGIO: Yes, but I'd only known him for twenty minutes. I ran into him at the Borghis' house, these people who were giving a party. He was leaning against a wall and not saying a word to anyone. He looked very bored. I was bored, too. He seemed to have a friendly face, and we chatted a bit. I brought him here. As soon as we got here, Stefano put on a Vivaldi record. *The Four Seasons.* It was lovely. I fell asleep on the couch. I don't know about him. You were with Angelica up in the bedroom. I'd had a lot of wine to drink. Stefano and Raniero made up a bed for me and I fell into it like a stone. I just haven't had time to ask you any questions, Raniero. And this morning we played chess. I know you're from Perugia and that you don't play chess very well. Other than that, I don't know anything. I haven't even understood exactly what it is you do for a living. (*Stefano enters with a tray.*) It took you all this time to cook a steak?

STEFANO: I went down to the bakery for a minute.

GIORGIO: This is supposed to be a fillet, rare?

STEFANO: It's not a fillet, it's a sirloin. But it's a very nice cut.

GIORGIO: Why is it so grey? (*Stefano exits with the tray.*) She won't eat it.

TECLA: No, she won't eat it. She isn't getting anything down, imagine trying to eat a steak. It's some bright idea of Stefano's. Poor Angelica. What a dreadful situation. She says she starts crying if she even thinks of eating. She's anorexic. That's what they call what she's got.

RANIERO: Did something happen to her?

TECLA: Nothing. Nothing out of the ordinary. She's anxious. She's got an anxiety neurosis. She wants to die.

RANIERO: Maybe she's not getting along with her husband?

GIORGIO: With Stefano? Poor Stefano. He's a martyr. She's got him nailed to the cross.

TECLA: Yes. She's really mean to him. But he doesn't seem to realize it. He doesn't know. She makes him stay awake the entire night

because she can't stand it if he's sleeping when she can't. And if
he goes out even just for a minute, she has a fit. Because she needs
him. It's that she doesn't make any distinction between him and
herself. She tortures him the same way she tortures herself. Exactly
the same.

Stefano re-enters with the tray.

GIORGIO: She didn't want it? Didn't she eat anything?
STEFANO: Nothing.
TECLA: Did you try with some milk and cognac?
STEFANO: No. Today she doesn't even want milk. She's nauseous.
GIORGIO: But she must be pregnant.
STEFANO: No. She's not pregnant.
GIORGIO: This girl I know, everything made her nauseous. She stopped
    eating, and it turned out she was pregnant.
STEFANO: You got some girl pregnant?
GIORGIO: No, of course she wasn't pregnant by me. Her boyfriend got
    her pregnant and she married him.
STEFANO: But she's not pregnant. (*He goes to the phone and dials a num-*
    ber.) Hello, Romoletto? Romoletto, call the attorney to the phone. I
    have something urgent to tell him. He's sleeping? Wake him up, Ro-
    moletto, please. It's urgent. I know it's Sunday. He didn't go to bed
    until three this morning? Wake him up anyway. It's almost noon.
    Eight hours of sleep are more than enough for a grown man. I wish
    I'd slept eight hours. If you only knew how little I'd slept. That's no
    concern of yours? I know it's no concern of yours. Please don't be
    rude, Romoletto. I'm asking you nicely, go wake him up. Tell him
    it's about Angelica. It's urgent. Thank you, okay. I'll hold on.
GIORGIO: Who's Romoletto?
TECLA: His butler. A queer.
RANIERO: He's queer, too?
TECLA: Him? Who? No, not Cencio. He's Angelica's ex-husband. He's
    got plenty of women.
GIORGIO: Butlers are often queer. Ours is a queer, too. A sad queer.
    Before he came to work for us he lived with a tailor. They must
    have been lovers. He's filled the servant's quarters where he sleeps
    with pictures of the tailor, their house, the grounds, his grave. He
    has a gorgeous grave. He's dead. He was a famous tailor. He used
    to dress princesses.

STEFANO: Hello, Cencio? Damn, I've been waiting for an hour. Yes,
I know it takes you a while to wake up. I know you didn't go to
bed until four this morning. I know. Romoletto told me. I'm sorry.
Listen, Cencio, Angelica wants you to come over for a few minutes. No, without the baby. She doesn't want to see the baby; she's
afraid it'll make her cry. Very, very badly. A horrible night. I read
the letter you wrote to her yesterday. A terrible letter. Excuse me
for saying so, Cencio, but it was a terrible letter. Vague, superficial.
Falsely affectionate. And only ten lines besides. You could have put
yourself out a little more. You write novels a thousand pages long
that end up in the editor's wastebasket and then when you have to
write a letter to the person who was your wife you can't find more
than a few dull little words. Excuse me, excuse me. I don't have
anything against your novels. You should go right ahead and write
all the novels you like. The thing is, Angelica wants to see you for a
minute. No. Not tomorrow. Today. Angelica isn't doing well. She's
in a state of mental anguish and I'm afraid. She heard you were getting married. She wants to know when you're getting married and
to whom. She found it very strange that you hadn't said anything
to her about it yet. Oh, really? It's really still all up in the air? That
may be, but even if you've only got the vaguest of plans, Angelica
should be the first person you tell. They don't concern her? Your
vague plans don't concern her? On the contrary, they concern her
a great deal. Your vague plans are connected to the future of your
daughter. In any case, Angelica wanted to know more about this
boarding school in Switzerland that you say you've seen. For now,
Angelica doesn't feel she can have Ilaria with her. She's too sick.
But if you're really getting married or if your job is requiring you
to move around a lot, your daughter needs to be settled either in
a good boarding school or else at home with Signora Carafa. The
three of us ought to be able to talk this out together. Me, too. Yes,
me too because I'm involved in this question given that Angelica is
my wife now and the issue of her peace of mind is very near to my
heart. So we'll expect you today? Today is difficult for you? What
do you mean today is difficult for you? Find a few minutes, a few
minutes for Christ's sake. Excuse me. I know you have things to
do. You have to be in Naples tonight? But it isn't even noon yet. I
know it's raining. But you have a car. I know we're far away. The
house is definitely out of the way. Although it's your house. No,
all I mean is that if it weren't for you, it would never have entered

our minds to live in this area. Yes, yes. Of course, I'm extremely
grateful to you for giving us this house. Because it's a lovely house.
Inconvenient, but beautiful. Damp. Yes, it's damp. I know you were
born here. But the house is old now and the walls soak up the rain.
And it's true we've never paid you a fair amount for rent. Eighty
thousand lire per month is hardly anything. But that doesn't really
have anything to do with what we're talking about. Let's not get
money matters mixed up in a situation that's already complicated.
Exactly, we should definitely clear up the question of the house,
too. Anyway, you ought to be able to dedicate a fraction of your
day to someone who is ill and who once was very dear to you. I'm
not being sentimental. I'm just stating the facts. Come over. We've
got some friends of ours here, too. Tecla, Giorgio, Raniero. Raniero
is someone you haven't met. I know, you know everyone, but you
haven't met Raniero. You want to come to lunch? Come to lunch
then. What? Bring some prosciutto? There's no need, we have food
here. What? Yes, Angelica does like prosciutto, but that's crazy. You
haven't understood a thing I've been saying. Angelica is very ill
and she hasn't been able to get anything down for several days. She
can't eat. Everything makes her nauseous. No, she's not pregnant.
Yes, that might be a solution, but she's not pregnant and I don't
know what else to do for her. Yes, goodbye Cencio. See you later.
(*He hangs up the phone.*)

TECLA: So is Cencio coming?

STEFANO: Yes, he's coming to lunch. In the afternoon he'll continue on
to Naples. They're holding his party's convention there.

GIORGIO: But is he really getting married?

STEFANO: That's what people are saying. He maintains that it's a vague
possibility. That the two of them still have to think it over.

GIORGIO: And what's this girlfriend of his like? Have you seen her?

STEFANO: Yes. I saw them together the other night at the Opera Theatre.
They were putting on *Ernani*. She's an attractive girl. I'm told she's either Hungarian or Romanian. A tiny little thing. Skinny. With a great
big head of black hair and a nose that looks like it's been squashed
flat. She looks like a little black poodle. She had on a leather jacket.
He pulled her around behind him like she was his pet dog.

GIORGIO: Nice legs?

STEFANO: I don't know. I didn't see her legs. She was wearing pants.
She had on some kind of palazzo pants.

GIORGIO: She was wearing palazzo pants with a leather jacket?

STEFANO: Yes. I think so. The production of *Ernani* was good but the tenor was pretty worthless.

TECLA: Did you and Cencio talk to each other?

STEFANO: For a minute. In fact, we were saying that the tenor was pretty worthless.

GIORGIO: Cencio was born here? In this house?

STEFANO: Yes. In this house. I think even in this very room.

TECLA: That has no effect on me. That doesn't affect me in the slightest.

GIORGIO: It doesn't affect me, either. I'm thinking I may leave, if he's coming to lunch now.

STEFANO: Don't you move a muscle. I want you to stay here. Everything will be a lot simpler. (*Exits.*)

TECLA: We can't leave. Don't you see that our being here is a comfort to him?

RANIERO: But maybe it's better if I go.

TECLA: Why?

RANIERO: Because I'm a stranger. Maybe they don't really feel like having strangers here. Given that they've found themselves in a rather delicate situation, from what I've been able to gather.

GIORGIO: It might be that strangers are exactly what you need at a time like this. They come in handy. They bring a breath of fresh air in with them when the atmosphere has gotten too suffocating.

RANIERO: What's this Cencio like? What does he do?

GIORGIO: He's a lawyer. He also writes poetry. He writes novels that are a thousand pages long. No one will publish them, but it doesn't matter to him. He's happy. He's more than happy. He's blissful. He lives in a state of eternal bliss. He plays the organ. He has an organ at his house. He does a little of everything. He's got his nose everywhere. First he was a socialist, then a communist, then he was in the PSI, and now he's a republican.[3] He was a registered member, but they threw him out. Didn't bother him. He's very rich, but he gets a kick out of dressing like a ragamuffin. He only wears linen or velvet, but always with his clothes a mess, wrinkled and frayed, and he walks slowly around the streets, smoking a cigar, with his curls blowing in the wind. He's got this head of blond curls and blue eyes that always seem to be laughing. He looks like a shepherd. A goatherd. He strolls along with the soft, light step of a goatherd, walking slowly with his cigar, up and down the length of his long, endless days.

TECLA: He was Angelica's husband. They were together for four years.

They have a baby that he takes care of. Angelica was the one who
dumped him, but as soon as she dumped him she regretted it
and wanted him back again. She went to live in Paris and gave
up men. She was painting. She painted cats. She even had a show
in Paris, which was a success. Kokoschka[4] came to it. But she felt
homesick for the baby and so she came back to Italy. She got back
with Cencio for a few months. Then she tried to kill herself with
sleeping pills. They saved her. She and Cencio got a divorce and
she married Stefano. As soon as she married him, she discovered
she'd probably made a mistake. But she doesn't know how to live
by herself. She doesn't know how to live with a man or without a
man. And she doesn't know how to live with the baby or without
her. Angelica would like to have the baby with her, but she understands she's too ill. The baby is with her father. It's not that Cencio
is anything special when it comes to being a father. It's not like he
spends much time with the poor thing. He's put her in the care of
a nanny. There's not much room in his endless days for his daughter. But in those few moments when he does stay at home with his
child, he's joyful and affectionate with her. Angelica, on the other
hand, doesn't know how to be with the baby, not even for a minute. She gets anxious, she gets upset, she starts crying. And it's not
as though she's ever really managed to get over Cencio. She can't
leave him alone. She writes him letters. And now that he may be
getting married, she's tormented by jealousy. It's a kind of senseless
jealousy, because I don't really believe she's still in love with him.
Her jealousy is just a pretext for making herself feel worse. She's
been going downhill over the last several days. She isn't eating
anymore.

Stefano and Angelica enter.

STEFANO: Here's Angelica. This is Raniero. I don't recall his last name.
RANIERO: Camerana.
STEFANO: Camerana. The Cameranas are always from Siena, or so your
mother says. But he's from Perugia. Call your mom, Angelica. She
said you should call her as soon as you got up.
ANGELICA: I'll call her.
RANIERO: I'm afraid I'm in the way here. It was raining last night. We'd
had a lot of wine to drink. Stefano told me to stay and sleep over.
But now perhaps I ought to be on my way.

ANGELICA: No, why? It's Sunday. Isn't it Sunday? You can stay as long as you like. Stefano enjoys having people around the house. He finds having to be alone with me hard to bear. As a matter of fact, I am a bit unbearable. Cencio is coming soon, my ex-husband. Do you know Cencio?

RANIERO: No. I don't know anyone here. I haven't been in Rome long. Stefano has been very kind. Without knowing me, he invited me to stay over and spend the night. I feel right at home with all of you. It seems to me I've known you all for a long, long time. Even with you, I have the impression that I've seen you somewhere before.

ANGELICA: And where would that have been? Last year at Marienbad?[5]

RANIERO: I don't know where. It's just an impression. A pleasant impression. I've a rather closed personality, and I usually find myself uneasy around people I don't know.

ANGELICA: No. We've never seen each other before. Your face is new to me. A new face at last. I'm sick of always seeing the same faces.

GIORGIO: Thanks.

ANGELICA: Your face isn't old or new to me. I barely even see it. It's like that end table there or the wall. Something I'm accustomed to seeing, something that doesn't trouble me and that doesn't cause me any problems.

GIORGIO: So disagreeable.

ANGELICA: You misunderstand me. In fact, I've just said something very kind. If I didn't have that end table or that wall in front of me right now, I'd feel a void. It's the same thing with you.

GIORGIO: And Stefano? Is he also like an end table?

ANGELICA: Stefano?

GIORGIO: Yes, Stefano. It strikes me that you treat him like your end table.

ANGELICA: I married Stefano.

GIORGIO: You married him, but now you've put him to work as an end table. You spill anything you like all over him, you put things on top of him and you take them away again, you tear him and shake him, and it never even enters your mind to consider whether he can bear the weight or not.

ANGELICA: You're forgetting that I'm ill. You can't just tell me your opinions like that. You can't just tell me anything that jumps into your head to say. You have to use some caution with me.

GIORGIO: You shouldn't rely so heavily on the fact that you're ill, Angelica. We're all ill, in one way or another. We all have something evil in our souls, something that's scratched up, something bruised, something wounded. The essential thing is not to get fixated on the place that aches. The essential thing is to live and let other people live.

ANGELICA: Don't get on a moral high horse with me. I'm sicker than other people. I can't manage to live or to let others live. Is it true that I treat you like an end table, Stefano?

STEFANO: I've got a bit of a headache today. I should go into the kitchen and get lunch started. There's the soup from yesterday. I'll make some risotto.

ANGELICA: Make risotto, but don't tell me what you're making. And don't mention soup to me, for God's sake, Stefano.

STEFANO: I got up all of a sudden in the night last night, and I sat here and I wanted to work, but I couldn't manage to put down a single word. I've been blocked for quite a few days now. I've run aground on a sentence. I need to find some way to get beyond that sentence. Otherwise, that's the end of it.

RANIERO: Are you writing a book?

STEFANO: I'm writing a book about Thomas Mann. I should be having some peace and quiet.

GIORGIO: You're a martyr, Stefano. You're a victim. Your wife has trimmed your wings.

STEFANO: I don't think I ever had such big wings.

GIORGIO: Big or small, she's trimming them with a pair of fingernail scissors.

TECLA: On the other hand, maybe he's growing enormous wings living the way he does. He's turning into an angel.

STEFANO: Angelica loves angels. In her paintings there's never anything but angels and cats.

ANGELICA: I love angels because they don't eat.

TECLA: And why do you like cats?

ANGELICA: Cats seem like the children of angels. But I don't want you talking to me about angels or cats. I don't want to remember my paintings. It's been quite a while since I stopped painting.

GIORGIO: A person can't talk to you about paintings. A person can't talk to you about eating. So now a person can't really talk to you about anything.

The telephone rings.

STEFANO: Hello? Oh, Signora Carafa. Here's Angelica. We were all just here having a little chat. Angelica? Yes, she's wearing enough clothes. She has on a flannel shirt and a sweater. Her dark red sweater. Let me give her to you.

ANGELICA: Hello, Mom? Hi. I'm fine. We're waiting for Cencio to come for lunch. Hmm? Cencio? Yes, he said he was coming over for lunch. Hmm? Mom, I don't know. I don't know. He's getting married, he's not getting married, I don't know. No, he's not coming with the little one. Today she has to go to rehearsals for her recital. The one at school. By the way, don't forget that you need to buy seven metres of lemon yellow organza silk for her costume. For the recital, right? It's only two weeks away. She has to play the Flower Fairy. Yes, Ilaria loves playing dress up. Like her father. She adores performing and being an actress. Go buy the organza tomorrow and also some rayon in the same colour for the lining. And some bias tape. It's closed tomorrow? Right, it's a holiday. The day after tomorrow, then. Don't forget. Okay. I'll tell Cencio to send her to lunch with you tomorrow. Yes. Mom, please, make whatever you want but I'm asking you not to tell me about it. The idea of polenta pudding gives me the shivers. Yes, the little one likes it. No. No, I'm not pregnant. I don't need to take the rabbit test. I assure you that I'm not pregnant. I can't go into the details, mom; we have people here. Yes, we should put a phone jack in our room. I'll call the telephone people. No, we don't need your housekeeper. For this lunch? It's not really even a lunch. We're just eating, that's all. Me? I don't even sit at the table. Mom, can we please not talk about it? I don't know. We'll use paper plates. Why will that make us look bad? Guests? They're not guests, they're old friends. Camerana? Who's a Camerana? Oh, right. No, I laid eyes on him today for the first time. What does he do for a living? I don't know. Okay, Mom, bye. (*Hangs up the phone.*) What do you do for a living, Raniero? My mother wants to know what you do for a living. We can use '*tu*' with one another, can't we?

RANIERO: I work with an editor.

ANGELICA: Which editor?

RANIERO: His name is Volpato.

ANGELICA: Oh. Volpato? It seems to me that Cencio sent one of his novels to him once. But he didn't want it. Cencio isn't lucky with his novels. No one publishes them. Not even that editor Volpato, who really must be the biggest cretin on earth.

GIORGIO: Why are you insulting his editor? What do you know about anything?

ANGELICA: It's really raining. Poor Cencio. I'm sorry he's coming in all this rain.

STEFANO: But you're the one who told me to call him to come over. You said you absolutely needed to see him.

TECLA: Look, I don't feel sorry for him. It's not like he's walking over here. He has a car. It's late. He ought to be here by now.

GIORGIO: He drives very slowly. He drives the car as if he were driving a horse and buggy.

STEFANO: Then I'm going into the kitchen. I can start getting the onions cut in the meantime.

ANGELICA: Cut whatever you want to cut, but don't tell me about it.

TECLA: I'll go with you so I can help. So will Giorgio. Come on, Giorgio.

Stefano, Tecla, and Giorgio exit.

ANGELICA: So you're with Volpato. What do you do there for Volpato? Do you read novels for him when they arrive?

RANIERO: That, too.

ANGELICA: You sure don't talk much! Here, we don't do anything but talk. Not you, though. Perhaps we seem stupid to you. You've got one of those faces where a person can't tell what you're thinking by looking at you. Maybe we seem too stupid for you to waste any of your words on us.

RANIERO: I'm always by myself. I've lost the habit of talking. I haven't been in Rome long. I don't know anyone.

ANGELICA: Why do you stay by yourself so much? Don't you have a girlfriend or a wife?

RANIERO: No.

ANGELICA: Not here or anywhere else? You don't have a girlfriend anywhere?

RANIERO: No.

ANGELICA: Being with you is hard work. You don't talk. You need a pair of pliers if you want to tear a word out of you. What do you usually do on Sunday afternoons? When you don't go to work for Volpato, where do you go?

RANIERO: On Sundays, Volpato usually invites me to his house.

ANGELICA: Is he pleasant to be around?

RANIERO: Volpato? Yes, he's pleasant to be around. He's very quiet.

ANGELICA: What fun that must be. You and him sitting at the table without saying a word. How are the two of you running a publishing company if you never say anything? If you don't talk things over, don't discuss things together? What in God's name kind of books do you publish?

RANIERO: I toss out a word every now and then. A half-hour later he tosses back another one. We publish lots of books. It isn't necessary to discuss anything. We're more or less always in agreement.

ANGELICA: Does Volpato have a wife?

RANIERO: No, he doesn't have a wife.

ANGELICA: Is he a queer?

RANIERO: No, I don't think so.

ANGELICA: Are you a queer?

RANIERO: Me? No.

ANGELICA: I knew it. When someone's a queer I can tell immediately. Why were you saying earlier that you thought you'd seen me before? Where have you seen me?

RANIERO: I've never seen you before. But it seems to me I've known you forever. As if you were my sister or my mother.

ANGELICA: I seem like your mother to you? How could I seem like your mother? I'm the same age as you. I might even be younger. I'm a little feeble right now, and my skin is drawn because I don't eat or sleep. But everyone tells me I give the impression of being a young girl. I have a six-year-old daughter. Would you say that I had a six-year-old daughter? Do you have a mother and a sister at home?

RANIERO: My mother is dead. My sister is married in America.

ANGELICA: If you feel as though you've known me forever, why don't you talk to me? Why don't you make me talk?

RANIERO: Your daughter lives with her father?

ANGELICA: Yes, with Cencio. But he travels a lot, and now it seems as though he's going to be getting married. So they may put her in boarding school. Or else she'll live with my mother, I don't know. I can't keep her with me. I don't have the peace of mind you need to live with a child. Ilaria gets on my nerves. I want her here, but then when she's here I get nervous. And then I suffer because she's not with me. Do you understand? Cencio says I don't have any maternal instinct. I don't know. I dream about my daughter every night. I've made all kinds of mistakes like that in my life, one after another. I didn't get along with Cencio. I think we're both too narcissistic. Each of us wanted all the space for himself. But as soon as I left him I was in despair. I married Stefano. He's so good with

me that the better he is the more I hate him. But if he goes out for a
half-hour I'm in despair. So now Cencio has a girlfriend and maybe
he'll marry her. It's making me suffer. It's making me suffer atro-
ciously. I don't know the reason why. There's no logical explanation.
I'm ill and I want to die. At least that would make everyone feel
better. The only one who'll cry over me will be my mother.

RANIERO: (*At the window.*) There's a car stopped in front of the gate.
Someone's getting out.

ANGELICA: Cencio.

RANIERO: Someone with curly blond hair is getting out. He's wearing
a raincoat and velvet pants. A girl's getting out, too. A girl with a
leather jacket.

ANGELICA: A girl? With a leather jacket? (*She goes to the window.*) Stefano! Stefano!

Giorgio enters.

GIORGIO: Stefano went out to meet Cencio at the gate.

ANGELICA: The girl is here, too. Why did he bring her here? I don't
want to see her. I don't want her to set foot in this house. You two
go down and tell her to leave.

GIORGIO: Calm down. Can't you behave with a little bit of dignity?
With a little presence of mind? You don't really want to make some
jealous scene. You'd just make yourself look ridiculous. The world
has changed. It's moving forward. No one makes jealous scenes
anymore.

ANGELICA: I said I don't want her to set foot in this house!

STEFANO: (*Entering.*) Angelica, Cencio has come with his girlfriend. He
made a mistake. He should have come by himself. But they're already here. They saw some guys beating each other up in the street
and one of them was bleeding. The girlfriend is really upset. She
needs a cognac. She's very pale. She must be pregnant.

ACT TWO

[*The same house. After lunch, later the same day.*]

Giorgio, Tecla, and Raniero are in the room.
Stefano enters, goes to the phone, and dials a number.

STEFANO: Hello, mom? Hi, Mom. Oh, yeah? You were just having
some hot chocolate? You and Signora Borbona? How nice. Are you
watching television? There's a soccer game on? Sorry, but what do
you care about soccer? It's the Rome vs. Lazio game? Oh, Signora
Borbona has a cousin on the Lazio team. No, pretty bad. I have
some bad news for you. We have to move. Within a month. Uh-
huh. Cencio wants the house back. They're evicting him from the
house where he's staying. He found out a couple of hours ago. Of
course, this is his house. His father had it built. Cencio was born
here. Of course he could find himself another house if he wanted
to, but he doesn't want to. Yes, we've had a stormy Sunday. Cencio
came over. I called him because Angelica wanted to see him. But he
stupidly decided to bring his girlfriend along. He might marry her.
Apparently, he's going to. When, I don't know. Anyway, I believe he
wanted to show her the house in the meantime. So Angelica locked
herself in her room and hasn't wanted to come out. Tecla has been
with her. Sure, it's understandable. But there are a few things that
have to be decided if he's really going to marry her. The future of
their daughter. Whether he gets married or not, he'll need to be
thinking about putting her in a good boarding school. But it was
impossible to talk about any of that today. He showed up with his
girlfriend, and he dragged her behind him through all the rooms
like someone pulling a pet dog along on a leash. She is a pet dog,
a little black poodle. Face completely hidden in this jungle of hair,
and behind the hair you can see two pale, terrified eyes looking out.
She's tiny, skinny, with freckles all over and a leather jacket. She
saw some people in a brawl on the street and got scared. She must
be pregnant. As soon as they got here I had to let her stretch out
on the sofa. I gave her some cognac. Poor little sparrow. They went
through the entire house. They looked at everything. Except our
bedroom, of course, where Angelica had barricaded herself. Cencio
wanted to knock but I stopped him. He insisted on seeing Angelica,
because he said that was the reason he'd come in the first place. I
tried to explain to him that there was no need for that, that Angelica
was ill. So he gave up. He flung open all the closets without asking if I minded. True, they are his closets, but they have our things
inside. Every now and then the girlfriend said something I didn't
understand. She's Hungarian. It seemed to me she was saying she
didn't like the house. It seemed to me she was saying it was damp.
In fact, it is damp. Cencio said he was going to have some Dutch

stoves put in. They run on wood and they give off a lot of heat.
There's nothing to do about it. He's decided to come here to live
and come here to live he will. He's a terrible egotist, even I know
that. But he doesn't have a clue. He doesn't know. So then you can't
even manage to hate him. You can't even take solace in the great
refuge of hate. There he was, blissful, peaceful, smiling, big as
life with that golden cherub's head of his. He's not worried about
Angelica – he said he'd come back to see her another day, when he
gets back from Naples. He ate three bowls of risotto. Huh? How
was I supposed to throw him out? I don't know how these tough-
guy routines are supposed to go. Besides, I felt sorry for that girl.
So young, and practically numb with cold. Yes, they're gone now.
They were headed for Naples in the car. There's a republican party
convention in Naples. I had to tell Angelica about the house. She
had a big crying jag. She's very attached to this house, as you know.
She spent her first years with Cencio here. Her daughter started
walking here. I called Dr Vlad. He told me to give her an injection
of Seronal. It's a tranquillizer. She calmed down after the injection.
She's still in bed. Dr Vlad also told me he knew of an apartment.
I'll go see it tomorrow. It's in Prati. I don't know how many rooms
there are. Mom, you're going to have to lend me some money. I
don't have any. Yes, for the move and for the deposit. You need to
come up with three months in advance. It's generally like that. Yes,
it's a snag. Mom, I don't feel comfortable asking Signora Carafa.
She's already given us a lot of things. She gave us a refrigerator, a
washing machine. It doesn't work, but she didn't know that. It's not
like she's rich either. Huh? No, she's not rich. No, she doesn't own
a mink. Come on. You're kidding. No, your eyes are playing tricks
on you. It's African bear. What do you mean there are no bears in
Africa. Yes, there are. Okay, let's not get bogged down in discussing Signora Carafa's furs. You could sell Aunt Rosina's stocks. The
Montedison. They're down? No, they're up. Or else, you could sell
the forest land. What do you mean, what forest land? The forest
land in Vallepiana. But it's such a little piece of land. Or you could
take out a loan on your apartment. We have to buy some furniture.
We don't have anything – everything here is Cencio's, all of it. No,
no one is thinking of throwing you naked into the streets in your
old age. I'm begging you not to turn this into a melodrama. All
I'm asking for is a small loan. There are some people who owe me

money. There's an editor who owes me some money. I'll pay the
whole thing back to you. No, we can't live with you or with Signora
Carafa. No, not even for one day. Angelica can't bear you or her
mother. What does that mean, she ought to adapt, mom? Angelica
is ill. It's not that she's spoiled; she's ill. Yes it's a cross. But it's a
cross that I've chosen to bear. No, I'm not Jesus Christ. I'm not an
angel. Oh, no, listen: Don't start crying. Don't worry about it. Go
back to your hot chocolate. I should slam who around? Oh, you
mean Cencio. But I don't know how to act like that. I'm not cut out
for it. I'm not a violent guy. And anyway, he's within his rights – the
house is his. I probably should have hit him. He took one of my ties
with him. He saw it in the closet and he just put it on. The plaid
one. No, I didn't feel like grabbing it back from him. I'm not going
to get possessive over a tie at this point. No, don't swear, Mom, not
at your age. Plus in front of Signora Borbona. Oh, for God's sake,
Mom, stop crying. I have enough on my mind without you crying. I'll call you back when you've calmed down. (*He hangs up the
receiver.*)

TECLA: That apartment of Dr Vlad's – I know which one it is. He tried
to get me to take it. It belongs to some relative of his. Don't bother
going out to see it because it's a toilet. It stinks like a toilet. No, if
you want to find a house, you'll need to make an appointment with
an agency.

STEFANO: The idea of having to empty out all these closets frightens
me. It seems impossible. In two years you really fill up a house.
Papers. Letters. Books. Old rags.

RANIERO: If you need to, please put me to work. I'll come and help you
move.

TECLA: I'll come, too. And so will Giorgio, right Giorgio?

STEFANO: Thank you. I have to say that your presence here has been a
big help to me today. Raniero's face is a comfort. It's a face I barely
know – yesterday I didn't know he existed, and yet I look at it and I
draw a sense of tranquillity from it. I have a headache. I'd like some
tea.

TECLA: I've already put the water on to boil. Maybe Angelica will even
want a little tea if she wakes up.

STEFANO: Unlikely.

TECLA: He's a monster. He's a monster, that Cencio. I still feel stunned.

GIORGIO: He's a dog, yes.

TECLA: Don't insult dogs. Istanbul can hear you.

GIORGIO: Now that he's taken the house back, is he taking Istanbul back, too?

STEFANO: I think so. Istanbul is his as well.

TECLA: And the cats. The cats are his, too?

STEFANO: Yes, even the cats.

TECLA: Angelica loves those cats.

GIORGIO: From the way he was petting the cats, I got the feeling they were his.

STEFANO: Oh, but he touches everything as if it were his. He's the master of the universe. He's happy.

GIORGIO: Yes, he considers himself the master of the universe, but at the same time he moves with the sweetness and simplicity of a goatherd. He moves slowly, as if he had a flock of goats following him. He's like one of those ancient tribal kings – even though they were kings, they still led their flocks out to pasture. He dresses completely in corduroy like a shepherd. Like a king or an outlaw.

TECLA: You have a soft spot for him, Giorgio. You gave him a discount on shirts. You didn't have to do that.

GIORGIO: When he comes into the store, my father would give him the shirt off his back anyway. My father adores him. He throws himself at his feet. They talk about Freud.

RANIERO: Is he interested in psychoanalysis?

STEFANO: What isn't he interested in? He's got his nose in everything. He sticks his blond head and that big, red nose anywhere he feels like. The universe holds no secrets for him because it belongs to him. He swims around like some enormous, phosphorescent, rainbow-coloured fish. He slides down into the abyssal depths, swallowing smaller fish as if he were breathing. The humiliations, the bitterness, the sad things that come along in life don't touch him; they can't dim his splendour. There are women who leave him, friends who shower him with insults, editors who reject his books. But he finds a reason for everything. He finds a flattering explanation that leaves him looking good. Nothing interferes with his blissful roaming of the earth. The sea is still his. The universe is his.

TECLA: That girl. That poor girl. He can't really be in love with her. At one point today he got irritated with her and told her off because she broke a glass.

GIORGIO: Are the glasses his?

STEFANO: His.

TECLA: If he marries her, he'll make her miserable. I'm going to hope for her sake that he doesn't marry her. I'll go make the tea. (*Exits.*)

STEFANO: He found himself someone so small and terrified on purpose. Angelica was too strong and overbearing a personality for him. They couldn't get along for very long. Angelica used to stand up to him. She told him he was wrong. Piece by piece she dismantled the castles he'd constructed out of all those flattering arguments and explanations. He's indifferent to humiliation, but perhaps in some way, on some small patch of his skin, he feels her stingers go in and it bothers him. He doesn't want women around who bother him. He wants little fish. Sparrows.

GIORGIO: That girl is going to leave him. Women leave him. At a certain point they can't stand him anymore. But they never quite manage to forget him. Even after they've left him, they go on pursuing him. Like Angelica. You made a mistake when you married Angelica, Stefano. You came through the wrong door. You've gotten caught up in an endless tangle of complications.

STEFANO: I knew I was making a mistake. I preferred to make a mistake rather than live without her.

GIORGIO: But happiness is mutual, you know. If you can't be happy with her, she can't be happy with you either.

STEFANO: Angelica needs me. Happiness isn't the main problem.

GIORGIO: So what is the main problem? Raniero, why aren't you saying anything? Even you must have some kind of an opinion, don't you? I'm glad you're here – you seem very agreeable to me – but you can't seem to force a single word out of your own mouth.

Tecla and Angelica enter.

TECLA: Here's the tea.

ANGELICA: I don't want any tea. I want to go outside for a little walk in the garden. I can't stand this house anymore, now that I know we have to leave it. I've started to hate it. Stefano, when are you going to see that house that Dr Vlad has?

STEFANO: That house is out of the question. Tecla has seen it and she says it's a horror. A toilet.

ANGELICA: So look at the ads in the newspaper. Use the phone. Houses don't drop out of the sky, you know. You have to look for them.

STEFANO: Tomorrow. Today is Sunday.

ANGELICA: Raniero, take a little walk with me?

RANIERO: Gladly.

GIORGIO: He said 'gladly.' He said a word. What a miracle. Imagine what a joy a stroll in the garden will be. He wears his silence around him like a funeral wreath.

TECLA: Yes, he keeps his mouth shut, but it's not as if he's gloomy. He does nothing to make me think of graveyards or of anything depressing. Not all silences are equal. His is a lively silence, intense – one that actively listens and keeps you company.

GIORGIO: Nobody knows what he's thinking. Maybe he thinks we're all idiots and he can't wait until he's free of us. See, even now he doesn't say anything. He ought to say something, even if only for the sake of good manners.

TECLA: He has very good manners. His manners are a lot better than yours. He's quiet because he has good manners. We talk so much because we're rude.

RANIERO: I would have left if I didn't enjoy being with you.

ANGELICA: I'm going to keep my mouth shut, too. I don't feel much like talking. Come on, Raniero.

STEFANO: Don't stay out long. It's cold. You shouldn't tire yourself out, Angelica. Remember that you haven't eaten anything since yesterday.

TECLA: Not exactly nothing. She had a little piece of chicken. About the size of my thumb.

Angelica and Raniero exit.

GIORGIO: Imagine her not remembering that she hasn't eaten since yesterday. Her little fast is the only thing on her mind. She's deliberately refusing to eat in order to make everyone worry and feel sorry for her. You ought to stop paying attention to her. She doesn't want to eat? Then she'll die. If you treated her with a little more indifference, even with a certain amount of brutality if need be, I'll bet she'd start eating again soon enough.

TECLA: She's sick. Her rejection of food is a death wish.

GIORGIO: What if we were to discover that at night, in secret, when no one can see her, she's been slipping downstairs to the kitchen to fill up on bread and sausages?

TECLA: There aren't any sausages in this house.

STEFANO: No, plus that isn't what she's doing. If only she were. You can see how run down she is. How wasted.

TECLA: On the contrary, she's better today. Her colour is improved. The fact that Cencio came here with his girlfriend – he disrespected her. But in some way it must also have been a relief. Maybe she understood that it's finished with him, that it's a closed book.

GIORGIO: They were divorced three years ago. She even married someone else. Doesn't get much more closed than that.

TECLA: And in the end she took his rotten little trick about the house fairly well. She cried, she had her fit of hysterics, but then she calmed down. She ate that little bit of chicken. She's gone out for a walk with Raniero. (*At the window.*) I see them. They're on the path. They're talking. It even looks like Raniero is talking. He's waving his hands around.

GIORGIO: This Raniero, he's going to make Angelica cheat on you, Stefano. You'll see. It's the quiet waters that destroy the fields.

STEFANO: Not the fields. The bridges.

GIORGIO: The fields.

STEFANO: The bridges.[6]

GIORGIO: Would you rather see Angelica run off with Raniero to eat steak or stay with you, about to collapse from refusing food?

STEFANO: I'd rather she eat steak.

GIORGIO: Far away from you? With Raniero?

STEFANO: Yes.

GIORGIO: Fine. As soon as they come up, I'll tell them. But there's no understanding why you married her. You say you knew everything – you knew she'd be unhappy and so would you. And so?

STEFANO: So I married her because she needed me.

GIORGIO: The wrong door. You really came through the wrong door.

TECLA: Raniero is a new person. New people bring out Angelica's curiosity, they intrigue her. It isn't anything more than that. She put some powder on her face, she put on some lipstick. She hasn't done that for a while. And now she's even wearing her new black dress. She wouldn't have worn it for me or for you, Giorgio; she's seen too much of us. We don't matter anymore. She feels better. While she was getting dressed she told me that she wanted to tell Cencio to give her the baby for a month or two. She wants to take her to Cortina.

STEFANO: To Cortina? And who's going to give her money to go to Cortina with the baby? I don't have any.

TECLA: Cencio will give her money. It's his daughter.

STEFANO: Cencio? You're in for a shock. Cencio wouldn't give her the

money even to go to Frascati. (*The phone rings.*) Hello? Who is it?
Cencio? Oh, hi. What? What's happened to you? The suspension?
I'm sorry. Excuse me for asking, but what can I do about it? Oh. I
understand. I understand. Okay. I'll ask Giorgio. Where are you?
On the highway at the Monteporzio Catone[7] rest stop. Waiting for a
part to arrive.

GIORGIO: What's happened to him?

STEFANO: He's had a problem with the car. They weren't doing anything wrong, but the car broke down. The suspension went out.
He's at the Monteporzio Catone rest stop waiting for them to fix the
car. He wants some help. He wants you to go out there in your car.
The girlfriend is cold and she's frightened. He wants you to pick
her up and bring her back here.

GIORGIO: She's frightened. She was frightened well before the accident.
She was frightened before she was born. And why is she cold?
Aren't there any restaurants along the highway?

STEFANO: He says she gets bored if she has to sit in a restaurant by herself. He's staying with the mechanics so he can oversee the repairs.
They might finish tonight, they might not. But he doesn't trust
mechanics. He wants some help and some advice.

GIORGIO: Okay. Look's like it's up to me.

STEFANO: (*On the phone.*) Okay, Cencio. Giorgio is coming now. Rest
stop. Monteporzio Catone. Okay. Bye. (*Hangs up the receiver.*) He
also says could you bring him some money. He's afraid he doesn't
have enough money with him. Seems that replacing the suspension
costs a lot. He also called Romoletto, his butler, but he'd gone out
for a walk. He forgot the chequebook at home.

GIORGIO: But isn't he supposed to go to Naples? Why did he go off on a
trip without any extra cash?

STEFANO: That I don't know.

GIORGIO: How is it possible that he doesn't have any friends other than
us? How is it possible that he has to make all these requests of us?
Money, the house, hospitality, help – everything? Doesn't he have
the world at his feet? Isn't he the master of the universe? Isn't he the
king of kings?

Angelica and Raniero enter.

ANGELICA: What's the matter? What are you all talking about? Where
are you going, Giorgio? Why are you wearing your raincoat?

STEFANO: Cencio has had a little problem with the car. Right nearby. Nothing serious. Something to do with the suspension.

ANGELICA: Then he's not dead?

STEFANO: Of course not. He's terrific. It's just that his car has broken down.

TECLA: But why is he asking Giorgio to bring her here where Angelica doesn't want her? Can't he take her somewhere else?

GIORGIO: And where shall I take her? If I don't bring her here, I don't know where I'm going to take her.

ANGELICA: Bring who here?

GIORGIO: If I at least liked the girl. But I don't. She has too many freckles. She's cute, but she's not my type. I won't know what to talk about.

TECLA: There won't be much to talk about. She doesn't know a syllable of Italian.

GIORGIO: Raniero, come with me?

ANGELICA: No. I want Raniero to stay here. He said he'd enjoy listening to some records. And I don't want that girl here. This is my house, until I hear otherwise.

TECLA: Who knows how she can be that cold? They always heat those restaurants along the highway enough to kill you.

STEFANO: She'll be tired. She'll be sleepy. Poor little sparrow.

ANGELICA: Why should she be sleepy at five in the afternoon? I can't tell you how much your endless, universal pity for everyone disgusts me.

GIORGIO: If he didn't have a little pity, how would he be able to stand living with a pest like you?

ANGELICA: Don't you think it might be that Stefano stays with me because he loves me? Has anything like that ever entered your mind?

GIORGIO: There's no love that can survive a pest like you. I'd prefer a wife who cheated on me to one like you who made me worry all the time. Plus you don't let him sleep when he's tired or go out when he feels like it. No, if he stays with you, it's only because he has a compassionate soul.

TECLA: Better get a move on, Giorgio. By now the girl will be dead of boredom in that bar.

Giorgio exits.

ANGELICA: Is it true that I'm a pest? Do you think I'm a pest, too, Raniero?

RANIERO: I really don't know.

ANGELICA: Always such evasive, cautious, polite answers. Always in such a deep, polite voice. What a bore.

TECLA: Sometimes you say people have to treat you cautiously because you're sick. And sometimes you want to be treated in some entirely different way. No one knows how to behave around you. Was Raniero talking when the two of you were in the garden? It looked to me like he was talking. He was waving his hands around.

ANGELICA: Of course not. He was waving his hands to warm them up because he was cold. I was still doing all the talking. He didn't open his mouth. Every once in a while, he asked some question. Questions are the great tool of those who long for silence. They interrogate others in order to defend themselves, so they aren't required to say anything about themselves. I know nothing about him. All I know is that he works with some editor named Volpato. On the other hand, I told him the whole grand story of my entire life. I certainly needed to tell it to someone. I'm surrounded by people who know everything about me. All of you, Dr Vlad. Telling my story to you no longer gives me any pleasure.

RANIERO: And telling it to Dr Vlad?

ANGELICA: That's therapy. That's analysis. Being in analysis doesn't give you pleasure – on the contrary, it makes you feel terrible. But I don't want to talk about Dr Vlad. One should never speak about one's own analyst in public. Never.

RANIERO: And why is that?

ANGELICA: Because that's the law of analysis, my friend. You wouldn't understand. But never mind Dr Vlad. I'm always happy to tell my life story to anyone who doesn't know it.

TECLA: It's not like you've had such an extraordinary life. To hear you tell it, a person would get the idea that you'd lived through who knows what adventures. You haven't exactly been exploring the North Pole.

ANGELICA: Yes, I have had an extraordinary life. My life with Cencio was extraordinary.

TECLA: You argued from morning to night. What was so extraordinary about that?

ANGELICA: Cencio is an extraordinary man. He hurt me some, but he's an exceptional man, a unique man. I don't know if you realize it, Raniero, you only saw him for that half-hour he was here. I am sorry he showed up with that girl. An ordinary little bourgeois.

STEFANO: But you don't know her.

ANGELICA: I watched from the crack of the door. Ugly. Insignificant. All freckly. With that ugly leather jacket. One of those leather jackets that everyone's wearing nowadays. Without the slightest personality. No light. Plus with that Piedmontese accent. I can't bear a Piedmontese accent.

STEFANO: How can she have a Piedmontese accent? She's Hungarian. She doesn't speak a syllable of Italian.

ANGELICA: She will. I heard a Piedmontese accent. Maybe she's pretending to be Hungarian and she's really from Saluzzo.[8] And to think that within a month Cencio and his girlfriend will be here together on these very armchairs. They'll be petting my cats. They'll be playing with Istanbul. Cencio will surely want the cats back. I've no desire to get into a fight with him over the cats. Although they are mine. I painted all kinds of pictures of them, so by now they're more mine than his. But I'm not going to fight about it. I'll leave it all to him, if it's that important to him.

RANIERO: It's strange. You're thinking about the house, about the cats, about Istanbul. But don't you think about your own daughter? Have you ever done anything to get your daughter back with you?

ANGELICA: So you haven't understood a thing, Raniero. It's strange. I've talked to you so much, but you don't understand. I dream about my daughter every night. I wake up in tears. But I know I'm too sick to keep her with me. Ilaria will go to boarding school, or with my mom. I won't be able to give her anything. It weighs on me. I'm infecting her with my neurosis.

TECLA: It's true. Angelica is too sick to have her daughter with her. Maybe in a little while, as soon as she's better, she'll be able to take her daughter with her to Cortina for a while, to ski. To Cortina, or some other place where it isn't so expensive. Maybe to Chianciano.

ANGELICA: What am I going to do at Chianciano? Am I supposed to ski at Chianciano?

TECLA: People go to Chianciano for the waters. The air there is very healthy. I've been there. You see, Raniero, people aren't all the same. If I had a daughter and someone had the nerve to try to take her away from me, I'd tear their eyes out. To tell the truth, I don't know what I'd give to have a child. Sometimes I think I'd like to adopt an orphan or just have a baby with the first guy that passes by.

ANGELICA: Raniero.

RANIERO: What?

ANGELICA: I wasn't saying it to you. I was saying it to Tecla. I said to her, 'Raniero.' I was advising her to have a baby with you.

TECLA: Don't talk such stupid nonsense. Raniero is a boy. I'm at least ten years older than him. He doesn't know what to make of me. Besides, I barely know him.

ANGELICA: You want to have a baby with the first guy that passes by? The first guy to pass by is him.

RANIERO: In what sense am I the first guy to pass by? I wasn't really passing by. I wasn't passing by here. I was going in an entirely different direction. Giorgio took me by the jacket, and he brought me here.

ANGELICA: Because you had a very agreeable way about you.

RANIERO: Does he pick up everyone who has an agreeable way about him and bring them here?

ANGELICA: Why? Are you sick of being here? We're still better than that editor of yours, Volpato. Less boring.

RANIERO: My editor Volpato isn't at all boring.

ANGELICA: So go back to your fabulous Volpato, then. We'll be terrific, even without you.

RANIERO: But I'm not at all sick of being here. I like it here. If I didn't like it here, I'd have left, as I already told you. I have the sense I've known all of you for a long time. I feel right at home here.

ANGELICA: And meanwhile you won't tell us what the hell home is like?

RANIERO: Like here.

ANGELICA: Strange. It doesn't seem possible to me. It seems to me that we're all rather strange, that what goes on in this house is well outside of what most people would consider ordinary.

STEFANO: I'm going to make supper. Will you be eating, Angelica?

ANGELICA: I don't know. Perhaps a little later. For now, please don't mention supper to me. (*Stefano exits. The telephone rings.*) Hello? Mom? Oh, Mom, hi. Fine. Cencio? Yes, he came over. He came with his girlfriend. Sure he did. He brought her here. Why are you stunned? What's so strange about that? The world goes on, mom, the world changes. You're from another era. But that's not at all to say that your time was so much better than this one. What? No, she's not a whore. She's rather bourgeois. Not cute. All freckly. Changing the subject, do you know, mom, that we're supposed to move? Soon. Within a month. You're stunned? And why is that? This is Cencio's house, it's his. They're evicting him from the house

where he's staying. And he's getting married. As far as the baby
goes, we still haven't decided anything. Maybe we'll put her in
boarding school. Or else with you. Yes. Yes, I know. Imagine, Ilaria
is so attached to the nanny that she doesn't even realize that her
father's getting married. She may do better with you than in boarding school, in the sense that she won't have to leave her nanny. Yes,
certainly, in all ways she'd be better off with you. What? Are you
crying? Mom. I can't stand it when you cry on the telephone. I've
been thinking that as soon as I'm better I'll leave with the baby
for Chianciano. Yes. The waters there are good for the liver, too.
Either Chianciano or some other place. I don't know yet. But first
we have to finish this move. I don't know, but we'll find a house,
everyone does. No, Mom, it's not a dirty trick for him to do this
to me because it's his house. Plus, haven't you always said that it
wasn't decent for us to be here, me and Stefano, in Cencio's house?
And haven't you always said it was damp? He's having some Dutch
stoves put in. Give Ilaria a call this evening; she's home alone with
the nanny. Cencio went to Naples. That is he had left, but then he
had an accident and now he's on the highway with his car in ruins.
No, he's not dead. He's terrific. You know, Mom, I think you might
need to give us some furniture. For the new house. Mom, you know
very well that we don't even have a mattress – nothing here is ours.
Stefano's mother? Stefano's mother has four chairs to her name. I
can't take them away from her. Mom, I'm going to let you go. I have
things to do. I want to wash my hair. Egg whites? Yes. I know that
they're good for your hair. Yes, I ate. I don't remember – it was quite
a few hours ago. Some chicken. Yes, it was boiled and yes it was
tender. But I don't want to remember it now. Bye, Mom. (*Hangs up
the receiver.*)

TECLA: You're washing your hair now? But it's evening.
ANGELICA: I don't know.
TECLA: You wash your hair with egg whites?
ANGELICA: Don't talk to me about eggs.

Giorgio enters.

GIORGIO: I'm back. It's so cold! The wind is blowing and it's pouring.
My shoes are soaked. Give me some slippers.
ANGELICA: Take those, under the couch there. They're mine.
GIORGIO: What big feet you have.

ANGELICA: They're too big for me, you idiot.

TECLA: And the girlfriend?

GIORGIO: I left her in the kitchen with Stefano. She was frozen. She's eating an apple. What a mess that girl is! I'm giving you all fair warning that she'll be sleeping here. Cencio left for Naples. She was too tired to make the trip. It's already evening.

ANGELICA: But I told you before that I don't want her here. I said so and I repeated myself. You all treat me like a crazy woman, and when I talk it's as if I were talking to the wind.

GIORGIO: You could learn from your husband to be a little more welcoming, hospitable, and compassionate.

ANGELICA: Welcoming to Cencio's girlfriend? To the girl that he's going to marry?

GIORGIO: Who knows if he'll marry her?

TECLA: What about the suspension?

GIORGIO: The suspension has been replaced. I had to shell out 40,000 lire. I'll never see them again. Cencio isn't in the habit of returning money. He forgets. I found him at the service station haranguing the mechanics. He was proselytizing for his party, explaining the ins and outs of the republicans.

TECLA: And the girlfriend?

GIORGIO: The girlfriend was sitting in the bar, perched on a stool. She was eating popcorn.

ANGELICA: Don't tell me what she eats or what she was eating.

GIORGIO: You're such a bore, Angelica. You're so monotonous. I'm fed up with your neuroses. The girlfriend's probably neurotic, too, but at least she's always hungry. She consoles herself by eating. They must have had a fight, her and Cencio. Maybe that's why she didn't want to go to Naples. I didn't understand what they were saying. They were speaking Hungarian.

ANGELICA: Cencio doesn't know Hungarian.

GIORGIO: On the contrary, he does. He learned it with those Linguaphone records. In the end he climbed into the car alone with a bottle of wine and an Alemagna panettone.[9] When all's said and done, he must be happy to be free of her. He told me to bring her here and let her stay tonight. So I threw her in my Cinquecento[10] and I even wrapped her up in a blanket. Her hands were purple. Tomorrow I'll have to call Romoletto to get him to come over with the keys. The butler.

TECLA: What keys?

GIORGIO: The keys to who knows what room where the girlfriend is staying. Some kind of attic on the Campo dei Fiori. Property of Romoletto. Sort of a bachelor pad.

TECLA: So now they're using butlers' bachelor pads.

ANGELICA: Why didn't they take the keys with them?

GIORGIO: You're asking too much. I don't know.

ANGELICA: Won't Romoletto wind up installing himself here for the night tomorrow, too?

TECLA: It wouldn't be such a bad thing. You could get him to clean the whole house up.

Stefano enters.

STEFANO: She ate an apple and a hardboiled egg. I gave her some sheets and blankets and got her settled in the study. But she's pretty run down. She doesn't feel well. Poor little sparrow.

TECLA: Is she pregnant?

STEFANO: Of course she's pregnant. You should go sit with her for a while, Tecla. Ask her if she wants some camomile tea.

TECLA: In what language shall I ask her? I don't know Hungarian.

STEFANO: Explain yourself with gestures. I explained myself with gestures. Afterwards, we'll have supper.

Tecla exits.

ANGELICA: I won't have supper. I won't touch a thing.

GIORGIO: And none of us gives a crap.

ANGELICA: I don't like having her here. You could all have had the tact and the consideration to have taken her somewhere else. To that attic or I don't know where. Why must I spend the night under the same roof as the woman my husband is seeing?

GIORGIO: Because he's not your husband anymore. Your husband – who is right here – is Stefano.

STEFANO: And that's no woman. She's just a young girl. A little sparrow fallen from the nest. A black poodle. A little dog.

Tecla enters.

TECLA: She didn't want camomile tea. She wanted some wine. We explained ourselves with gestures.

GIORGIO: Maybe she's an alcoholic. Maybe she's a drug addict.

STEFANO: Of course not. Not a drug addict or an alcoholic. She's a little sparrow, a poor little sparrow who got caught in the rain.

ANGELICA: We all understand that she's a little sparrow. I'm so sick of your pity.

TECLA: You should take a look at her shoes. They're completely soaked through. And they're falling apart. She needs to put them on the stove to dry. Give me some newspaper. I'll stuff them with newspaper or they'll dry out like a piece of salt cod.

ANGELICA: Quiet. Don't talk about codfish.

GIORGIO: Why does she have shoes that are falling apart? Doesn't she have any money?

TECLA: Maybe she doesn't have any money. Maybe she just has other things on her mind. She doesn't remember to take her shoes in to be fixed when they need to be.

GIORGIO: And Cencio? Doesn't Cencio tell her to get her shoes fixed? Doesn't he look at her shoes? He's about to marry her and he doesn't look to see if her feet are dry?

ANGELICA: Cencio is too busy to attend to things like that. He's too intelligent a person to be thinking about shoes.

GIORGIO: About other people's shoes. He thinks about his own. He had a pair of fancy boots with fur lining on his own feet. He bought them in Oslo. He showed them to me. They must be extremely warm.

ANGELICA: When our daughter was born, he and I were staying at a hotel in Terminillo. One night I felt pains, but he didn't pay any attention to me. He told me they weren't labour pains and that it was just indigestion. He was writing a novel and he didn't want to be interrupted. I had to call my mother. My mother came up with the Red Cross[11] and took me to a clinic in Rome. A little bit after that, Ilaria was born in the ambulance. He arrived at the clinic after she was already born. He came into the delivery room with a cigar in his mouth. A nurse snatched it away. That's the kind of man he is. I was sick – I was having pains and he was saying it was the prawns. We'd eaten prawns for dinner. He said maybe they'd gone bad. That it had been a mistake to eat prawns in Terminillo. And instead I was giving birth. See – that's what he's like. Imagine him worrying about what shoes she's wearing.

GIORGIO: You're talking about prawns. You're making progress. Maybe you're starting to get hungry.

ANGELICA: I was distracted. Even with all that, he's an extraordinary man. None of you know him. You couldn't understand.

RANIERO: But you went looking for his opposite. You ran away from him.

TECLA: Yes. Stefano is his opposite. Yes.

STEFANO: I wouldn't want to be compared to Cencio. You don't put people on the balance scales like that. I am different from Cencio. There's no relationship between us. By chance, we chose the same woman. But for such contrasting reasons that it's as if you were talking about two different women.

GIORGIO: Cencio probably didn't choose a thing. He doesn't choose women. He finds them. He finds them underfoot while he's out taking a walk. Or else they suddenly attach themselves to his velvet coat. Then they dump him. He doesn't dump them. He would keep all of them. They dump him but then they don't know how to break loose. They swarm around him like bees to honey. And he goes blissfully on his way, a cigar in his mouth.

ANGELICA: Did you say honey?

GIORGIO: What?

ANGELICA: You were talking about honey. I feel as though I could very happily eat a little piece of toast, with honey and butter.

STEFANO: I'm sorry. There isn't any honey in the house. No butter either. You'll have to wait until tomorrow.

ACT THREE

[*The same house. The next day.*]

Stefano, Tecla, and Raniero are in the room. The phone rings.

STEFANO: Hello, Signora Carafa? Good morning, Signora Carafa. I'm able to announce that your daughter drank a big mug of caffe latte along with some bread, butter, honey, and cookies. Yesterday she got a craving for honey and so this morning I went down and bought some at the bakery. What? No, she has these sudden urges, but she's not pregnant. Better that way? Perhaps it's better that way. The move? What move? Oh, yes, we're supposed to move. No, I have the newspaper but I haven't glanced over the ads yet.

Oh really? You can give us some wool mattresses? Thanks. Yes, Angelica prefers the PermaFlex ones, but it doesn't matter. Sure, the wool ones are healthier. Thanks. I seem hoarse to you? A little hoarseness – must be from being tired. Yesterday evening we were up late with friends. Yes, they're all still here. Because it's their vacation until tomorrow. Me? My book? It's moving along, moving along fine. No, the housekeeper hasn't come, not today either. She must have thought it was a holiday. Or maybe she's not coming back. We'll look for another one. No, I assure you that the house is not falling apart. Signora Carafa, would you mind if I called you back later? Yes, I'll have Angelica call you as soon as she gets up. Thanks. (*Hangs up the receiver. Dials a number.*) Hello, mom? Mom, listen. Bad, bad. A horrendous night. No, if only Angelica had slept. She's better. She drank a glass of milk. No, what happened instead is that that girl – you know, Cencio's girlfriend – she didn't feel well. Yes, she was sleeping here; he left for Naples. She slept in the study. At some point in the night I heard crying. I ran down and she was sick. She was having pains. No, not labour pains, no. She only just got pregnant. She was burning up. She had quite a fever. I called Dr Vlad. I didn't have another doctor on hand. He was very kind. He came right away. He even knows a little Hungarian. His grandmother on his mother's side was Hungarian. He said it was an attack of appendicitis. He put her in his Millequattro and he rushed her to the Maria del Rosario Medical Clinic. They're going to have to operate on her. I tried to find Cencio in Naples – I phoned his party headquarters. I still haven't had any luck turning him up. Mom, the Maria del Rosario Medical Clinic is pretty close to your house. It's on Via Piave. You take the #77. I'd like it if you went to see the girlfriend, in Room 11, and take her a nightgown, some nice bath soap, and a comb. We forgot to give her a night-gown in all the confusion here. No, she slept here in her sweater. Her bag got left in Cencio's car, in the trunk. He forgot to give it to her. And I haven't had any luck in finding Cencio's butler either, who has the key to the attic room where she's staying. So that's what I know. Don't ask me so many things; it's a complicated story. You go to the store and buy a nightgown. I don't know her size. I know she's a small, thin girl. Don't ask me so many questions. Oh, that's true. Today's a holiday and the clothing stores are closed. Okay, listen – take her one of yours. It doesn't matter whether it has a collar or not. Mom, she's a poor young girl all alone in a foreign country, pregnant, and in the middle of an appendicitis attack. They're hoping she doesn't lose the baby. Oh, you bet. Yes, she's definitely pregnant. She took the rabbit test and it was positive. (*Hangs up the receiver.*)

GIORGIO: So is your mother going over? Is she taking her a nightgown? Is a nightgown really all that important to a woman?

STEFANO: Yes, it must be important. It must provide some sense of stability. Dr Vlad phoned me to make sure she had one.

GIORGIO: Wouldn't it have been simpler if Dr Vlad had gotten her one himself? When he saw that all she had was a sweater?

STEFANO: You want too much from Dr Vlad. It's not like he can waste his time on a nightgown. He has patients to attend to. Besides, he's been more than kind. He's gone out of his way. He even had to come up with the deposit for the clinic. He left a cheque.

TECLA: That's money he'll never see again.

GIORGIO: Try to find Cencio again at the republican party headquarters.

TECLA: We called a little while ago. He isn't there. We left word that they should have him call us here as soon as they see him. Anyway, imagine him getting upset over an attack of appendicitis. He'll come, sure, but when it's convenient for him. Maybe tomorrow.

GIORGIO: My suspicion is that Dr Vlad doesn't know Hungarian. He may not even be a real doctor. His history is rather murky. Thirty years ago, before the war, he was working in a hospital in Berlin. That's what he says. But who knows if it's true? Sometimes I have the suspicion that he's telling lies. You know, just to put on airs.

TECLA: So?

GIORGIO: So maybe his diagnosis was wrong and it wasn't appendicitis at all.

STEFANO: And what was it?

GIORGIO: And who knows?

STEFANO: Let's not go casting doubts on Dr Vlad. It could be bad for Angelica. He's her analyst. She needs to feel secure with him.

GIORGIO: If I were one of his patients, I'd tell him not to wear those ties he wears. I'd tell him to dress more austerely. I'd feel uneasy if I had to tell the facts of my life to those multicoloured bow ties. They make him seem frivolous. Frivolous and a little bit like a country bumpkin, besides.[12]

STEFANO: We owe him a pile of money. Angelica has already had I don't know how many sessions.

TECLA: How tired you must be, poor Stefano. You seem exhausted. I'm tired myself. And I hurt my finger while I was crushing ice with the meat hammer. My fingernail has turned black. And I couldn't find the ice pack. I found it in with the coal. How in the world did it end up there?

STEFANO: I don't know.

GIORGIO: What a night. The girl howling, the ice needing to be crushed, Istanbul barking, coffee for Dr Vlad. We're falling apart after a night like that. Everyone except Angelica, who hasn't budged from her bed.

STEFANO: Angelica is ill. Did you know that? Besides, she doesn't want Dr Vlad to see her in curlers. He's her analyst. It's a delicate relationship.

GIORGIO: One ought to be able to show oneself to one's analyst in any condition. Even naked as a jaybird. Angelica isn't ill. She's fine. She drank a mug full of milk. What you need to do is ignore her. What you need to do is not let her have her way. Find something else to worry about.

STEFANO: Plus her bathrobe is a little old, a little worn out. She's ashamed of it.

GIORGIO: You never get ashamed in front of your own analyst. That's the law of analysis. (*Angelica enters.*) Was the caffe latte good?

ANGELICA: Don't worry about me. Ignore me. I heard everything you all were saying. The walls here are thin.

GIORGIO: Isn't this an old house? Old houses have thick walls.

ANGELICA: Not this one. This one has thin walls. Stefano, have you looked at the ads in the newspaper? We need to get moving on looking for a house.

TECLA: He's had other things on his mind than looking at ads. With all this confusion.

GIORGIO: There you are in your bathrobe, Angelica. You're ashamed of the bathrobe with Dr Vlad, but with us, on the other hand, you're not ashamed. And you've still got curlers on your head.

ANGELICA: No, I don't feel ashamed of anything in front of all of you. I've known you for a long time. It doesn't matter to me if you see me ugly and in disarray.

GIORGIO: But you've only known Raniero for a short time. For just two days. He's a new face.

ANGELICA: It's not new anymore. I've gotten used to seeing it. It seems as though I've known him for a very long time. As if I were his sister or his mother. He no longer intrigues me.

GIORGIO: Does Dr Vlad intrigue you?

ANGELICA: He doesn't intrigue me. He's my analyst. It's a delicate, complicated relationship – one you're not in a position to understand.

RANIERO: I'm comfortable here with you. It's not really important to me to arouse other people's curiosity. I'd rather you saw me as a wall or a table. Something that's always been there.

TECLA: What wonderful manners. Such a well-bred voice, so kind. A lovely timbre in that voice. It's a shame that you make your voice heard so rarely, Raniero.

ANGELICA: You could go live with him, Tecla. You don't have a man. You're alone. You're living in that utterly dreary little apartment.

TECLA: Stop talking stupid. There's too much of an age difference between him and me. Besides, I don't know what you have against my apartment. It's not dreary. It's got plenty of light. You wish you two could find a comfortable little house like mine.

ANGELICA: For the love of God. I'd commit suicide immediately in a house like yours. Tecla, you wouldn't be ugly if you dressed differently. You have all these dresses made out of thick, bulky material and covered with buttons. Look at what you're wearing today. It's got so many buttons it looks like some kind of control panel.

GIORGIO: I don't think Raniero wants to live with Tecla even if she gets rid of the buttons. Maybe he's already got oceans of women. He's handsome. Or else it could be that he's queer. We don't know. Since he doesn't talk, it might be anything at all. It's pointless to make all these plans for him.

TECLA: I'm not making plans for anyone. Angelica's the one who's talking random nonsense. By this point I've resigned myself to being alone. I'm unlucky in relationships with men. My relationships are always so difficult, so entangled. But I would like a child. I'll adopt one. I'm going to adopt an earthquake orphan.

GIORGIO: Raniero is one of those closed types. We could sit here on this couch for five years talking without hearing one drop of information from him about his life. In the meantime, we'd have been pouring the details of our lives over him by the litre. Because looking at him, you get the urge to tell him the world. You'd be a good analyst, Raniero. Yours is the kind of silence that invites confession. I think an analyst ought to be like you, completely attentive and silent. Dr Vlad is too frivolous and chatty.

STEFANO: Do me a favour, Giorgio, leave Dr Vlad out of this.

ANGELICA: Yes, leave him out of this. Don't you dare even mention his name. You aren't worth so much as his big toe.

GIORGIO: Don't make me think about Dr Vlad's toes. I've seen them. They're hideous. In the summer, we go swimming in Ostia – me, my father, and Dr Vlad.

ANGELICA: I'm sorry you woke him up last night for that stupid appendicitis.

GIORGIO: You wake him up at night every time you're feeling anxious. Do you think your anxiety attacks are any more pleasant than appendicitis? Or is it that you think you have the right to wake him up but other people don't?

ANGELICA: You should leave if you're in the mood to offend me. I don't wish to be offended.

RANIERO: Would it be possible to listen to some Vivaldi records? I love music. Though I'm not a true connoisseur. I don't actually own any records.

ANGELICA: Why don't you have any records? Are you poor?

GIORGIO: He's not obliged to respond to that. He may not want you to know if he's poor or not. A person can't really know everything about everybody else.

ANGELICA: We have quite a few records, for example, though we're rather poor all the same. But not so much. When it comes down to it, we have what we need.

TECLA: If you're leaving this house, you're going to need some beds, some mattresses, and some furniture.

ANGELICA: Don't make me think about it. This morning I have no interest in thinking about the fact that we've got to leave here. It seems to me we won't be comfortable in any another house.

TECLA: But yesterday you hated this house.

ANGELICA: I love it and I hate it. Like everything I have. Everything in my life. Even my daughter. It's terrible what I'm saying. I love and I hate even the baby.

GIORGIO: And Stefano.

ANGELICA: Stefano, too. All of it. Everything I have.

GIORGIO: *Odi et amo. Fortasse quid hoc faciam requiris.*[13]

TECLA: Don't start talking Latin now. I don't know Latin. I never studied it. I went to technical school.

ANGELICA: That's why I'm in such bad shape. That's why I'm always so annoying. It's terrible hating what you love. It's the most terrible thing in the world.

GIORGIO: Any possibility you might think a little less about yourself and a little more about others?

ANGELICA: Don't get on your moral high horse with me. It's not like you're someone who thinks all that much of others.

GIORGIO: More than you anyway.

The telephone rings.

TECLA: Could that be Cencio?

STEFANO: Hello? Who is it? Yes. Yes, it's long distance from Naples. Hello, Cencio? Ah, no, Romoletto. Romoletto, you're in Naples, too? What? I can't hear you. From the airport? Oh yeah? What? Why is he going to Jerusalem? With Vadim, the director. Huh? Oh, I see. I see. Listen, Romoletto. Call him to the phone for a minute. I need to tell him something urgent. Oh, yeah? Listen, that Hungarian girl. I don't even know her name. She's recuperating at the Maria del Rosario Hospital. Oh, he knows? He already knows the whole thing? I see. Roses? But when is he coming back? Fifteen? Fifteen roses?[14] Listen, Romoletto. Romoletto! Damn, the line went dead. (*Hangs up the receiver.*)

TECLA: What's happened?

STEFANO: Cencio is taking a plane for Jerusalem with Vadim, the director. They've given him a part in a film. A small part. He'll be the Prophet Ezekiel. It's a film about the Bible. Cencio called Romoletto last night and had him come to Naples to bring him some underwear and a coat. Yesterday, Cencio ran into Vadim in a restaurant in Naples. They're friends. Vadim suggested that he leave with him right away for Palestine, where they're shooting the film.

GIORGIO: Does the Prophet Ezekiel look like Cencio?

STEFANO: Evidently.

ANGELICA: They'll put a white beard on him all the way down to his feet. He'll have on long pants and a robe. Dressing up is his grand passion. He's a very gifted actor. He's a man who's good at everything he does.

TECLA: And the girlfriend?

DEBORA: Romoletto knew that she'd been taken to the clinic. He found out last night from Dr Vlad. So that's how Cencio found out as well. But now the Prophet Ezekiel is the only thing in his head and he's not thinking about anything else. Romoletto was rather put out

because he was the one who had to bring clothes to Naples. Put
out, but proud to be the butler of a prophet.

GIORGIO: But prophets don't have butlers.

STEFANO: They put me in charge of sending a huge bunch of roses to
Room 11. Cencio will be back in two or three weeks.

TECLA: And the republican party convention?

STEFANO: Romoletto said Cencio gave his speech first thing this morning at the convention. They booed him. His motion was rejected.
But now he's at the airport, about to fly to Jerusalem with Vadim,
the director. Cencio didn't come to the phone to talk to me. He was
busy getting his passport stamped.

GIORGIO: What a man. They boo him at the republican convention but
then he goes off, happy, with Vadim, the director. Tomorrow he'll
be the Prophet Ezekiel with a beard and a robe.

ANGELICA: We'll need to call my mother to take the baby to her house
while he's away. Poor Ilaria, poor baby girl. Her father is the
Prophet Ezekiel and her mother is a woman unfit to live in this
world.

GIORGIO: I don't feel sorry for your daughter. Because children have no
need of parents. The less they have their parents underfoot the better off they are. And I don't feel sorry for you, either. You're getting
along in the world just fine. You drank a whole mug of caffe latte.

RANIERO: A person can drink caffe latte and feel hopeless all the same.

GIORGIO: He has spoken. The oracle has spoken.

TECLA: I feel sorry for that girl. In the clinic without so much as a dog
to keep her company. I'm going to go visit her. I'll take her some
magazines. I've never had an operation for appendicitis, but I
remember when they took my tonsils out. It was awful. Plus what
kind of life will she have with Cencio? Poor soul. What kind of life
can she expect?

GIORGIO: And the roses? Who's going to deal with the roses?

STEFANO: Yes, we'll need to deal with the roses, too. Look up the
number of a florist. In the yellow pages. (*The telephone rings.*) Hello,
hello? Who is it? Oh, Signora Carafa. We were just about to call
you. Oh, so the baby and the nanny are already with you? Good.
Because Cencio has left for Jerusalem. Oh, you know. Yes, he's
playing the part of the Prophet Ezekiel. Come on, don't say that.
What do you expect? That's the kind of man he is. Let it go. Yes, I
think the Prophet Ezekiel probably was used to behaving differ-

ently. Hmm? What did you say, Angelica? Angelica is telling me
something. Oh, yes. Please remember the organza silk. And the lining, too, and some bias tape. Seven metres. Oh right, everything's
closed today. Tomorrow. Thanks. What? Tomorrow you're sending
the mattress maker over? But there's no real hurry on those mattresses. There's at least a month. Maybe more. And we still haven't
found a house. Yes, a wool mattress is an extremely healthy way to
sleep. Sure. What? My mother? My mother called you? Oh, from
the clinic? I'm sorry, there was no point in her calling you. I didn't
want you to have to get mixed up in the business with that girl.
Yes, she's Hungarian. Yes, in fact she is the girl that Cencio says he
wants to marry. But who knows if he'll actually marry her? No one
knows. No, she's not a drug addict. I don't believe so. What? Oh,
yes, you know a doctor at the Maria del Rosario Medical Clinic? Of
course you should talk to him. Sure. Advice is always useful. Even
in medical clinics. Especially in medical clinics. Room 11. You're
going to take her some eau de cologne? Thanks. Thanks. She must
feel alone, that poor girl. You're a very good person. But of course,
go right ahead and talk with the doctor you know. It seems like
a terrific idea to me. Yes, in addition to having appendicitis, she's
also pregnant. Yes, go ahead and say that she took the rabbit test.
She explained it to me with gestures. The rabbit test came back
positive.

December 1968

Notes

1 Tecla says she's the daughter of a *portinaio,* but the word describes a con-
cept that is less widespread in an anglophone context, especially in the
twenty-first century. The *portinaio* is something like the 'super' or building
manager in an apartment block, though that does not capture the lowliness
of the work in an Italian context. The *portinaio* typically lives onsite and is
responsible for cleaning the building, doing repairs and small errands, etc.
The *portinaio's* quarters are not infrequently below ground and somewhat
shabby.
2 A neighbourhood in the north-northeast of Rome, originally planned in the
1920s on the English 'garden city' model.

3 The PSI, or Italian Socialist Party, was a moderate or 'light' leftist party (it disbanded in 1994). The Italian Republican Party (PRI) is the oldest political party in Italy, tracing its roots to the Risorgimento.

4 Oskar Kokoschka (1886–1980), a Viennese expressionist painter and print-maker often grouped with Egon Schiele and Gustav Klimt, was widely exhibited across Europe by the 1930s. As Nazi influence grew, however, Kokoschka's work was denounced as 'degenerate,' and hundreds of his paintings were stripped from German museums in the year before the Anschluss.

5 The title of a 1961 film by French *nouvelle vague* director Alain Resnais.

6 The saying is *'acqua cheta rompe [or rovina] i ponti'*; Stefano is correct.

7 Frascati is a community in the hilly Castelli Romani ('Castles of Rome') area, about thirty kilometres southeast of the centre of Rome; Monte Porzio Catone is nearby. Neither location is, thus, very far from the house where the play is set. Cortina, conversely, is a rather exclusive winter-sport resort in the Dolomites.

8 Saluzzo, whose history dates back some 1100 years, is located in the Piedmont region, one of the historical centres of Jewish Italy. Today, Saluzzo remains primarily an agricultural and industrial area; at the time *The Wrong Door* was written, the population of Saluzzo was roughly 16,000.

9 A famous brand of panettone.

10 The '500' is a small, boxy Fiat that enjoyed great popularity.

11 The Italian Red Cross is also a provider of local ambulance services.

12 Ginzburg's own analyst made the mistake of wearing a bow tie at one of their last sessions. She wrote, 'One day I found him wearing a bow tie, his shirt buttoned up at the collar. That bow tie on an austere, Jewish man struck me as stupid, the most stupid symbol of frivolousness. I didn't even bother to tell him about it, or about how useless my relationship with him had become. I suddenly stopped going to see him, and I mailed him, along with a few brief words, the last of the money I owed.' 'La Mia Psicanalisi,' in *Mai devi domandarmi* (Einaudi, 1991, 46; my translation).

13 This appears to be a paraphrase, perhaps intentionally misquoted, of lines from a poem of Catullus: *'Odi et amo. Quare id faciam, fortasse requiris. Nescio, sed fieri sentio et excrucior.'* Roughly, the quote translates into English as 'I hate and I love. Why I do so, you may well ask of me. I do not know, but the feeling comes upon me, and I am crucified.'

14 Though it may seem strange to give a bunch of fifteen roses rather than, say, a dozen, it is useful to bear in mind that, in Italy, flowers are not typically given in even numbers. Rather, the number of roses in a bouquet may

betoken a reference meaningful only to the giver or receiver; as a general matter, not a few Italians favour giving flowers in multiples of three. Here, what significance the number fifteen may have for Cencio (or for Romoletto) is anyone's guess.

Dialogue

A PLAY IN ONE ACT

Cast:
Francesco
Marta
Concetta (offstage)

ACT ONE

[The interior of a small apartment in Rome.]

FRANCESCO: So?

MARTA: What?

FRANCESCO: Wasn't there something you wanted to tell me?

MARTA: I don't feel like it anymore.

FRANCESCO: Talk. I'm listening.

MARTA: Quiet. The baby's crying.

FRANCESCO: No. It's a cat in the courtyard.

MARTA: What time do you have?

FRANCESCO: I don't have the time. I left my watch in the bathroom. The bathtub is full of clothes that need to be washed. If some poor devil wants to take a bath, what's he supposed to do?

MARTA: It must be morning. I heard the church bells. I heard eight chimes. Concetta always comes late. The agreement was that she would come at eight, but she doesn't get here before nine. We owe her a month's salary, and she gets her revenge by coming late.

FRANCESCO: That's if she even comes. Sometimes she doesn't come at all. If she doesn't come, what's going to happen with all those clothes? Why don't you pay her?

MARTA: With money that I'll be getting from where?

FRANCESCO: I saw you doing the wash last night. What were you washing?

MARTA: I washed something. Your sports shirt.

FRANCESCO: Which one of my sports shirts?

MARTA: Your pale blue sports shirt.

FRANCESCO: Oh, and what am I going to wear this morning?

MARTA: You have lots of sports shirts.

FRANCESCO: Yes, but that's the only one I like. The pale blue one. My pale blue shirt. You washed it – why?

MARTA: It smelled bad.

FRANCESCO: No, it did not smell bad. I never smell bad.

MARTA: You're mistaken.

FRANCESCO: The bathtub is full of clothes. You could have washed those and left my pale blue shirt alone. Why don't you put all those clothes somewhere else? I want to take a bath this morning. So I won't smell anymore. Put them out on the balcony.

MARTA: Not on the balcony. The balcony is where I put the baby in her playpen. I don't keep dirty clothes near my baby.

FRANCESCO: So?

MARTA: What? There, I think Concetta's here. I heard the key.

FRANCESCO: You said you wanted to tell me something.

MARTA: I don't remember.

FRANCESCO: Go to hell! I want you to tell me right now whatever it was you said you wanted to tell me.

MARTA: Nothing.

FRANCESCO: I was sleepy earlier. I didn't come to bed until around two o'clock. I wrote to my brother. Then I went downstairs to put the letter in the mail. I had a cappuccino. I ran into Michele and walked around with him for a while.

MARTA: Where?

FRANCESCO: Like I said, for a walk. He'd come downstairs because of the dog. They've got the terrace, but every evening he has to take him out for a walk around the block anyway. If not, he suffers.

MARTA: Who suffers?

FRANCESCO: The dog. It's a kind of slavery, owning a dog. In the city. Not in the country. Sure, they've got a butler, but he told them he didn't want to hear another word about taking the dog out. Do you like him?

MARTA: The butler?

FRANCESCO: No, the dog. Do you like him?

MARTA: Yes.

FRANCESCO: I don't. He's too small. He looks like a little frog. A hairy little frog. I like big dogs. I liked that other one, the one that died on them.

MARTA: Yes. He was a beauty.

FRANCESCO: Uh-huh. He had a lot of spirit. Affectionate. He died because he ate a hairpin.

MARTA: It wasn't a hairpin. It was a curler.

FRANCESCO: Peritonitis.

MARTA: Right. It was one of Angelica's curlers.

FRANCESCO: But they blamed the butler. They said he should have been paying more attention. They even fired him.

MARTA: Why are you telling me things I already know?

FRANCESCO: But then they took him back. They don't know how to get along without a butler. The butler said he'd be willing to come back, but he didn't want to have anything more to do with any dogs. He's very disagreeable, that butler. There's something phony about him. This new dog of theirs – no, I don't like him. You aren't interested in dogs. But I am. We used to have a dog when I was a little boy, my brother and I. We loved him like crazy. We kept him in the country. At our house in Raparola. I'm so sorry we don't have that house anymore. I'd fill it up with dogs.

MARTA: (*Calling.*) Concetta!

FRANCESCO: Don't call her. Just wait. It's not that late.

MARTA: I want her to get the baby up and put her on the balcony.

FRANCESCO: On the balcony? But it's raining. I noticed it was raining.

MARTA: Oh really? It's raining? I left the wash outside on the line. Concetta! (*She gets up and faces the door.*) Concetta. Please go and get the baby up. Put her in the living room. Give her her milk, with two slices of Melba toast. Make up the shopping list. Get the laundry off the balcony. But first make some coffee.

FRANCESCO: Not for me, I don't want any coffee now. When I get up, I want a real breakfast.

CONCETTA'S VOICE: May I also have a couple of slices of Melba toast? The bread is all dried out.

MARTA: Yes, sure. Go ahead and eat.

FRANCESCO: Go ahead and eat! If I get up and find there's no more Melba toast, I'm going to pitch a fit. Is it really our job to keep Concetta in Melba toast? Bread isn't good enough?

MARTA: But she said it was dry.

FRANCESCO: If this is the way things are headed, I don't know how we'll end up.

MARTA: It won't be two slices of Melba toast that ruin us.

FRANCESCO: No, but it's everything together.

MARTA: If you eat Melba toast, why shouldn't she eat some, too? Aren't we all equal?

FRANCESCO: Yes, we're all equal. But I'm on a diet.

MARTA: Her too.

FRANCESCO: A diet, her too?

MARTA: Yes, sure. She weighs eighty kilos.

FRANCESCO: Damn.

MARTA: The only one who isn't eating Melba toast is me.

FRANCESCO: Please don't start acting like some kind of victim.

MARTA: How much did you ask your brother for?

FRANCESCO: Three hundred thousand.

MARTA: Four hundred thousand would have been better.

FRANCESCO: That seems exaggerated.

MARTA: We've got the phone. The payment on the refrigerator. Concetta. Plus I've still got to pay for my poncho.

FRANCESCO: Your what?

MARTA: My poncho. Twenty-five thousand lire.

FRANCESCO: That whatchamacallit with the fringe? Couldn't you at least have done without buying a poncho at a time like this?

MARTA: It's Angelica's fault. She made me go with her to see this Mexican friend of hers who makes them by hand. A little hole in the rear of a courtyard. It was full of ponchos. Elena bought four of them. Plus a pair of slippers, all furry, for Michele.

FRANCESCO: Michele was wearing those slippers the other night. He went outside in slippers. He says they're quite comfortable. Between the fur on the dog and the fur on his slippers, I wasn't seeing anything but fur. Has she been nice to you?

MARTA: Who?

FRANCESCO: Angelica.

MARTA: No.

FRANCESCO: Not to me either. I don't know why they keep her in the house. I'd tell her to go screw herself.

MARTA: Elena loves her very much. She's her sister.

FRANCESCO: It hardly seems possible that she's Elena's sister. Elena is so sweet, so simple. Angelica, on the other hand, is a snob. All kinds of

Mexican women friends pretending to be poor. Maybe they're even
pretending to be Mexican. Don't let them palm any more ponchos
off on you. Be a little careful.

MARTA: It's not as though I knew you'd lost your job. It was all so sudden.

FRANCESCO: I didn't lose my job. If I wanted, they'd keep me on. If I
agreed to go to Brussels. You didn't want to go to Brussels.

MARTA: It must be a sad city. The climate's humid. The baby would
always be coming down with bronchitis.

FRANCESCO: There are wonderful children in Brussels. All pink and
white and bursting with health. It doesn't matter. Enough. Subject
closed.

MARTA: I think I've found a job.

FRANCESCO: Oh really? What job?

FRANCESCO: On television. Michele found it for me.

FRANCESCO: Oh, Michele. Is that what you wanted to tell me earlier?

MARTA: No.

FRANCESCO: Strange, Michele didn't say anything to me about it –
about finding you a job. Even though we were together for quite a
while yesterday evening. We walked around for some time, back
and forth. I kept my eyes glued to his slippers. I've never seen
slippers like that before. Enormous, fur everywhere. I thought they
were ridiculous, but fascinating. I would never wear them. Don't
buy me any like that, you understand? So. What's the job?

MARTA: With old people. With old people in a nursing home.

FRANCESCO: And what do you know about old people in nursing
homes?

MARTA: I don't know anything about it. It's an investigation. I'm supposed to go around to all the nursing homes. Talk with the old
people.

FRANCESCO: How much are they paying you?

MARTA: I think 150,000.

FRANCESCO: And who are you going to leave the baby with while
you're going around to all these nursing homes?

MARTA: I'll leave her with Concetta.

FRANCESCO: But Concetta is an idiot.

MARTA: She's not such an idiot. Plus she's had all those children.

FRANCESCO: But they're all dead.

MARTA: The husband's an alcoholic. They were born delicate and that's
why they died.

FRANCESCO: Oh, her husband's an alcoholic?

MARTA: Yes. He used to beat her. He even broke some of her teeth. That's why it's hard for her to eat bread. He took all their coffee cups and he threw them out the window.

FRANCESCO: And where's this husband now?

MARTA: Where is he? He's in a mental hospital.

FRANCESCO: A hundred and fifty thousand lire just this one time isn't going to help much. They'll send you around everywhere in taxis. You won't take the bus because you don't know your way around the city. But it doesn't matter, I'm glad. Michele was very kind to come up with this job for you. Did you thank him?

MARTA: Yes.

FRANCESCO: Strange. He didn't say anything to me. He never even mentioned your name. He seemed very serious. Depressed. I asked him what was wrong, but he didn't tell me. He changed the subject. He's read my whole novel. You know, he liked it. The only thing he said was that I should change the ending. At the boat.

MARTA: What boat?

FRANCESCO: What do you mean, what boat? Don't you remember, he goes to sit next to the boat? He shakes the sand out of his sandals and looks out toward Corsica?

MARTA: Right.

FRANCESCO: He doesn't like that part. He says it's sentimental.

MARTA: Was he alone?

FRANCESCO: Who?

MARTA: Michele?

FRANCESCO: Oh. Yes. He was alone. Elena stayed upstairs, on the terrace, with Angelica. I wanted to go up and say hello to them, but he said it was better not to, that they were both depressed. Maybe they'd had a fight. I don't know.

MARTA: Who?

FRANCESCO: Them. The two sisters. Or else Elena and Michele. I'm telling you, I don't know why they keep that Angelica in the house. She's virtually installed herself there. She's moved all her furniture in. Now they'll never get rid of her. I'm sure Elena loves her, but him – if you ask me, he can't stand her. Poor Michele. To have your wife's sister just drop into your lap. From one day to the next, just like that. Because she's a widow. Watch out that you don't bring your sister here. I won't stand for it.

MARTA: My sister is hardly a widow.

FRANCESCO: If she ends up a widow, don't bring her here to me.

MARTA: A very strange personality.

FRANCESCO: Who?

MARTA: Angelica.

FRANCESCO: Anyway, he didn't talk about you at all the other evening. Michele, I mean. He talked about everything except you.

MARTA: But you said he was quiet.

FRANCESCO: Quiet? No, he talked. But he was depressed. (*Pause.*) What's worrying me is that this job is just something you dreamed up on your own. That it's not a sure thing. Otherwise he would have said something to me about it.

MARTA: It's more than a sure thing.

FRANCESCO: It's such a shame you never finished high school. You always leave things half done. If you had a diploma you could find a job as a substitute teacher. It would be a steady salary every month.

MARTA: It's not my fault that I didn't finish high school. My mother made me study classical dance.

FRANCESCO: Your mother clearly had no common sense. You're not cut out for classical dance, it's obvious. You have no grace at all when you move.

MARTA: Anyway, I eventually left it.

FRANCESCO: Sure. You always leave things half done. You don't stick to anything. Really, not to anything.

MARTA: Why don't you go find a job as a substitute teacher yourself, since you've finished high school?

FRANCESCO: Because then I wouldn't have time to write anymore. I even asked Michele for his advice. He feels I should continue as I have been. A screenplay here and there, now and then an article. You want to know the truth? Deep down I'm happy not to have gone to Brussels. But not because of the weather. Because of the job. Since I haven't had a job, I feel so good. So free. Free like Michele.

MARTA: But he's a writer.

FRANCESCO: Ah. Because I'm what exactly?

MARTA: He has his books published.

FRANCESCO: He has published a book or two. I still haven't. That simply means that he's been luckier than I've been. Maybe he's even better. I don't know. However, I also write and therefore I'm a writer. Don't you agree?

MARTA: Yes.

FRANCESCO: If money is the issue, he never has a cent either. And yet he manages to live as if he were rolling in it. How he does it I don't know. They have that beautiful house. The terrace. All those aza-leas. A butler. All those beautiful cats. A lovely dog.

MARTA: But you said you didn't like that dog.

FRANCESCO: No, no, I don't like it; it looks like a frog. It's bowlegged. But it's an expensive dog. He eats a pile of meat. Not table scraps either. He has to buy meat specially for the dog. Elena is wonderful. She gets up early every morning, she makes sure the cats are taken care of, she waters all those plants. She gets the whole house shin-ing. I don't think their butler really does anything.

MARTA: How do you know she makes sure the cats are taken care of early every morning?

FRANCESCO: I've seen her. One morning when we had to go to Naples. I went upstairs and she was there, on the terrace, in her night shirt, barefoot, with all that long black hair of hers tumbling down. She was feeding the cats and the dog. What a beautiful woman. So full of life. Her eyes look like black cherries.

MARTA: And Angelica?

FRANCESCO: What about Angelica?

MARTA: Angelica, meanwhile, what was she doing?

FRANCESCO: I don't know. She was sleeping. Why are you so interested in Angelica? She was sleeping. No, then she came out too with a little cup of coffee, wearing a baby-doll nightie.

MARTA: And what's she like, in a baby-doll nightie – ugly?

FRANCESCO: Yes, because she's bowlegged. The butler was sleeping. He never made an appearance. He takes sleeping pills because he suf-fers from insomnia. So in the mornings he sleeps in. I don't under-stand why they keep him.

MARTA: Because they say he's neurotic. They feel sorry for him.

FRANCESCO: Anyway, Elena cooks; she does everything around the house. It's a real shame you don't know how to cook. You know what a savings it would be.

MARTA: No one ever taught me.

FRANCESCO: You can always learn.

MARTA: From who?

FRANCESCO: I don't know. From Elena. Instead of going over there to gossip, you could tell her to teach you something. Or else from Concetta. Although Concetta is an idiot. Plus she doesn't know how to cook.

MARTA: Don't talk so loud. You can hear everything from in there.

FRANCESCO: As soon as we pay her, I say we should look for another housekeeper.

MARTA: No, Concetta suits me just fine.

FRANCESCO: That's because you demand too little. It's one of your defects – you demand too little. You adapt. She doesn't clean, she never dusts. There's half an inch of dust on my desk. It doesn't matter to you. You adapt. This house, for example. You know how ugly this house is. But nothing matters to you.

MARTA: We don't pay much here. Everyone says we're paying very little.

FRANCESCO: We don't pay much, but it's an ugly house. Noisy. Dark. There's no place here where a person can really feel comfortable.

MARTA: There's the living room.

FRANCESCO: You can call it a living room. It's a hole. Anyway, you keep it in constant disorder. With the baby's pajamas thrown all over the place. How come the baby has so many pairs of pajamas?

MARTA: She has six.

FRANCESCO: I seem to find all six pairs of those pajamas everywhere. On my desk. On all the chairs. Slung over the toilet bowl. In with my shoes. (*Pause.*) For example, Elena and Michele – I would never dare ask them to come here. I would be ashamed. Do you realize that we've never had them over even one time?

MARTA: Never.

FRANCESCO: We always go to their place. It's not nice. If we had a different house, maybe even with a terrace, we could have our friends over in the evening. We shouldn't always have to go out ourselves. We'd save on the babysitter. Don't you think?

MARTA: Yes.

FRANCESCO: In the summer we could sit out on the terrace and enjoy the air. You remember how cool it is, even in August, on Michele's terrace. If we had a terrace like that, we could save on vacations. Instead, it's our bad luck to die of boredom at Soriano del Cimino, because otherwise we'd suffocate to death in this hole of an apartment.

MARTA: We have a balcony.

FRANCESCO: A balcony the size of a closet. No air, and it smells like the courtyard. If you could even manage to keep a few plants out there. My mother gave you two pots of geraniums. They're dead.

MARTA: Because they didn't have any roots.

FRANCESCO: Because you forgot to water them. Not because of the roots. Who told you they didn't have any roots?

MARTA: Concetta said so.

FRANCESCO: Concetta is an idiot. Don't repeat the opinions of an idiot. (*Pause.*) As soon as I have my novel ready, I'm going to give it to Michele. He'll take it to an editor. To Vallecchi. He's said he would take it to Vallecchi. I just have to revise the ending. By the boat.

MARTA: Yes.

FRANCESCO: I could even win a prize with that novel. The Salsomaggiore. I could win the Salsomaggiore. Michele is on the jury. It's a million lire, the Salsomaggiore. Did you know that?

MARTA: Yes.

FRANCESCO: Then, between the Salsomaggiore, the foreign translations, et cetera, we could look for another house.

MARTA: As soon as the money arrives from your brother, I'll buy a crib for Memé. The cradle has gotten too cramped.

FRANCESCO: Isn't she too small to be sleeping in a crib already?

MARTA: No, she's ten months old. It's the cradle that's too small. (*Pause.*) I saw a beautiful crib, made of wood and painted red. Thirty thousand lire.

FRANCESCO: Is that what you wanted to tell me?

MARTA: No.

FRANCESCO: Thirty thousand lire! Damn, that's expensive! Always so grand. At Upim[1] they have very nice cribs at ten or twelve thousand.

MARTA: Yes, but this one expands. She can sleep in it until she's eight years old. Plus it's red. It matches the blanket.

FRANCESCO: Who the hell cares if it matches the blanket? The house you live in is a pit and yet you let yourself get bogged down in all these details. But you shouldn't give the cradle away anyway. It could still come in handy if we have other children.

MARTA: I already promised it to my sister. She's pregnant.

FRANCESCO: Your sister's pregnant? Again?

MARTA: Yes.

FRANCESCO: Damn.

MARTA: I don't believe we'll have any more children.

FRANCESCO: Don't you want some more children? Didn't you used to say that you wanted at least four?

MARTA: It's exhausting.

FRANCESCO: Of course it's exhausting. Everything's exhausting. She's some kind of nitwit, your sister is. They don't have a cent. They're going to live on caffe latte.

MARTA: She got a job.

FRANCESCO: What job?

MARTA: She just has to answer the phone. Attach some stamps.

FRANCESCO: Where?

MARTA: Onto letters, I guess.

FRANCESCO: I'm saying where, in what kind of office?

MARTA: It's a notary's office, I think. On Via Arenula.

FRANCESCO: You're always so imprecise. You never remember anything exactly. It's your sister; you should find out where she works, right?

MARTA: On Via Arenula.

FRANCESCO: And when she's out, who stays with the children?

MARTA: Her mother-in-law.

FRANCESCO: Sure. She has her mother-in-law living with her. My mother lives far away. Anyway, she wouldn't be right for it. She has a heart murmur.

MARTA: Aside from the fact that she has a heart murmur, she wouldn't spend so much as a half-hour looking after the baby. She's not the type. She has no patience. She's always playing canasta.

FRANCESCO: Poor thing. She's all alone, and she plays a little canasta. What's wrong with that?

MARTA: Nothing. But she's no good with children.

FRANCESCO: What has my mother ever done to you, poor woman? You're always so nasty when you talk about her.

MARTA: She hasn't done anything to me. She can't stand me. I can't stand her either. We could be living in the dirt, she wouldn't lend us ten cents. It's always your brother we have to write to. It doesn't matter. Enough. Subject closed.

FRANCESCO: Yours was even less cut out for bringing up children. She had no common sense. And she was obsessed with antiques.

MARTA: Better that than canasta. Anyway, mine's dead.

FRANCESCO: But your sister was wonderful. She found herself a reliable job. With a steady salary every month. If you do a good job with this investigation, maybe they'll take you on permanently at the television station. If Michele vouches for you. I'm sure he'll vouch for you. He's the kind of guy who puts himself out for others. And he's very fond of me. He loves me very much. Anyway, if you get a permanent job, you could even put the baby in daycare.

MARTA: No. I'm not putting the baby in daycare. Signora Bea put hers in daycare and she came down with German measles.

FRANCESCO: Signora Bea? And who is she?

MARTA: The woman who lives down below, right?

FRANCESCO: She got German measles when?

MARTA: Now.

FRANCESCO: You took Memé to play with the baby downstairs the day before yesterday? She could have gotten German measles.

MARTA: No. She's not contagious anymore.

FRANCESCO: It takes forty days for them not to be contagious.

MARTA: Forty days for measles. For German measles, it's fifteen.

FRANCESCO: But you took her over there the day before yesterday!

MARTA: They didn't say anything to me about German measles. They told me afterwards. Anyway, I didn't know what to do. I didn't know who to leave her with. I had to go out. Concetta hadn't come.

FRANCESCO: Where did you have to go that was so urgent?

MARTA: To see Michele.

FRANCESCO: At Michele's house?

MARTA: No. Out.

FRANCESCO: Out where?

MARTA: In Piazza Navona.

FRANCESCO: Well, you could have taken the baby to Piazza Navona. It would have been better than leaving her there with German measles.

MARTA: But I had to talk to Michele.

FRANCESCO: She could definitely have gotten German measles.

MARTA: Maybe it's not German measles. Maybe it's tertian fever.[2]

FRANCESCO: Make up your mind.

MARTA: Plus it was raining.

FRANCESCO: Elena and Michele are a minute away. You can take the baby to Elena whenever you want. You can leave her there the entire day. Elena will take care of her better than Signora Bea. Plus Angelica is there. Angelica doesn't have a thing to do. She gets bored. She listens to records. You could even take the baby there today. They've told me so time after time. I don't like Angelica much. But she's kind. She adores children.

MARTA: But I've stopped being friends with Angelica.

FRANCESCO: You've stopped being friends with Angelica? Because of that whatchamacallit, that poncho?

MARTA: No.

FRANCESCO: Give her the money right away. I'll find you 20,000 lire.
   Maybe I'll even ask my mother for it.

MARTA: The poncho has nothing to do with it.

FRANCESCO: I don't like Angelica much, but she's always very, very
   kind. She lends me her car when I need it. The Mercedes. She's lent
   you her clothes lots of times. That sweater that you've got on the
   chair, isn't that hers?

MARTA: Yes.

FRANCESCO: Give it back to her. Give it right back to her.

MARTA: But the sweater has nothing to do with it.

FRANCESCO: She's Elena's sister. I like Elena a great deal. She's such a
   simple person, so generous. I don't know how many times she's
   made me spaghetti at two in the morning. Really, Michele and
   Elena are the only friends I have in Rome. The only people I feel
   comfortable with. And Angelica doesn't even bother me when I'm
   with them. I can tolerate her. I don't even want to know why you
   argued. Stupid nonsense. Women gossiping. A sweater.

MARTA: My God, I told you the sweater has nothing to do with it.

FRANCESCO: I don't want to know why you argued. I'm not at all curious to know. Now you've started fighting with my friends. Michele
   is an extraordinary man. Unique. His friendship matters to me a
   great deal. I owe him a lot. So do you. He found you a job. Now I
   guess that idea's shot.

MARTA: I stopped being friends with Angelica. Not with Michele.

FRANCESCO: You stopped being friends – you've stopped making sense,
   that's what you've stopped doing. And may a person ask why?

MARTA: It's a long story. Difficult to explain.

FRANCESCO: We should take a trip to Spain, with the three of them. As
   soon as the money from my brother comes. You make up with her
   right away, you understand?

MARTA: I don't think I'll come to Spain.

FRANCESCO: You're not coming? Never mind then. I'll go. You stay
   home. I can't wait to be travelling around Spain with Michele.

MARTA: I don't think Michele's going to come either.

FRANCESCO: And why is that?

MARTA: Just because. I don't think so. Besides, if I went I wouldn't
   know where to leave the baby.

FRANCESCO: With my brother, right? Haven't we said you could leave
   the baby in Bologna with my brother?

MARTA: The weather is terrible in Bologna.

FRANCESCO: It's terrible in Bologna?

MARTA: Yes.

FRANCESCO: Drop dead. (*Pause.*) What about Elena? Have you stopped being friends with Elena?

MARTA: No. Not with Elena. Because she doesn't know anything.

FRANCESCO: She doesn't know what?

MARTA: Nothing. I've only stopped being friends with Angelica.

FRANCESCO: You've stopped being friends, you've stopped being friends – I ought to stop you right in the face!

MARTA: Don't shout!

FRANCESCO: Do you want to tell me what in hell happened?

MARTA: Angelica feels no affection for you at all. She thinks you're a social climber.

FRANCESCO: And I don't feel any affection for her either. Social climber! And where am I supposed to be climbing, since I don't seem to be getting any higher?

MARTA: Social climber means someone who is hoping to get higher. Maybe without ever getting to the top.

FRANCESCO: Social climber! Do I seem like a social climber to you?

MARTA: No. Not to me.

FRANCESCO: Gossip. Women chattering. What do the opinions of some moron matter to me? Now I understand why Michele was so serious yesterday evening. Because he was unhappy about all the gossip the two of you have been up to. That's why he told me not to come up. So I wouldn't have to run into that moron.

MARTA: Maybe.

FRANCESCO: The only thing I ask of you is that you not fight with my friends. Understood?

MARTA: Yes.

FRANCESCO: Is this what you wanted to tell me earlier?

MARTA: No.

FRANCESCO: You want to tell me what the hell you wanted to tell me?

MARTA: Turn off the light.

FRANCESCO: Why should I turn off the light?

MARTA: Because I want to talk in the dark.

FRANCESCO: (*Turns off the light.*) There. It's off. Talk.

MARTA: You remember that trip?

FRANCESCO: What trip?

MARTA: To the Marche, hmm?

FRANCESCO: When we went to the Marche, two months ago? When the
  car broke down?
MARTA: Yes.
FRANCESCO: It broke down because they put the wrong oil in it. I told
  Angelica about it. She doesn't know how to drive a Mercedes any-
  way. It's too much for her. But it's important to her to have a Mer-
  cedes, because she's a snob.
MARTA: Yes. She's a snob.
FRANCESCO: So?
MARTA: So that's how everything started.
FRANCESCO: What started?
MARTA: Don't you understand?
FRANCESCO: No. I don't understand anything. I must be stupid.
MARTA: In Urbino. In the piazza at Urbino. That's when we said it
  started.
FRANCESCO: We said? Who?
MARTA: Us.
FRANCESCO: Us who?
MARTA: The two of us.

Silence.

FRANCESCO: You and Michele.
MARTA: Yes.
FRANCESCO: You're in love with Michele!
MARTA: Yes.
FRANCESCO: And him?
MARTA: Him too.
FRANCESCO: He's in love with you, too?
MARTA: Yes.
FRANCESCO: No. That's impossible. (*Silence.*) In the Marche?
MARTA: Yes. In the Marche. At Urbino. In the piazza at Urbino. There
  was a terrible wind. You were messing around inside the car. An-
  gelica and Elena had gone into a store and they were buying some
  caciocavallo.[3] There was a terrible wind and I was afraid the baby
  would get cold.
FRANCESCO: And then?
MARTA: Then we went into that restaurant to eat. They brought me
  some milk for the baby. There were red tablecloths on the tables,
  and there was an owl.

FRANCESCO: I don't remember any owl. I don't remember anything.

MARTA: It was only two months ago. It was in March. But it was cold. Memé's hands were frozen. In the restaurant there, they had a huge stove lit and we were getting warm by it. They brought us some polenta and some wine. You ordered the agnolotti,[4] but they didn't have any ready. You had to wait.

FRANCESCO: Why are you describing all these details? What do I care about all that?

MARTA: Nothing. Just that … I remember. I remember everything. But Memé was crying and Michele, to calm her down, started singing. He sang a song. 'Drink up! Empty cup! Bring on more bottles of wine!'[5]

FRANCESCO: So?

MARTA: Nothing. It started that day. I remember everything because that was the day it started. Angelica had said something unpleasant. She said how annoying babies are when you're travelling. Especially when they're spoiled.

FRANCESCO: I have a vague memory.

MARTA: I brought her along because who would I have left her with otherwise?

FRANCESCO: Go on.

MARTA: It's not exactly true that Angelica adores children. You said earlier that she adores children. It's not true.

FRANCESCO: Go on.

MARTA: Nothing. There isn't any more. That's it.

FRANCESCO: What do you mean, that's it?

MARTA: Yes. I think Angelica realized that day that something had happened. That's why she was nasty about the baby.

FRANCESCO: I don't care about Angelica. Or about 'drink up' either. I would like to know if you plan to leave me.

MARTA: I don't know.

FRANCESCO: You can't not know.

MARTA: And yet I'm telling you that I don't know.

FRANCESCO: What are your intentions?

MARTA: I don't have any intentions. I have a lot of very mixed-up ideas. And I feel very unhappy.

FRANCESCO: Can I turn on the light?

MARTA: If you want.

FRANCESCO: (*He turns the light back on.*) Afterwards? What happened afterwards? After 'drink up,' what happened?

MARTA: Nothing. Practically nothing. We went to put the caciocavallo in the car, Michele and I. The baby stayed behind in Elena's arms.

FRANCESCO: And you talked?

MARTA: No. Not that day. Later. Three days later. One evening at Ancona. We went dancing, me and Michele. You and Elena were sleepy. We went. They had a kind of a cantina there where people were dancing.

FRANCESCO: He told you that he loved you.

MARTA: Yes.

FRANCESCO: And afterwards?

MARTA: Afterwards nothing. We came back to Rome.

FRANCESCO: And you went to meet each other? You had dates?

MARTA: Sometimes.

FRANCESCO: Where? In a hotel?

MARTA: No. He has a sort of a studio in an attic. A room where he goes to write.

FRANCESCO: I know it. I've been there. It's near Piazza Navona.

MARTA: Yes.

FRANCESCO: Michele loves pretty women. I know. He's quite picky when it comes to women. You're not especially pretty. Can you tell me how this happened?

MARTA: I don't know.

FRANCESCO: You have an ugly complexion. Sort of mustard-coloured. And you're bowlegged. Like the dog. Evidently he's got a weakness for bow legs.

MARTA: Evidently.

FRANCESCO: Angelica's bowlegged, too. He surrounds himself with people with bow legs. His wife, on the other hand, isn't bowlegged. She's gorgeous.

MARTA: Yes.

FRANCESCO: And ten times more beautiful than you.

MARTA: I know.

FRANCESCO: Ten? Not ten. A thousand, a thousand times.

MARTA: I'm not really all that bowlegged.

FRANCESCO: Bowlegged enough.

MARTA: I feel so unhappy. I'm cold.

FRANCESCO: Put on that sweater. Angelica's sweater. Put it on. (*Pause. Marta puts on the sweater.*) And Angelica? Did Angelica find out? Is that why you stopped being friends with her?

MARTA: Yes.

FRANCESCO: How did she find out? Did she figure it out? Or did she see the two of you together?

MARTA: She saw us in a café. But she had already figured it out.

FRANCESCO: Sharper than me. I'm stupid. I'm distracted. I never thought about it. It was the furthest thing from my mind.

MARTA: Because you've never paid very much attention to me.

FRANCESCO: That's true. I've always paid more attention to your faults. Your skin. Your bow legs.

MARTA: I'm not really all that bowlegged.

FRANCESCO: Bowlegged enough.

MARTA: If you want to say mean things to me, go right ahead.

FRANCESCO: You were like my feet and my hands. A man doesn't look at his hands that closely. He knows he has them and that's enough. He glances at them for a moment, notices the hairs, the freckles. But he doesn't know them. He doesn't find some cosmic significance in them.

MARTA: You're talking strangely.

FRANCESCO: I'm talking strangely. Sometimes I talk strangely.

MARTA: The thing is, you were never in love with me. I've never understood why you married me.

FRANCESCO: And you? Why did you?

MARTA: I don't know. It seemed to me that I did love you. I was very confused. I still am. Even now my head is so jumbled. It's just that I get so tremendously flustered when I think I love someone.

FRANCESCO: My brother told me I shouldn't marry you. He said you were flighty.

MARTA: It's true that I'm flighty. I feel empty-headed and confused.

FRANCESCO: My brother told me I ought to choose a sensible woman, with both feet on the ground. Like his wife.

MARTA: I've never been able to stand them, either your brother or his wife.

FRANCESCO: I know. You were always chilly to them! Apart from constantly telling me to ask him to lend us money.

MARTA: They've got plenty of it.

FRANCESCO: When they came for Christmas, with the children, you gave them quite an icy reception. They had brought so many beautiful gifts.

MARTA: I was not icy. I was friendly enough but I couldn't find anything to say to them, or them to me for that matter.

FRANCESCO: You refused to cook. I had to take everyone out to a restaurant.

MARTA: I don't know how to cook. Besides, Memé had a fever.

FRANCESCO: What are your intentions?

MARTA: I told you, I don't have any intentions.

FRANCESCO: Are you thinking of going to live with Michele?

MARTA: I don't know. Angelica says that if he leaves Elena, she might even kill herself.

FRANCESCO: Of course not, she won't kill herself. She'll cheer up. She'll find someone else right away. She's so beautiful.

MARTA: Why don't you take Elena, if you like her so much?

FRANCESCO: I like her as a person. Not as a woman. As a woman she makes me uneasy. She's too beautiful. Too tall. With too much hair. Anyway, I don't need anyone. In the end, I do just as well alone.

MARTA: You'll write. You'll finish your novel. You'll give it to Vallecchi.

FRANCESCO: Don't mention Vallecchi's name to me!

MARTA: Don't shout! (*Pause.*) He has a house. He has a house in the country. At Poggio Mirteto.

FRANCESCO: He who?

MARTA: Him, Michele. He inherited it from an uncle of his.

FRANCESCO: Would you two go live there?

MARTA: Maybe. We've talked about it. It's a little dilapidated, as houses go. But we could live in it. He won't have any money – he'll have to give all the money he has to Elena. We could live there on fairly little. I could do some work from time to time, an occasional investigative report for the television station. He'll write.

FRANCESCO: So you do have intentions. You even have plans.

MARTA: The baby will be fine there. There are chickens. She'll have fresh eggs every day.

FRANCESCO: The baby?

MARTA: Yes. There's even a vineyard with grapes.

FRANCESCO: You've thought of everything, haven't you?

MARTA: There's a big meadow behind the house. There are geese. The baby can chase the geese.

FRANCESCO: She doesn't know how to walk yet, how is she supposed to chase geese?

MARTA: Later. When she learns how to walk.

FRANCESCO: Have you seen these geese?

MARTA: No, Michele told me about them.

FRANCESCO: You've decided that the baby will live with the two of you?

MARTA: And where should she live?

FRANCESCO: I'm her father, aren't I?

MARTA: It's always seemed to me that the baby's not very important to you. You've always said that you don't have a strong paternal instinct.

FRANCESCO: But she's mine. She's mine, too. Unless you know something I don't, the baby is mine, too.

MARTA: I won't leave without the baby.

FRANCESCO: So then you won't leave. It's not like you're obligated.

MARTA: She's tiny, the baby. She can't be without me. And I can't be without her.

FRANCESCO: You don't have such a strong maternal instinct either. You're always dumping her on the neighbour downstairs. With Signora Bea.

MARTA: What do I dump? I don't dump anything!

FRANCESCO: Don't shout! (*Pause.*) You and the baby at Poggio Mirteto. With Michele. Elena in Rome, still in her house with the terrace. And me? Where am I?

MARTA: Don't you want to stay here?

FRANCESCO: In this house? No. I hate this house. I don't want to stay here even a half an hour longer. I hate it.

MARTA: You could go back to your mother's.

FRANCESCO: No. I can't even imagine it. I wouldn't be able to tolerate her. She'd talk to me about you. Just to say that she can't stand you. I want some place where people are going to talk to me about other things.

MARTA: But do we have to decide all this right now – where you're going to live and where I'm going to live?

FRANCESCO: I can't stand uncertain situations. (*Silence.*) I used to have a stable life, up until a few minutes ago. I believed it was stable. I had a wife. I had some friends. One friend. Now the whole thing's caved in. It seemed like a morning like so many others. Are you crying? Why are you crying? What have you lost? You've hardly lost anything at all. You found yourself a man who loves you. And even a house in the country.

MARTA: Be quiet, I'm pleading with you. I feel hopeless.

FRANCESCO: I don't understand why.

MARTA: I'm confused. My head is killing me. (*Pause. Francesco gets up and gets dressed.*) You're getting dressed? Now?

FRANCESCO: Yes. I'm leaving. I hate this room. I think I'll go to Bologna, to my brother's. I feel like seeing my brother. Where's my sports shirt? The pale blue one?

MARTA: I washed it. It's wet.

FRANCESCO: Doesn't matter. Give it to me anyway. I'll take it wrapped in cellophane. And the baby's pajamas? Get up. Get out the baby's pajama's.

MARTA: The baby? You're not really taking the baby with you?

FRANCESCO: Yes. I'm taking her to Bologna with me. I've decided.

MARTA: No, I won't let you take the baby away!

FRANCESCO: Don't shout!

MARTA: She could have caught German measles. I don't want her to get sick in your brother's house.

FRANCESCO: She doesn't have German measles yet.

MARTA: She probably caught them, though. She'll spread German measles to all your brother's children.

FRANCESCO: I don't give a damn about my brother's children. I'm ordering you to get the baby's things ready immediately!

MARTA: Don't shout like that!

A bell is heard.

FRANCESCO: Who's that?

MARTA: I don't know.

Knocking is heard at the door.

CONCETTA'S VOICE: Someone's brought a letter. It's for the Signora

FRANCESCO: Give it here. (*He takes the letter.*) It's for you. Michele's handwriting.

Marta reads the letter.

CONCETTA'S VOICE: If you give me some money, I'll go down and do the shopping.

MARTA: Give her some money.

CONCETTA'S VOICE: Shall I bring the baby in?

MARTA: No. Leave her where she is.

CONCETTA'S VOICE: I'm going then.

MARTA: Yes. (*She reads the letter.*)

FRANCESCO: (*Packing a bag.*) What's he have to say?

MARTA: They're leaving.

FRANCESCO: Who?

MARTA: All of them. Angelica, Elena, Michele.

FRANCESCO: Going where?

MARTA: To Spain.

FRANCESCO: All of a sudden? Just like that?

MARTA: He doesn't have the heart to leave Elena. He must have talked to her last night. He doesn't have the heart to do it. They're leaving. He didn't tell her anything.

FRANCESCO: He didn't tell her anything. About you. He didn't tell Elena.

MARTA: No. He never will tell her anything. He doesn't have the heart to leave her. He isn't brave enough.

FRANCESCO: I'd considered him braver.

MARTA: Elena is ill. She has a heart murmur.

FRANCESCO: Like my mother.

MARTA: Like your mother.

FRANCESCO: So?

MARTA: So that's the end of that.

FRANCESCO: (*He sits on the bed.*) Let me see the letter.

MARTA: No. (*She folds the letter. She gets up. She puts the letter in her purse. She looks for a cigarette and lights it. She goes back to the bed.*) I'm cold. I'm freezing to death.

FRANCESCO: Cover yourself up. You're turning blue. Your teeth are chattering. (*Pause.*) Will you see him before he goes?

MARTA: No. They're leaving now.

FRANCESCO: Are they going in the Mercedes?

MARTA: I don't know.

FRANCESCO: And us? What are we going to do now?

MARTA: I don't know. (*Pause.*) Didn't you want to go to Bologna?

FRANCESCO: I'll go. Maybe not now. Perhaps tomorrow.

MARTA: Why tomorrow?

FRANCESCO: So as not to leave you alone here.

MARTA: Tomorrow will be just like today.

FRANCESCO: Of course, I can't give you anything. I won't be able to give you anything at all anymore. We already live here together like two people who barely know each other.

MARTA: I feel terrible.

FRANCESCO: Do you want me to bring you the baby?

MARTA: No. (*Pause.*) Go see if she's all right. Then come back.

FRANCESCO: (*Leaves the room. Then returns.*) She's fine. She's playing. (*Pause.*) For her it's a morning like every other. (*He opens the shutters.*) It's really raining. Good thing I didn't take her to Bologna.

Pause.

MARTA: I feel terrible.

FRANCESCO: (*He touches her hand. Then her forehead.*) You're hot. Looks to me like you have a fever. (*Pause.*) What if you're the one who's coming down with German measles?

MARTA: No. I don't have German measles.

FRANCESCO: It's a good thing we didn't go to Spain. Otherwise, who knows, you might have come down with German measles on the trip.

MARTA: Don't mention that place to me.

FRANCESCO: Spain?

MARTA: Yes. Don't mention it.

FRANCESCO: I heard the key. Concetta's back.

MARTA: Back already?

FRANCESCO: Yes.

CONCETTA'S VOICE: Ma'am, may I come in for a moment?

MARTA: Go see what she wants.

Francesco leaves the room. Then he returns.

FRANCESCO: That was Michele's butler. He brought the dog over. He's asking us to keep it here until they come back. He says he doesn't want to be responsible.

MARTA: And what did you say?

FRANCESCO: Me? Nothing? I told him to leave it. It's out back.

MARTA: I don't want to see that dog!

FRANCESCO: But what's he done to you, the poor beast? He's out there on the rug. He's cold, he got rained on. He's a little frog. A hairy little frog. Of course I'm going to take care of him until they come back. This is hardly his fault.

MARTA: I don't want to see that dog!

FRANCESCO: Don't shout!

May 1970

Notes

1 More or less the Italian equivalent of Sears.

2 'Tertian fever,' by one definition, is a name, dating to the Middle Ages, for what modern doctors recognize as a form of malaria. In Dumas's *The Man in the Iron Mask*, for example, Minister Fouquet suffers from Tertian fever. Here, however, Ginzburg appears to refer to one of those mysterious ailments of childhood – a 'third-day fever' – that is, an intermittent fever of unknown origin, especially one that returns every few days.

3 'Caciocavallo' is a mild, hand-shaped or 'stretched' cow's-milk cheese that comes in gourd or pear shapes and is tied and hung on string. Some say caciocavallo was originally made from mare's milk, giving rise to its name.

4 A ravioli-type stuffed pasta, crescent-shaped, but more doughy and often prepared with a ham, cheese, and spice filling.

5 The reference is to a drinking song popular among soldiers in the First World War and still heard as a folk song in the Italian Alpine region. There are numerous verses and several versions, some more richly peppered than others with local dialect. All versions, however, seem to share the refrain – *'vinassa vinassa, e fiaschi de vin'* (which Marta quotes slightly inaccurately in the original). Unfortunately, the song is a bit difficult to make sense of without an explanation. *'Fiaschi de vin'* is easy enough – bottles of wine, specifically those in straw holders. But *vinassa*, related to the French *vinasse*, is the residue left in the barrel after wine is fermented; it can also refer to the lees in a bottle or the dregs in a glass. In a figurative sense, it simply means cheap wine. A verse common to a number of versions has the singer say: 'If my colour is pale, if I'm white as a rag, I don't want the doctor. No, I don't want the doctor. [I want] *vinassa vinassa, e fiaschi de vin.*' The translation here is an attempt to render the sense of the song but obviously does not reflect its literal meaning.

The Wig

[A room in a roadside hotel north of Rome.]

A woman is seated on the bed. She picks up the telephone receiver.

Hello? Signorina, I would like to make a call to Milan – 80 18 96. I had also asked for a soft-boiled egg. They brought me my tea, but not the egg. The tea was like water. Yes, signorina. It doesn't matter. No, my husband doesn't drink tea; he'll have a caffe latte later on. Now, if you would connect me with Milan. Hmm? The number I just said. Oh God, now I can't find it. 80 18 96. No, I don't want to dial direct. I told you earlier I didn't want to dial direct.

She stands in front of a mirror and begins to put on makeup. From the next room comes the sound of whistling.

Massimo? I am now informing you that I have asked to be connected with Milan. Stop whistling. My skin is so dry and yellow – it's disgusting. It's no wonder, though, given the night I had. The mattress couldn't have had more lumps in it. And I was cold. The blankets in this hotel are like cobwebs. And I am also informing you that my nose hurts. It's swollen. And it won't stop bleeding. Massimo, the cotton is still coming out all covered with blood. Seeing my own blood makes me feel sick. Other people's, no. Mine, yes. If you have the nerve to slap me again, I'll take off and that'll be the last you see of me. My jaw hurts – and my nose. My God, come out of the damn bathroom. Even though, when you do come out, you're going to seem dirtier than you did before you went in. It's strange. Me, even if I don't bathe, I seem clean. This wig has come to the end of its days. It's turned into a dish rag, thanks to the little trip you sent it on. There's still mud all over it.

Too bad. It was a gift from you. The only gift you ever gave me in six years of marriage. That's because you're stingy. You're stingy when it comes to me. With yourself you're quite generous. You bought yourself that jacket. Considering we're broke, you could have done without that. It doesn't really suit you anyway. You're too short to wear raspberry velvet. This damn hotel! I ordered a soft-boiled egg and they won't bring it to me.

The phone rings.

There. That's my mother.

Hello, mom? Hi, mom. I've been asking them to place the call for an hour. I don't dial direct because Massimo doesn't want me to. He's a miser. He's not a miser when it comes to his clothing. I was just saying that he'd bought himself a velvet jacket, raspberry-coloured. A horrible thing. Little him – you can't imagine what he looks like. It's been a while since you've seen him – he's let his hair grow, you've hardly ever seen him with long hair. He's got this long, gold-coloured mustache coming down on both sides and this golden mane down to his shoulders. Yes, it's been a while since I've called, but I wrote to you. I didn't write you that he'd let his hair grow? Odd.

You know where I'm calling from? From Montesauro. A town on the crest of a hill. It's snowing. We're in a hotel called Collodoro. No, it's not a nice hotel. On the contrary. I asked for an egg and it has yet to arrive. I had to put a heavy sweater on over my night shirt because I was freezing. What are we doing here? Well, I certainly don't know what we're doing here. No kids. The girls are in Rome. They're with the housekeeper. No, they were happy with the housekeeper. She's a cheerful woman. Always singing. Yes, she's trustworthy. She's wonderful. She doesn't know how to do anything, but she's great. I'm lucky? Lucky in what? In housekeepers? Yes, I'm lucky in housekeepers, but in everything else I've got miserable luck.

Yes, exactly. Good thing we didn't drag the girls along. Because it's snowing. And then we were leaving to go to Todi and the Dauphine stalled on the freeway. It made an ugly noise and then it stalled. It was snowing. We were in bad shape. We pulled out our bags and the paintings and we started walking. We walked a half-hour. Then we finally found a rest stop. Our feet were soaked. No boots. Why not? Because I didn't bring them. When we were leaving Rome, the weather was beautiful. I had my reindeer jacket and my black maxi-skirt. No, no leggings. We called a mechanic, and they towed the Dauphine. Apparently the battery will have to be changed. The mechanic recommended this hotel. Last night all we had for supper were a couple of old meatballs. My feet were like blocks of ice. Massimo got a hair crosswise and stormed off with his bed into the bathroom. He says he sleeps better when he's alone.

Mom, I had a specific reason for calling you. We need some money. We left Rome with very little. Because of course we couldn't have known that the battery would quit. Could you wire me a money order for 200,000 lire? Oh, yeah. I'm sorry. Maybe I'll be able to pay you back. Eighty thousand for the battery, the rest will come in handy here. More than handy – essential. It was Saturday when we left and we couldn't go to the bank. Anyway … what do we have in the bank? Nothing. Practically nothing. We were thinking we'd arrive in Todi the same evening, and we'd pull something together one way or another. We've got friends in Todi. You'll have to wire the money. Send it express – don't send it the regular way. We're here and Massimo's nerves are a wreck. He has some hair crosswise. And you know he's got a lot of them. It's a mane. Earlier he hauled off and slapped me and he made my nose bleed. My nose is still stuffed with cotton, and my night shirt is covered with blood. No, Mom, it's true. I'm not making anything up. Me? What did I do to him? Nothing. All I said was that I don't find his paintings all that beautiful. They're all the same. He's always painting these fields full of flowers, with one huge eye hanging overhead. I'll tell you the truth, I'm fed up with that eye. I even dream about it at night. It's a huge, wide-open eye, with long eyelashes that curl up. It's huge, it's yellow. It looks like a fried egg.

Mom. Please pay attention. Write it down. Put your glasses on, otherwise you'll write it down wrong and you won't understand what you've written. Albergo Collodoro. Not Pollodoro. Collodoro. Montesauro. Province of Todi. What do you mean it's not a province? It's a province.[1] Keep in mind that it's snowing here. I already said that, yes. Until your money order comes we can't go anywhere. Not much, we haven't got much at all. What we've got isn't even enough to pay for the hotel. We don't have any common sense? Could be. We'll stay with a friend of ours in Todi, a girl named Rosaria, who's a social worker. Rosaria is supposed to introduce us to some old lawyer who buys paintings. We're going to take him six paintings. All with the usual eye. No, we can't call Rosaria from here and ask her for a loan. Massimo says it would be bad manners. Besides, Rosaria is completely penniless. Massimo brought a book with him but I don't have anything to read. Just an old issue of *Annabella* that I found here. No transistor radio. I didn't bring it. Right now he's immersed in the bathtub with his book. It's a book entitled *The Psychology of the Unconscious*. Freud, I think. He's gotten into the habit of reading while he takes a bath. He stays in the bathtub for hours, then he comes out dirtier and more dishevelled than he was when he went in. Oh here, they've brought me my egg. No, don't hang up, wait. I'll talk while I eat. I asked for some bread sticks. They've brought me a roll that's like a rock. What? Is the egg fresh? Yes, it seems fresh. Mom, I'm in the middle of a disaster and you're worried about whether the egg is fresh.

Mom. I don't think Massimo and I can stay together. I don't know. I can't stand him anymore. He can't stand me either. We're constantly fighting. It's not just that we're going through a difficult time, Mom, it's worse than that. We had an enormous fight just before we left. We were at the dining room table. I told him I didn't feel like coming with him to Todi. He answered me in English that if I didn't leave with him he'd kick me right out the door. He was speaking English because the girls were there. I told him in English that he couldn't kick me out because the house is mine – we bought it with the money dad left me. He put it in the girls' name, but I have the right to use it. Massimo was eating a persimmon, and he took that persimmon and he squashed it on the floor. So I grabbed a spoon and started to clean. The girls weren't frightened; actually, they were amused. While I was bent over cleaning, he tore the wig off my head and flung it out the window. My wig went flying out onto the roof of the garage and landed in a puddle of rain water. So I had to send the maid downstairs to where this pharmacist lives, and the maid and the pharmacist fished my wig out with a broom, soaking wet and covered with mud. So then I told the maid to get the children dressed and take them to the Villa Borghese. When I was alone with Massimo this immense rage came over me all of a sudden, and I started kicking the paintings he had leaning up against the wall in the entry way. He let out a howl like some wild animal, so I locked myself up in the bedroom and started brushing out my wig. After a little while he begged me to open the door. He was almost crying. He asked me to forgive him and he pleaded with me to come to Todi with him because he says I encourage him. I don't know how he can say that I encourage him when I tell him the same thing over and over: that I don't like his paintings all that much and that I think that eye of his is a joke. Anyway, I said I'd come with him, although it would have been better if I'd stayed at home because as soon as we were in the car we started arguing again.

Mom, I know. He isn't a bad guy. He has a good heart. He's pretty quick with his fists, but he has a good heart. I know. But I can't stand him anymore. Yes, he's successful. Pretty much. Yes, a *succès d'estime*. Certainly. Of course, he's healthy as can be. I'm as healthy as can be. The girls, too. Mom, what has our health got to do with anything? Yes, I know. We have two darling girls. One overlooks things for the sake of the children. I know. But I can't stand him anymore. I know. I've had two children with him but now I can't stand him anymore.

Mom, I have to tell you the truth. I have someone. What? No, Massimo knows very well. I've let him know in all kinds of ways. No, no. Don't turn this into some big drama or I'll never tell you anything again. I have someone. His name is Francesco. Of course not a lover; lover isn't exactly the right word. He's barely touched me. Hardly ever. He doesn't have time. He's always super busy. He's the publisher of a weekly magazine. He's a political man. Yes, famous. Rich? Of course not rich. He's completely penniless. He has to take care of all those children. His. He has six children. No, he's not a nice-looking young man. He's not so nice looking and he's not young. He's forty-nine years old. Yes, mom. He's not so nice looking because he's a little bald and he has an enormous nose besides. Yes, enormous. What do I see in him? What do I see in him. Well, I don't know.

But I'm not a home wrecker. His wife doesn't give a damn. They're more or less separated. He stays on the floor upstairs. He has an enormous apartment. On Via del Gesù. The wife and the kids live on the floor below. But the kids go upstairs all the time. I couldn't even describe to you the chaos in that apartment. Doorbells, typewriters, people calling on the telephone, children. You're always stumbling over one child or another. And the wife is always going out to do the shopping because they keep separate kitchens. The wife? Yes, she's very nice to me. She's a beautiful woman. A little chubby. They're maniacs in the kitchen, both of them, him and her. He's always got so much to do but every so often he goes into the kitchen to keep an eye on his pasta sauce. They're very Catholic. Leftists, but Catholic. Of course I would end up with a couple of Catholics.

The real mess is that now I'm afraid I'm pregnant. No, not by Massimo. By Francesco. No, he's hardly ever touched me, but the one time he did almost touch me I wound up pregnant. It was a Sunday. We bolted the door. No, not in our house, in his house. On Via del Gesù.

The children called and called and we didn't open the door. It was terrible. I'm speaking to you softly because Massimo doesn't know this. No, he doesn't know that I'm pregnant. No, no I haven't told him. I haven't even told Francesco. When I go back to Rome, I'll tell him. I don't want to have an abortion. I can't even think about it. I want this baby. Yes, mom, it will have an enormous nose. It doesn't matter to me what kind of nose it has. I want to live with Francesco. No, I haven't lost my mind. I'm in love. The problem is that he doesn't want to. He doesn't have time. He doesn't have any room for me. No, the apartment is enormous. If I go to stay with him there's room for me and the girls – there's a ton of rooms. He doesn't have room for me in his life. He's got too many things in his life that are tying him down. His life is full. So I don't know how I'll manage. I'm in bad shape. I'll get over it. You say I'll get over it, but I want to live with him no matter how we do it. I've made up my mind. Unfortunately, he doesn't want to. But I'll convince him. Yes, he's in love with me, too, very much, but he's confused. To him it doesn't seem like a sure thing. Besides, he says that together he and I would end up running a nursery school. Understand? You want to do what? Come down and talk to who? To Massimo? You're not going to get anything out of talking to Massimo. No. Don't you move. You stay there instead and send me that money order. But wire it. Bye, mom. I'll let you go now. You're scared? Come on. Don't be scared. Everything will work out, you'll see. How, I don't know. No, I'm not crazy. I'd better hang up because we've already spent a pile of money on this long-distance call. Remember about the money order. Albergo Collodoro. Collodoro. Yes, thanks, mom.

She hangs up the receiver, goes back to the mirror, and starts putting on makeup again.

Massimo! I am informing you that my mother will send the money tomorrow. Poor mom. She's a little alarmed. Shocked, really. Shocked and alarmed. I told her the whole story. I've even told her something that you don't know yet. That I'm pregnant. I made love with Francesco only a couple of times, but I ended up pregnant. Did you hear me? Yes, you must have heard me because you've stopped whistling. It's still snowing. What we're going to do today, God only knows. Shut up in this room. If I at least had a puzzle magazine. Massimo! The bathroom's flooding. The water's coming all the way in here. Your paintings have gotten a little wet. I'm going to dry them especially carefully with some cotton. You'll see. I'll take good care of your paintings even if I don't like them. You, on the other hand, are careless with my things. You destroy them. My poor wig, reduced to its current pitiful state thanks to you. You bought that for me. Remember? With the money from one of your paintings. It was one of the first that you sold. It was a simple meadow scene. But there was already an eye – a little, tiny eye that had settled on a flower, like a bug. That was four years ago. We were happy. Sometimes I feel such nostalgia for those days. When I loved you. You didn't have that overgrown mustache. You didn't have that dishevelled mane of hair that you have now. You wore your hair in a crew cut. Your head looked like a toothbrush. You know, I don't really believe that man is going to buy a single one of your paintings. It's some fantasy of Rosaria's. It was totally pointless to come here. I'm so cold. Come out of that bathroom or I am going to shoot you. I'm pregnant – do you understand? Pregnant by Francesco. And I don't want an abortion. I'm going to live with Francesco, and I'm taking the girls with me. It's not like the girls mean anything to you anyway. You can stay there, on Via dei Cerchi. I'll leave you the house. I can't give it to you because it belongs to the girls. You'll pay me rent. Seventy thousand lire a month. No, eighty. I'll stay on Via del Gesù. God, my nose is bleeding again. Come out of that bathroom and help me. Bring me a towel. My sweater's all stained. I don't have another sweater, just this one. (*She knocks loudly on the bathroom door. She shoves against the door, which opens.*) He's not here. God, he's not here. Where's he gone? His clothes aren't here. He must have gone out through the door on the terrace. He can't really be gone. He can't really have deserted me here in this ridiculous town.

She picks up the phone.

Hello, Signorina. Have you seen my husband by any chance? Oh really? He's in the dining room? What's he doing? Drinking a caffe latte. Tell him to come back up right away. Tell him I'm sick. I feel sick. Tell him to stop drinking coffee and come back up because I'm going nuts up here. I'm sick and I'm cold and I'm fed up and I'm desperate besides. If he doesn't come up right away, I'm going to take a pair of scissors and shred every last one of these idiotic paintings!

January 1971

Note

1 Todi, in fact, is not a province; it is a small city in the province of Perugia in Umbria.

The Armchair

A PLAY IN TWO ACTS

Cast:
Ada
Matteo
Ginevra

ACT ONE

[*An apartment in Rome, late afternoon.*]

*A room. Ada is seated at a table, cleaning artichokes. Matteo enters with a
briefcase. They kiss.*

ADA: Hi. I didn't expect you so soon. I didn't think you'd be getting
here until this evening.

MATTEO: I came as soon as it was over. I was fed up with it. It was raining. The hotel was damp. Not a cheerful place, Montecatini, in the
fall.

ADA: What was it you were doing in Montecatini? I don't remember.

MATTEO: You never remember anything. That damned conference was
there.

ADA: A conference on what?

MATTEO: The destruction of the environment. What are you doing with
all those artichokes?

ADA: I wanted to make a quiche. The custodian's wife gave me the
recipe.

MATTEO: I'm not hungry.

ADA: It's not for now. It's for supper. I've eaten already. I had some bread and butter. Do you want something?

MATTEO: No. I just told you I'm not hungry. I should write my article on the conference, but maybe not today. Tomorrow. We could invite someone to supper, since there's going to be a quiche. We could call Lea and Vittorio. I'll go call them a little later.

ADA: They're gone. They left yesterday morning. I took them to the airport. I cried. Lea cried, too. They'll be gone a year. Their friend is already here, in their apartment. She got here yesterday evening. She's staying until they get back.

MATTEO: They're gone already! Oh, no. I didn't give them a real goodbye, just a quick wave from the kitchen balcony. I was in a rush because I was so late. I didn't realize they were leaving before I got back. I thought I'd still have time to say goodbye. Did you say that friend of theirs is already here in the apartment?

ADA: Yes. A mother and daughter. I saw them yesterday evening, just for a second, on the kitchen balcony. The daughter's young, maybe twelve or thirteen. Her name is Maria Claudia. I heard her mother calling her.

MATTEO: Pretty?

ADA: No. Too much hair. She looks like a sheepdog. I didn't get a good look at the mother. She stuck her face out for a minute and then went right back inside. Lea told me she owns a ceramic shop.

MATTEO: Can a person make a living from a ceramic shop? Who buys ceramics?

ADA: She doesn't only sell ceramics. She also sells light fixtures, serving trays, hand-embroidered napkins. She sells a little bit of everything. It's sort of a department store. In a little alley behind Piazza Farnese.

MATTEO: I see. How long are Lea and Vittorio going to stay in America?

ADA: A year. Until next November.

MATTEO: So long? I'm sorry. I'll miss them. I was always glad to spend time with them. It was wonderful having them here just next door, able to call if we needed anything. There aren't really that many people here in Rome you can feel comfortable with. Whenever I go out on the landing, it's going to make me sad. What's this armchair?

ADA: It's an armchair.

MATTEO: How did it get dumped here?

ADA: It was my brother's.

MATTEO: Oh, right. I remember. It was your brother's, in the dining room. And what's it doing here?

ADA: They didn't know where to put it in their new house. The living room is small. They've already got a couch and two other armchairs.

MATTEO: So do we. We've already got a couch and two armchairs. What are we supposed to do with a third armchair, if you don't mind telling me?

ADA: We don't have any kids. They do, so they need more space. Anyway, I like it. I think it's nice. And it's really in good shape.

MATTEO: With coffee stains.

ADA: I'll get the stains out. I haven't had time to do it yet.

MATTEO: How are you going to get the stains out?

ADA: With a little bit of milk, I'm thinking.

MATTEO: Coffee comes out with milk?

ADA: I think so.

MATTEO: You think so? You think so? You're never certain of anything!

ADA: And you?

MATTEO: What about me?

ADA: Is there something you're certain of?

MATTEO: I'm certain I won't be able to stomach having this armchair here. It's horrendous. The more I look at it, the more horrendous it seems.

ADA: I told you, they didn't know where to put it. Plus they needed some money. The move cost them a lot. And my brother has lost his job.

MATTEO: Please don't tell me they made you pay for it.

ADA: I paid them, yes, sure. It's a nice armchair.

MATTEO: How much?

ADA: Not much.

MATTEO: Not much. How much?

ADA: Six hundred fifty thousand.

MATTEO: What? You gave him 650,000 lire for this disgusting armchair?

ADA: That's what they paid for it. More or less. That's what they told me. Some years ago. It's certainly worth more now. They got it in a shop on Via dei Coronari.

MATTEO: Those stripes! Those horrible stripes! Those arms all rolled up on the ends like a snail shell. I hate stripes. Grey and violet stripes. I hate them. They'll end up bringing me bad luck.

The bell rings. Ada opens the door, and Ginevra enters.

GINEVRA: Please excuse the bother. My name is Ginevra Teodori. I live next door. I'm a friend of Lea and Vittorio's. They lent me their apartment. We arrived yesterday evening, my daughter and I. Lea and Vittorio told me I could call on you if I needed something.

ADA: Of course. Do you need something?

GINEVRA: My phone has no dial tone. It was working this morning, and now all of a sudden it's out of order. Could I call telephone repair from your phone?

MATTEO: It's Saturday. No one answers the phone at the telephone repair on Saturday, you know.

ADA: That's not necessarily true. Once in a while they answer even on Saturday.

MATTEO: Go right ahead and try.

GINEVRA: (*Dials a number.*) No one's answering.

ADA: If you need to make a telephone call, you can call from here.

MATTEO: Of course. Have a seat. Have a seat on this armchair. It's new. It's actually old, as you can see, but it's new to this room.

GINEVRA: Thank you. I'm exhausted. I unpacked the bags and straightened up a little, and now I've got a terrible pain in my back. It's lumbago.

MATTEO: If you need an armchair over there, we can give you this one. Because we've already got two.

GINEVRA: Thank you, no. There are armchairs over there. What we don't have is an ironing board. Apparently they ironed on the kitchen table. But I'm not used to ironing on the table. I could really use an ironing board. I'll buy one. Other than that, I don't need anything. The apartment is fairly comfortable. I've been more or less homeless since last summer. We used to have an apartment in Parioli,[1] and they evicted us. We went to stay with my sister, my daughter and me. My sister doesn't have much room and we were sleeping in a tiny room with bunk beds. So yesterday evening, after I set the bags down and got into my house slippers, I took a breather. It hardly seemed possible that we finally had a house. Even my daughter was happy, I think, but I don't know, because you can never tell when my daughter is happy. She's thirteen. It's an ugly age. We have a difficult relationship. She doesn't study. This morning she told me there was no school and that she was going with some friends to Tivoli. There was no school because the boiler for the radiator was broken, she told me. She left without combing her hair. She never combs her hair. She wears eye shadow. She's so young, but she wears eye shadow. She says all the other girls are doing it. I told her to put her jacket on, but I saw that she didn't take it. She had her coral-coloured slacks and a synthetic wool sweater. Black. She's crazy for black.

MATTEO: Please go ahead and use the phone, if you need to.

GINEVRA: Thank you but not now. Right now I don't need to. It's too early. I will need to make a call to Umbertino, but later on. He's sleeping now.

MATTEO: Who's Umbertino?

GINEVRA: He's my daughter's father. My ex-husband. He's the conductor of an orchestra and he's always out late in the evening. He wants me to call him every three or four days to give him an update on his daughter. But at five in the afternoon. Not earlier and not later. Earlier, he's sleeping. Later, he goes out. It's always a problem for me, calling Umbertino. If I call him, he's annoyed. If I don't call him, he gets offended. Sometimes he's very sweet to me, sometimes he's so unpleasant. I will come back and bother you at five, if you don't mind.

MATTEO: I'm not sure we'll be home at five.

GINEVRA: If you're not home it doesn't matter. I'll go down and call from the bar. I didn't go down now because the stairs are so tiring. I've got a lot of pain in my back, as I was saying earlier.

MATTEO: The stairs? But there's an elevator.

GINEVRA: I won't take the elevator. It's so little. It makes me anxious. I took it yesterday evening because I had the bags, but I was thinking I wouldn't take it again.

MATTEO: How long will you be staying in the apartment? When are Lea and Vittorio coming back, exactly?

GINEVRA: They'll be back in a year, in November. I'll spend the summer looking for another apartment. But I don't want to think about that now.

MATTEO: A year is a long time. I'll miss them, Lea and Vittorio. I'm already feeling their absence.

ADA: They won't be back until next November. I've already told you that fifty times. Now you miss them, but when they were here, you argued with them.

MATTEO: I argued with them, but we got along. We used to talk about all kinds of things. I can't wait until they're back next door again.

ADA: You're not very polite to talk like that. When they come back, Signora Teodori will have to go.

GINEVRA: How do you know my last name?

ADA: You said it when you came in.

GINEVRA: And it stayed in your mind?

MATTEO: Everything stays in Ada's mind. It's only whatever I tell her
that she forgets immediately. But everything else she holds onto
with the greatest of care. She collects it and she saves it. Every little
crumb of information she comes across.

ADA: You're being impolite again. Someone's last name is not exactly a
crumb.

GINEVRA: I'll put my business card on the door. I'll pin it up with some
thumbtacks. Though I don't have any more thumbtacks. I ran out.

ADA: Do you want some thumbtacks? I must have some.

GINEVRA: It doesn't matter. There's no rush. I'll let you go. Meanwhile,
I'll just hope my telephone starts working again. Sometimes they
just fix themselves.

ADA: I'm not going out, though. Come right back and use the phone,
if you like. Right now, I'm going to make a quiche. Then maybe I'll
get a little work done.

GINEVRA: I'm going to rest today. I'm not going to open the store.

MATTEO: Are there ceramics in your store? Lamps, light fixtures, tablecloths?

GINEVRA: Yes. How did you know?

MATTEO: Ada told me.

GINEVRA: Yes, I've got a little of everything. Things made by local
craftspeople.

MATTEO: Ada doesn't actually do anything. She says she works, but it's
not a real job. She writes. She spends her afternoons writing. She
writes novels, stories, poems. Unfortunately, she can't find anyone
to publish them.

ADA: It's not important to me.

MATTEO: It's not important to you? So then why do you spend so much
time worrying about editors? I don't know how many times I've
seen those packages come back.

GINEVRA: I used to enjoy writing, too, when I was younger. But I didn't
keep up with it. It was Umbertino's fault. I used to ask him to read
the things I wrote, and he would say they were worthless. So I got
discouraged. Although even now, in the evenings, sometimes I try
to write something, some of the thoughts that are passing through
my mind. But then I immediately see Umberto standing there in
front of me. We haven't lived together for a long time, but I still see

him standing in front of me, with his big pale, severe, face, his bald head with a few little silver curls. And suddenly the urge to write goes right out of me.

MATTEO: I sometimes tell Ada that what she writes isn't worth much, too. But she doesn't lose heart. She's stubborn, Ada is. She's very stubborn.

GINEVRA: But I'm sure such harsh judgments aren't good for her. They don't help her.

MATTEO: So what should I do? Should I lie and say she's writing really gorgeous novels?

GINEVRA: I have the idea that sometimes it's healthy to lie. But I don't know. I'm going to let the two of you go. Thanks so much. (*Exits.*)

MATTEO: Six hundred fifty thousand lire! You are truly nuts!

ADA: My god, are you still thinking about the armchair?

MATTEO: You're nuts, I'm telling you! Why should we be giving money away to your brother? I'm already supporting your mother and your Aunt Giuseppina.

ADA: You're not supporting either my mother or Aunt Giuseppina. They loaned you money and you're paying them back month by month.

MATTEO: They gave me that loan a million years ago.

ADA: Yes. They gave you good money and you're paying them back in dribs and drabs with inflated lire.

MATTEO: Anyway, I don't want this armchair here. Give it back to them. Those stripes! Those hateful stripes! How can you keep an armchair in the house with grey and violet stripes? Those arms rolled up on the ends like a snail shell. Can you really not see how horrible it is? I don't know what you've been looking at. Plus I'm sure it's going to bring bad luck. It brought your brother bad luck. So much bad luck, in fact, that he lost his job.

ADA: Yes, he lost his job. The business went bankrupt. They let everyone go. But he'll certainly find something else.

MATTEO: He won't find anything. He's not looking. I ran into him on the street a few days ago. He was going to the movies. He said he was going to the movies because there was too much chaos in his house. His wife was packing up books. Now he's gotten it in his head that they ought to move. He was calmly going to the movies. Your brother is irresponsible.

ADA: He didn't know he was going to lose his job when they bought the house.

MATTEO: Meanwhile, they've bought themselves a house. And what about us, what are we doing? We're paying rent.

ADA: How did she seem to you?

MATTEO: Who? Our new neighbour? Well enough. She seemed fairly charming.

ADA: I like her a lot.

MATTEO: You like her because she said that harsh judgments are hurtful. She said it's better to lie. I don't know how to lie. From now on, I'm not going to read a thing you write. I don't want to lie and I don't want to hurt you. You have it in your mind that you're Sylvia Plath. You're not Sylvia Plath. Or at least I don't think you are. Sylvia Plath wouldn't have brought this horrendous armchair into the house.

A bell rings. Ginevra enters.

GINEVRA: Excuse me, oh Lord, excuse me. I've locked myself out. I went out onto the landing with a sack of garbage and there was a gust of wind and the door closed. I went down to the custodian, because I thought she would have the key, but no one was home.

ADA: The custodian is usually not home in the afternoons. She goes to see an aunt of hers who lives in Piazza Tuscolo.

GINEVRA: How am I going to get back in the house? I'll have to wait until Maria Claudia comes back from Tivoli. Let's hope Maria Claudia took her keys with her.

MATTEO: Why? Is there some chance she didn't?

GINEVRA: My God. It's so nerve-wracking to be locked out of the house.

MATTEO: Does it happen often?

ADA: Don't get upset. If worst come to worst, my husband will go find a locksmith who can open the door.

MATTEO: It's Saturday. Are you forgetting that it's Saturday? You won't find any locksmiths open on Saturday.

GINEVRA: You've been so kind to me. Let me stay here until Maria Claudia comes back home, or the custodian. If I have to wait out on the stairs I'll get cold and I'll feel anxious.

MATTEO: You already feel anxious. Didn't you say you were already anxious?

ADA: How could you think we'd make you wait on the stairs? Come sit with us. Would you like a cup of tea?

GINEVRA: No, thank you.

MATTEO: Come sit here. On the infamous armchair. That way, I won't
see those hateful stripes as much. Put your hands over the armrests
so I can't see the snail shells.

GINEVRA: Why? What have you got against the armchair?

MATTEO: Let's not talk about it. Do you know how much it cost? Six
hundred fifty thousand lire.

GINEVRA: That's not much. It's a beautiful armchair. It has personality.

MATTEO: A nasty personality.

GINEVRA: Go ahead with whatever you need to do. I'm just going to sit
here and be quiet. I won't be any bother.

MATTEO: You should go put a note on the door, to let Maria Grazia
know to come look for you here when she comes back from Tivoli.

GINEVRA: That's right. I hadn't even thought about it.

MATTEO: You should do it right away. It'll be the first thing she'll look
for. Go write it. In fact, I'll write it myself. (*Writes something on a
sheet of paper, leaves, and then returns.*)

ADA: What did you write?

MATTEO: I wrote: 'Ginevra is with the Almerighis. Ring the Almerighis'
bell next door.'

GINEVRA: How did you know that my name is Ginevra?

MATTEO: You said it when you came in.

ADA: But you're someone who keeps everything in his mind, too. You
collect information and you save it. But you were wrong about
her daughter's name. You said Maria Grazia. Her name is actually
Maria Claudia.

GINEVRA: Are you still going to make a quiche, Signora Almerighi?

ADA: Maybe. I don't know.

MATTEO: Why maybe? Didn't you say you were going to make a quiche
for supper?

ADA: Yes, but later I started thinking that I didn't really feel like it. I
only cook when I'm in a good mood. You've put me in a bad mood,
with all this business about the armchair.

MATTEO: So what are you going to do with all those artichokes?

ADA: Nothing. I'll put some oil-and-vinegar dressing on them.

GINEVRA: Even like that, with oil and vinegar, artichokes are delicious.

ADA: Stay and have supper with us. We've got plenty of artichokes. I
even have some eggs. Maria Claudia can eat with us, too.

GINEVRA: Really? Thank you. Do you think we might start using '*tu*'
with one another?

MATTEO: Absolutely, let's use '*tu*' with each other. We've only known each other a half-hour or an hour, I'm not sure which. But okay, let's use '*tu*' with one another.

GINEVRA: The kindness you two have shown me really is a comfort. Today has been a bad day for me. It's been a bad period.

MATTEO: But you said you took a breather yesterday evening.

GINEVRA: Yes, because we finally had a house. But everything else is a disaster.

MATTEO: The store? Maria Claudia? Umbertino?

GINEVRA: The store. Maria Claudia. All of it.

MATTEO: Aren't customers coming to the store?

GINEVRA: A few people come in. If you have friends here, bring them by the store. It's in Via dei Canestrari. On the corner.

MATTEO: We don't have all that many friends. We've got very few. We have Lea and Vittorio, but now they're in America.

ADA: That's not true. We have friends.

MATTEO: Very few. I have a rather nasty personality.

GINEVRA: Like the armchair.

MATTEO: The armchair is horrendous. Let's forget about it. No, I have a nasty personality, I never get along with anyone. Ada, on the other hand, has a sweet personality, too sweet. She gets along with everyone. She's a sheep. She doesn't choose people. She's pleasant to anyone she happens to meet. If I let her, she'd be perfectly capable of filling the house with swarms of imbeciles. But I don't let her. I wish she were more independent, that she had some friends of her own. Even imbeciles I couldn't stand. But she could see them away from the house. No chance of that. If I argue with someone, she complains that I'm too hard to get along with, but then she immediately stops seeing that person, too.

GINEVRA: I understand. Thinking back on when I lived with Umbertino, that's how things were then. He was friendly and hospitable, and I was withdrawn and sulky. But Umbertino was only pretending to be warm. In reality, he was critical of everyone when we were alone again, and I couldn't stand that.

MATTEO: It's 5:45. Shouldn't you call Umbertino?

GINEVRA: That's right. I forgot. It's too late now. By now, he's put on his white scarf and headed out to rehearsal.

Ada leaves the room for a moment, then returns.

ADA: Maria Claudia is back. I saw her on the balcony. I called to her and she said she had her keys. She never saw any card. It must have blown away.

GINEVRA: I'll go home, then. I'll be back at supper time with Maria Claudia. I have to warn you that Maria Claudia never says a word. She doesn't have a very warm personality. She's especially gloomy whenever she's with me. When she's with her girlfriends, she turns into a cheerful, talkative girl. But me, you understand, I put her in a bad mood. She wants to live with her father. She dotes on her father.

MATTEO: And Umbertino?

GINEVRA: Umbertino loves his freedom. He can't accept the responsibility of a daughter. He can't accept those kinds of bonds. I lived with Umbertino for six years. I think he thought it was six years too many. He couldn't stand me. He couldn't stand Maria Claudia. But I have to call him all the time to tell him how she's doing.

MATTEO: Maybe the quiche would work on Maria Claudia.

GINEVRA: No. Forget about it. Maria Claudia detests complicated dishes. She would live on hamburgers. Damn hamburgers! I do nothing but cook her hamburgers, day in and day out. I hate them.

ADA: I'm sorry. We don't have any hamburger in the house.

GINEVRA: Don't be silly! Eggs and artichokes will be wonderful!

ACT TWO

[*Six years later.*]

The identical room. Matteo enters with a briefcase. He takes off his raincoat and sits. The doorbell rings. Matteo opens the door. Ginevra enters. They kiss.

GINEVRA: Hi, Matteo.

MATTEO: Hello. What in the world are you doing in this neighbourhood?

GINEVRA: I went to see Leo and Vittorio and to see my house again – what was my house for a year. I thought I'd stop by to say hello. We haven't seen each other for so long. How are you?

MATTEO: I'm fine. I've just come back from Perugia. There was a round-table.

GINEVRA: A roundtable on what?

MATTEO: On soft technology.[2]

GINEVRA: What's soft technology?

MATTEO: It would take too long to explain.

GINEVRA: Nothing soft about you, though. You're tough as an old boot. But you're working on soft technology.

MATTEO: It's not that I'm working on it. I have to write an article about it. But not today. Today I'm resting.

GINEVRA: Everything's exactly the same here. The table, the oilcloth, the green drapes, and the infamous armchair. Didn't you want to give that away, the infamous armchair?

MATTEO: Yes, of course. Because it brings bad luck. From the day it entered this house, all kinds of things have happened. Ada's brother tried to commit suicide. Ada and I broke up. One of my aunts died. I had an automobile accident, you know, on the Anzio Road. I barely missed ending up in the next world. All kinds of things have happened.

GINEVRA: Your Aunt Giuseppina died?

MATTEO: Of course not, not Aunt Giuseppina. That one is still as lively and energetic as ever. I still have to send her money every month for an old loan she gave me years ago. A million years ago. If only Aunt Giuseppina had died. She's Ada's aunt. No, it was one of my aunts who died, my mother's sister. She was really very old. She was more than eighty. But I took it hard. She loved me very much. She left me a farm house, with a little bit of land, close to Bracciano. I may go there to live.

GINEVRA: You're going to live there? Near Bracciano? In the country?

MATTEO: I don't know. Maybe. It's an old farm house, really dilapidated. In its current condition, it's pretty much a cave. I'd have to spend some money on it. But once everything was put back into shape, it could be beautiful. I'm going there to live. I'm tired of the city.

GINEVRA: Maybe that's a good idea.

MATTEO: You can get to Rome in half an hour in the car.

GINEVRA: Sure.

MATTEO: Are Lea and Vittorio well? I don't see them anymore. We've stopped being friends. We barely say hello when we run into each other on the landing. We fought a long time ago. A little bit after they got back from America. I don't remember why anymore.

GINEVRA: They're fine.

MATTEO: You don't have that store anymore? The one on Via dei Canestrari?

GINEVRA: No, I haven't had the store for a while now. I make sweaters at home and sell them. I have a pretty big house on Via delle Convertite. I make a good living with the sweaters. It suits me a lot better than the store, because my expenses are low. I make some very beautiful sweaters. Ada came over and bought two of them. One for herself and one for her boyfriend.

MATTEO: How was Ada? I haven't seen her for quite a while.

GINEVRA: She was fine.

MATTEO: I remember that day when you happened by here for the first time. Your telephone was out of order. There wasn't any dial tone.

GINEVRA: Yes, I remember.

MATTEO: That was also the day when I found that armchair here. The infamous armchair. I knew it would bring me bad luck.

GINEVRA: But why do you think it's brought you bad luck? All the things you were telling me about aren't really bad luck. Ada's brother tried to commit suicide, but he didn't die. They saved him. One of your aunts died – who was more than eighty years old – but you inherited a farm house from her. You and Ada broke up, but maybe it was better that way. The two of you were unhappy together. She has a man now and she's happy.

MATTEO: He's hardly a man, he's a boy. He's fifteen years younger than she is. She met him through a publisher – one of those publishers that she was going around to with her terrible novels. She had a lot of terrible novels, and she used to go on pilgrimages from one publisher to another – never any success. He – the boy – was an editorial assistant or I don't know what in some small publishing house that wasn't making a cent. She never succeeded in getting them to publish anything of hers. She tried, but she didn't succeed. But he fell in love with her.

GINEVRA: Right. She told me the story.

MATTEO: In all honesty I do better alone because I have a nasty personality, as you know.

GINEVRA: So that means it isn't true that the armchair brought you bad luck. On the contrary, in a certain sense, it's even been lucky.

MATTEO: I remember when you came here. You had on velvet slacks and a red sweater. We became friends immediately. Almost immediately. You ate supper here. We had fried eggs.

GINEVRA: And an artichoke salad.

MATTEO: Yes. Maria Claudia was there, too. What's going on with Maria Claudia?

GINEVRA: She doesn't live with me anymore. She's living with a guy. She's pregnant.

MATTEO: Pregnant? But how old is she?

GINEVRA: Nineteen.

MATTEO: Nineteen? Has it been so long? She was a little girl then.

GINEVRA: It's been six years.

MATTEO: No, not really! Impossible! You're about to become a grand-mother, then. And Umbertino? Is Umbertino happy to be becoming a grandfather?

GINEVRA: Not happy or unhappy. He's also become a father again. He remarried and he has a little boy.

MATTEO: Why are people having all these children?

GINEVRA: I don't know.

MATTEO: And what does Maria Claudia look like now? Back then she had all that wild black hair. Ada used to say she looked like a sheep dog.

GINEVRA: She has short hair now and she's bleached it. She's blond now.

MATTEO: Blond and pregnant! I can't imagine it!

GINEVRA: Come visit me sometime so you can run into her.

MATTEO: I will. You know, one night I went to a concert where Umber-tino was conducting. I went just to see him, because you were al-ways mentioning his name. I saw a bald head with a cloud of silver curls around it. I don't know what the music was. Bach or Handel, I don't remember. I don't understand it, music I mean. After a little, I fell asleep.

GINEVRA: Umbertino gets more famous all the time. He tours Europe. I almost never see him.

MATTEO: You're still beautiful. I fell in love with you, that day when you happened by, first with the telephone with no dial tone, then when the door slammed shut and you didn't have your keys. Do you remember?

GINEVRA: Of course.

MATTEO: A little while after that, we made love. Do you remember how many times we made love?

GINEVRA: I don't know how many times.

MATTEO: We made love precisely three times. Once at Rocca di Papa. Once in Lucca. Once here, in this room because Ada had gone with Maria Claudia to the movies. I never told Ada anything about you, but she must have understood that something was going on.

Anyway, it wasn't hard to figure out. So that ruined things between me and her. It was all your fault.

GINEVRA: It wasn't my fault, and it wasn't the armchair's fault. When I came here for the first time, to this room, all those years ago, I understood immediately that something was in the process of falling apart.

MATTEO: We had a difficult relationship, it's true, long before you came.

GINEVRA: And before the armchair.

MATTEO: Yes, before the armchair.

GINEVRA: When something is falling apart, it doesn't take anything – a cat walking across the shingles, or a pigeon landing on the gutter. Isn't that the way it is? The shingles and the gutters and the walls and the rooms may collapse. But it's not the fault of the pigeon or the cat.

MATTEO: Yes, that's true.

GINEVRA: A cat or a pigeon. That's the role I would have played in your lives.

MATTEO: Could be.

GINEVRA: Could be! A cat or a pigeon! You're always so nice to people.

MATTEO: It wasn't me who said it. You did.

GINEVRA: Yes. But I was hoping you might have the courtesy to tell me I was wrong.

MATTEO: Why should I tell you you were wrong? Maybe that's just how it was.

GINEVRA: I don't remember anymore what happened after. You and Ada left on a trip. To Berlin or where was it?

MATTEO: To Prague. It was a disaster.

GINEVRA: I helped the two of you pack your bags. You left me the keys so I could come and water the plants. You had some plants out on the balcony. Are they still there?

MATTEO: No.

GINEVRA: It was summer. I was looking for a house. In the evenings I would come home exhausted and I didn't feel like coming over and taking care of your plants. I did come a few times, but the empty apartment made me feel so gloomy. So the plants shrivelled up. You two came back and the plants had dried up and Ada wanted to shrivel me up, too.

MATTEO: It had been a disaster in Prague.

GINEVRA: You said you never lied to Ada. But then you did lie to her after all. You never told her anything about me.

MATTEO: Yes, that's true.

GINEVRA: Of course, since I was nothing – a pigeon or a cat – what should you have told her?

MATTEO: Oh hush! You weren't a pigeon or a cat and you know it.

GINEVRA: So I wasn't a pigeon or a cat when you were thinking of me that summer in Prague?

MATTEO: No.

GINEVRA: I'm glad. It's never pleasant being a pigeon or a cat for someone.

MATTEO: How in the world did you happen to come by today?

GINEVRA: I told you. I was in the neighbourhood. On the landing, I thought I'd like to pay you a little visit. To find out how you were. But it's late now. I'm going to go.

MATTEO: I'm fine.

GINEVRA: I'm glad.

MATTEO: Do you see Ada often?

GINEVRA: From time to time.

MATTEO: Do you talk about me sometimes?

GINEVRA: Sometimes. Last year, for her birthday, I gave her a plant. A cactus. Maybe to pay her back for those plants of yours that I'd let shrivel up.

MATTEO: I used to torment Ada. I tormented her from morning to night. I'm reminded of it at times, and my conscience bothers me.

GINEVRA: Yes, you tormented her. I thought you were cruel. I believe I told you so, in those years, quite a few times.

MATTEO: It's good living alone. But in certain moments, like now, I feel nostalgic for Ada. I really miss her. I'd like to see her sometime. But she's never alone. That zero is always with her.

GINEVRA: He's a beautiful man, Ada's boyfriend.

MATTEO: He's not beautiful at all. Very tall with a big nose. They have an apartment on Via dell'Anima. A dark little rabbit hole of a place. I haven't seen it, but I'm told it's a dark little rabbit hole. They've always got to have the lights on when they're home. Who knows what came over you to have given them a cactus. A cactus is a big plant. They barely have room to move around as it is. They don't have money. He isn't working. That publisher fired him. Ada supports him. Ada works with her brother, the one who wanted to kill himself. They started up an insurance agency. I think with money from Aunt Giuseppina. All in all, things turned out well for everyone except me. Things even went well for you. Not bad at all. You're making sweaters.

GINEVRA: Yes. I make beautiful sweaters. I've been thinking of making a striped sweater, with violet and grey stripes, just like that armchair.

MATTEO: Ada came over one day to ask me for it, you know, the armchair. But I didn't give it to her. It's strange. I've gotten used to it. I couldn't do without it. I never sit in it, but I'm used to seeing it there.

GINEVRA: I understand. (*Goes toward the door.*)

MATTEO: Come on, you want to leave already? Why? Are you going back to see Lea and Vittorio? Listen, tell them they should come to visit me once in a while. It's ridiculous that we don't see each other anymore. To think they're just there on the other side of the wall.

GINEVRA: Why don't you go visit them yourself?

MATTEO: Me? Go visit them? No, I'd prefer it if they were the ones to come here. I don't remember why we fought, but it was nasty. They were unpleasant. They threw me out of the house. Onto the landing. They dumped me out on the landing. They were so rude. It was many years ago.

GINEVRA: I'll tell them to get in touch.

MATTEO: Listen, when you see Ada, tell her to come visit me. But by herself. Not with that zero.

GINEVRA: Okay, I'll tell her. And now I'd better say goodbye.

MATTEO: Are you leaving already? So soon? No, wait. I still have something I wanted to tell you.

GINEVRA: What?

MATTEO: I don't know anymore. Wait a minute. It was something important, really important, that I thought of the moment I saw you, and now it might be years before we see each other again. Wait a minute. It had something to do with … something to do with…. God, I don't know anymore.

April 1985

Notes

1 An elegant district in Rome.

2 The phrase '*tecnologie dolci*,' which translates literally as 'sweet' technologies, refers to no specific science or system, but is more generally used to connote any approach to development, agriculture, farming, industry, or

sometimes even to medicine or the social sciences that is considered en-
vironmentally friendly, 'green,' non-invasive, or self-renewing; Matteo's
response is, in fact, vague.

The Interview

A PLAY IN THREE ACTS

For Luca Coppola

Cast:
Marco
Ilaria
Stella
Signora Olimpia

This play unfolds in a house in the Tuscan countryside. It begins in the year 1978 and ends in the modern day.

ACT ONE

MARCO: Good morning.

ILARIA: Good morning, sir. And who might you be?

MARCO: I'm Marco Rozzi. I'm from *Aries*.

ILARIA: I'm from Libra.

MARCO: *Aries* is a weekly magazine. It's a weekly that my friend and I are doing. It's not my astrological sign, *Aries*. My sign is something else.

ILARIA: Are you looking for someone?

MARCO: I'm looking for Gianni Tiraboschi. I talked to him on the phone yesterday. He told me to come by this morning. I'm supposed to interview him.

ILARIA: He's not here.

MARCO: He's not here?

ILARIA: He left.

MARCO: No. He left? But I came from Rome just for this. The drive took three hours.

ILARIA: What kind of car do you have?

MARCO: A Centoventisette.[1] But what difference does it make what kind of car I have?

ILARIA: It doesn't. I was just asking.

MARCO: Can he really have gone? He gave me an appointment.

ILARIA: He left for Modena. They called him late yesterday afternoon. There was a roundtable. On income policies, I believe. Seems to me that's what he said. He probably forgot that he told you to come. He's very forgetful. Did he have your phone number?

MARCO: No. Stupidly, I never gave him my number and it's not listed.

ILARIA: It's still possible he may be back this afternoon. He took the car.

MARCO: What kind of car does he have?

ILARIA: A Morris Mini. But what difference does it make what kind of car he has?

MARCO: It doesn't. I was just asking. He might really be back this afternoon? Because I'd wait for him in that case.

ILARIA: Sure, wait for him. Modena isn't really all that far. It must be ninety kilometres.

MARCO: Do you think you might call him and ask what time he'll be back?

ILARIA: Call him where? He said he was going to Modena for a roundtable. He didn't say anything else. Where the roundtable might be, I don't know.

MARCO: I don't want to be a bother. I'll go down and wait in town, in a café.

ILARIA: Oh, no, wait for him here. Don't you move. Sit right down.

MARCO: Very lovely, this room. The whole house is lovely.

ILARIA: What do you see that's lovely? It's an old house and it's falling to pieces. It belonged to Gianni's parents. He came here when they died. He came to live here with his youngest sister, Stella. He has other brothers and sisters, but Stella's the only one he gets along with. He lived in Rome before that. Now he's come to hate Rome. He's right, because it's a hateful city. I hate Rome, too. But this house is quite isolated and there's nothing here. If you want to buy something to eat, you have to go all the way into town. It takes about a half-hour on foot. Here, there's just a little convenience store. They've got bread and salt. No, they've got coffee, too, but it's really the worst quality. I don't drive, and anyway, I don't have a car. Gianni's the only one with a car. I have a bicycle.

MARCO: It's lovely living in the country.

ILARIA: It's not lovely living in the country, but living in the city is terrible. Living in Rome is terrible. And where do you live, in Rome?

MARCO: In the Trastevere District.

ILARIA: Terrible. I lived there, too, for a while.

MARCO: Terrible? Not at all. I have a mansard apartment on Via della Lungara. I can see the Tiber from my window.

ILARIA: The Tiber is an ugly river. It's yellow. Full of rat urine. It's poisonous, rat urine is. If you drink even a drop of it, you'll die.

MARCO: But I don't drink from the Tiber. I look at it from my window. I don't think much about rat urine.

ILARIA: Why don't you think about it? Think about it.

MARCO: Will Gianni Tiraboschi really be back soon? It's very important to me to interview him. I was up until late last night writing out all my questions. I realized my tape recorder was broken and I had to bring one that belongs to a friend of mine. I left Rome early this morning. I even set the alarm because I have a tendency to oversleep. My Centoventisette is a bit broken down and I had to stop at the mechanic's because something wasn't working. It was so hot and I was sleepy and thirsty and I drank a lot of cold cappuccinos in a lot of highway rest stops. After Arezzo, for a while everything was going along smoothly. Then I got lost. Gianni Tiraboschi had given me street directions yesterday on the phone, but they were complicated and rather confusing. I got lost. Finally, I saw the playing field. He had mentioned a playing field, a fig tree, an intersection, and a traffic signal that doesn't work. After that there's a gravel road that goes up through the middle of a vineyard. That's what he told me. Finally, I saw the gate. I rang the bell, but no one came. I waited about ten minutes. There's a sign that says 'Dog Bites!' on the gate, but I didn't see hide nor hair of a dog. Lucky thing, because I don't exactly love dogs. Then this girl appeared and she let me in. A girl wearing jeans and a white T-shirt with a huge palm leaf on the front. With long blond hair and curls that went all the way to the bottom of her back. Beautiful hair.

ILARIA: That's Stella, Gianni's sister.

MARCO: She's very young. Fifteen or sixteen.

ILARIA: Seventeen.

MARCO: Very pretty. She told me I could park the car in the garden. I parked close to the wall, under an awning where there are some empty demijohns.

ILARIA: How do you know they're empty?

MARCO: I don't know. They seemed dusty.

ILARIA: They are empty, in fact.

MARCO: Still no dogs. I don't love dogs. My parents have a dog now and they're crazy about him. They live in Albissola.[2] When I go to Albissola for a visit that dog is always underfoot. He's ugly, fat, short, and bowlegged. I can't stand him. The last time he bit me. I had to be treated for rabies. My parents, both of them, were totally unperturbed. It was as if nothing had happened to me. They didn't even want me to get treated for rabies. They said I was exaggerating.

ILARIA: My parents aren't with me anymore. They died when I was young. My grandmother brought me up. She also died a long time ago. I don't have anyone left.

MARCO: But why do you have 'Dog Bites!' on your gate, given that there's neither hide nor hair to be seen of any dog?

ILARIA: We did have a dog, but he ran away. He ran away about ten days ago. Gianni doesn't want to take the sign down because he's hoping the dog might still come back. He never really was a biter. He was a small, rather tranquil dog. I'm speaking of him in the past tense because I don't believe he'll be back. The 'Dog Bites!' sign, of course, is meant for burglars.

MARCO: I got out of the car and we looked at each other. That girl and me. Stella. You said her name was Stella? She's pretty, that Stella. She was frowning and sucking on a lock of her hair. I told her about my appointment. She told me I could come up. She didn't say that Tiraboschi wasn't here. Her brother. Tiraboschi is her brother. She didn't tell me anything – not about Modena and not about the roundtable. She had a bucket and a scrub brush and she started washing the steps. I went inside the house and I came up here.

ILARIA: She loves to wash the steps. The house is filthy, but the steps are always freshly washed. The house is disgusting. Signora Olimpia comes on Mondays and Fridays. But Signora Olimpia isn't cut out for housecleaning. She spritzes a bottle of water on the floor, then she sits down, smokes a cigarette, and says she's tired. Then she says she has to go see her mother, who is elderly. They live right next to us, Signora Olimpia and her mother. They're the only neighbours we have. I leave the house filthy, too, because I don't feel cut out for housecleaning either.

MARCO: What are you cut out for?

ILARIA: I don't know. I still haven't figured that out. I make hand-

painted fabric. I don't dislike hand-painting fabric, but I feel as
though I'd rather be doing something else. What, I don't know. I
take my fabric to a woman in Florence. She makes dresses out of it
and sells them. She doesn't pay me much.

MARCO: Are you having money problems?

ILARIA: No. Big problems with money are one thing I don't have. My
grandmother left me two apartments in Rome and I've got those
rented out for a decent amount. Gianni's the one who has money
problems. He never has a cent. I have to help him out. When he
has a little bit of money, he gives it away. Gianni is very generous.
I'm sometimes rather stingy, on the other hand. Not always. From
time to time I get these major attacks of stinginess. But it makes me
furious that I get paid so little for the fabric. Are you having money
problems?

MARCO: Sometimes. But I'm trying to work more. I'm on assignment
with various magazines and newspapers. They pay me fairly well.
I have to help out my family. That dog they have eats a kilo of meat
everyday. And fresh eggs. I also have major attacks of stinginess
from time to time. (*Pause*.) That girl named Stella is Gianni Tiraboschi's sister. And you're his wife, right?

ILARIA: No. Gianni has a wife in Rome. He also has a child. A little
boy who's six. He's crazy for that little boy. He's nuts about him.
The wife is a huge bitch. She doesn't want a divorce, though he
doesn't want one either. No, I'm not his wife. I'm his companion.
His live-in. We began living together only a few months back, last
winter. I say 'living together' just as a figure of speech, because he's
never here. He's always dashing from one end of the planet to the
other. They're always calling him. It's incredible how much they call
him. It's a living arrangement that won't last long. Next October I
may go live in Australia.

MARCO: In Australia? What in the world for?

ILARIA: Because I have a cousin who lives there. In Melbourne. She
teaches ancient history at the university in Melbourne. She wrote
me to come live with her so I can help keep the house clean and
look after the children. She has four children. The oldest is twelve
and the youngest is three.

MARCO: Why would you go live in Australia if you're not having
money problems?

ILARIA: You know. To find out if I like living in Australia with my
cousin.

MARCO: But you don't feel cut out for housecleaning.

ILARIA: I don't feel cut out for housecleaning in Italy. It could be that I'll turn into a completely different person in Australia.

MARCO: What about the children? Do you feel cut out for taking care of children?

ILARIA: It depends on the children. It depends what day you ask me, too.

MARCO: And so?

ILARIA: So what?

MARCO: Are you going to have a hard time in Australia? With those four children, on days when you don't feel like looking after children?

ILARIA: Yes, I might have a hard time. In fact, I'm not sure what I'll do.

MARCO: You don't have children?

ILARIA: No, never had any. You?

MARCO: Me neither.

ILARIA: Gianni brings his son here sometimes. As soon as I lay eyes on him, I immediately feel exhausted. He's a good-looking boy, but he's spoiled and he has bad manners. His mother raised him badly. The Big Bitch. That's what people call her – The Big Bitch.

MARCO: Who calls her that?

ILARIA: I do.

MARCO: Won't you be sorry to leave Gianni when you go to Australia? Gianni Tiraboschi? Your companion? Your live-in?

ILARIA: Ours is a difficult living arrangement. He goes away a lot, but when he's here we don't do anything but argue. It's despicable the way we fight.

MARCO: About what?

ILARIA: About all kinds of things. About money. He's generous and I have these major attacks of stinginess. About the filthy house. About Signora Olimpia, because he thinks I treat her rudely sometimes. About his sister, because he thinks I talk down to her. About my fabric, because he thinks the colours are dull. About the aspirin that's past the expiration date and both of us forgot to buy more. About the dog that ran away. About the ants in the store room where we put the prosciutto. About my face, which is sad when he's happy or cheerful when he's sad. About the newspapers that I throw away and that he was saving. About the exhausted face he sees me make when he brings his son here. About the annoyed face he sees me make when he brings these certain friends of his over whom I find utterly boring. Or, on the other hand, about the fact that he brings people to the house so rarely and that I'm stuck here without anyone interesting to talk to. About the things that people fight about when they're in a difficult living arrangement. Haven't you ever lived with anyone?

MARCO: No, the only living arrangement I know is with my parents. I'm by myself in my apartment in Rome. (*Pause.*) But the two of you seem to be fighting over trifles.

ILARIA: Yes, over trifles. But those are the trifles born from the strain of difficult living arrangements.

MARCO: And how is it that Gianni Tiraboschi has the time to concern himself with so many trifles? Aspirin, ants? Isn't he always dashing from one end of the planet to the other?

ILARIA: Yes, but when he's here, he gives me no peace. He sticks his nose into everything.

MARCO: On the other hand, you don't really have all that much desire to go to Australia.

ILARIA: That's true.

MARCO: And so?

ILARIA: So ... I'll see. (*Pause.*) When I told Gianni that I might be going to Australia, he didn't say anything. But the next day he brought me five Linguaphone records. So I could do English exercises. I think it was his way of telling me I should hurry up and leave.

MARCO: I think so, too. It's not hard to believe that. (*Pause.*) May I ask you a question?

ILARIA: Yes. Go right ahead.

MARCO: Don't you feel humiliated staying with a person who maybe can't stand you anymore and that you can't stand? Why put up with a situation like that? Don't you have any pride?

ILARIA: Living together is difficult. But separations are difficult, too. (*Pause.*) Do you know Gianni personally?

MARCO: No, I don't know him personally. I've read his books. Plus I've heard him speak several times – in Milan, in Turin, in Rome. Seeing him has always made a big impression on me. So tall and thin, pale, with that scruffy black beard, those hands that he waves in the air, so refined, delicate, and white. He speaks very well.

ILARIA: He stutters though.

MARCO: He stutters, yes, a little. But what difference does it make? People like him like that. People are sick of speakers who talk so glibly, so randomly, in booming voices. He stumbles over his words. Plus it seems he has to work to pull every word up from the bottom of his belly. He has a hoarse, rusty sort of voice. It almost sounds like a hen clucking over her nest. You hear that hoarse, rusty, clucking voice in your ears for a long time afterwards. He's a wonderful speaker.

ILARIA: He's a wonderful stutterer of a speaker.

MARCO: You have a grudge against him. You're not objective.

ILARIA: The truth is the truth.

MARCO: I feel deep admiration for him. Yesterday, when I called him on the phone, that rusty voice captivated me. Later, I went to the kitchen to make myself a little supper, and I was talking to myself in a rusty, clucking voice. I often talk to myself. He was very kind on the phone. He gave me all those directions about how to find the right streets. The fig tree. The intersection. The traffic signal that doesn't work. It seemed as if he was delighted to meet me and to be interviewed. Then I get here and he's gone. Without leaving any word for me.

ILARIA: Gianni always agrees to be interviewed. Then, when it's time, he doesn't feel like it anymore. He takes off. He's done it lots of other times.

MARCO: But this time, did he really have to go to Modena? Did they call him? Was it urgent?

ILARIA: It seemed to be.

MARCO: And he'll be back this afternoon? You think he'll be back?

ILARIA: One hopes so. But you wait for him here.

MARCO: You're using 'tu' with me? Shall we use 'tu' with each other? How nice. You know, I'm from the old school. I tend to speak to people with 'Lei' when we've just met. But I'm wrong. It's lovely to use 'tu' with each other right away.

ILARIA: But you're young. You're young, but you're from the old school?

MARCO: I'm thirty. I'm young, but I'm from the old school.

ILARIA: Everything's lovely as far as you're concerned. This house is lovely. Stella's hair. The Tiber. Rat urine. Using 'tu.' I, on the other hand, find everything horrendous. We're very different. What sign are you?

MARCO: Taurus.

ILARIA: I'm a Libra.

MARCO: You already told me. I was still coming through the door when you told me.

ILARIA: Would you like some coffee?

MARCO: Love some.

ILARIA: Stella! Make some coffee.

Stella enters.

STELLA: We're out of coffee.

ILARIA: We're out of coffee? Too bad. It was for this reporter who came for your brother, to interview your brother. An interview that's going to be published in a weekly magazine.

MARCO: *Aries.*

ILARIA: *Aries.* Though I've never heard of *Aries* before.

STELLA: Neither have I.

MARCO: Because it hasn't come out yet. The first issue will come out in September. It will be a weekly magazine of politics, criticism, and culture. A friend of mine and I are doing it. Agostino Spada. Does either of you know Agostino Spada?

ILARIA: Never heard of him.

STELLA: Neither have I.

MARCO: He's very intelligent.

ILARIA: The reporter rang the bell at the gate and waited a good long while and nobody let him in. Why didn't you let him in?

STELLA: I was taking a shower. Why didn't you go down and let him in yourself?

ILARIA: I didn't hear him ring. You can't hear the bell from this room. And then, when you let him in, why didn't you tell him Gianni wasn't here?

STELLA: I don't like to talk to people I don't know. He might have been a burglar or something.

ILARIA: If he seemed like a burglar to you, why did you tell him to come in?

STELLA: Because I wanted you to deal with it.

ILARIA: Thank you. Very kind on your part.

MARCO: Did I frighten you, Stella? I'm sorry.

ILARIA: No, you didn't frighten her. Not a chance. Stella is never frightened of anything. She's got a tough hide. Besides, anyone could see right away that you're no burglar. With that sort of mustard-coloured pullover you're wearing.

STELLA: Why? What colour pullovers do burglars wear?

MARCO: You think my pullover is ugly?

ILARIA: No, quite the contrary. Honest. It's an honest pullover.

MARCO: My mother bought it for me. It's light. Because it's made of pure cotton. That's what my mother says. I don't pay much attention to what I wear. In the morning, I just fish around in my dresser for whatever I can find.

ILARIA: Stella, on the other hand, doesn't just fish around for whatever she can find. The minute she gets up she thinks about which one of her thirty tops to choose. This morning she chose this one with the enormous palm leaf on the front. She thinks it's an extraordinary find. To me it's a thing of horror. I almost prefer your mustard-coloured one.

STELLA: Is this reporter having lunch here?

ILARIA: Certainly. Where would you like him to have lunch? He's waiting for Gianni. Did you put the potatoes on to boil?

STELLA: Yes.

MARCO: While we wait for the potatoes to cook, couldn't I ask the two of you some questions about Gianni Tiraboschi? About Gianni? About his projects, his political ideology, his public activities?

ILARIA: No, don't ask me questions. I'd say stupid things. He'd get mad. He turns into a hyena when he gets mad.

STELLA: No, don't ask her questions. She hasn't read Gianni's books. She isn't acquainted with his political philosophy. She lives outside of reality. She lives in the clouds.

ILARIA: Why? Because you're so well acquainted with his political philosophy?

STELLA: More so than you.

ILARIA: So explain it.

STELLA: I can hardly explain it just like that, in two words.

ILARIA: Stop sucking on your hair. You have a marmalade stain on your T-shirt, right under the palm leaf. You ought to go comb your hair. The reporter thinks you have beautiful hair.

STELLA: You know how many potatoes there are?

ILARIA: How many?

STELLA: Exactly four.

ILARIA: Not very many.

STELLA: What shall we eat for lunch, you, me, and this reporter? We haven't gone shopping. We both forgot about it. Coffee's not the only thing we're out of. We're also out of wine. And oil, too. We're out of almost everything.

ILARIA: Go into town. Go ahead and take my bicycle. Yours is falling apart. It'll be quicker if you take mine. Buy whatever we need. You'll find some money in my drawer, in with my stockings. The drawer's open.

STELLA: So, if he is a burglar, now he knows where we keep the money.

ILARIA: We've established that he's not a burglar. Come on. Get a move on. Hurry.

STELLA: Where am I running to? It's almost two o'clock. All the stores are closed.

ILARIA: So late? How time flies.

MARCO: I have some fresh caciottine[3] in my car. In the trunk. I bought them at a rest stop on the way here.

STELLA: How many are there?

MARCO: I don't remember. But if you want, we can eat all of them.

STELLA: Give me the keys to the trunk.

ILARIA: You're using 'tu' with him? Even though you just met?

STELLA: You're using 'tu' and you've just met him. You've never seen him before now.

ILARIA: Go see how the potatoes are cooking.

STELLA: How should they be cooking? They're cooking.

ILARIA: Boiled potatoes with salt, even without olive oil, are the best thing in the world.

MARCO: That's true.

STELLA: The keys to the trunk. (*Exits.*)

ILARIA: She's lazy. She's very lazy. Why didn't she go into town to do the shopping? She didn't forget. She didn't feel like going. She was hoping I would go. She's lazy. She finished high school but she doesn't want to continue her studies. She says she wants to work in theatre. Or else she says art restoration. She says lots of things. In the meantime, though, she isn't budging from here. She's very disorganized. You should see her room. Clothes and undershirts scattered all over the floor. Overflowing ashtrays. Stinking rubber-soled shoes piled up in the top of the closet. To get her to do anything you have to get down on your knees.

MARCO: She's very pretty.

Stella enters.

STELLA: Gianni called. He says he's not coming back today. He has to go to Milan. They called him. It's urgent. I told him about the reporter. He said he's really very sorry. He'd forgotten that he told

you to come. He was in a hurry on the phone because he was running out of change. He asked if you could come back another time.

MARCO: Damn him.

STELLA: Damn him? No, damn you. He's my brother. Don't say damn
to my brother. If you do, I'll rip your mustard-coloured pullover
right off your back. Made of pure cotton.

MARCO: Come on. It's just something you say. Can you imagine that I'd
even dream of cursing him? I have enormous admiration for him.
I'm just upset. Upset and disappointed. I needed to do the interview today because there won't be any time later. It was supposed
to come out in the first issue. It was supposed to be a long interview
– covering all his projects, all his public activities. It doesn't matter.
I'll come back another time. The interview could even come out in
the second issue. Never mind. Journalists have to be very patient.

STELLA: Are you still having lunch here?

ILARIA: Certainly he's having lunch here. You don't really mean to
send him out into this heat wave, furious and on an empty stomach?

MARCO: I'm not all that furious. To tell the truth, it's been a pleasure to
meet you both and I'm enjoying being here with you. Let's eat those
four potatoes together and then I'll get in my car and *vaya con dios*.
I'll be out of your hair, as the saying goes.

STELLA: Potatoes and fresh caciottine. You're forgetting we have those,
too.

MARCO: And fresh caciottine. Of course. I bought them to give to a
neighbour as a gift. She's got a passion for fresh caciottine. It doesn't
matter. I'll buy some more on my way back.

STELLA: We've got a passion for caciottine, too. I've already brought
them up.

MARCO: How many are there?

STELLA: There are exactly four.

MARCO: Today's the day for number four. It keeps turning up. Four
potatoes. Four caciottine. Four children in Melbourne.

STELLA: What children?

ILARIA: But we're only three.

MARCO: No, we're four. Gianni Tiraboschi is here with us. Gianni. He's
far away, in Modena or Milan or I'm not sure where, but I feel his
presence. This is his house. This is the armchair where he surely
always sits. He's here.

ILARIA: Stella, go set the table.

Stella exits.

MARCO: She's Stella. And you? What's your name? You've told me your sign, but you haven't told me your name. You've told me all kinds of other things about you, and for that I'm very grateful. It doesn't often happen that people speak to me with so much faith and trust. You've spoken to me as if I were an old friend of yours. What's your name?

ILARIA: My name is Ilaria.

MARCO: And your last name?

ILARIA: Rossetti. But what do you care? Probably, when you come back the next time, I won't be here.

MARCO: Because you'll be in Australia.

ILARIA: I'll probably be in Australia. But I have to get moving on my English studies. I should start immediately. I still haven't touched those Linguaphone records. I haven't even opened the package. I'll open it today, as soon as you're on your way.

MARCO: But what will Stella do when you leave? Her brother is always running around. She can't be left alone – she's so young – in this big, lonely house.

ILARIA: I don't know. I'm not exactly her nursemaid.

MARCO: Why don't you and Gianni send her to Rome? She could attend the Academy of Dramatic Arts. I have a friend who teaches there. I could recommend her to my friend.

ILARIA: Stella will do whatever she feels like. I can't worry too much about other people. They'll have to take care of themselves.

MARCO: Maybe I could give Stella some advice. Now, I mean, while we're sitting down to eat. What do you think? Wouldn't the Academy of Dramatic Arts be a good idea?

ILARIA: Maybe. I don't know. She'll have to take care of herself. All I need is to start worrying about how things are going to turn out for Stella. A girl who means nothing to me. We've found ourselves together here purely by chance. I really need to think solely of myself. I learned to think of myself when I was a very small child. I've told you I have no parents. I don't have anyone left. People don't give a damn about me and I really don't give all that much of a damn about them. Come on, let's go down and eat.

ACT TWO

[*The same house, a year and five months later.*]

MARCO: Good morning.

ILARIA: Good morning, sir. And who might you be?

MARCO: Who am I? I'm Marco Rozzi. You don't recognize me. I came here some time ago. Exactly a year and five months ago. I'd come to interview Gianni Tiraboschi. He wasn't here and I was supposed to come back the following month. But then I didn't come back. Do you remember? I even ate here.

ILARIA: Oh, certainly. But weren't we using *tu* with each other the last time?

MARCO: In fact, we were.

ILARIA: I didn't recognize you. This room is dark. I was here reading and I started to doze off. Is it still snowing outside? Yes, it's snowing. What time is it? Three? Three in the afternoon and it seems like night. Do you mind turning on the light? That lamp that's on the table there. Thanks. Who opened the gate for you?

MARCO: Stella let me in. I came from Rome. I called yesterday evening. Gianni Tiraboschi answered. Gianni. I'm supposed to interview him. You recall that I didn't find him in last time? He told me to come by today, early in the afternoon. So here I am.

ILARIA: It was summer the last time you came. August. It seems to me it was August. We didn't see each other again after that. You got together with Stella, in Rome. Not with me.

MARCO: Exactly. (*Pause.*) Stella was a little surprised when she let me in. She might have been a little upset, too. Anyway, she told me I could go right up. May I take off my jacket?

ILARIA: It's more than a jacket, it's a fur coat. Take it off and put it there.

MARCO: Yes, I got together with Stella in Rome. Actually, we saw quite a bit of each other for a few months. Then she vanished. She made herself pretty scarce after that.

ILARIA: I know.

MARCO: You know. She must have told you. She must have said a few things at least. Obviously.

ILARIA: A few things.

MARCO: At the beginning she seemed happy to be living in Rome. I convinced her to enrol in the Academy of Dramatic Arts. I recommended her to a friend of mine there. That time when I came by, a year and five months ago, that one single time, I convinced her. I found her a boarding house in Rome, modest but reasonable. On Via Crescenzio. Pensione Sorriso. But she didn't treat me very well. We saw each other almost every day. Did you know that I wanted to marry her? I thought very seriously about it. I was quite taken. She never told me no; she would always say she had to think it over. That seemed more than fair to me. Then I took her to visit my parents at Albissola. My mother gave her a ring. It might have been a little premature to give her the ring, but my mother is like that. She was very pleased that I was getting married. She was rushing things. My mother is from the old school. If I bring a girl around, she immediately thinks there's an engagement. Stella put the ring on her finger. She seemed happy. Then we went back to Rome, and the whole way she was morose and sullen, and she wouldn't say one single word to me. Maybe she didn't like my parents. I don't know. The following week, she vanished. Vanished, I'm telling you. I went to look for her at the boarding house and they told me she'd left with her luggage. I even went to the Academy of Dramatic Arts, and they told me they didn't see her anymore. I called her here a number of times, but no one answered.

ILARIA: I don't hear the phone. It rings down below and I don't hear it from this room. If Gianni is away, no one answers the phone. But Stella did come back here to live. She told me she didn't like Rome. She enrolled in the University in Florence. She wants to study costume history. She goes to Florence fairly often. She has a boyfriend. Swiss. Whether she really attends the university, I don't know. She's told me nothing about Albissola or the ring. She may well have sold the ring, because I've never seen it.

MARCO: It was a beautiful ring. It belonged to my family. My mother gave it to her with so much joy but with a certain sense of unease, as well. I told you that my mother is from the old school. She thought she ought to give my fiancée a ring. They treated her as though she were my fiancée. My father was still there, then. Then he died.

ILARIA: Stella told me some things about you, but very little. She told me that the reporter who came by here once had convinced her to move to Rome, then he fell in love with her, and she didn't know how to get herself out of a relationship that felt both misguided and oppressive. It was cold at the Pensione Sorriso, she told me, and everyone at the Academy was unpleasant. So she came back here. It

was last spring, it seems to me. She came back with her suitcase full
of dirty clothes and with a serious cough. I never saw any ring. She
got into some debt in Rome. She'd gotten some friends of Gianni's
to lend her money. I had to pay it back because Gianni never has
a cent. But I told her that the next time she'd have to take care of
herself. I told her that I'm not exactly her nanny.

MARCO: I lent her some money, too.

ILARIA: Oh, really? How much did you lend her?

MARCO: I don't remember. It doesn't matter. Money doesn't matter to
me. I've said goodbye to it. But the way she treated me did offend
me. She vanished. Just like that – from one moment to the next,
without a word. I thought of coming here to look for her, but then I
gave up on the idea. Here, no one answers the phone. I told myself
that maybe you had left and who knew where Gianni was. And
anyway, Gianni and I had never met in person. Lots of times when
Stella was in Rome I asked her to arrange an introduction. She
didn't tell me no, but she kept putting it off. Maybe Gianni doesn't
even know that his sister and I had a relationship. Yesterday evening, when I called him, I asked myself whether he knew anything.

ILARIA: Who knows? I've never spoken to him about it, but it's possible
that Stella did. But he's very distracted anyway. He immediately
forgets other people's business. His sister's business, too. Sometimes, he even forgets his own business.

MARCO: Yesterday evening on the phone I told him my name and I told
him that I'd come by for an interview a year and five months ago, in
vain. He remembered that missed interview. Or at least he said he
remembered.

ILARIA: He was lying. He never remembers anything.

MARCO: He asked me to forgive him. He gave me an appointment for
today. He was very kind. He repeated the usual street directions.
The fig tree. The intersection. The traffic signal that doesn't work.
Just like the last time. Exactly the same. I heard his rusty voice over
the phone. I'm the opposite of Gianni. I never forget anything. I
remember that the last time you said you wanted to go live in Australia. You didn't go?

ILARIA: No. As you see, I'm still here.

MARCO: When Stella vanished, I was close to having a nervous breakdown. I wasn't sleeping anymore. I was very much in love with
her. I was quite taken. Then my father got sick and I had to go to
Albissola to take care of him. He died. My mother moved to Rome,

with her dog, and came to live with me. In my attic. But the three of us were going crazy in that attic – me, the dog, and my mother. We looked for an apartment. Now we live on Piazza Santa Emerenziana.

ILARIA: Terrible place.

MARCO: Yes. I don't see the Tiber anymore from my window. I don't see the rat urine anymore. Remember that you were telling me about the rat urine?

ILARIA: I certainly do remember.

MARCO: You remember lots of things, too, like me. I sublet my apartment to a friend of mine. Agostino Spada. Did I talk to you about Agostino Spada?

ILARIA: Yes. The one you were doing *Aries* with. The one who was very intelligent.

MARCO: Yes. *Aries* never did get published. Not even one issue. It died before it was born. Now Agostino Spada and I are doing a monthly magazine. *The Ace of Clubs*. That's what it's called. The first issue should be out within a month. That's why I'm here. There'll be a long interview with Gianni Tiraboschi in the first issue. Covering all his projects, all his public activities. A long interview, with photos. He promised he'd give me some photographs, too. I brought my tape recorder. I have it down in the car, in the trunk. That's why I'm here. Only for that. I have no desire to see Stella again. Not at all. That's all dead and buried. I didn't say anything to her at the gate, and I won't say anything to her. It's over, with Stella. No, I've come for *The Ace of Clubs*. But seeing you gives me such pleasure. I've thought about you often, and with affection. Almost with friendship. Certainly, with friendship. It was summer. August. It was the month of August exactly.

ILARIA: I have some bad new for you, though. Gianni isn't here.

MARCO: Isn't here? How can he not be here?

ILARIA: He left. He left this morning at dawn. His wife called him late yesterday evening. The Big Bitch. The one people call The Big Bitch. Before she didn't want a divorce, The Big Bitch, but now she does. She's got a fiancé. Now Gianni wants a divorce, too. So she made an appointment with the attorney for today. I don't know at what time. They were supposed to work out all the details about their son. Gianni told me all of this in a hurry, then he rushed down to his car, and he left for Rome. He didn't say much about you. He must have forgotten that he'd told you to come. But you can wait for him. He might be back before nightfall. Do you want some coffee?

MARCO: No. Give me the attorney's phone number. I'll call him.

ILARIA: I don't know who the attorney is. And I'm certainly not calling The Big Bitch at home. You can call her if you want.

MARCO: Give me The Big Bitch's number.

ILARIA: Go downstairs. The phone is down below in the study. I know the number by heart. I'll write it down for you on this piece of paper.

MARCO: You don't call The Big Bitch, but you know her telephone number by heart?

ILARIA: Yes. I used to call her sometimes before. I have no trouble keeping telephone numbers in my head.

Marco exits. He reappears a few moments later.

MARCO: No one's answering. I'll wait a while. Do you think Gianni might be back this evening before nightfall?

ILARIA: I don't know. It's possible. Be patient. Reporters always have to be very patient.

MARCO: I'll wait a while. Damn. Damn it to hell. I gave him my telephone number. He could have warned me first thing this morning. I was in the car for five hours. I had to take it very slowly because of the snow. I had to put the chains on. Except for the snow, this is about what it was like the last time. I rang the bell and wound up having to wait a quarter of an hour before Stella came to let me in. The 'Dog Bites' sign isn't on the gate anymore, but now there's a dog in the garden instead, who launched himself at my pants leg. He didn't bite me, but he didn't miss by much. A white poodle, very filthy, kind of an ugly thing. But still better than my mother's dog. How come the 'Dog Bites' sign isn't there anymore?

ILARIA: I don't know. I think the wind blew it away.

MARCO: Stella doesn't have her hair down loose across her shoulders anymore. She has it all gathered up on the top of her head in a big bun. It's a shame. She was very pretty with her hair down. This way, her nose shows more. She has a rather huge nose. A potato.

ILARIA: What have you got against potatoes?

MARCO: Nothing. Because boiled, with salt, they're the best thing in the world.

ILARIA: Exactly.

MARCO: See how well I remember what you said? (*Pause.*) But I don't like noses like potatoes. It's a shame. Stella was so much cuter before, when she used to put that lock of hair in her mouth. Nothing about her matters to me anymore. We looked each other over. She was frowning and chewing her lip. She seemed a little stunned and embarrassed. She said to me, 'Oh, you're here?' Then silence. She pulled down the sleeves of her cardigan. She has an enormous black cardigan that goes down almost to her knees, with a red velvet heart sewn over her chest. I asked her if I could go up. She nodded. I parked the car under the awning. The empty demijohns aren't there anymore. Instead there's a mattress with the springs poking out, buried under the snow. But nothing about Stella matters to me anymore. Total indifference. I just don't think she should do her hair in that style. Women are so stupid!

ILARIA: Why? Because men are so intelligent?

MARCO: No, men are stupid, too. If I think about all the idiotic things I've done in my time on this Earth, I get shivers up and down my spine. So many mistakes, so many futile, pointless relationships. The wrong friends, the wrong women. How could I have fallen in love with Stella? What nonsense that was. I should have understood right off that she wasn't the right girl for me. And yet I suffered. I suffered like a dog for her. But let's not talk about dogs. Go ahead, get me some coffee. Strange, I'm furious because Gianni isn't here, but finding myself back in this room is such a pleasure. Who knows why it's such a pleasure? It's not like it's a beautiful room. The covers on the armchairs are in a pitiful state. There are mildew stains on the walls. The curtains are torn. What would it take to sew them up? My mother would already have done it.

ILARIA: You said it was a beautiful house when you were here before.

MARCO: Because I was younger. I was a year and five months younger. Now that I'm older, I see everything more clearly. Plus it was summer then and now it's winter. The house seemed more beautiful in the sun. It's cold in this room. Don't you have an electric heater?

ILARIA: We have a fire going in the fireplace.

MARCO: Yes, but it's a miserable fire. You probably used green wood. It makes smoke, but it doesn't burn. Plus the fireplace may be drawing badly.

ILARIA: Stella! Make some coffee.

MARCO: It's certainly colder here than it was at Pensione Sorriso.

Stella enters.

STELLA: The coffee is from the convenience store. It's really bad. You can hardly drink it.

MARCO: Hi, Stella.

STELLA: Hi. We already said hello to each other earlier. At the gate.

MARCO: Yes, but now I'm saying hello to you again. You've changed. You've gained weight and you've put your hair up. With that big bun on the top of your head.

STELLA: I'm going into town. I'll take the car. We're out of coffee and wine.

MARCO: Just like the last time I was here.

STELLA: I should also take the car to the mechanic. It's making an odd noise.

ILARIA: Careful that you don't wind up stuck in the middle of the street in this snow.

STELLA: That's my problem.

ILARIA: Take the car to the mechanic who's down below on the main street. Not to the one next to the bakery because that guy has no idea what he's doing.

STELLA: That's my problem.

ILARIA: No, it's not your problem because the car is mine. I bought it with my treasury bond. (*Stella exits*.) I bought the car three months ago. It's a Diane. I wanted to get a licence but I still haven't gotten one. Stella got hers, though. She goes to Florence a lot. She has a boyfriend there, as I've told you. A Swiss guy. He doesn't seem so bad.

MARCO: Nothing about her matters to me anymore. Really nothing. It's just that when I wake up I feel empty, useless. A used-up rag that nobody wants. I look at the squalor of my life and my thoughts and it's all a kind of daze. Then I get up and things get better. I go to Largo Argentina, to a bar where I meet my friend, Agostino Spada. He's a small man, Agostino Spada, with a fringe of blond hair that falls over his eyes. I cheer up as soon as I see him. I immediately feel less bothered by what I was thinking. We were in Turin together a few days ago, the two of us, to see a dance concert. Gianni Tiraboschi was speaking on Sunday morning, at a movie theatre downtown. We saw the posters and we went to hear him. He was talking about the *Scala Mobile*.[4] I admire him, Gianni Tiraboschi. Gianni. Right at the moment I hate him, too, because he told me to come by and he isn't here. But I admire him hugely. I could never stop admiring him. Agostino admires him, too. There was

an enormous crowd in that movie theatre. And there he was on
the dais, tall, with his messy black beard all curly and dishevelled,
wearing a checkered shirt. He was also wearing suspenders. These
ugly suspenders pulled all the way up his chest. Who else in the
world wears suspenders? No one wears them anymore. Only him.
Every once in a while he would raise his beautiful, delicate hands
in the air, so white. We were enchanted to listen to him, Agostino
Spada and me.

ILARIA: Was he stuttering?

MARCO: Oh sure. He was stuttering a ton. At the end there was an
ocean of applause. I wanted to go congratulate him, to ask him if I
could interview him, but Agostino stopped me. As a matter of fact
he was right: How could I go over in the middle of all those people
to talk to him about *The Ace of Clubs*? It would have been grotesque.
On the train, on the way back, we were having a discussion about I
don't know what, me and Agostino, and we realized we were both
stuttering and talking in rusty, clucking voices. We burst out laughing. It was a very cheerful trip back.

ILARIA: I don't go to hear him speak anymore. I used to go, but not
anymore. He doesn't want me to.

MARCO: Why doesn't he want you to?

ILARIA: Because he says that when he sees me there, in the middle of
all the other people, he feels uneasy and he stutters worse. He says
he immediately starts being afraid he'll say something wrong. I
usually don't understand anything he's saying – nothing, not even
a syllable, because he talks about politics and other things I know
nothing about. But he says that the expression on my face makes
him uneasy. And even if he can't see my face because I've gone to
sit somewhere far away from the stage, he may see my hair from
a distance and my blouse and feel embarrassed and insecure. He
says I judge him, even though I don't understand a syllable of his
speeches, and that makes him feel uneasy.

MARCO: Is it true that you judge him?

ILARIA: Yes, I judge him. I sniff the words he's using to see what they
smell like. He says he detests the way I sniff at his words.

MARCO: And his wife, The Big Bitch? The one you call The Big Bitch?
Does The Big Bitch go hear him speak sometimes?

ILARIA: Oh sure, she goes sometimes. She plants herself there, tall,
with her hair all teased and her devious eyes, and that porcelain
face. She has a very tiny nose, a very tiny mouth, this wide, smooth

forehead, and this pale blond hair all teased up. She always wears a little scarf around her neck and a string of pearls.

MARCO: Is she pretty?

ILARIA: They say she's pretty. I don't find her pretty at all. She doesn't understand a word either, when Gianni speaks, I'd be willing to swear, but she pretends to understand everything. She's a great faker. She frowns and curls her lips, and then she makes comments using sentences she's learned reading the newspapers. The Big Bitch reads all the newspapers. She may not understand anything, but she reads them all. She makes a show out of sniffing around, but the truth is that it's beyond her capacity to smell anything. Gianni says she's a gifted, highly cultured woman. He's never understood what a great faker she is. They've lived together for a long time. They even had a child together, and he's never understood that when she frowns and curls her lips she doesn't have the slightest original thought in her head. At a certain point he couldn't stand her anymore, but he continued to say that the two of them had magnificent exchanges of ideas together. With me on the other hand, there were never any magnificent exchanges of ideas. There never was any true mutual understanding. That's what he thinks.

MARCO: And you? Is that what you think?

ILARIA: I don't think anything. All I know is that it was despicable the way we always fought.

MARCO: But didn't you want to go live in Australia? Why didn't you go?

ILARIA: Last winter I was about to leave. I hadn't learned much English, but I was leaving anyway. Then Gianni told me that if I was leaving, he was leaving with me. He was in a crisis at that point, Gianni was. He was very depressed. Everything was going wrong for him. He was tired of the roundtables, tired of dashing around from one city to another, tired of standing on podiums and giving speeches. He wanted to leave Italy. We wrote to my cousin in Melbourne and she found him a one-year position at the University of Sydney. Both of us got to work studying English with the Linguaphone records. He doesn't know languages just like I don't know languages, and he very much admires those that do. We went to Florence and we bought some things for Australia – some shirts, socks. But then he got an invitation to Mexico City for a conference on world hunger. He accepted. That was at the end of February. He told me: 'When I come back we'll get organized for the trip to

Australia.' He came back ten days later and after that we didn't
leave – not him and not me.

MARCO: Why not?

ILARIA: He came back and I immediately realized that something had
happened. He wasn't depressed anymore. He was cheerful all the
time. He was kind to me, affectionate in a way he'd never been.
He'd fallen in love with some girl at the conference in Mexico City.

MARCO: Mexican?

ILARIA: No, Italian. From Puglia. Brindisi, to be exact. She studied to be
an interpreter and she knows English very well. She translated all
his speeches at the conference into English. A month ago, we went
to supper with a group of people one evening in a restaurant in
Florence, and she was there, too. Lucianella is her name. Lucianella
Calabrò. As soon as I saw her I understood immediately. I hated her
immediately.

MARCO: A Little Bitch?

ILARIA: Yes. Very different from The Big Bitch. A tiny, emaciated thing,
with enormous green eyes and this forest of frizzy hair. She dresses
a little bit like a gypsy, with long skirts, sandals, hoops in her ears,
chains around her neck, and bracelets. The Big Bitch has pearls. The
Little Bitch has bracelets. She barely speaks, The Little Bitch, and
she fixes those enormous eyes on you – piercing, nasty. She sniffs
around and she judges you. But she judges in a resentful, nasty-
minded way. I judge without being nasty-minded; she judges out of
nastiness. That's the difference between her and me. It's a substan-
tial difference. Gianni and I came back home and in the car I told
him I understood what was going on. I told him I was leaving him.
He said, in fact, that we ought to break up. He wanted a cappuccino
and we stopped at a rest stop. We sat there and we watched the sun
come up. There we were, the two of us, right next to one another, silent, chilled to the bone. He was playing with his beard. I was playing with the rim of my cap. He covered his hands with his eyes.
When he took his hands away I saw that his eyes were red. He told
me he'd never loved me as much as he did now that we were going
to be leaving one another. He was stuttering. He stuttered so much
that I barely managed to understand the words he was saying. He
told me he was sure the girl would get tired of him very quickly. So
young. Younger than Stella. A child.

MARCO: And then?

ILARIA: He saw her like a child. On the other hand, I saw her as an old

snake. She may have been young, but she had all the wrinkles of
an old snake. We got back into the car. By then it was day time and
the sun was out. He told me not to go to Australia, not so far away.
I could look for an apartment in Florence instead, so we could still
see each other every now and then and spend time together. Separations are difficult. I also felt that I'd never loved him as much as I
did in that moment, as we were going back home, numb from the
cold, and stinking from all those hours at the table in the rest stop.

MARCO: And then?

ILARIA: Then nothing. I'm looking for that apartment in Florence. I've
put myself in the hands of an agency. He's still dashing off in the
car from one place to another. They call him to go everywhere.
He also goes to Brindisi a lot, where The Little Bitch lives with her
family. He dashes from Genoa to Brindisi, from Brindisi to Milan.
The Little Bitch often follows him around on his trips and to his
conferences, with her long skirts, with that forest of frizzy, puffy,
black hair, with all those bracelets. She goes and listens in the midst
of all those people and she watches him with those enormous eyes
of hers, piercing, nasty. She's a witch, The Little Bitch. A little witch.
A snake. But he's in love. He's lost his head over her. He doesn't
remember anything anymore. He used to love his baby son so
much; he was crazy about him. Now, he doesn't even remember his
birthday. If he happens to go to Rome he doesn't call to see him. I
don't believe he's seen him for quite a while. The baby had to go to
corrective gymnastics classes last fall, and Gianni kept the therapist's bill in his pocket for weeks. Because he's forgetful, but also
out of indifference. Finally the therapist called, furious, and I ended
up paying the bill myself. The day of the baby's birthday, The
Big Bitch called here and I answered. She was indignant because
nobody had heard from Gianni – not a gift, not a word – and she
said the baby had been crying and that he'd gotten a fever besides.
That was probably a lie because The Big Bitch is a big liar. But she
caused a huge scene with me on the phone, as if it had all been my
fault. I was speaking to her in monosyllables, ice-cold, but at a certain point I couldn't stop myself from telling her that I had paid for
the corrective gymnastics classes. Keep in mind that The Big Bitch
couldn't be richer – in fact, she's a millionaire, because her father
has a chain of hotels, but she's stingy and plus she has the idea that
Gianni absolutely must pay for certain things having to do with the
baby. Since she wouldn't quit shouting at me, I made Stella come to

the phone and the two of them started talking between themselves about The Little Bitch. They were saying she was nuisance, and a viper, and probably a gold digger. In the end, I told Stella to stop talking so long on the phone because long-distance calls are expensive. Of course, The Big Bitch was the one who called and she was paying, the millionaire. But all the same, I didn't like them wasting money and I didn't like that it was the two of them of the phone, screaming and saying awful things while meanwhile Gianni and The Little Bitch were happily flitting around the city.

MARCO: I heard footsteps on the stairs. Someone's coming.

ILARIA: It's Signora Olimpia. I recognize the sound of her slippers.

Signora Olimpia enters.

SIGNORA OLIMPIA: I brought four fresh eggs. I put them in the kitchen. While I was downstairs, there were two telephone calls. Stella wound up stuck in the street with her car. She called from a bar in town. She wound up having to go into town on foot. Her shoes and socks got soaked. She wants the reporter to come get her in town in his car since he's here.

ILARIA: I guessed the car would break down.

SIGNORA OLIMPIA: The other call was from Gianni. He says he's sleeping in Rome because he's very tired. He's leaving for Brindisi tomorrow morning. He doesn't know when he'll be back. Then he asked whether someone had come for him – a reporter – and I told him yes. He said he was truly mortified. It slipped his mind that he'd given him an appointment and he remembered too late. He asks the reporter to forgive him. And he wishes you would come back another time.

MARCO: Damn him! I'm going to die without ever having interviewed him!

ILARIA: Don't say 'damn him.' If anyone says 'damn him,' it should be me. Go get Stella in town, if you don't mind. At the bar in town. There's only one bar. Grab that ugly fake-fur jacket of yours and put it on. Be patient. Journalists have to be very patient. Later you can have supper and spend the night here. You can hardly go back to Rome in the dark with all this snow.

SIGNORA OLIMPIA: For supper you have this morning's soup. It just needs to be reheated.

MARCO: Potato soup.

SIGNORA OLIMPIA: Without potatoes. It's made with carrots and cab-
   bage. May I go along now? Do you need anything?

ILARIA: Soup without potatoes. You can go.

MARCO: Plus four eggs.

ILARIA: Plus four eggs. Last time you said it was the day for the number four.

MARCO: You remember so many things.

ILARIA: Hurry up. Go get Stella. She'll be frozen and irritable. She'll
   want to get back home.

MARCO: Yes, I'll go right away. I'll bring her right home.

ILARIA: The last time there were four of us – we three and Gianni, who
   wasn't here but was here all the same. This time we make five. The
   three of us, Gianni who isn't here but is here all the same, and The
   Little Bitch, who's here, too. I feel her presence in this room, on this
   couch. She's sitting right next to us and looking at us with her nasty
   eyes.

ACT THREE

[*The same house, eight years later.*]

MARCO: Good morning.

ILARIA: Good morning, sir. And who might you be?

MARCO: I'm Marco, Ilaria. Marco Rozzi. Do you still remember me?

ILARIA: Marco Rozzi, who? Marco Rozzi. Oh, yes. But so much time
   has passed. Why didn't you keep in touch? We wrote each other a
   couple of times – then we didn't write anymore. Sit down.

MARCO: I tried calling a few times, but no one answered. Then I lost the
   number and it isn't in the directory. I didn't get an answer to the last
   letter I wrote you.

ILARIA: I seem to remember that you came here twice to interview
   Gianni. Both times he was nowhere to be found. Isn't that right?

MARCO: In fact it is. You don't know how much I've thought about
   you over the years. About you, about Stella, and about the time
   we spent together, in this room and also in the room downstairs
   where there used to be, if I'm not mistaken, an oval table with a lace
   tablecloth and a big credenza with glass doors. So today I was passing through Arezzo and the idea came into my head that I should
   make a detour. To see if you were all still here. I've brought some

bottles of wine and some fresh caciottine. I have them in the trunk
of my car. I remembered that the two of you really like fresh caciottine – you and Stella. Stella didn't open the gate for me this time.
Instead, an elderly woman wearing a plaid oilcloth apron let me in.
It seemed to me I'd seen her before.

ILARIA: That's Signora Olimpia. She's our neighbour and she cleans for
us. You've certainly seen her. I remember that you have.

MARCO: Yes, yes. I remember, too. Anyway, she acted as though she
recognized me, too. Even though all these years have passed. I
parked the car on the slab. I remembered there used to be an awning but it's not there anymore. Instead there's a rusty bathtub with
some dried-up mortar in the bottom. I didn't see any dogs, though I
did see a cat or two.

ILARIA: What kind of car do you have? (*She looks out the window.*) Oh,
look, you have a big car. Luxurious.

MARCO: It's a Volvo.

ILARIA: A Volvo. I don't know about cars, but I know that Volvos are
very expensive. Are you earning a good salary? Once, if I'm not
mistaken, you were pretty broke. Now I see you looking elegant.
Apart from that though, you hardly seem very different from the
way you were years ago. You've only lost a little hair.

MARCO: You're not much different either. It's strange, I can never remember people's features, but your face has stayed very sharply in
my memory. (*Pause.*) And Stella? What's new with Stella?

ILARIA: Stella has been here for the last little while, but she lives in
Milan now. She's out at the moment. I think she's gone into the
woods to pick mushrooms. She'll be back soon. You'll see her.
She lives in Milan with a guy named Pierre. He's a French Swiss.
They've been together for years. They aren't married because nowadays people don't get married. They don't have any children. He's
a graphic designer, but his interest is in cooking. They wrote a book
together on peasant cooking. It was a success and they made a little
money. People call them to come to their houses to prepare buffet
suppers. They show up in the afternoon with big bags, they prepare
all kinds of strange dishes, and they don't spend much. Or at least
they say they don't spend much. I don't know. But people call them.

MARCO: And you? What are you doing? At one time, you were hand-
painting fabric.

ILARIA: I quit. I wasn't bringing anything in. Maybe my fabrics weren't
all that great to start with. I do translations from French. I never did

manage to learn English. I don't make much of a living. You don't get paid well for translations.

MARCO: And didn't you go to Australia? To Melbourne? To be with those four children in Melbourne?

ILARIA: No. My cousin isn't in Melbourne anymore. She's divorced and she lives in America.

MARCO: Those babies must be shaving by now.

ILARIA: Shaving. Do children get whiskers so quickly? How many years has it been since I wanted to go to Australia?

MARCO: Ten years. Ten years have passed since I came here for the first time and you told me you wanted to go to Australia. Stella had her hair loose and we ate potatoes. I'd come from *Aries*, from the magazine *Aries*, which was never published. It was ten years ago. I'm sure of it. It was the year Moro was assassinated.[5]

ILARIA: Ten years ago? How time flies.

MARCO: The first time I came in summer. The second time in winter. The second time it was snowing and I slept here.

ILARIA: You slept with Stella.

MARCO: No, you're wrong. I wanted to make love with her that evening, but she sent me away. Maybe you saw me going into her room. But I came back out almost immediately. She put her two hands on my shoulders and she shoved me out. I still recall those hands on my shoulders. They were like pliers. So I went back to my room. The guest room. I recall there was a painting of Vittorio Emanuele III.

ILARIA: It's still there. It belonged to Gianni's father. He was a monarchist, Gianni's father.

MARCO: I'd drunk a little wine that evening and my head was really spinning. I remember the next morning you came down to the kitchen and made me some coffee. You had on a little pale-blue bathrobe, all worn out, short as it could be, covered with stains. I wanted to send you a bathrobe as a gift from Rome. But then I never did.

ILARIA: Why didn't you?

MARCO: I don't know. It seemed too intimate a gift. I'm – you know, I'm from the old school. Plus I didn't have any money just then. I sent you a box of chocolates instead. Do you remember?

ILARIA: No, that I don't remember.

MARCO: It was a huge box of chocolates. I spent quite a lot on it. I remember because right after I bought it, I had a major attack of

stinginess. At that point I really didn't have any money. You wrote
me and you didn't thank me. You don't remember?

ILARIA: No.

MARCO: Stella, on the other hand, didn't come down that morning
when I left. I haven't seen her since. She had thrown me out of her
room with hands that felt like pliers. I was a little bit drunk. So is
Stella happy with this man of hers? They prepare buffet suppers.
Do they get paid well? Is she rich?

ILARIA: Fairly rich. Sometimes she lends me some money.

MARCO: Are you having money problems?

ILARIA: No, it's worse than that. I don't have a cent anymore. The translations pay so badly. I told you that I had two apartments in Rome?
Well, I sold them. The money I got seemed like a lot at the time, but
by now it's almost gone. It went pretty fast.

MARCO: Not much has changed in this room. The curtains are still
unravelling at the hems, just like years ago. The fire in the fireplace
is weak. It's really quite cold today and it's damp, even though it's
spring. The first time I came it was summer, the second time it was
winter, and now it's spring. On my fourth trip I'll come in the fall.
That stain on the wall has gotten bigger and yellower. Evidently,
rain is coming in from the roof. Don't you have money to get the
roof fixed? The springs are poking out of the armchairs. The carpets
and the covers on the armchairs are worn out. I can give you a loan
if you need it. I told you I'm earning a good living. Pretty good. I'm
not rich, but I'm earning a decent living.

ILARIA: You have a Volvo. A Volvo is a rich man's car.

MARCO: I got it used.

ILARIA: No, you shouldn't give me any loans. I'm grateful, but it's not
necessary. I'll figure something out.

MARCO: How is it that you sold those apartments?

ILARIA: Why are you so surprised? I sold them because we absolutely
needed the money. Did I talk to you about The Little Bitch? A girl.
Gianni was hopelessly in love with her. For a while the two of them
lived together here. I'd gone to live in Florence. Didn't I tell you that
I was going to Florence to live? Gianni was completely out of his
mind. She was more than a bitch, she was a witch. She was asking
Gianni for money and he ran up debts. I always ended up being
the one who paid them off. I would see him – he'd come visit me
almost every day and he would tell me all about her and him. Then
she took off. She left him alone. She had another guy – or other

men, I don't know. Her name was Lucianella. Lucianella Calabrò. The name gives me a chill when I say it. She left him, and that was when things started going downhill for him. He loathed everything he was doing – all the people he was spending time with and all the places he used to go. That was about seven years ago. Now he never leaves his room. Did you know that Gianni was ill?

MARCO: Yes, I knew. Someone told me. I didn't dare ask. I didn't know if you wanted to talk about it. I didn't even know if the two of you were still together. And where is Gianni now?

ILARIA: He's upstairs.

MARCO: He's upstairs. So I can finally meet him? I've yet to meet him in person, you know. Can I finally meet him? Can I shake his hand?

ILARIA: Oh, no. Don't even think about it. He never wants anyone to come to his room. He doesn't see strangers.

MARCO: But for a second. Just for a second. I beg you. I admired him so much.

ILARIA: Why say that? You don't admire him anymore?

MARCO: Come on. I still admire him. I feel immense admiration for him. I used the past tense – who knows why I used the past tense? I have all his books at home. I'm always rereading them. I take great care of them. I had them all rebound. Because you can't find his books around anymore. They've been out of print for quite a while. And so you came back here to live with him? When he was left alone?

ILARIA: He asked me to come back and I did.

MARCO: But what exactly is wrong with Gianni? What's his illness?

ILARIA: I don't know. He doesn't have a real illness. But it's almost worse than if he did. The doctors say he has a depressive syndrome. He stays closed up in his room, like I said. He doesn't do anything anymore. He's in there, motionless, sitting in an arm-chair. The man who always used to go dashing around in his car from one city to another. It isn't only because of that viper that he's been reduced to this, but that's when it started, when she left him, and now I hate that viper to death. He doesn't even go see his son anymore. He loved his son so much when he was little, and now he doesn't go see him anymore. They come here once in a while, the boy and his mother. The Big Bitch. The one that used to be called The Big Bitch. But Gianni almost always refuses to see the boy. I really feel sorry for the boy. He stays here for a few hours, next to his mother, silent, dignified. He resembles Gianni physically – Gianni the way he was years ago. He's tall, slender, lanky, and he also stutters a bit. He's sixteen years old. He doesn't have to shave yet but it won't be long. He's in his fourth year in the science academy. He was a naughty baby, spoiled, and now he's turned into a serious, quiet boy, a bit sad. People change. It's incredible how people change. Even The Big Bitch isn't the same anymore. Her hair is completely grey, and she pulls it all the way back, tight, and piles it on top of her head in a little bun. She doesn't have pearls anymore and now she dresses only in blacks and greys, a bit like a nun. It seems like she was supposed to get remarried, but then she didn't. She started an organization for children whose parents are in prison. She turned out to be a better person than she seemed. She's almost not a bitch anymore, if I have to be honest. She comes to visit us often, with the boy. She lends us money. Why not, she's a millionaire.

MARCO: And Gianni? What's Gianni like now?

ILARIA: Oh, Gianni's unrecognizable. His beard is completely grey and so is his hair. He's gotten fat.

MARCO: And the voice? Is the voice still the same? Rusty, clucking, hoarse?

ILARIA: The voice is still the same. But days go by without him pronouncing a single word.

MARCO: I'm sorry. I'm so very sorry.

ILARIA: I don't know why I've told you all this. I don't see anyone; no one ever comes by. In the beginning, Gianni's friends came to ask about him. They wanted to go up to his room, but he refused to see them, and so they quit coming. The minute you walked in, this great desire to talk immediately came over me. Though we know each other so little. You came twice – three times including today. The first time you were doing a weekly magazine, *Aries*. The second time you were doing a monthly, *The Ace of Clubs*. And how are things with *The Ace of Clubs*?

MARCO: My god, what a memory you have. You really do remember everything!

ILARIA: I've found myself thinking of you often, too, just as you've often found yourself thinking of us. The times you came here we chatted for quite a long time.

MARCO: Two issues of *The Ace of Clubs* came out. The second issue was impounded because there was an article about Andreotti[6] that some people judged to be defamatory. We almost got sued, my friend

Agostino Spada and me. You remember that I spoke to you about Agostino Spada? The lawsuit never happened, but we'd run out of money and *The Ace of Clubs* died.

ILARIA: And how are things with your friend Agostino Spada?

MARCO: He's fine. But I never see him now. We took different roads. He isn't working as a reporter anymore. He has a job in a travel agency.

ILARIA: And you, what are you doing?

MARCO: Me? I'm not a reporter, either. I write screenplays for the movies.

ILARIA: I recall that you were living with your mother and her dog. And now?

MARCO: I'm still with my mother and her dog.

ILARIA: Still the same dog?

MARCO: Still the same dog. They're both quite old by now, the dog and my mother.

ILARIA: And you never got married?

MARCO: I got married and I was separated almost immediately. After not even a year. We were living together – me, my wife, my mother, and the dog. Living with other people is difficult.

ILARIA: Yes.

MARCO: Sometimes necessary, though.

ILARIA: Damnably necessary.

MARCO: Exactly. My wife died last summer in Acapulco in a car accident. Our son lives with his grandmother on his mother's side.

ILARIA: And why doesn't he live with you?

MARCO: He's very close to his grandmother. He grew up with her.

ILARIA: What was she doing in Acapulco? Your wife I mean.

MARCO: She was there for work. Five of them were travelling in a car. They crashed, and she was the only one who died.

ILARIA: The poor thing.

Stella enters.

STELLA: I was in the woods and I gathered a bunch of mushrooms. My knapsack is full of them. I put them in the kitchen. But it was pouring, and I'm soaked from head to toe.

MARCO: Good morning, Stella.

STELLA: Good morning. Who are you?

MARCO: I'm Marco. Don't you recognize me? Marco.

STELLA: Oh, yes. I didn't recognize you. It's quite a while since I've seen you. You've changed. You've lost a lot of hair.

MARCO: You've changed, too, but you're still pretty. You've cut your hair. It's straight now, and you've dyed it brown. The first time I came here, though, you had it blond, all curly and falling down across your shoulders. I remember, when you were in Rome, that my friends complimented your hair. After you left, they still talked about you for a while at the Academy of Dramatic Arts.

STELLA: Don't mention the Academy of Dramatic Arts to me. They were all hateful. I have a hateful memory of that place.

MARCO: I understand you're doing peasant cooking now.

STELLA: Yes. Though it's not exactly a novelty. When have I ever done gourmet cooking? We've always found ourselves rather short of money around here.

MARCO: I brought some fresh caciottine and some wine. I remembered that the two of you like caciottine quite a bit. I have them in the car, in the trunk.

STELLA: Is that your Volvo outside?

ILARIA: Of course it's his. Whose do you think it is? It's not like anybody else has come by. He was passing through Arezzo and he made a detour.

STELLA: You have a Volvo. But it used to be that you never had a cent.

MARCO: Yes, but I'm earning a good living now. Pretty good. I thought I would stop by and say hello to the two of you. I remembered the way. But it's all changed a lot. The playing field is still there, but now it's in the middle of a housing circle. The traffic signal that didn't used to work is working now and there's quite a line of cars backed up there. The fig tree has disappeared.

STELLA: Of course everything has changed. Did you think you'd find everything the way it was? The fig tree – did you think you'd find that?

MARCO: Would you make me some coffee? Or are you out?

STELLA: No, we're not out. I'll go make some. (*Exits.*)

ILARIA: So you were telling me about your wife who died in Acapulco. What kind of work did she do?

MARCO: Do you know who my wife was?

ILARIA: No. How would I know? Who was she?

MARCO: Lucianella.

ILARIA: Who?

MARCO: Lucianella Calabrò.

ILARIA: The Little Bitch!

MARCO: If you could please not call her that. She was my wife and now she's dead.

ILARIA: You married The Little Bitch!

MARCO: Why are you so surprised? It's a small world.

ILARIA: No, it's big. It's enormous. But we keep crossing paths at the same points, as if there were only a few of us, when there's actually an endless number of us. When did you get together with her? Was she, by chance, still with Gianni and you stole her from him?

MARCO: Yes, to tell the truth, that's how it was. I stole her from him. I met her one evening at a buffet supper. Gianni wasn't with her but she talked about him a lot. I stole her from him. I was proud to have a girl who used to be with Gianni. At the same time, my conscience bothered me. She wanted to become a movie actress. I was starting to work in the movies then and she wanted me to introduce her to movie people. I advised her to enrol in the Academy of Dramatic Arts.

ILARIA: You're fixated on the Academy of Dramatic Arts. If you like a girl, the first thing you do is send her there.

MARCO: She didn't have any success as an actress, though. She didn't have any talent. She left Gianni and took an attic apartment that I was paying for. She was always asking me for money, too. I ran up debts. I pawned my mother's jewellery. Then she got pregnant, and I married her. When the baby was born, I thought she'd be different, but she was the same. She was making love with everyone who happened along. She went to bed with all my friends – even with Agostino Spada, I think. No, I'm sure of it. She couldn't stand me anymore. She couldn't stand my mother or the baby or the dog. We split up. She took the baby to her mother's in Brindisi. Sometimes I would run into her on the street. Each time she seemed smaller, more fragile, with those sandals and bracelets, and wearing gowns made out of that kind of fabric that rustles when you walk. She would look around with those enormous eyes – desperate, terrified. They weren't evil eyes. They were desperate and hungry for who knows what. How she ended up in Acapulco, I don't know. They said she was there as an interpreter or maybe she followed someone there.

ILARIA: That's where she died?

MARCO: Yes, that's where she died.

ILARIA: I hated that girl so much. Now, all of a sudden, I find it difficult to hate her. It's difficult to hate the dead.

MARCO: It's impossible.

ILARIA: Impossible? You're right, perhaps it's impossible. But why? If someone scratches you and bites you and wounds you and makes you suffer, don't all those wounds remain even when he's dead?

MARCO: The wounds remain, but you don't know what to do with your hate anymore. So it just falls out of your arms like a bundle of wet straw.

ILARIA: Yes. That's true. But I think it's strange. And maybe now I should hate you because you stole Gianni's girlfriend from him. And yet I don't. I don't hate you. I've always thought of you as innocent and naive, and that's how I continue to think of you. It's just that before I used to remember you with pleasure, even if I'd only seen you twice, and from now on I won't be able to remember you with that same pleasure. Now it's as if something else has gotten mixed into your personality – something that hurts me when I think about it.

Stella enters.

STELLA: Here's your coffee. It took me a while to bring it because I was upstairs in Gianni's room. I told him there was a reporter here who had come to interview him before, but he was always away, so the reporter never found him at home. Then he said he remembered the reporter and he remembered that he'd had him come from a long way away for nothing, and he felt bad about that. He said that he'd accept an interview now. For the magazine *War and Peace*, he said. Does a magazine called *War and Peace* exist?

MARCO: It used to exist. But it's been out of business for a long time.

STELLA: He wants you to come up. He combed his hair and he washed his face. He's even changed his shirt. Can you imagine? It's been years since he wanted to talk to anyone. And anyway, by now it's been years since anyone has asked to see him. How many years must it be, Ilaria? Do you remember?

ILARIA: No, no I don't remember. But I'm very glad. That's wonderful.

MARCO: What's wonderful?

ILARIA: Drink your coffee. Hurry. Go on up to Gianni's room. It's on the floor above, to the right along the hallway. You said you'd be happy to shake his hand.

MARCO: To shake his hand, yes. For a moment. But I don't feel up to interviewing him now. I'm not a reporter anymore. I'm not on assignment with any magazine or newspaper. Nobody in the newspaper business remembers my name anymore. I do something else now. I write movie scripts.

ILARIA: It doesn't matter in the slightest.

MARCO: It doesn't matter? What do you mean it doesn't matter? If I'm telling you I don't feel up to it? I don't have any questions ready. I'm not prepared.

ILARIA: Do you have a tape recorder?

MARCO: Here? No.

ILARIA: In your Volvo, don't you have a tape recorder?

MARCO: No. Why should I travel with a tape recorder? I have one at home, in Rome.

ILARIA: It doesn't matter. Stella has a tape recorder. It's small but it works well enough. She has it in her room. She'll go get it now. You go in and sit there, next to Gianni. You get seated there quietly with the tape recorder on the writing desk, and you ask him some questions, all the questions that reporters usually ask. About his projects, about all his public activities. You don't feel like doing it, I can tell. You've turned pale. You even seem a little frightened. Didn't you know that things always happen when we don't want them to anymore? But now you have to act as though time had never passed. As though you were the person you once were – a reporter – and as if he were the person he once was, when he never slept and he wrote his books all night long and at daybreak they'd call him and he'd go dashing off in his car from one city to the other. When he'd stand at podiums in front of people and give speeches. When he'd lift his beautiful white hands into the air. Did he stutter? He stuttered, sure, but it didn't matter. People were enchanted listening to him. They applauded. There was an ocean of applause. You can give the interview to whatever magazine you want. To any newspaper or magazine that's willing to take it. You'll figure something out. Perhaps you'll even create a magazine or a newspaper just for this—one single issue. It doesn't matter. As long as people remember Gianni Tiraboschi. The famous Gianni Tiraboschi. One of the finest men Italy has ever produced.

August 1988

Notes

1 Another sporty but 'sensible' Italian model from Fiat, the 127 was manufactured from 1971 through the early 1980s and remains popular among car

enthusiasts. The Morris Mini referenced a few lines later was a small British model manufactured by the famous Austin Motor Company.

2 A small town in the Province of Savona, in Liguria.

3 'Caciottine' describes a mild, semi-soft Italian cheese, usually made of sheep's milk and formed into small, irregularly shaped balls.

4 Literally 'the escalator,' *la scala mobile* was an increase, based on an index of the annual cost of living, in the pay scales and pensions of public employees.

5 The 1978 kidnapping and assassination of Italian Prime Minister Aldo Moro remains perhaps the most infamous and shocking event in modern Italian history. Italians of a certain age recall 'where they were' when they learned of Moro's death, just as Americans recall their whereabouts when the death of President Kennedy was announced.

6 Giulio Andreotti (b. 1919) is a fixture in Italian politics, having begun his public career as a member of the Constituent Assembly that drafted Italy's postwar constitution in 1946. A mainstay of the Christian Democrat party (Democrazia Cristiana), he served three terms as prime minister and has also held the offices of minister of the interior (twice), defence minister (twice), foreign minister, and other positions. He has several times been indicted and investigated for Mafia connections and bribe-taking. Since 1991, he has served in the Italian parliament as an appointed lifetime senator.

The Cormorant[1]

Cast:
Fiorella
Dario

FIORELLA: Hi, there. I'm not interrupting, am I? I was just passing by and I thought I'd come up.

DARIO: Bad idea. You know I work in the morning. I've got an article to finish and my nerves are shot. But yeah, come on in, have a seat. Take the couch.

FIORELLA: Oh, yeah, I really like this couch. It's so soft! When I was living here, I spent entire days on this couch. How long has it been since I left? A year? At least, I'd say. It was April, I think. You'd been hitting me because I said something that irritated you. What was it I'd said …? Who knows? I don't remember. I do remember that I packed in five minutes, and you weren't exactly telling me not to go. You didn't move a muscle. You didn't even help me carry my bag down the stairs. I see you've still got the same old typewriter, that old piece of junk. How come you don't get yourself a computer? I'm going to take my sandals off, do you mind? Aren't these sandals cute? Cute and deadly. I've got a blister right here, on my heel. You don't have a Band-Aid, do you?

DARIO: No.

FIORELLA: I've been running around the entire morning. I need to find a job. My head hurts, and I've even got my period. A blister on my heel and my period. I don't know how I could be in any worse shape. I don't suppose you've got any Sanadon tablets? No, of course you don't. There's never anything you really need in this house. What's your article on?

DARIO: Cormorants.

FIORELLA: Cormorants? What's a cormorant?

DARIO: What planet do you live on? Haven't you seen them on TV or in the newspapers, those cormorants all covered with crude oil? During the Gulf War?

FIORELLA: Oh, right. Those were cormorants, those birds that were coming out of the water, all black, all covered in oil? But the Gulf War has been over for quite a while. What's there to say about cormorants?

DARIO: The war isn't over because wars are never over. There are always hundreds of things to say about wars, about disasters, about cormorants. About sea turtles. About seals. About whales. About all the poor animals that suffer because of what people do. About the species that are on their way to extinction. About the oceans that have become inhospitable to marine life. About the burning rain forests in the Amazon. Why do you go out of the house in the morning wearing gold-coloured sandals?

FIORELLA: Because I like gold-coloured sandals. In the morning or in the evening. Write your article, go on. Get a move on. In the meantime, I'll just rest here and watch you work. Why are you still in your pajamas, by the way?

DARIO: I have to iron a pair of slacks. I don't feel like wearing wrinkled slacks.

FIORELLA: If you want, I'll iron them for you.

DARIO: You? When we were together, you wouldn't even iron so much as a handkerchief for me. You took your clothes to your mom's so she could iron them.

FIORELLA: Now I iron, though. I learned how. My sister always leaves me a big pile of ironing. She's working and she's got two little kids. Anyway, they're supporting me. Me, I don't have a job.

DARIO: What about your mother? Doesn't your mother iron anymore?

FIORELLA: My mother is dead.

DARIO: No! When did she die?

FIORELLA: Two weeks ago. She had a heart attack. You didn't know? There was a notice in the *Messaggero*.

DARIO: I never read the obituaries. I'm sorry to hear that. I'd have called you.

FIORELLA: My mother couldn't stand you. Because you hit me. She said, 'He acts like he's so progressive, this great big pacifist, and then he's a woman-beater.' But you know, as far as I was concerned, I didn't

really mind when you hit me. That evening, while I was walking
down the stairs with my bag, I had a huge desire to turn right back
around. I was thinking you'd call me back. But not you, no way. I
had a fight with my sister this morning. We hit each other because
I hated her and she hated me. You know why I showed up here?
Because I really wanted to see your face. It's the face of a friend, a
face that's special to me. It was even when you were hitting me. I
cried when you hit me, but deep down inside I felt like laughing.
It's strange, isn't it? I must be very old-fashioned somehow, just
like your typewriter. I like getting hit. I like a good slap in the face.
Nowadays, women aren't like that anymore. I'm a member of a species that's on its way to extinction.

DARIO: Could be.

FIORELLA: I couldn't come back here to live, could I? You don't want
that, do you?

DARIO: No.

FIORELLA: Not even for a little while? Just to give it another try?

DARIO: No. Look, I'm not alone here. I've got a girl with me.

FIORELLA: A girl? Where is she?

DARIO: She's asleep in there.

FIORELLA: The other times I came, there wasn't any girl.

DARIO: She hasn't been here long. A week.

FIORELLA: And you like her?

DARIO: I think so.

FIORELLA: I see. She's not going to iron your slacks either, you know.
You're going to have to iron them yourself. You're not lucky that
way. You always wind up with women who don't know how to
iron. Now I know how, but it's too late.

DARIO: Exactly.

FIORELLA: Let me stay for a little while, though, okay? If she wakes
up, her I mean, I'll explain it to her – that I'm tired, that my mother
died. I'm not in good shape. I'm not going back to my sister's and
I don't have anywhere else to go. My feet hurt, my eyes hurt, my
shoulders hurt. I feel like I'm dirty all over, all smeared with something. I feel like one of those cormorants. I feel like I'm wallowing
in crude oil. Write, write. Write your article. Say that cormorants
are everywhere you look. Say you've even got one in your very
own house. Covered with oil. Do you think I'm ever getting up off
this couch? Never. Oh, my head is spinning. Don't touch me. I'm
all smeared with oil. You wouldn't have a little cognac, would you?

What am I saying? There's never anything in this house. Nothing, ever.

1991

Note

1 As reported by Domenico Scarpa, editor of the authoritative Italian edition of Ginzburg's plays, Ginzburg wrote *The Cormorant* at the request of the organizer of the Mittelfest Festival, held each July in Cividale del Friuli, in the province of Udine. Ginzburg's five-minute 'microdrama' was performed at Mittelfest on 19 July 1991, just three months before Ginzburg passed away during the night between 7 and 8 October 1991. Scarpa, ed., *Natalia Ginzburg: Tutto il teatro* (Turin: Einaudi, 2005, 409).